Acclaim for T. Christian Miller's

Blood Money
Wasted Billions, Lost Lives, and Corporate Greed in Iraq

"An investigative masterpiece. . . . The evidence Miller presents seems persuasive beyond a reasonable doubt. . . . *Blood Money* is not an antiwar book. It is an antigreed book. . . . Miller is no armchair journalist merely echoing what others have written previously. As is clear from the book, he has traveled throughout Iraq, placing his own life in danger. . . . The book gives the names of those who are guilty of immoral or illegal behavior, rarely uses anonymous sources, recognizes the efforts of those trying to help, and — unlike so much other reporting about Iraq — treats the much-persecuted whistle-blowers with the respect they deserve."
 — Steve Weinberg, *Boston Globe*

"The story is seeping out in ever more incriminating detail, thanks to well-sourced chronicles like . . . *Blood Money*."
 — Frank Rich, *New York Times*

"Compelling. . . . *Blood Money* renders untenable the claim that when it comes to managing national security affairs, the tough-minded Republicans (in contrast to the wimpy Democrats) are the party of competence and sound judgment."
 — Andrew J. Bacevich, *Los Angeles Times Book Review*

"Searing. . . . Readers interested in understanding the political and economic dynamics behind the faltering campaign in Iraq will appreciate this investigation of the money trail between Iraq and Washington, DC."
 — Vanessa Bush, *Booklist*

"Miller's collection of riveting, disheartening narratives chronicles the spendthrift methods of the coalition behind the Iraq invasion, featuring so many spurious entrepreneurs, opportunistic politicians, and greedy contractors that it almost requires a pen and paper to keep track of them all. . . . Miller's important account fascinates throughout with the breadth and depth of the ongoing debacle."
— *Publishers Weekly*

"Miller's book is a needed corrective, providing the reader objective metrics to quantify the pace and progress of the reconstruction. . . . *Blood Money* can't help but install outrage in the reader. It's a damning indictment of an administration's hubris and complacency, and a vital chronicle of a mission that remains unaccomplished."
— Elbert Ventura, *San Francisco Chronicle*

"A book sure to fascinate — and anger — its readers."
— *Kirkus Reviews* (starred review)

"Miller fills in the missing piece: the staggering incompetence and corruption of the U.S.-led reconstruction effort. . . . One of the many virtues of his book is its balance. . . . *Blood Money* provides the best account yet of the pitfalls of contracting security out to private companies."
— Michael Hirsh, *Washington Post*

"A dogged reporter, Miller follows the money trail and uncovers escalating tales of thievery." — Edward Nawotka, *Bloomberg News*

"I hope everyone will read T. Christian Miller's book on contractor corruption in Iraq and its deadly consequences. It should give us all some much-needed perspective."
— Tom Palaima, *Austin American-Statesman*

BLOOD MONEY

MONEY

Wasted Billions, Lost Lives, and Corporate Greed in Iraq

T. CHRISTIAN MILLER

BACK BAY BOOKS

Little, Brown and Company

New York Boston London

Back Bay Books / Little, Brown and Company
Hachette Book Group USA
237 Park Avenue, New York, NY 10169
Visit our Web site at www.HachetteBookGroupUSA.com

Originally published in hardcover by
Little, Brown and Company, August 2006
First Back Bay paperback edition, May 2007

Library of Congress Cataloging-in-Publication Data
Miller, T. Christian.
    Blood money : wasted billions, lost lives, and corporate greed in Iraq / T. Christian
Miller. — 1st ed.
        p. cm.
    Includes bibliographical references and index.
    ISBN 978-0-316-16627-0 (hc) / 978-0-316-16628-7 (pb)
    1. Iraq War, 2003– — Economic aspects.   2. Bush, George W. (George Walker),
1946–   3. Iraq War, 2003– — Moral and ethical aspects — United States.   4. Iraq
War, 2003– — Equipment and supplies.   5. Petroleum industry and trade — Political
aspects — United States.   6. United States — Politics and government — 2001–   I. Title.
DS79.76. M47   2006
956.7044'31 — dc22   2006015074

10 9 8 7 6 5 4 3 2 1

Q-MART

Map by George W. Ward

Printed in the United States of America

To my parents, who always had faith; to my wife and children, who always had patience; and finally, to Doris Turck, who always had hope

Contents

"There is no price tag on chaos — or salvation."
— Allen W. Dulles, *The Marshall Plan*

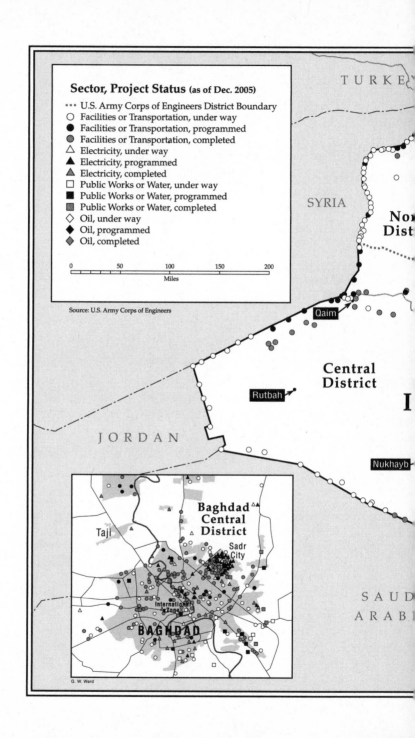

Sector, Project Status (as of Dec. 2005)

- ••• U.S. Army Corps of Engineers District Boundary
- ○ Facilities or Transportation, under way
- ● Facilities or Transportation, programmed
- ◉ Facilities or Transportation, completed
- △ Electricity, under way
- ▲ Electricity, programmed
- ◮ Electricity, completed
- □ Public Works or Water, under way
- ■ Public Works or Water, programmed
- ▨ Public Works or Water, completed
- ◇ Oil, under way
- ◆ Oil, programmed
- ◈ Oil, completed

0   50   100   150   200
Miles

Source: U.S. Army Corps of Engineers

TURKE

SYRIA

No
Dist

Qaim

Central
District

Rutbah

JORDAN

Nukhayb

Baghdad
Central
District

Taji

Sadr
City

International
Zone

BAGHDAD

SAUD
ARAB

G. W. Ward

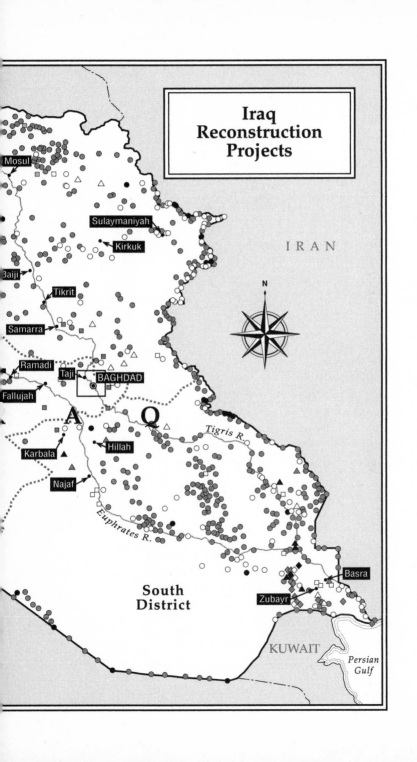

Time Line of Key Events
in Iraq War and Reconstruction

9/11/01   Al Qaeda terrorists fly planes into the World Trade Center and the Pentagon. Bush administration officials begin discussing the possibility of attacking Iraq.

1/29/02   In his State of the Union address, President Bush declares that Iraq forms an "axis of evil" with Iran and North Korea.

4/9/02   The State Department launches the Future of Iraq project. The earliest plans for postwar Iraq emerge during Deputies Lunches at the White House among senior officials from the Pentagon, CIA, State Department, and other agencies.

10/10/02   U.S. Congress passes resolution giving Bush the power to use force in Iraq "as he deems to be necessary and appropriate."

11/8/02   United Nations approves resolution 1441 warning Iraq of "serious consequences" if Saddam Hussein fails to comply with sanctions and arms inspections.

11/11/02   The Pentagon awards Halliburton Company subsidiary KBR the first rebuilding contract, to plan for postwar repair of Iraq's oil industry. USAID and other agencies develop first detailed plans for providing emergency food, shelter, and medical supplies.

1/20/03   Bush signs a presidential directive creating the Office of Reconstruction and Humanitarian Assistance. Headed by retired general Jay Garner, it is the first U.S. reconstruction agency.

1/27/03   UN chief weapons inspector Hans Blix raises questions about Saddam's compliance during a briefing at the UN Security Council.

2/5/03   Secretary of State Colin Powell goes to the United Nations to make a case for war.

3/8/03   U.S. Army Corps of Engineers awards Halliburton a contract worth up to $7 billion to rehabilitate Iraq's oil industry.

3/17/03   Bush issues ultimatum requiring Saddam and sons to leave Iraq within forty-eight hours.

3/19/03   Invasion of Iraq begins with strikes against suspected Saddam hideout. U.S. Army and Marines begin ground invasion the next day. Oil engineers from Halliburton follow forty-eight hours later.

4/9/03   U.S. forces seize control of Baghdad. Jubilant Iraqis and U.S. Marines topple statue of Saddam in Firdos Square. "Liberation Day" proclaimed. Looting spreads across Iraq.

4/12/03   Congress approves first installment of U.S. reconstruction aid to Iraq, totaling $2.4 billion.

4/17/03   USAID awards San Francisco–based Bechtel Corporation the second major reconstruction contract, worth $680 million, to rebuild schools and electricity, water, and sewage treatment plants.

4/21/03   General Garner arrives in Baghdad after weeks in Kuwait and establishes operations in the Green Zone, a former Saddam palace in central Baghdad. He finds most government buildings looted.

4/22/03   Halliburton gets Iraqi oil flowing for first time since the invasion.

5/1/03   Bush flies onto the U.S. aircraft carrier *Abraham Lincoln* to announce the end of "major combat" and the beginning of the reconstruction effort.

5/12/03   Ambassador L. Paul Bremer III arrives to lead the Coalition Provisional Authority, the American occupation government. Bechtel begins repair work on Iraq's power grid, which is producing about 300 megawatts of electricity.

6/15/03   The U.S.-controlled Program Review Board begins spending Iraqi oil revenues held in the Development Fund for Iraq. More than $20 billion will eventually pass through the fund.

July 03   Coalition reconstruction chief David L. Nash and chief financial officer David Oliver begin putting together a list of construction projects that form the basis for the rebuilding of Iraq.

7/13/03   The Iraqi Governing Council is established to help draft a new constitution.

7/22/03   Saddam's sons, Uday and Qsay, are killed in a shootout with U.S. forces at their hideout in Mosul amid growing signs of Iraqi insurgency.

August 03   Car bomb attacks against the embassy of Jordan and the United Nations compound. The United States is left largely alone to carry out the rebuilding as international interest fades in the face of violence.

8/8/03   In remarks to reporters, Bush says the goal of the reconstruction is to make Iraq's infrastructure the "best in the region."

9/7/03   Bush announces that he will seek $20 billion in additional funds for the reconstruction of Iraq and says that the United States will "spend what is necessary" to achieve victory.

10/5/03   Electricity production reaches U.S. goal of 4,400 megawatts. New goal set of 6,000 megawatts by June 2004.

10/23/03   Madrid conference where international donors pledge an additional $13 billion to the reconstruction of Iraq. Most of the money is never delivered, as international donors back out.

11/2/03   Congress approves $18.4 billion for the second installment of reconstruction money. Called the Iraqi Relief and Reconstruction Fund, it's the largest aid package for any single country since the Marshall Plan.

12/9/03   Paul Wolfowitz, U.S. deputy defense secretary, bars France, Germany, and other noncoalition companies from receiving major reconstruction contracts. State Department and Pentagon bicker over control of money, resulting in delays.

12/13/03   Saddam Hussein captured by U.S. troops in farmhouse near Tikrit.

1/28/04   David Kay, the chief American weapons inspector in Iraq, tells Senate that no weapons of mass destruction have been found and that prewar intelligence was wrong.

March 04   Major rebuilding contracts awarded to American multinationals, including Bechtel, Fluor, Washington Group International,

Office. IRMO oversees USAID, the Project and Contracting Office, and other agencies involved in rebuilding. Iraq reaches peak postwar oil production of 2.5 million barrels per day. Iraqi Defense Ministry official Ziad Cattan, a U.S. appointee, signs first of weapons and equipment contracts worth nearly $1.3 billion paid with Iraqi funds. Iraqis later accuse Cattan of corruption in connection with most of the contracts.

9/14/04   State Department announces revised rebuilding strategy. Billions of dollars redirected to security, resulting in money taken away from water, health, and electricity projects. United States also decides to turn over more responsibility to Iraqis to run recently built infrastructure.

11/7/04   American forces begin assault to retake Fallujah from insurgents. Later in the month commanders announce city is under control.

1/30/05   Iraqis vote to select a transitional government to draft a constitution. First free and fair election in modern Arab history. United Iraqi Alliance, a coalition of Shiite groups, wins nearly half the votes.

After voting is complete, Stuart Bowen, special inspector general for the reconstruction of Iraq, announces the result of an audit of the Development Fund for Iraq. Nearly $9 billion cannot be properly accounted for.

4/7/05   Ibrahim Jafaari chosen as new prime minister.

4/28/05   Iraqi National Assembly approves new cabinet after months of partisan bickering between Sunnis, Shiites, and Kurds.

5/11/05   Third major U.S. reconstruction aid installment for $5.4 billion signed into law, nearly all of it for training and equipping security forces.

6/21/05   Zalmay Khalilzad takes over as U.S. ambassador to Iraq. Begins a new policy of more aggressive engagement with Iraqis, from politics to rebuilding issues.

9/10/05   American and Iraqi forces begin major assault on insurgents in Tal Afar in northern Iraq. Operation concludes three days later, with two hundred insurgents declared dead.

10/15/05   Iraqi constitution adopted by popular vote.

10/19/05   Saddam Hussein trial begins.

11/11/05   Secretary of State Condoleezza Rice announces formation of first Provincial Reconstruction Team in Mosul, the newest rebuilding initiative.

12/5/05   Project and Contracting Office, the first rebuilding agency, is formally disbanded and folded into the U.S. Army Corps of Engineers.

12/7/05   In his first-ever speech on the rebuilding of Iraq, President Bush acknowledges that "reconstruction has not always gone as well as we had hoped."

12/8/05   Army Corps brigadier general Bill McCoy announces that the United States "never intended to completely rebuild Iraq."

12/15/05   Parliamentary elections held for first permanent Iraqi government since fall of Saddam Hussein.

4/22/06   Nouri Maliki named prime minister to replace Jafaari.

5/20/06   First permanent Iraqi cabinet named. Almost 90 percent of reconstruction money contracted out, with most projects scheduled for completion by end of 2006.

BLOOD MONEY

Promises

In a packed room on Capitol Hill, Paul Wolfowitz was making promises.

The war in Iraq was far from over, the deputy defense secretary told a long row of congressmen a week after the March 2003 invasion. But the United States was prepared to rush in after Saddam Hussein's defeat to begin rebuilding the country. The plans were ready. The expertise was there. And so was the money.

"There's a lot of money to pay for this," Wolfowitz said, adding, "We are dealing with a country that can really finance its own reconstruction and relatively soon."

Wolfowitz was wrong on nearly every point that afternoon. Neither the plans, nor the experts, nor the money was in place. They would eventually join the weapons of mass destruction as another of Iraq's mirages. The team that President Bush had designated to oversee the reconstruction had met in full for the first time only thirty-four days earlier, huddling in secret on a snowy day at the National Defense University in Washington, DC.[1] Handpicked by the Pentagon, the team was woefully understaffed and unprepared for what lay ahead. They lacked expertise in the Middle East. They did not have enough translators.[2]

The biggest mistake of all, though, was to say that U.S. taxpayers would not bear the burden of rebuilding a nation with the third largest petroleum reserves in the world. Three years after Wolfowitz's speech, the United States had committed more than $30 billion to rebuilding Iraq — more than the budgets of the Departments of Transportation, Interior, and Commerce combined.[3] No other country had received as much foreign aid in the history of the United States, not even any of the war-ravaged nations that took part in World War II's Marshall Plan, which ushered in modern Europe. But the restoration of Iraq fell far short of that effort's lofty achievements. It did not spark an economic renewal. It did not win the trust of a shattered people. And it has not made Iraq more peaceful.

The story of the failure of the reconstruction of Iraq is as broad, sweeping, and tragic as the war itself. Thousands of dedicated Americans worked long hours, in horrendous conditions and relentless violence, to make the reconstruction a success. Civilian bureaucrats gave up comfortable lives for lengthy tours of duty in Iraq. American soldiers reinvented themselves as school painters and village well repairmen. American businessmen put careers on hold and their safety on the line to give the Iraqis power, water, and hope. Many of them made the ultimate sacrifice: more than five hundred contractors have died trying to make Iraq a better place.

Their efforts were not matched at the highest levels of the Bush administration. Wolfowitz's miscalculation was only the beginning of a nation-building process crafted with all the care of a sand castle. There was never any single figure, never any single agency, that took control of the reconstruction effort. Responsibility drifted between different agencies and people, as money flew out the door and policy was hatched on the fly. The rebuilding program was like an enormous bulldozer with a cinder block on the gas pedal, grinding blindly forward but accomplishing little.

As the administration poured more and more money into the effort, one astonishingly slapdash act followed another. A motley assortment of retired Republican operatives, U.S. businessmen, and Iraqi exiles with dubious histories and doubtful motives were the first recipients of the largesse. So too were massive U.S. corporations like Halliburton and Bechtel, which received secret invitations to bid on government contracts worth hundreds of millions of dollars, profit guaranteed. With contracts in hand, the businesses hired poor laborers from places like backwoods America and rural Nepal to work for cheap, sending them to their slaughter in Iraq's wastelands.

Political appointees in Washington jostled to make sure friends got in on the action. Americans in Baghdad picked a used car dealer to buy weapons for the Iraqi military, an international arms broker to transport building supplies, and a self-described mercenary to protect government workers. In some cases U.S. officials handed out bricks of cash to pay contractors, keeping some for themselves to buy luxury cars and Breitling watches. Billions of dollars in Iraqi and U.S. money went missing. As the effort ground on, U.S. officials repeatedly changed strategies. Money drained away as security costs mounted. Projects were cut back. Goals were rarely set and rarely met. Achievements were tallied like body counts: another hundred schools painted, another clinic opened, another thousand Iraqis employed — statistics that said little about the reality on the ground. It was rebuilding without a foreman or blue-prints.

It was supposed to be different, to display America at its finest. As with U.S. efforts in Japan and Germany, the idea was to create a free, prosperous, and democratic society. New power plants would light towns once darkened during the rule of Saddam Hussein. Water plants whose shuttering contributed to the death of tens of thousands of Iraqi children would spring to life again. The U.S. government and industry would send its best technocrats to teach Iraqis the latest in health care, modern management, and law enforcement.

There was more to the effort than altruism, of course. Restoring Iraq had the concrete, strategic goal of protecting American lives. The idea was to pacify the country by making life better for its long-suffering people. New jobs would provide work for young, unemployed Iraqis who were easy fodder for recruitment by insurgents. Better services would allay fears that the United States had invaded simply to gain access to Iraq's oil wealth. The improvements would be a barrier to violence. Why battle a nation — even an occupier — that is working hard to make life better for all?

Beyond Iraq, the restoration was supposed to play an important role in the wider war on terror. A free and democratic Iraq, with open markets and a rising GDP, would become a democratic oasis in the deserts of the Middle East. Autocratic Arab leaders would be forced to reform. The political, economic, and social repression that created simmering rage among the Muslim masses would ease. A generation of young men angered by America's support of corrupt despots would see the United States as less of a threat, perhaps even an ally in their own struggle for self-rule. Angry editorials would replace suicide bombing as a means of expression. The United States would be safer because of it.

The results? After three years Iraqis have less power in their homes than under Saddam. Hospital neonatal units lose electricity, and doctors watch children die. Families suffer through withering 130-degree summers. Factories shut down because there is not enough electricity to power their machines. Oil production is far below its prewar peak. Pipelines in the north are bombed repeatedly. Oil tankers in the south sit empty at the port for days. Poor Iraqis in Baghdad slums suffer through outbreaks of easily preventable diseases like hepatitis for lack of clean water or health care. Children step through puddles of raw sewage on their way to school.

There have been successes, to be sure. Hundreds of thousands of Iraqi troops have been trained. Tens of thousands of Iraqi children have been vaccinated. Thousands of schools have been restored, updated with new textbooks, school supplies, and modern plumbing. Scores of government office buildings, police stations, and border outposts have been refurbished. The vast marshlands of southern Iraq, devastated after Saddam drained them to punish rebellious Shiites, are on their way to recovery. But those achievements have not been enough to markedly improve the lives of average Iraqis.

The clearest sign of the program's failure is the unabated violence. Thousands of American soldiers have now died fighting those same angry young men who were supposed to have jobs. Private contractors, aid workers, and idealistic civil servants have been killed working on projects that were supposed to produce a grateful populace. Tens of thousands of Iraqis have died in a vicious guerrilla war and sectarian conflict that draws its ground troops from the simmering resentment of ordinary Iraqis.

In almost every way the rebuilding has fallen short. The Bush administration and the neoconservative architects who conceived and supported the war have not built their nation on a hill. U.S. military commanders have not seen a decline in attacks against soldiers. Contractors have suffered, their funding cut, their reputations tarnished, and their employees killed. But the most disappointed group of all may be the Iraqis themselves, many of whom believed the United States could help restore a nation wracked by dictatorship, two wars, and a dozen years of sanctions. Month after month Iraqis have frequently expressed amazement at the lack of progress. How could a country that put a man on the moon not manage to make the toilets flush in a slum in downtown Baghdad?

This book is an attempt to answer that question, a plainspoken way of asking how it was possible that the most economically and militarily powerful nation on earth could fail at so vital a task as rebuilding a nation. The book will also serve, I hope, as a warning. As of this writing, the United States appears intent on retreating from its ambitious plans to rebuild Iraq. In the face of continuing reports of waste and abuse, the Bush administration has limited funding to continue the current program. Most of the reconstruction will be finished by the end of 2006. The last American power plants and water treatment stations will be completed a year later. Nor has the administration committed sufficient money to help the Iraqis pay for the operations and maintenance of complex infrastructure projects that have cost billions of dollars to build. The lack of money puts the American investment in Iraq at risk. The administration's move to back away from the rebuilding flies in the face of historical precedent. A RAND Corporation study showed that prior successful nation-building efforts in places like Germany and Japan took a minimum of five years to implement. "While staying long does not guarantee success, leaving early ensures failure," the report concludes.[4]

Even now, it is not too late to find a new path. Surely if we owe the Iraqis anything, it is the chance to stabilize Iraq. American leadership has so far lacked the intelligence and integrity to accomplish the basic moral imperative to better the lives of a people devastated by American firepower and authoritarian cruelty. That does not mean matters must continue in that way. In the end, Wolfowitz and company had one thing right: rebuilding Iraq is one of the most important goals to making America, and the world, a safer place. The tragedy is that reconstruction has so far not succeeded. If it does not, we will all pay the price — in lives lost, in money wasted, in opportunity squandered.

Part I
Cowboy Days

1

Man of Honor

While his fellow soldiers prepared to unleash one of the most spectacular land assaults in modern military history, Col. Ted Westhusing was studying old wars. He was in the final months of writing his doctoral dissertation at Emory University's department of philosophy in the spring of 2003. His topic was honor. As the Third Infantry Division charged into Iraq, Westhusing pored over ancient Greek texts like those once preserved in Baghdad's libraries, comparing them to modern Civil War novels and accounts of valor in America's more recent wars. He was an archaeologist carefully sifting the history of human violence: Achilles' savagery at Troy, Gen. Robert E. Lee's compassion to an underling at Gettysburg, Gen. Matthew Ridgway's turnaround of the Eighth Army's retreat in Korea. He sought an understanding of what the Greeks called *arete* — skill, excellence, or virtue — because Westhusing wanted to know, exactly, what honor meant for the modern American soldier. "Born to be a warrior, I desire these answers not just for philosophical reasons, but for self-knowledge," he wrote.[1]

Westhusing stood out on Emory's leafy green campus, which is not far from downtown Atlanta. He was twice as old as some of his fellow graduate students, with a buzz cut that grayed at the temples. They showed up for class in shorts and flip-flops, Westhusing in slacks and loafers. They stayed out late at campus bars, Westhusing had a wife and three children. They were younger, but he was faster. Intensely competitive, he had a physique as lean and hard as an ax head. He could often be seen jogging through the hilly neighborhoods around campus in camouflage and combat boots, a full rucksack strapped to his back. He challenged his fellow students to race. "I'm ten years older than you, man. You wouldn't last five minutes in the army!" he'd shout as he ran past.[2] And he finished his dissertation in three years — a year or two earlier than most students. The story about his dissertation defense was campus legend. Supposedly he had walked into the room in full dress uniform, took a seat in front of his advisers, and placed his sidearm wordlessly on the desk in front of him. It was apocryphal, but it spoke to his Pattonesque reputation: bullheaded, self-assured, and packed with military bravado.

Westhusing's unwavering belief in the United States made him a maverick in another way. In a department of professional skeptics, Westhusing was a believer. He saw things in black and white, true or false, right or wrong. There was no room for relativism in Westhusing's world. He was a deeply faithful Catholic who attended Mass nearly every Sunday. His ardent, unalloyed patriotism burned brightly in the coffee shops and classrooms of the mostly liberal institution. He loved his country, loved serving it, loved defending it. "We have the finest fighting force to ever exist, and we will get the job done, no matter what it is," he said.[3] Some found his conviction exhilarating. Westhusing got into fierce debates with fellow students, leaving newspaper clippings in mailboxes with comments circled in pen. He loved arguing about Aristotle and Epictetus, Kant and Wittgenstein. "He enjoyed being the voice of dissent. He definitely had a strong contrarian streak," said Aaron Fichtelberg, a fellow student who went on to become a professor at the University of Delaware, when we spoke of Westhusing in the fall of 2005.

Others found him rigid and inflexible. It was almost as if he wasn't interested in digging too deeply into the issues, afraid of the moral ambiguities he might find. One of his fellow graduate students suggested a reading by liberal philosopher Martha Nussbaum that questioned the value of patriotism. Westhusing refused even to attend the discussion group. Instead he sent a typed three-page response criticizing the article. "There were clearly things that Ted was not willing to question. One of them was patriotism," Fichtelberg told me.

Westhusing stood out in the military too. He had graduated third in his class at West Point. He became a Ranger and special forces instructor with the legendary Eighty-second Airborne, serving in some of the world's hot spots: East Berlin before the wall tumbled, Central America during the proxy wars between the United States and the Soviet Union, the demilitarized zone between North and South Korea. He loved working with soldiers in the field, but it wasn't enough. He thought he could have more influence by training America's next generation of officers. He decided to teach at West Point.

There he returned to his devotion: honor. For Westhusing, honor was what set the soldier apart from the rest of society. It gave a soldier meaning, the military strength, and society structure. At West Point he became one of the army's top ethicists, contributing to military journals and grappling with the toughest issues of modern war. Emory was a chance to deepen his knowledge. He learned ancient Greek and modern Italian. When he graduated in 2003, he was one of only fourteen out of eighty thousand officers in the army with a PhD in philosophy.

Westhusing had only one regret about his immersion in academia — he had never seen combat. It gnawed at him that he missed the first Gulf War, which happened while he was earning his master's. He had also not seen action in Bosnia, Kosovo, or any other of America's myriad conflicts. "He used to say he never had a shot fired at him in anger. There was a twinge of disappointment as he said that," Fichtelberg said. Westhusing's interest, after all, was in applied ethics. He was not interested in philosophy for its own sake. He had written about the thresholds of knowledge necessary before a commander could order an air strike, and about the rules of engagement that governed when a soldier could open fire during a peacekeeping mission. The classroom was good enough for discussion. But the battlefield was where you tested ideals. "War is the hardest place to make moral judgments," he wrote.

THE THINKING WARRIOR

Westhusing was born in 1960, the third child in a closely knit family of seven siblings that grew up in Texas and Oklahoma. His father, Keith Westhusing, served in the Korean War and had been a commander in the Navy Reserve. He was a geophysicist who worked with NASA during the moon mission, and the Westhusing kids had grown up with the children of the Apollo astronauts. The family moved from Texas to Oklahoma when Westhusing was in the eighth grade, settling in Jenks, an outlying suburb of Tulsa across the Arkansas River from Oral Roberts University. Tim Westhusing, the oldest of the siblings, said his younger brother played the role of mediator in the competitive family, which spent summer vacations engaged in tennis and basketball tournaments with one another. "He was the one who could really calm down a family of nine. He was the diplomat," said Tim, a telecommunications executive.

Although small, Ted Westhusing played basketball for the Jenks High School Trojans as a starting guard. He was intensely driven. Joe Holladay, who coached Westhusing before going on to become an assistant coach at the University of North Carolina, recalled him showing up at the gym at 7 a.m. to get in a hundred extra practice shots. The team nearly won the state championship his senior year. "There was never a question of how hard he played or how much effort he put into something," Holladay said. "Whatever he did, he did well. He was the cream of the crop. Ted was special."

Westhusing was academically talented as well, with a flair for math and science. He was a National Merit Scholar and the vice president of a fellowship of Christian athletes. (He would have been the school's valedictorian if not for a B in driver's education.) Both students and teachers knew there was something different about Westhusing. "He was very bright and a successful athlete, but he didn't boast about it," said Mike Means, the Jenks principal who coached Westhusing. "He had a maturity level as far as his character and values."

Westhusing thought about going to Notre Dame or Duke University, but decided on West Point. His mother, Terry, had had to evacuate with her family when Pearl Harbor was attacked, and Westhusing had always been intrigued by his family's military past. The nation's oldest military academy also appealed to the competitor in Westhusing. Only one of every ten applicants is accepted. The median grade point average of the entering class is 3.5; 20 percent are class presidents; 60 percent are varsity team captains.[4] The roster of graduates includes many heroes of American military history, from Robert E. Lee (class of 1829) to Gen. John "Black Jack" Pershing (class of 1886) to Dwight D. Eisenhower (1915) to Norman Schwarzkopf (1956).

When Westhusing entered West Point in 1979, the tradition-bound institution was in the midst of turmoil. The first female cadets were going through the system; within a year the academy would name the first black first captain, the leader of the cadet corps. A revelation in 1976 that scores of cadets had cheated on their engineering exams had resulted in congressional hearings, public outcry, and a commitment from the army to reemphasize the academy's moral code. From the moment they entered, cadets were taught to value duty, honor, and country and drilled in West Point's strict moral code: A cadet will not lie, cheat, or steal — or tolerate those who do.

Westhusing embraced the code's austere demands. As an underclassman, he was the honor representative for his company, serving on the cadet committee that reviews any violations and makes recommendations on punishment. As a senior, or firstie, Westhusing was the honor captain, the highest-ranking ethics position in the cadet corps. It is a position of tremendous responsibility, with the ability to make decisions that can destroy the future of would-be officers. Each year, some one hundred cases of honor violations come before the committee. They range from accusations of lying to cheating to stealing. Most infractions result in punishments such as being forced to repeat a year of school, but about 10 percent bring the ultimate sanction: the offender is separated — expelled — from the class. Col. Tim Trainor, a classmate and West Point professor, said Westhusing was strict but sympathetic to cadets' problems. He remembered him as "introspective." Lt. Col. William Bland, another classmate and professor, said Westhusing managed to maintain the cadets' respect despite being a disciplinarian. "He was a smart guy, a thoughtful guy, a caring guy. He was pensive," Bland said. As honor captain "you do a lot of thinking."

BEGUILING VIRTUE

After graduation, Westhusing became an infantry platoon leader. He took Ranger and Airborne training and went through jungle warfare courses in Panama. He rose to become division operations officer and chief of staff for the Eighty-second Airborne, based at Fort Bragg, North Carolina, where he worked with Gen. David Petraeus. He loved commanding soldiers. Westhusing told friends that one of his favorite postings was near the demilitarized zone between North and South Korea. He lived with his platoon, far from the comforts of base. "He liked it because he was with his people. He was living with them. 'That's the way you lead soldiers,' he said. 'You lead them by being with them, rather than being at a comfortable villa,'" his dissertation adviser, Nick Fotion, told me.

Nonetheless, Westhusing was always drawn to intellectual pursuits. In his doctoral dissertation, he wrote about visiting the remote village of Chipyong-ni in South Korea, the site of a famed defensive stand by U.S. and French forces during the Korean War. He "walked and studied in detail" the battlefield in an effort to distinguish "false from true honor," he wrote in his doctoral dissertation. "War is brutal; courage remains supreme," he wrote.

"True self-knowledge in the form of the moral virtue of 'honor' demands warrior recognition of that brute, vulgar fact."

He went to Emory twice, once for his master's degree in the early 1990s and a second time in 2000 to get his doctorate. He chose Emory partly because the philosophy department had one of the nation's few programs in applied military ethics, but also because of its reputation as a bastion of classical Greek philosophy. Westhusing had little truck with modern epistemology (he told one friend that society had "taken the wrong road after Descartes"). He loved Socrates, Aristotle, Plato. His favorite saying was by Socrates from Plato's *Phaedo:* "Those philosophizing rightly are practicing to die."

"He saw himself as a person of antiquity. He felt much more engaged in ancient Greece than the modern world. He was an anachronism," Fichtelberg recalled. To master ancient Greek, Westhusing took an intensive summer course at the University of Texas. His professor, Tom Palaima, remembered how Westhusing jumped at the chance to participate in the Aristophanes play *The Acharnians.* Westhusing played the role of Lamachus, a braggart, buffoonish general. He seemed to enjoy the chance to poke fun at himself and his beloved military. "He took to the role, and the self-irony to do it. He was just tremendous," Palaima remembered.

Westhusing's 352-page doctoral dissertation is a dense, searching, and sometimes personal effort to define the ideal spirit for a modern American soldier. His lantern held high, he plucked specific examples from history and picked each apart in a search for the perfect warrior. Achilles was a fierce fighter, adept with his spear and physically fit. But he desecrated Hector's corpse and selfishly pouted on the sidelines as the Trojans nearly destroyed the Greeks. Ridgway was a brave leader of men, but, Westhusing noted, some considered him too eager for his own glory. The bridge between the sometimes competing virtues of competition and cooperation was honor, a soldier's desire for approval from his fellow man and his country. Westhusing called it a "beguiling virtue" — difficult to define and difficult to recognize. The job of the American soldier was to embrace the true form.

Westhusing cautioned that devotion to honor could be taken too far. The "regimental honor" of the British infantry in the Victorian era was so extreme that officers suffering even a slight moral lapse would occasionally commit suicide rather than face disgrace. Westhusing called it a "monster" of a notion. "This sense of regimental honor tends to prevent and transfigure

both greatness of mind and extended benevolence," two of the requirements needed for true honor, he said.

VERIFICATION

As planned, Westhusing returned to teach philosophy and English at West
Point. He was made an "academy professor," the military's equivalent of
tenure. With a guaranteed lifetime assignment, he settled into life on campus with his wife, Michelle, and their three young children. He played basketball on the weekends, and exulted in being able to beat cadets on a
bicycle ride up a nearby mountain. He was not particularly outgoing. He
had his family and a few close friends. His relationships with his colleagues
were professional and courteous. Westhusing kept himself busy outside
academia as well. He and Palaima served as consultants for a Discovery
Channel re-creation of the battle at Troy. He went to a conference in St.
Louis that tried to link Achilles to modern-day Iraq.

As always, he remained deeply involved with ethics. He worked with the
cadet honor program as faculty adviser. Westhusing commented forcefully
to Tom Palaima when his former professor wrote a newspaper column ques-
tioning an apparently inadvertent instance of plagiarism in a book by *New
York Times* correspondent Chris Hedges, *War Is a Force That Gives Us Meaning.* Palaima, who was a columnist for a local newspaper, believed that
Hedges had copied a passage from a Hemingway novel without giving due
credit.[5] Westhusing scoffed at excuses. "Do you know what this would garner
Hedges in the circles I run in? If truly 'inadvertent,' and if Hedges were a
cadet, he might be lucky to garner only a 100-hour 'slug.' That is, he spends
100 hours of his free time marching back and forth in the hot sun in Central
Area under full dress uniform pondering the consequences of his failure (a
slug). If intentional, Hedges would get the boot. Kicked out. Gone."

Westhusing was restless, however. The war in Iraq raged on, always in
the headlines. Westhusing believed in the effort there, deeply, fervently. He
had once criticized Clinton for using soldiers in the rebuilding of Bosnia.
Westhusing's attitude, a friend said, "was, 'They are trained to kill people,
not build schools and bridges.'" But now he saw the war as a way to spread
democracy, to make life better for Iraqis. It was also personal. Iraq was a way
to "obtain 'verification' . . . and to lend authenticity to his status, not only as
a soldier, but as an instructor at West Point," his father, Keith Westhusing,
said. He believed that the war would make him a better soldier, a better

professor, a better man. When Westhusing got a call in the fall of 2004 from one of his former commanders in the Eighty-second Airborne, he didn't hesitate. "He wanted to serve, he wanted to use his skills, maybe he wanted some glory," recalled Fotion, his dissertation adviser at Emory. "He wanted to go."

When Westhusing finally shipped out for Iraq in January, he was as excited as he had ever been. His long, careful study had paid off. He was going to be doing what he had always wanted, serving his country in war. He had been assigned to one of America's most important missions in the rebuilding of Iraq, training new Iraqi security forces to relieve the burden shouldered by American troops. He was not just teaching a new generation of soldiers to be officers. He was teaching a new nation about honor and freedom and democracy. The future looked so bright.

2

High Noon

On the morning of September 11, 2001, Al Qaeda terrorists used hijacked planes to kill nearly three thousand people in New York City, Washington, DC, and Pennsylvania. Only five hours later, with smoke still wafting in the corridors from the strike against the Pentagon, Defense Secretary Donald Rumsfeld had Saddam Hussein, Iraq's dictator, in his sights. At a meeting in the operations center deep in the Pentagon, he made no secret of his desired targets. "Hit S.H. @ same time — not only UBL [sic]," Rumsfeld wondered aloud, according to the notes of one aide, who used abbreviations for Saddam Hussein and Osama bin Laden, the leader of the terrorist organization Al Qaeda.[1]

President George W. Bush instead decided to first launch an attack against Afghanistan, whose Taliban government had sheltered and supported bin Laden for years. Nevertheless, at a retreat at Camp David four days after the September 11 attacks, Bush told Gen. Hugh Shelton, then chairman of the Joint Chiefs of Staff, that he would deal with Saddam in due time. "We will get this guy, but at a time and place of our choosing," he said.[2] And even as the Afghanistan campaign unfolded during the fall of 2002, the Pentagon was busy updating OPLAN 1003-98, the military's preexisting secret plan for invading Iraq.

The updates were necessary because Rumsfeld wanted a new approach, an attack that used fewer soldiers and required less time to prepare. He ordered Gen. Tommy Franks, the commander of CENTCOM, or Central Command, the U.S. military command responsible for operations in the Middle East, to cut down the 400,000 soldiers envisioned by the existing plan and compress the time needed to deploy them overseas. In December 2002, Franks provided Bush a first look at a new invasion plan. It incorporated successful strategies from the Gulf War in 1991 and the current war in Afghanistan. Precision bombing and Tomahawk missile attacks could be used to target Saddam, his leadership circle, and elite Iraqi military units like the Special Republican Guard. Special forces operations could penetrate Iraq and protect the oil infrastructure. Under the best-case scenario, with full support from international partners, the United States could have 230,000 troops in the region within three months. It was an invasion at almost half the cost of the Gulf War.[3]

That January, in the most watched State of the Union address since President Bill Clinton's speech during the Monica Lewinsky sex scandal, Bush laid out a bold foreign policy agenda. No longer would America sit back while rogue nations developed weapons of mass destruction. The danger was too great that they would fall into the hands of terrorists, who could use them against the United States and its allies. Three countries — North Korea, Iran, and Iraq — formed an "axis of evil," Bush declared. "I will not wait on events, while dangers gather. I will not stand by, as peril draws closer and closer. The United States of America will not permit the world's most dangerous regimes to threaten us with the world's most destructive weapons," he said to loud applause. The speech was the first sign that America would henceforth act preemptively, to strike other nations before they had a chance to attack. The administration formalized the doctrine of preemption in June, with an address by Bush to the graduating cadets of West Point, the army's premier incubator of military talent. The days of waiting to be attacked, he said, were over.

The newly aggressive stance was a result of the Bush administration's thinking on the dangers of the post-9/11 world. The biggest threat to the United States, the president and his team believed, was the combination of a terrorist organization like Al Qaeda with weapons of mass destruction, and all three states that Bush mentioned had shown a willingness to manufacture chemical, nuclear, or biological weapons. North Korea was the furthest along in the development of a nuclear weapon, and Iran had the deepest ties to terrorist groups. But Iraq was the country in the Bush administration's crosshairs.

There were a number of reasons for this. Of the three, Iraq was the easiest target, while Iran and North Korea both posed difficult strategic problems. North Korea was within artillery range of South Korea's capital, Seoul. Iran had an enormous population and support among European allies of the United States. Saddam Hussein, on the other hand, was already the subject of international condemnation. Indeed, after the first Gulf War the United Nations had imposed sanctions on Iraq that had undermined his military and his hold on political power. Saddam was weak, friendless, and dangerous.

Vice President Dick Cheney and Deputy Defense Secretary Paul Wolfowitz were the strongest advocates in the administration for attacking Saddam. Both men had played a role in the first Gulf War, with Cheney having been the secretary of defense and Wolfowitz his chief policy official. Partly their interest in attacking Iraq was due to unfinished business. The American-led coalition in 1991 had stopped short of removing Saddam from power, a decision that both Cheney and Wolfowitz had come to regret. Subsequently Saddam had viciously attacked the Shiites and Kurds who responded to American calls for an uprising, slaughtering thousands of them with chemical weapons. He spent the next twelve years defying the weapons inspectors who were supposed to halt his weapons program and firing at American and British aircraft patrolling no-fly zones designed to contain him. The September 11 attacks gave the United States an "opportunity," as Rumsfeld once put it, to finish Saddam off.[4]

"After 9/11, Saddam Hussein had to go," one senior U.S. official close to Rumsfeld told me. "There was an inevitability about his need to go. We needed to pick up all the gauntlets that we had thrown down. He had to go. It was for others to decide whether we needed an excuse."

Cheney and Wolfowitz were part of a group of Republicans within the administration who saw Saddam's overthrow as a way to remake the map of the Arab world. Neoconservatives such as Richard Perle, who headed the Defense Policy Board, a Pentagon advisory panel, and Doug Feith, who was Wolfowitz's deputy, had long advocated Saddam's removal. They had worked to pass the 1998 Iraq Liberation Act under Clinton, which made the despot's ouster official American policy. The neoconservatives believed that getting rid of Saddam would give the United States the opportunity to create a democratic, free, and open society in the Middle East, one of the world's most politically and economically backward regions. Such a nation would help turn around the deep-seated animosity of the Arab street toward the United States, which had long backed autocratic regimes and was blamed for Israeli attacks on Palestinians. "We've got an obligation to go stand up a democracy," Cheney said. "We've got to fundamentally change the place."[5]

DIPLOMATIC ENDS

By the summer of 2002, the drumbeat of war was growing louder. In Washington the question was not whether the United States would attack Iraq, but when. Secretary of State Colin Powell was among the cabinet members most reluctant to rush into an invasion. In August he visited Bush to deliver his famous "Pottery Barn" warning. An invasion of Iraq would wreck the country, Powell said, and the United States would be responsible for fixing it. He also urged Bush to go to the United Nations to win international support for any military action he might take. Cheney was more skeptical, but Powell was joined in his pleas by Prime Minister Tony Blair of Britain and other close allies. Bush agreed.[6]

That fall the Bush administration made its case for war. In a speech to the Veterans of Foreign Wars national convention in Nashville, Cheney proclaimed that there was "no doubt" that Saddam possessed weapons of mass destruction. "He is amassing them to use against our friends, against our allies, and against us," the vice president said. Then National Security Adviser Condoleezza Rice warned on CNN that the United States had all the evidence needed, arguing, "We don't want the smoking gun to be a mushroom cloud." A new National Intelligence Estimate report — the combined view of America's intelligence agencies — asserted that Iraq was producing chemical and biological weapons and was on its way toward having a nuclear device. There were caveats, to be sure, but the consensus was that Saddam possessed weapons of mass destruction.

At the same time, top Bush officials declared there were links between Saddam and Al Qaeda. Cheney's office pointed to a supposed meeting in Prague between Mohammed Atta, one of the 9/11 hijackers, and Iraqi intelligence agencies, while Feith produced a long list of contacts between the two groups that was leaked to the *Weekly Standard,* a magazine that championed the neoconservative viewpoint. These claims were controversial and shaky, even within the Bush administration. Although the National Intelligence Estimate noted that Saddam might turn to Al Qaeda if threatened, it held such an estimation in "low confidence." Private doubt did not translate into public misgivings, however.

In October both the House and Senate approved a resolution authorizing Bush to use force against Iraq. In both cases the resolution was approved by margins greater than for the first Gulf War. Time would later show that Saddam had neither weapons of mass destruction nor links to Al Qaeda. But Congress had cleared the way for the war.

The United Nations proved a more difficult battle. Powell fought for weeks to gain a new resolution approving the use of force against Iraq for violating the already-imposed United Nations sanctions. In November he accepted a compromise solution. By a unanimous vote, the United Nations Security Council — including Britain, France, Russia, even Syria — passed resolution 1441, which found Iraq in "material breach" of its obligations to disarm. The resolution warned of "serious consequences" if Iraq did not allow the return of weapons inspectors, who had been expelled in 1998, and produce a new accounting for its weapons program. The language was not an endorsement for an invasion, but the Bush administration believed it vague enough to allow the United States to unilaterally decide to go to war if needed.

In December, Iraq produced a nearly twelve-thousand-page report to account for its weapons programs, showing that all stockpiles had been destroyed. United Nations weapons inspectors, led by Hans Blix of Sweden, began examining Iraqi military bases and presidential compounds, even those areas which had been off limits under the previous inspections regime. Blix found nothing, though when he delivered his first report in January 2003, he accused Saddam of refusing to fully cooperate. Iraq had not accounted for the final whereabouts of 6,500 bombs loaded with chemical weapons, or more than 2,000 gallons of anthrax. Stocks of the deadly biological agent still "might exist," Blix said.

The next day Bush gave his State of the Union speech, in which he boldly claimed that the British government had reports that Saddam was attempting to obtain uranium for possible use in a nuclear weapon from an African country. While technically true — the British had received such a report — the CIA did not consider it solid intelligence, and Stephen Hadley, then deputy national security adviser, would eventually apologize for accidentally including the phrase in the speech. That apology, however, was not forthcoming at the time — nor was any clarification from the Bush administration.

Some of Bush's closest advisers believed that the president had already made up his mind to go to war. Bush had become frustrated with bickering at the United Nations. He believed that Saddam was playing the same games that he always had, delaying action in order to survive. "Time is not on our side here. Probably going to have to, we're going to have to go to war," Bush told Rice in early January. She believed that he had made the decision to fight.[7] At the end of the month, just after his State of the Union speech, Bush met with Prime Minister Blair in the Oval Office. Bush told Blair that the United States would go to war, no matter the outcome of diplomatic efforts to obtain a second resolution authorizing force against Saddam. Bush "commented that he was not itching to go to war, but we could not allow Saddam to go on playing with us," according to notes of the meeting by an aide to Blair.[8]

In February, Powell made a dramatic appearance at the United Nations to attempt to show that Iraq had lied. Bush chose to send the secretary because he was the most credible spokesman for the administration, the person most capable of convincing the world that war with Iraq was necessary. Before arriving in New York, Powell had spent four days reviewing the best CIA intelligence. Much of the evidence was weak, and he tossed it out.

At the United Nations, Powell highlighted Iraq's acquisition of precisely machined aluminum tubes. The tubes, he told the world, could be used to enrich uranium and were evidence of a renewed interest in making a nuclear bomb. Powell also focused on the testimony of an Iraqi defector who claimed that Iraq was using trucks as mobile weapons labs to develop and test biological weapons. Curveball, as the defector was known, turned out to be an emotionally unstable Iraqi with a history of fabricating evidence.[9] "We know that Saddam Hussein is determined to keep his weapons of mass destruction. He's determined to make more," Powell said.

But as Powell tried to win support for the second UN resolution for force, it was clear that he did not have the votes. His argument was further undermined by Blix's second report, which was much more equivocal about the existence of Saddam's weapons program. By February his men had inspected thousands of sites and turned up no evidence of a weapons program. France, which held a veto, was emphatic that it would not approve a war measure. Nothing would justify a war, said Dominique de Villepin, the French foreign minister.

With that, diplomacy was over. Bush decided that the United States did not need a new resolution from the United Nations. "This needs to end," he told Rice.[10] On the morning of March 17, the administration withdrew its proposal from the United Nations. That evening Bush appeared on national television to announce that he was giving Saddam Hussein and his sons forty-eight hours to leave Iraq. If they did not, the United States would attack. The risk of waiting for Iraq or Al Qaeda to strike first was too great, he said. "We choose to meet that threat now, where it arises, before it can appear suddenly in our skies and cities," Bush said.

Two days later, Bush ordered Tomahawk missiles and two F-117s to hit a compound in Baghdad where Saddam was believed to be staying. As was often the case with the intelligence leading to the war, the tip was wrong.

DEPUTIES' LUNCHES

Unlike war operations, which fell solely under the purview of the Defense Department, no single U.S. agency was in charge of planning for postwar Iraq. In the spring of 2002, top officials from the National Security Council, the Pentagon, and the State Department began holding meetings at the White House to plan for the possibility of an invasion and its aftermath. The tightest security prevailed. Since the Bush administration was publicly pursuing diplomacy to disarm Saddam Hussein of his suspected weapons of mass destruction, the meetings were kept secret from all but cabinet officials, undersecretaries, and their deputies, a senior U.S. official told me. The meetings, which took place generally once a week over lunch, were given the innocuous-sounding name of Deputies' Lunches. Neither the public nor the rest of the government would know their true purpose. The tactic worked: news of the lunches never leaked.

Among the regular attendees were Deputy Defense Secretary Wolfowitz and his deputy, Douglas Feith; Deputy Secretary of State Richard Armitage and Undersecretary of State Marc Grossman; Deputy CIA Director John E. McLaughlin; and Frank Miller and Zalmay Khalilzad from the National Security Council. The lunches evolved into an informal bull session for a country's future. Who would run the country after Saddam's fall? How would the country's police and legal system function? How would the Iraqi people obtain food, water, and electricity? How should Iraq divide up its oil revenues? The meetings served only to talk about the issues. There was no real, detailed planning involved.

The State Department took the job of reaching out to Iraqi exiles. On April 9, 2002, State convened its first meeting of the Future of Iraq project.[11] Led by Thomas Warrick, a midlevel career civil servant with extensive contacts in Iraq's exile community, the project brought together more than two hundred Iraqis and seventeen different federal agencies, ranging from the CIA to the U.S. Agency for International Development (USAID) to the Defense Department. Over the next year the group held a series of meetings to plan for the transition to post-Saddam Iraq. Not all the meetings were productive. The Iraqis involved frequently skipped scheduled teleconferences and ignored their duties to produce recommendations. Nor was the process particularly smooth. At one contentious gathering in London, the various Iraqi factions got into a public spat in the middle of a press conference over the best form of government after Baghdad's fall.[12] "This is a complete disaster for Iraq," declared Kanan Makiya, a prominent Iraqi dissident who was a favorite of senior Pentagon officials because of his embrace of liberal democracy.[13]

While the Future of Iraq project did not produce a complete and coherent plan, the group became the most sustained effort by the U.S. government to understand the realities it would face in postwar Iraq. The two-thousand-page report the group produced spanned thirteen volumes, covering topics from education to health to agriculture. Some of the reports within were no more than white papers, lengthy descriptions that simply described the state of Iraq's infrastructure, political structure, and economy. In other places there were plenty of practical suggestions. The team in charge of Iraq's judicial code produced six hundred pages of reforms. Suggestions for Iraq's infrastructure included "mini–power stations" to ease the expected collapse of Iraq's electrical system and "networks in a box" to create a temporary cellular phone system. Perhaps most ambitious was the idea of using the 500,000 men in Iraq's armed forces as muscle for the reconstruction. The soldiers could be trained to repair airports, bridges, dams, and other infrastructure, providing manpower and a cheap alternative to expensive U.S. contractors.[14]

The Pentagon's planning for a postwar civilian administration fell to Feith, an owlish corporate lawyer and one of the administration's most vocal neoconservatives. Feith had worked for Richard Perle during the Reagan administration and was a champion of Israel and the hard-line Likud Party. He also believed deeply in the overthrow of Saddam Hussein. As preparations for war became more intense in fall 2002, Feith created the Office of Special Plans. The name was deliberately misleading. "Iraq Planning Office might have undercut our diplomatic efforts with regard to Iraq and the UN and elsewhere," he later admitted.[15] The thirty or so staffers focused much of their time on preventing a humanitarian disaster following the invasion. They worried about food shortages and outbreaks of disease.

They wanted to make sure that any weapons of mass destruction were quickly found and destroyed.

Feith created a second group focused solely on Iraq's biggest prize: oil. Oil deserved special attention for several reasons, one being Saddam's willingness to turn it into a weapon. During the first Gulf War, Saddam's soldiers had used C4 explosives to light fire to more than seven hundred oil wells in Kuwait. The resulting fires burned for months, crippled Kuwait's economy, and cast eight-hundred-mile-long plumes of smoke into the air. Feith appointed one of his most trusted deputies as leader of the Energy Infrastructure Group, a former law partner named Michael Mobbs. Mobbs launched a study on the state of Iraq's oil infrastructure. Though never publicly announced, it concluded that the oil system was in far worse shape than previously believed. Pumping levels were off and the refining system was decrepit.[16] Mobbs decided that no U.S. government agency had the expertise necessary to simultaneously extinguish oil well fires and reignite the country's petroleum industry. In what was essentially the first contracting decision of the reconstruction of Iraq, Mobbs paved the way for the Pentagon to hire out the job to Halliburton, a company formerly run by Vice President Dick Cheney.

The military also carried out planning for Phase IV operations — the name given to the period following the fall of Baghdad. As the occupation commander, General Franks had overall responsibility for the governance of Iraq, but he never showed much enthusiasm for the job. Franks urged the reconstruction on other U.S. agencies like the State Department, telling the president that the military did not do nation building very well.[17] Indeed he wanted to get in and out of Iraq as quickly as possible. (Unlike many senior officers, Franks had not served in the Balkans, the military's most recent experience in rebuilding.) "There wasn't a whole lot of intellectual energy being focused on Phase Four," said Lt. Col. John Agoglia, one of CENTCOM's chief planners.[18] Upon his arrival in Baghdad after the fall of Saddam, Franks told his commanders to begin planning for a withdrawal of forces in thirty to sixty days.[19]

For their part the Joint Chiefs of Staff conducted their own plan for a military administration of Iraq. They anticipated the creation of a headquarters in Iraq that would coordinate different U.S. agencies before turning over control to an American ambassador. Rumsfeld modified the plan to ensure that the Defense Department had the lead in postwar efforts. This was a significant switch. The State Department had been in charge of nation building ever since the U.S. Army oversaw the reconstruction of Japan and Germany immediately after World War II. Rumsfeld wanted a unified command, however, and Powell did not object.[20]

The Joint Chiefs' planning effort was not embraced by either CENT-COM or Rumsfeld's civilian staff. Hoping to bridge the gap, Lt. Gen. George Casey, then head of the Joint Chiefs' planning operations and later chief commander in Iraq, appointed Brig. Gen. Steve Hawkins of the U.S. Army Corps of Engineers to assist CENTCOM. The reception Hawkins received was so frosty that he was reduced to cadging office supplies from a trade fair held at CENTCOM headquarters in Tampa.[21] Notepads and ballpoint pens were the least of it. Rumsfeld's office simply did not bother to respond to suggestions. Some in the Joint Chiefs took to calling the civilian operations in the Pentagon "the black hole."[22]

Yet more planning was carried out by Lt. Gen. David McKiernan, the land commander for the war. McKiernan's staff created a plan called Eclipse II, after the post–World War II plan for Germany. Eclipse II called for the coalition forces to support either a military or civilian government for two months. The military's role was to secure infrastructure, help restore basic services, and maintain public order. But as one of McKiernan's aides noticed, the war "plans" were internally inconsistent. The attack strategy called for the destruction of Saddam's methods for commanding and controlling his forces. Eclipse II, however, relied heavily on Iraqi military and bureaucrats to help with the reconstruction. The two strategies were at odds.

But whatever the plan and whatever the planning, the military, from Rumsfeld to Franks and down the chain of command, was not interested in nation building. None of the military plans were particularly detailed. They were so poorly coordinated and distributed that on-the-ground commanders were ignorant of them. The Third Infantry Division that seized Baghdad issued a report in the aftermath of the war complaining about the lack of direction. "Higher headquarters did not provide the Third Infantry Division (Mechanized) with a plan for Phase IV."[23] "I have a war to fight," Franks would say.[24] And for him and many others at the Pentagon, that was enough.

HAPPINESS FOR IRAQ

The Deputies' Lunches were supposed to be the linchpin that linked together the federal government's vast bureaucracy on rebuilding Iraq. But the secretive meetings had neither the firepower nor the visibility to bridge the fundamental divide in the Bush administration between the State Department and the CIA on one side and the Pentagon and the vice president's office on the other.

At State, career Arabists were wary of the Pentagon and its plans to convert Iraq into a liberal democracy. At a meeting in Michigan with Iraqi Americans, Warrick, the Iraq expert from the State Department, had issued a sharp warning about Wolfowitz, the war's philosophical architect: "If you work with Paul Wolfowitz, the State Department will not give you anything," he told those at the meeting.[25] At the Pentagon, Wolfowitz, Feith, and the rest of the neoconservatives believed the State Department was too cautious, too committed to the status quo. They believed it possible the United States would conquer Iraq, turn over control to the Iraqis, and depart quickly. After that, Iraq could be turned into a democracy. The reconstruction, such as it was, would be mostly emergency aid aimed at helping the Iraqis establish their own government.

The dispute became especially sharp over a single man: Ahmed Chalabi, fifty-nine, a portly MIT graduate and convicted bank swindler. The scion of a wealthy banking family that fled Iraq in 1956, Chalabi spent years organizing exile opposition to Saddam. He developed a network of agents to pass intelligence on to the CIA, much of it later proven false. He was also instrumental in convincing Congress and the Clinton administration to pass the Iraq Liberation Act. The Pentagon saw Chalabi as a man who could guide Iraq along the path of liberal democracy. The State Department and the CIA considered him an untrustworthy charlatan.

The divide doomed the effort to develop a single, coordinated strategy for postwar Iraq. Planning happened throughout the government, but it was fragmented and incoherent. The State Department, in particular, was shut out of the process. Many of the recommendations in the Future of Iraq project were never adopted by the Pentagon. "Nobody listened to us," recalled Mohammed Faour, a former major in Iraq's special forces who chaired the project's defense working group. "We were just put aside."[26] The reasons for this had more to do with politics than with questions of strategy or merit.

"No matter what their policy disagreements, U.S. officials should never have allowed their personal feelings to poison the interagency process. But, of course, they did," said David L. Phillips, a State Department contractor who was a leader in the Future of Iraq process. "Personal animosities combined with different postwar approaches would ultimately destroy the Future of Iraq Project."[27]

Anyone skilled at reading the subtle clues of a government hearing could see how wide the rift had grown. Feith, representing the Pentagon, and Grossman, from State, testified before the Senate Foreign Relations Committee on February 11, two months before the invasion. Grossman described the Future of Iraq project in some detail, including two-year scenarios for rebuilding Iraq's education, health, water and sanitation, electricity, shelter, transportation, rule of law, agriculture, communications, and economic and financial policies. Feith, on the other hand, was evasive and vague. He refused to say how much the reconstruction would cost, or who would pay for it. He dodged questions about which other countries would pitch in to help. He referred to the Pentagon's plans for restoring Iraq's oil three times, but barely mentioned other reconstruction tasks.

When pressed about the possibility of the rebuilding effort's lasting for two years, Feith pointedly noted that it was not him but his "esteemed colleague" Grossman who had supplied the number. In a phrase that could have come straight from *Alice in Wonderland,* Feith said that the Defense Department's time line was based on having "a commitment to stay and a commitment to leave." If Grossman was the schoolboy eager to please, Feith was the insider holding on to his secrets. "It is very hard to tell you precisely what we plan to do because so much . . . depends on how events unfold," Feith said. "But I could tell you that a great deal of thought has been given to the kinds of considerations that [are] crucial to the success of our policy and the possibility of happiness for Iraq in the future."

The performance angered both Democrats and Republicans. Their objections were remarkably prescient. "It's very important to be very level with the American public about this," said Senator Christopher Dodd of Connecticut. "It's going to be very expensive, it's going to take a long, long time, and we're going to be there for years in pulling this together." Such foresight didn't translate into action. Neither Feith, nor anybody else, was ever forced to prove that the United States had any real plan in place.

NO PLAN

Responsive or not, even Feith realized the level of coordination was a problem. So in a last-minute effort to pull together the decentralized planning that had gone on across the government, from the U.S. military to

USAID, he helped set up a new agency to oversee Iraq's reconstruction. In January, Bush signed National Security Presidential Directive No. 24, which Feith had drafted with Hadley, the deputy national security adviser. The directive created the Office of Reconstruction and Humanitarian Assistance, known as ORHA. The new agency was supposed to synthesize the plans created by disparate agencies, then deploy in the field in Iraq as an "expeditionary unit."

Jay Garner was given the nearly impossible task of making it happen. Garner, who was handpicked by Rumsfeld, was a retired general who had fought in the first Gulf War and then ran the emergency relief effort afterward to care for the Kurds. The feeding and housing of thousands of refugees fleeing Saddam Hussein had been a high point in his career. At his office in the Pentagon, Garner hung up thank-you notes in crayon from Kurdish children.[28] By all accounts he prevented a humanitarian disaster. When he left Kurds surrounded him, chanting, "Yes to America!"

Garner spent the last part of his career involved in the implementation of the Star Wars missile shield initiative, retiring in 1997 as a three-star general. It had been on a presidential panel on space and missile defense that he had gotten to know Rumsfeld, who was the chairman. After retiring from the military, Garner had gone on to become president of SYColeman, a subsidiary of defense contractor L-3 Communications Corporation. When Feith called, Garner required some convincing to take the job. He was wearing a business suit, delivering a year-end earnings report for his company. "I've got a company here I'm running that's got about two thousand people, and I've got a wife I've been married to for over forty years," Garner told Feith. "I've got to get permission from both."

Permission granted, Garner took the job and stepped into his Pentagon office for the first time on January 17 — kicking off the mission to finalize plans for the rebuilding of Iraq. He hired old military buddies as trusted aides, then convened all the players together at the National Defense University in Washington on a snowy February 21 for a "rock drill" — a term Garner used as metaphor for turning over rocks to discover hidden problems. What they found wasn't pretty. It was the first meeting of all the different agencies that would rebuild Iraq, and while nobody there could have known that the invasion would begin in precisely twenty-six days, they knew that the war was imminent. The session was dominated by more questions than answers. Gordon W. Rudd, assigned as a historian to the ORHA team, was at first annoyed by a man sitting near him in the auditorium who continually interjected comments and questions. "Then I realized he was better informed than we were," he said. It was the State Department's Tom Warrick. On the job for over a month, Garner had never met the man who had spent a year working on Iraq's reconstruction.[29]

The rock drill confirmed for many of those involved in the reconstruction that the U.S. program was in trouble before it even began. "The messiah could not have organized a sufficient relief and reconstruction or humanitarian effort in that short a time," said Judith Yaphe, a former CIA analyst who attended the session.[30] Larry Crandall, a former USAID director, remembered going into Garner's suite of offices in the Pentagon and seeing one wall covered with about two dozen 8½ by 11 sheets of paper. They seemed to contain basic lessons on economics, rather than development strategies. "I looked around and looked at my colleague and said, 'Hmmmm,' and started asking questions of some of the staff who were responsible for those pieces of paper on the wall. Then we began to think these people really don't get it," Crandall said. "There was no plan."[31]

Inevitably Garner stepped into the crossfire of the ongoing, ever escalating war between the State Department and the Pentagon about control over postwar Iraq. Garner invited Warrick and another State Department official, Megan O'Sullivan, to join ORHA. A few weeks later Rumsfeld told Garner to strike their names. Garner later discovered that Cheney himself had blocked the appointments. The vice president had decided that Warrick and O'Sullivan were too moderate in their approach to Iraq.[32] Later Rumsfeld personally blocked eight other State Department volunteers from going to Iraq; he thought they were not high profile enough to take over important ministries like oil and electricity. Secretary of State Colin Powell took it as yet another attack, and he called Rumsfeld to complain. Eventually Rumsfeld approved O'Sullivan and four of the names, but only after several more weeks of delay.

VACUUM

With the bureaucratic battle raging in Washington, Garner set up shop in the real war zone. On March 16 he flew to Kuwait and established headquarters in seaside villas at the Hilton Hotel south of the capital. The war began three days later, with Tomahawk missiles streaking toward Baghdad. As coalition military forces began their drive toward Baghdad on March 20, Garner and his expeditionary force of three hundred diplomats, soldiers, and private contractors watched CNN and waited for the end. Garner spent his days surrounded by his military buddies, the "Space Cowboys" who had come out of retirement for the reconstruction. He wore open-neck shirts and exuded confidence. Over dinners, he talked of being home by August.[33]

The handful of people from the State Department in Kuwait were growing increasingly nervous. They felt locked out of Garner's inner circle, cut off from Washington, and reduced to getting news on the war's progress from CNN. One remembered watching footage of the Iraqi government ministries burn with horror. How was the United States supposed to run a government without any buildings? Robin Raphel, the steely, blue-eyed former ambassador to Tunisia who would later head the State Department's reconstruction work, recalled a spreading sense of doom. The United States was not a colonial power. It did not have the ability to run a postwar country. "I was saying when we were in Kuwait, when it was gallows humor time, 'Don't worry, within weeks, we will be on our knees to the UN because we can't do this.' "[34]

Baghdad fell on April 9. For almost two more weeks, Garner's team stewed in Kuwait, blocked from going in by continued fighting. Finally Garner appealed directly to Tommy Franks, an old friend, and got permission to fly in. A stocky, can-do guy, Garner himself had grown nervous over the delay in getting to Iraq. "If you are absent too long, while expectations are created for our government . . . a vacuum occurs," Garner told reporters in Kuwait a few days before heading for Baghdad. "And if you are not there, the vacuum gets filled in ways you don't want."

Garner and a small staff arrived in Baghdad on April 21, with the rest of his group arriving a few days later in a convoy of Chevy Suburbans.[35] They set up shop in the Republican Palace, the site of cabinet meetings for Saddam's government. The condition of the massive, sprawling compound along the banks of the Tigris was the first clue that the rebuilding effort was in trouble. The windows had been blown out. A fine layer of dust covered everything. There was no electricity or running water. The only food was military rations. People slept on cots, some of them under wet towels to cool off. There were only a handful of portable toilets. Communications were abysmal. The Americans had only satellite phones; using them required going outside and pointing the phone toward the sky to pick up a signal. Frustrated U.S. officials frequently could not call the United States; they could not even call each other. Nobody had even thought to bring the ubiquitous two-way Motorola radios available in any RadioShack back home, and the military had none to spare. David Dunford, a former ambassador to Oman who traveled to Iraq with Garner, was appalled. "In southern Arizona, when I go on a bird-watching trip, we have two-way radios. These guys had no radios."[36]

Outside in the streets of Baghdad, the situation was even worse. As Garner's team ventured out to ministries, they were shocked by what they found. Looters had stripped government buildings bare. Ministry buildings were hollow shells, robbed of desks, chairs, even the metal rebar between walls. Electrical and oil plants had been trashed, their consoles smashed in a deliberate effort to sabotage the country's power grid. Government computers could be found on sale in the street for the equivalent of $35. Seventeen of twenty-one Iraqi ministry buildings were destroyed.[37] One senior adviser recalled meeting with a minister in an empty room, standing as they spoke because there were no chairs to sit on. "Our planning process was that we needed to immediately [restore] the ministries, because that's the only way that you get government services back and get the country functioning again," Garner said. "But what happens is when we get there, they're not there anymore."[38]

Also not there were many of the problems that *had* been anticipated by those planning for the reconstruction in Washington. There were no outbreaks of cholera. There were no food shortages. Special forces units had managed to prevent attacks against the oil wells. (Halliburton wound up putting out exactly nine wellhead fires.) The planners had, in essence, planned for the wrong war. No apologies were forthcoming. Feith said that the Pentagon simply placed its bets on the wrong disaster, like a poker player misreading a tell. Feith's planners foresaw disorder and looting, but concentrated on risks such as oil well fires, a refugee exodus, or famine. "When you plan . . . you [assess] various risks and you say, 'You can't do everything,'" he said. "That's life."[39]

Instead what Garner and his team found was a society on the brink of collapse — physically, morally, and intellectually. Two bloody wars, a dozen years of sanctions, and, most of all, three decades of brutal dictatorship had broken Iraq. Every power plant in the country was near collapse. The telephone system was destroyed in the bombing. The intelligentsia had fled or been ground into submission. The business class was crushed under one of the world's most warped economies. Ordinary Iraqis were fearful, hopeless, and given to paranoia. For all its talk of democracy, the U.S. government had not understood the reality of dictatorship.

Dunford, the retired ambassador to Oman, was one of those held up from deploying to Iraq by the fight between the State and Defense Departments. When he finally got approval to go to Iraq in mid-April, the war had already begun. Dunford was given the job of rebuilding Iraq's foreign ministry. His instructions consisted of a five-page paper written by a State Department summer intern. He had no list of Iraq's ambassadors abroad or even the location of its embassies. He created stationery for the new ministry by scanning in a letterhead that he found in the rubble of the old ministry building, which had been burned by looters. To communicate with ambassadors abroad about Iraq's new Ministry of Foreign Affairs, he set up a Hotmail account: iraqmfa@hotmail.com. "We had no instructions or guidance on how to do this; we just did it," he recalled.[40]

Both in Iraq and in Washington, concerns grew over the chaos in Iraq. There were grumblings that Garner was spending too much time in the Green Zone, as the Republican Palace came to be called. Iraqis complained that they had no power, no water, no political direction. Garner attempted to organize political meetings with Iraqis in both Baghdad and southern Iraq, but they turned into a chaos of shouting and finger-pointing. Back in the United States, meanwhile, the bureaucracy was moving without any sense of urgency. USAID was in charge of restoring the power system. But in Washington the agency didn't even award a contract to do the work until April 17 — nearly a month after the invasion began.

Soon after his arrival in Baghdad, Garner got a call from Rumsfeld. His replacement was on the way. Bush had decided to appoint a new civilian authority in Iraq, Ambassador L. Paul Bremer III, a State Department counterterrorism expert who went by his nickname, Jerry. The Pentagon insisted that Garner was not pushed out, that the plan was always to replace him with a more senior diplomat. But his abrupt departure interrupted Garner's work and left both Iraqis and Congress with the idea that the United States was scrambling to fix a mess. Garner himself was surprised by the call, which, like many things in Iraq that involved Rumsfeld, was both decisive and lacking in specifics.

"How long do you want me to stay?" Garner asked Rumsfeld.

"You and Jerry work it out," Rumsfeld responded.[41]

On May 1 President Bush was flown onto the deck of the USS *Abraham Lincoln*. Standing on the deck beneath a banner that said "Mission Accomplished," he declared that "major combat" had ended. With considerably less fanfare, he also announced that the rebuilding of Iraq had begun. "Our coalition will stay until our work is done and then we will leave and we will leave behind a free Iraq," he said. Eleven days later Bremer arrived in Baghdad. ORHA was dissolved and replaced by the Coalition Provisional Authority. By the end of the month, Garner quietly left Iraq. The first act of the reconstruction was over.

Feith insisted in an interview nearly three years after the invasion that the Bush administration had planned appropriately for Iraq. At the time, he was writing his own book on Iraq, and documents were stacked everywhere in the library of his home in suburban Washington. The papers were a physical record of the debate over the war in Iraq within the Bush administration, living proof, he claimed, of the planning that had been done. His office, he admitted to me, had not drawn up detailed plans — that was the military's job. Indeed, Feith said, his five-page, bullet-point outlines for reconstructing a nation were all that could be expected of a high-level official. "They're both called plans, and some journalists and others get confused by the terminology."

Feith acknowledged that ORHA had not worked as he had hoped. He told me that he envisioned ORHA as a "module" to plug into Central Command, which had responsibility for postwar Iraq. Franks would work with Garner, who would then serve as the military's bridge to the civilian world of the State Department and USAID. Instead the two sides did not get along. Each referred to the other as "they." The lack of coordination exposed a fundamental weakness: the U.S. bureaucracy was not set up for occupation.

"ORHA became part of CENTCOM when ORHA deployed to Kuwait. But the ORHA and CENTCOM people never got to the point where they talked as if they were in the same organization. The integration was not what was hoped for," Feith told me. "It's hard to get organizations to integrate, especially when they haven't practiced working jointly together over many years. This is true even among military organizations. It's even harder when you're talking about integrating civilian and military bodies. This has been a problem in the U.S. government for decades."

UTTERLY BROKEN

Jerry Bremer got a glimpse into the fundamental misunderstanding of Iraq's infrastructure and economy on his first night in Iraq. After driving in from the airport, he was greeted at the Republican Palace by the smell of diesel fuel and of sewage overflowing from the portable toilets. That evening he held a "warts and all" briefing with the senior advisers, the Americans assigned to each of Iraq's ministries to get them operating again. Pete Gibson, the senior adviser to the Electricity Ministry, told Bremer that the entire country was only generating about 300 megawatts of power — not enough to light a small city in the United States.[42]

Over the next month, Bremer got ever grimmer reports from his senior advisers. The oil industry was suffering from a lack of investment that extended back a decade. Although Iraq sat over an ocean of oil, its refineries could not make enough gasoline or cooking fuel to supply internal needs. Long lines were forming at gas stations and riots were breaking out. The economy was on the verge of collapse. The country's state-owned industries, the lumbering, bloated remnants of Saddam's socialist government, were broke, requiring nearly $1 billion a year in subsidies to stay afloat. The value of the Iraqi dinar was swinging wildly on informal street exchanges. Half of Iraq's fifteen thousand schools were in need of repair. There was only one schoolbook for every six children. Crumbling pipes had slashed the availability of fresh, clean drinking water. None of Baghdad's sanitation plants were working, sending a half-million gallons of raw sewage into the Tigris River every day.[43] Bremer was stunned. A frantic series of briefings in Washington had not prepared him for how badly Iraq had decayed under the twelve years of sanctions imposed against Saddam by the United Nations and the United States.

"Nobody had given me a sense of how utterly broken this country was," Bremer said.[44]

THE CIRCUS

The enormity of these physical plant problems demanded Bremer's complete attention. But instead he was immersed in the politics of forming a new Iraqi government. In doing so he made two controversial decisions that dramatically affected the prospects for success. First he issued an order that purged all senior Baath Party officials from public office. The Pentagon believed that the purge was necessary to prove to the Iraqis that the United States was serious about removing Saddam and his cronies from power. But since membership in the party had been a requirement for advancement, Bremer's order effectively removed all of the most experienced public administrators. Senior advisers to the ministries suddenly found themselves working with third- and fourth-tier bureaucrats who had no idea how to run a massive organization. Nor were they used to showing initiative.

The second order disbanded the Iraqi army. Bremer described the decision as recognition of reality. The Iraqi army had disappeared in the face of the invading coalition forces. But Garner's lieutenants had tracked down several Iraqi generals, and in meetings they had spoken of bringing these generals into the process of building a new country. The sudden change of plans created deep resentment in Iraq's military leadership, especially among the Sunnis at the top of the hierarchy, who would go on to lead the Iraqi-based insurgency. And since those disbanded included troops of all ranks, Bremer created 500,000 potential enemies with a pen stroke. Rather than rebuild their country, as the State Department's Future of Iraq project had envisioned, many of Iraq's soldiers turned into its destroyers.

Meanwhile responsibility for actually rebuilding the country drifted, spread among U.S. senior advisers in different ministries, the military's civil affairs soldiers, and U.S. agencies like USAID and the U.S. Army Corps of Engineers. There was no one person that Bremer tasked with the job of rebuilding. Instead it all fell on Bremer, one man juggling the formation of a new government, consultation with the military about an ongoing campaign, and the establishment of a new society. Among those priorities, the reconstruction came last.

Back in Washington a frantic effort began to find people to serve in Iraq. Responsibility for the task fell to the personnel office at the White House responsible for doling out political jobs at the Pentagon. The two people in charge were Jim O'Beirne and Jerry Jones. Jones had served in a similar position in the Nixon and Ford administrations. O'Beirne was a fixture on the conservative scene, and his wife, Kate O'Beirne, was the Washington editor for the *National Review*. The two men turned to those they knew best: Republicans and friends from past and present administrations, some with questionable qualifications. Among them was Darrell Trent, a sixty-six-year-old former Transportation Department secretary and friend of Donald Rumsfeld. Trent was hired to head Iraq's Transportation and Communications Ministry and would later be fired after he began negotiations to sell off Iraq's state airline to a company involved in the Oil-for-Food corruption scandal. Another was Thomas Foley, a Republican donor, business school classmate of President Bush's, and corporate bailout specialist placed in charge of selling off Iraq's state-owned businesses. His effort to privatize the economy was widely regarded as a failure. Still another

Bush administration pick was Bernie Kerick, the New York police commissioner and tabloid fixture, thanks to a high-powered mistress and alleged Mafia connections. He was given the job of training a new police force and would leave within months. Another appointee was Mike Karem, a consultant involved in the 1980s Housing and Urban Development scandal. The senior adviser to the Ministry of Housing and Construction, he would be forced out after coalition officials accused him of meeting in private to cut deals between American contractors and Iraqi counterparts. Devotion to the Republican cause became one of the factors in the hiring process. One job applicant was quizzed on his views of *Roe v. Wade*.[45] O'Beirne would strongly deny that political allegiance played a role in hiring. But the cavalcade of political appointees became a joke: "They don't call it the Republican Palace for nothing."[46]

Young, conservative college graduates with no experience were also favorite job recruits. They included Jay Hallen, a twenty-four-year-old Yale graduate who had applied for a job at the White House. A political science major, Hallen was instead put in charge of opening Baghdad's new stock market. Hallen was surprised when he was told to report for duty in a month's time. "Needless to say, I was in a mild state of shock," he said.[47] Another was Simone Ledeen, the twenty-nine-year-old daughter of Michael Ledeen, a leading neoconservative and scholar at the conservative American Enterprise Institute. She became a de facto budget director for the reconstruction. At one point the Pentagon contacted the Heritage Foundation and asked the conservative think tank for its database of job applicants. The résumés provided the coalition with recruits who were young, passionate, extremely ideological, and inexperienced. Lt. Col. Brad Jackson, a coalition adviser, said he was bombarded by impractical requests for information from Ledeen's budget team. "There were a lot of people who, being political science majors, didn't know what an income statement was, who were asking the impossible. . . . That was giving us ulcers, quite frankly," Jackson said. Ledeen herself was aware of the young staffers' shortcomings: "We knew we were overwhelmed," she said.[48] James Dobbins, a RAND analyst and reconstruction expert, later coined a term that perfectly captured the mix of good intention and questionable competence. The coalition staff, he said, was filled with "heroic amateurs."

As the White House sent young and old to act as Iraq's new government, the war sharks came flooding in — businessmen who sensed the opportunity in chaos. One of the first was Victor Bout, a Russian arms broker accused of violating UN sanctions. Contractors and coalition officials began using air-lines owned by air fleet companies linked to Bout to bring in electrical equipment and other supplies. The CIA warned about the associations with Bout, but companies tied to his network were among the few in the world that would risk flying into Baghdad's dangerous airport to deliver the goods.[49] Another businessman was A. Huda Farouki, a Washington socialite who was a close friend of Ahmed Chalabi. Farouki's firm had been bailed out of bankruptcy in the 1990s by a loan from Chalabi's Jordan bank. Al-though Farouki had no experience in arms dealing, his firms won an $80 million contract to guard Iraq's oil pipelines and a second to supply its fledgling army with weapons and equipment. Then there was Dale Stoffel, a former naval intelligence officer. Stoffel had once been accused in a Human Rights Watch report as an arms trafficker. He had also been accused, then exonerated, in a deal with Boeing airlines to supply the firm a top-secret Russian undersea missile for testing purposes. Stoffel would wind up in the middle of a messy deal to sell tanks to the Iraqis, and was killed in a myste-rious attack by men claiming to be insurgents.

Given such a cast of characters, the hallways and meeting rooms at the Republican Palace that hot, sweaty summer took on the air of the cantina bar in *Star Wars*. Twenty-somethings from America outfitted by the Gap mixed with U.S. military brass in desert boots. Iraqi expats in Dolce and Gabbana camouflage cut deals with Sunni tribal leaders in headdresses and robes. Outside, beefy Fijians, wiry Nepalese, and heavily muscled South African security guards ripped through Baghdad's streets in ar-mored SUVs, machine guns sticking out the windows. Truckers from Pak-istan and India drove fuel-laden rigs to gas stations, where they were besieged by mobs of angry Iraqis. American engineers in hard hats and goggles poked into Iraq's power plants and were stunned to find equip-ment still in operation that had been installed some fifty years earlier.

Senior American and British officials who had spent their lives in gov-ernment service were aghast. The Bush administration had hoped to show the Iraqis the benefits of a democracy. Instead they were providing a cir-cus, a Looney Tunes version of government, hatched on the fly, delivered at random, and operating without instruction. There seemed to be no rules, except that it helped to have good friends and ideological sympathies with the Bush administration's inner circle. On the ground there were no refer-ees, no adult supervision. Anything was possible; and the Iraqis were wait-ing to see what their new overlords would do.

"There was very much the sense that we were getting in way over our heads within weeks," said Robin Raphel. "We all knew it. It was very obvious to me that we couldn't do this, we could not run a country that we did not understand. . . . It was very much amateur hour."[50]

Nation-building experts have another name for the period right after the collapse of a government: "the golden hour," a reference to the trauma room dictum that there is a limited window of time in which to save a person's life. A new government has a brief chance to demonstrate that it represents a change for the better. In Iraq the summer of 2003 was the golden hour — but for businessmen, not the Iraqis. The Bush administration had ignored scenarios that contrasted with their rosy vision of postwar success. When the facts on the ground proved different, they had no idea what lay ahead, or how much it would cost. The patient was on the table, dying, and nobody knew what to do.

3

Back at the Ranch

At 7:30 one morning in July 2003, with the temperature in his office already past 100 degrees, Jerry Bremer got a visit from his money man, a crusty former nuclear submarine commander named David Oliver. All that month Bremer's advisers had reported on the decrepit state of Iraq's infrastructure. It came down to this: If Iraq was a used car, the United States bought it just before the engine blew. Now there was more bad news. Iraq's oil revenue would not be nearly enough to get the country moving again. In fact the coalition government would run out of money by December. "Boss, we're going broke," said Oliver, the budget director.[1]

Oliver's analysis was the Bush administration's first inkling that the reconstruction was going to cost far more than planned. Initially Bush dedicated $2.4 billion to the task. But over three years, the United States doled out more than $30 billion to the reconstruction of Iraq. The amount was more in constant dollars than any single nation in Europe received under the Marshall Plan. It was three times the total given to Germany, which, unlike Iraq, saw its infrastructure *and* cities leveled by wartime bombing. Thirty billion dollars is more than the annual GDP of Luxembourg, El Salvador, or Jordan — more, in fact, than that of most nations on earth. As a company, Iraq would have ranked among the top fifty largest revenue-earners in the United States.

Looking at just the numbers, it seems hard to fault President Bush or Congress for a lack of generosity when it came to rebuilding Iraq. But then, much of the money didn't go to Iraq. Billion by billion, politicians in Washington could not resist such an enormous pot of money. They constantly intervened in Iraq's reconstruction to benefit friends, constituents, and occasionally business partners. Usually the intervention did more to aid American corporations than impoverished Iraqis. The favors were passed out in typical Washington style — behind closed doors, between lobbyists and politicians, at committee meetings that left no trace of fingerprints. What appeared to be a remarkably generous foreign aid package was in fact a remarkable program of domestic handouts and corporate welfare. For a predominantly Muslim country, Iraq became an especially rich source of pork.

Bush launched the reconstruction of Iraq a week after the invasion. His $2.4 billion proposal (mostly for humanitarian aid and the repair of oil and electricity plants) was a relatively modest sum, and lawmakers wondered whether the amount was sufficient. In an appearance before Congress, Paul Wolfowitz assured them it would be. Rebuilding, he suggested, would take only six months. And the burden wouldn't fall only on America. Coalition partners would kick in money. Wolfowitz further boasted that Iraq would pay for its own reconstruction. The country's oil reserves were capable of generating up to $100 billion over the next three years, more than enough to cover costs.

While $2.4 billion was, in the scale of things, a puny amount, it was still a tidy sum for the firm that could get its hands on it. And plenty of firms had their hands out, most of them heavy donors to both parties, with well-connected lobbyists. The first infusion of cash was awarded to a handful of American multinationals in a contracting process fraught with controversy. On March 8 the U.S. Army Corps of Engineers awarded a Halliburton subsidiary called KBR the first big prize of the war: a contract worth up to $7 billion — to be paid with U.S. and Iraqi funds — to put out oil fires. The contract was negotiated in secret and no other companies were allowed to compete. The company's former CEO was Vice President Dick Cheney. When news of the KBR deal broke, Democrats pounced: "Given the suspicion that many Americans have about why we're going to war, and the constant speculation that we're at war for oil, I think the vice president should do everything he can . . . to remove even the appearance of a conflict of interest," said Representative Maxine Waters, the outspoken California Democrat. Nobody at the White House seemed concerned.

A month later Bechtel Corporation, the privately held San Francisco engineering firm whose board included Washington heavyweights such as Reagan's former secretary of state George Shultz, won the second biggest prize of the war. USAID awarded the company a $680 million deal in a secretive process in which only select, well-known U.S. multinational corporations were invited to participate. Bechtel's contract was supposed to become the primary vehicle to rebuild Iraq. The company would construct every bridge, road, power plant, and school that the federal government deemed necessary. Antiwar protesters held demonstrations at the entrance to the company's headquarters in San Francisco for two weeks to no real effect. The United States had contracted out nation building.

THE BUSINESS MODEL

As Bremer and Oliver analyzed the figures that summer day, it became clear that the $2.4 billion was only a down payment on the repairs needed to get Iraq running again. Oliver and a military buddy, a soft-spoken, white-haired former admiral named David L. Nash, went around to the U.S. senior advisers conducting what they called an "unconstrained drill." Each American adviser had been tasked with talking to his or her U.S.-appointed counterparts in Iraqi ministries to come up with a list of projects in need of funding. The result was heavy on bricks and mortar — new schools, hospitals, and power — and was more of a Christmas list than a plan for building a new democracy. USAID had anticipated taking responsibility for the reconstruction. After being pushed aside by the Pentagon, some of the agency's employees couldn't believe the haphazard approach. "It wasn't just a matter of fixing a road or fixing an electric plant, refilling stores or fixing schools; it was a matter of [how] to make those many activities politically meaningful," said Larry Crandall, a former USAID director in Haiti who rose to become the second in command for the reconstruction in Iraq. Not told to restrict their Santa lists, the Iraqi ministers and those beneath them found it easy to assume that all their wishes would come true. "There was a lot of lip service for months and months and months," Crandall recalled, "and it created a lot of disillusion on the part of the individuals who were talking serious reconstruction, who were talking serious economic development."[2]

In late July, Bremer made his first trip back to the United States, hoping to convince the White House to add $5 billion.[3] He got far more than he hoped, thanks to Doug Feith. Like Oliver and Nash, Feith had little experience in post-conflict development. He approached the rebuilding more or less like a business. His office did an analysis that concluded that increased reconstruction spending would decrease spending down the road on military operations. The faster Iraq rebuilt, the sooner U.S. troops could come home. It was a matter of input and output. There was not a lot of thought given to whether Iraq's shattered economy could handle such a large infusion of cash; whether the Iraqis had the training and management abilities to run such a big investment; or whether the country could support such projects in the future. Feith compared it to a corporation analyzing how much it could save by "front loading" an investment, and he urged Bremer to think bigger.

Two weeks after Bremer's visit, the administration rolled out an aggressive public relations campaign to prepare Congress and the American people for the news that the price tag for Iraq was going to soar. After a morning of fishing with Cheney, Bush met with reporters at his ranch in Crawford, Texas. Iraq was improving, he told them, and there were even better days ahead. "In a lot of places, the infrastructure is as good as it was at prewar levels, which is satisfactory, but it's not the ultimate aim. The ultimate aim is for the infrastructure to be the best in the region."[4]

His declaration came just as the White House was put on notice that the occupation was about to become more difficult. In August car bombs obliterated the Jordanian embassy and the United Nations compound in Baghdad. Sergio Vieira de Mello, the UN mission leader, was killed, and shortly thereafter the United Nations, with all its expertise in postconflict development, pulled out its workers. Many international agencies followed suit.

In September, Bush formally broke the news: the White House wanted $87 billion for the war in Iraq. Most of the money was for the military, which was burning $4 billion per month, but $20.3 billion was dedicated to the reconstruction of Iraq and Afghanistan. Over the next month, the administration laid out its plans in greater detail. Bremer provided Congress with a laundry list of projects, developed from Oliver and Nash's unconstrained drill and a World Bank assessment that found the country was in need of $55 billion in investment. Since the last time that the Bush administration had checked in — which was not frequently — the price of everything had gone up. The biggest items were power, security, oil, and water. The administration's proposal included $5.7 billion to rebuild the country's electrical system, $5.1 billion to train and equip security forces, $3.7 billion to supply potable water to 90 percent of the population, and an additional $2.1 billion to rebuild the oil industry.

The price tag caused panic in Congress. With the election year coming up, Democrats seized upon Bremer's request as evidence that the administration had planned too little, too late for Iraq. Others decried the "obscene profits" flowing toward contractors. Even the normally disciplined Republicans rebelled. "It is very hard for me to go home to explain why you have to give $20 billion to a country sitting on $1 trillion worth of oil," said plainspoken South Carolina senator Lindsey O. Graham.[5]

Despite the objections, Bush got almost everything he asked for. Public Law 108-106 set aside $18.4 billion for the reconstruction of Iraq. Nash and Oliver's Christmas list had been approved. Bush signed the bill at a White House ceremony on November 6, 2003. He called the reconstruction bill the "greatest commitment of its kind since the Marshall Plan." "By this action, we show the generous spirit of our country, and we serve the interest of our country," Bush said.

He could hardly have done more to signal the importance of the effort. But it would become quickly tangled in bureaucratic hoops, corporate greed, and violence. One of those interfering in the process was the president's wife.

HOSPITAL ON A HILL

As the White House put together its funding package to rebuild Iraq during the summer of 2003, Laura Bush asked an old Bush family friend to tour Iraq to develop recommendations for improving health care. John P. Howe III readily agreed. The Bushes had come to know Howe in Texas, where George Bush had been governor. Howe served as the president of the University of Texas Health Science Center in San Antonio, one of the state's leading medical institutions. After a waterskiing accident convinced him to step down in 2000, he went looking for a new challenge and a higher national profile.[6] He found them as president of Project HOPE, a Virginia-based international health group that had built its fame on an eponymous hospital ship. The ship, which had visited developing countries throughout the world, was mothballed in 1974, and Project HOPE was now involved mostly in health projects around the globe, from AIDS education in Africa to a children's hospital in Shanghai.

What Howe found in Iraq was a health care system in almost complete collapse. Once the best in the Arab world, Iraq's system had deteriorated badly under twelve years of UN sanctions. The Health Ministry estimated that as many as 25 percent of Iraq's eighteen thousand physicians fled the country after the U.S.-led invasion. Those who remained had no access to continuing education. Medical supplies and equipment were shoddy, the product of the graft-riddled Oil-for-Food program, which swapped Iraqi oil for humanitarian supplies under the UN sanctions regime. Hospitals and health clinics were in disrepair. In one survey, fewer than one-third of Iraq's clinics had "relatively clean" toilets. Women and children suffered the most. In southern Iraq, 150 out of 1,000 children were dying before reaching the age of five — the highest rate in the Middle East. Life expectancy in Iraq had fallen to under sixty years.

Howe called the trip "eye opening."[7] Confronted by Third World health care, Howe suggested a First World solution, one that provided a potential public relations boost to his charity, its corporate backers, and the Bushes. Howe convinced Mrs. Bush that Iraq would be an ideal place for a high-end children's hospital, similar to ones Project HOPE had started in Poland and China. Howe worked with Shirin Tahir-Kheli, Condoleezza Rice's senior director for democracy, human rights, and international operations, to develop a plan for a $500 million hospital on a hill. It would be a state-of-the-art pediatric care center, offering specialized care for children's cancer, high-risk pregnancies, and burn treatment, as well as an advanced plastic surgery clinic. The United States would pay for building the hospital, through USAID's contract with Bechtel. Howe promised his group would take care of the rest: Project HOPE would supply the training for Iraqi staff and administrators. Medicine, supplies, and equipment would come from Project HOPE's corporate backers, who provided most of the charity's revenue. In exchange, pharmaceutical and medical technology firms like Pfizer, GlaxoSmithKline, and Johnson & Johnson Healthcare Systems would have an Iraqi showcase for their products.

Within Project HOPE, the proposal stirred concern. The children's hospital in Krakow had been a logistical and financial strain. There were internal complaints that Howe, who always enjoyed the spotlight, was putting his desire for publicity over the charity's primary mission of humanitarian assistance. HOPE stands for Health Opportunities for People, but some disgruntled staff began to refer to it as Howe's Own Personal Enterprise. One former senior executive said the hospital proposal showed that Howe was "more interested in chasing dollars than quality programs."

The plan also caused an uproar among the international health experts at USAID. There was no doubt that Iraq needed a children's hospital. But Iraq needed lots of things. A new, expensive hospital was not its top priority. The country was in dire need of the basics: new clinics, clean water supplies, vaccines, and public health campaigns. It was a question of medical economics. Far more children's lives could be saved by spending $500 million on basic medicine rather than a new hospital.

Richard Garfield, a public health professor at Columbia University, is one of the world's leading experts on Iraq's health care system. As a consultant for USAID and the World Health Organization, he made repeated trips to Iraq over a decade, first during the sanctions period and then after the U.S. invasion. USAID asked Garfield to analyze the hospital plan. When he asked for more information, he got an eight-page fax sent from Iraq. It was nearly illegible and details were scarce. "Everyone at AID was moaning and groaning. Everybody understood that this was the wrong thing to do," Garfield told me. "It's infinitely quicker and cheaper to rehabilitate an old hospital. It was clear that this new hospital, a symbol of American support, would not provide services for at least eight years. It was cynical." Agency experts tried to block the project. Senior USAID officials overruled them. The White House wanted the hospital. "We ended up . . . agreeing to disagree," one senior U.S. official told me.

COMING TO PASS

When the hospital proposal reached Congress, it faced more skepticism. Both Democrats and Republicans opposed it. Representative Jim Kolbe, the moderate Arizona Republican in charge of foreign operations for the House Appropriations Committee, blocked it altogether. He didn't understand how a country without reliable electricity or water supply could support such a high-end facility. "Why should we build a hospital for kids first when kids in Iraq need clean water?" one staffer asked. Senator Patrick Leahy, the Vermont Democrat, agreed to enough funding to pay for architectural plans, but didn't want to go any further. "We don't doubt there are needs. But we have questions. This was a politically driven initiative which wasn't a reflection of the best public health needs that the country had," a Senate staff member told me. In response both Kolbe and Leahy received visits from the White House. In the meetings National Security Council staffers made it clear that Laura Bush herself wanted the hospital built. Leahy and Kolbe reluctantly agreed to approve it with modifications.

The compromise drastically cut the size and cost of the hospital, to $50 million. Project HOPE would raise $30 million for the training and equipment. The hospital would have ninety-four beds and include private pediatric oncology suites, a linear accelerator, and modern CAT scan equipment — all unheard-of features in Iraq. But the hospital would also be retooled to offer general medical services as well. "Of course we want to improve health care in Iraq, but we should focus on solving the most immediate and pervasive problems like the lack of safe water, child immunizations, and community clinics that can meet the basic needs of large numbers of people," Leahy said after the negotiation's conclusion. "I am concerned about spending large sums on a state-of-the-art hospital that may be more the result of political pressure than the best use of taxpayer dollars."

The White House said the Iraqis supported the hospital. Some did, but for reasons different from those of the administration. Under Saddam, the Iraqi Health Ministry had documented an eightfold higher incidence of childhood cancer in Iraq than in the West. The problem was especially bad in Basra, where leukemia in children had rocketed 70 percent since 1989. Saddam used the increased cancer rates as a propaganda weapon. He blamed them on the first Gulf War, when U.S. forces used shells hardened with depleted uranium. It was an article of faith among Iraqis that the shells caused the higher cancer rates, although there was no scientific proof. As the Iraqis saw it, an oncology hospital in Basra was simply a way for the son to expiate the sins of the father. "It would be more useful for the Basra people to have a modern pediatric hospital than to spend any cash on other services. Children in Basra are suffering more than in any other part of Iraq," said Faisal Ahmed, a banker in Basra who had once been a top police official.

Others Iraqis were more dubious. Fakhir Mousawi, the director general of the city, was struggling to get electricity, provide clean drinking water, and clear away the rotting piles of vegetables and scrap metal heaped alongside Basra's potholed roads. More than 80 percent of the city government's office equipment, supplies, and vehicles were looted after Saddam's fall. City officials had been reduced to renting cars to move around town. "I would prefer that that money be spent on the services and infrastructure that we need right now," Mousawi said. The reduced sum of $50 million amounted to a small fortune if used wisely on public health needs.

For her part, Laura Bush acknowledged supporting the hospital when a colleague of mine surprised her with a question during an interview in

2004. She did not want to discuss details, though, because final approval was still pending. "It will be a hospital with new, good equipment," she said. "We hope that can come to pass."

MYSTERY IN BASRA

Eighteen months later, it did. Laura Bush's gift to the people of Iraq began to rise in a dusty lot on the outskirts of Basra. When I visited in August 2005, about two dozen Iraqis in blue jumpsuits and yellow hard hats were hauling rebar around the thirteen-acre site. They were subcontractors of a Lebanese company that in turn was subcontracted to Bechtel. Cranes were unloading bundles of steel. Dust blasted across the lot, which was surrounded by a ten-foot-high concrete wall of gray cinder block. Outside, armed guards patrolled with jumpsuits that bore the label South Action Security and Protection Company. The foreman on-site, who did not want to reveal his name for fear of becoming a target of insurgents, said a police officer had been killed just down the road earlier in the month. "We are struggling. Security is not the best," he said.

From the street the hospital appeared to be a fortress, or perhaps a prison. Across the way, Iraqi shepherds sold sheep from ramshackle roadside stands crafted from wood and corrugated tin. The air was filled with bleating, rushing cars, and the scent of manure. It was hard to imagine a gleaming hospital rising amid the clamor. It was even harder to tell whether Iraqis would appreciate the gesture. Much had changed in Iraq since the project was first proposed, and there was no longer any effort to identify the project as an American gift. Even in Basra, a relatively quiet spot, it was simply too dangerous to tie the hospital to the United States. The sign out front said it was being built by the Iraqi Ministry of Health.

The secrecy gave the project an air of mystery. Some in Basra said Koreans were involved. Others thought the wife of the president had ordered its construction. Even Abdulamir Khafaji, the head of the pediatrics department for Basra's largest hospital, was unsure what was being built. Khafaji was surprised when I told him it was supposed to be a children's hospital. Sitting on an overstuffed couch in his office, he waved his hand at the hospital around him, built in 1938. Cracks ran through the plaster. Some of the walls along the narrow hallways seemed to be buckling. His own pediatric ward did not have enough space, requiring two and even three children to share beds. Nor did his nurses or doctors have up-to-date training.

Khafaji shook his head at the notion that America was building a new pediatric clinic in his own town without his knowledge. He later e-mailed me a twenty-four-page PowerPoint presentation and asked me to forward it to Bush. He had his own ideas for health care reform. "We have more important priorities to solve our urgent health problems," Khafaji said.

Laura Bush's hospital was emblematic of the problems with U.S. efforts to improve the Iraqi health care system. Again and again, the focus was on construction, not education, on infusing American corporations with cash, not providing ordinary Iraqis with a better life. America's single biggest health initiative was a $500 million contract to build clinics and hospitals given to Parsons Corporation, one of the country's largest engineering firms. It was like hiring Frank Gehry to design a tool shed. The plans called for simple, two-story brick structures scattered in neighborhoods throughout Iraq. Iraq's preexisting hospitals needed cleaning, refurbishment, and equipment. Both could have been done by Iraqi firms. "When you're talking about highly specialized work, like the oil industry or the generation of electricity, it makes sense to use these expert firms," said Karen Durham-Aguilera, who oversaw reconstruction programs for the Army Corps of Engineers. "When you're talking about brick-and-mortar work, when you're talking about small healthcare facilities . . . it does not make sense."

Another major health care initiative also faltered thanks to problems with a contractor. In April 2003 the USAID issued a $43 million contract to Abt Associates, a Massachusetts consulting firm, to modernize the Iraqi Health Ministry and provide needed supplies. But the company, which worked on health care issues throughout the developing world, quickly ran into problems, according to an audit by the USAID inspector general. Company officials were slow to mobilize, and once they did, they bickered with Iraqis and Coalition Provisional Authority officials. One Abt manager "did not recognize" the CPA as a "legitimate authority," the audit said. Medical kits intended for six hundred clinics were delivered eight months late and contained damaged or useless equipment. One USAID subcontractor involved in the delivery said he had "never witnessed such a debacle" in twenty years of working with the agency. In the end, USAID officials cut Abt's contract, paying it only $23 million. "I saw enormous incompetence, which was more costly than even Iraqi corruption," said Richard Garfield, who was in Iraq during the time Abt was working. The United States, he told me, "was pouring money down the drain."

FAILING THE CHILDREN

Although reliable statistics were scarce, U.S. spending did not seem to markedly improve Iraq's bleak health care landscape. One year after the invasion, easily treatable conditions such as diarrhea and respiratory illness accounted for 70 percent of deaths among children, according to a 2004 Iraqi Health Ministry study. One year later, a UN study found that a third of the children in southern and central Iraq were malnourished, the same as in 2003. Even U.S. officials involved in the effort were angered: "If the amount of child mortality under Saddam and since the conflict [had] happened in the States, things would be in an uproar," I was told by one U.S. official. "We could be doing more than we are." A study by RAND in 2006 underscored the consequences of the U.S. failure to improve health care in Iraq. The study examined seven nation-building efforts since World War II and found that health care improvements played a crucial role in the success of rebuilding. Most important, the study found a link between health care and security. American officials handing out powdered milk to Japanese schoolchildren after World War II helped build good will that played a role in maintaining a benign security environment. The final conclusion was blunt: "Nation-building efforts cannot be successful unless adequate attention is paid to health," the study said.[8]

But the priorities of the Bush administration's own health experts were of only occasional concern in Washington. USAID officials ticked off achievements, issuing monthly press releases to praise improvements. A public health campaign resulted in polio vaccinations for 98 percent of Iraqi children. The U.S. dramatically increased pay for doctors and nurses. It raised the Health Ministry budget from $16 million under Saddam to $210 million in 2003. There was a training program for nurses and doctors. The U.S. focus on buildings like Laura Bush's hospital, a spokeswoman said, would pay off as well. "We're building for the future," said Heather Layman, a USAID spokeswoman. "Our belief is that planning for the future and setting ambitious goals ultimately helps the Iraqis achieve their goals."

The ambition was clear at a gala reception that Laura Bush hosted on a chilly night in Washington in October 2005. Held at the Andrew W. Mellon Auditorium, an elegant 8,000-square-foot ballroom a few blocks from the White House, the dinner was designed to raise more than $1 million for the Project HOPE hospital. Gilded columns shot to the ceiling, where four crystal chandeliers hung. In the cavernous central hall, diners in black tuxedos and evening gowns sat at tables set with silver and decorated with red roses. Laura Bush, Condoleezza Rice, and John Howe congratulated each other on the hospital project. "The sickest and most severely injured children of Iraq desperately need our help," Howe said. "We will touch their hearts and the hearts of their families. We can't fail the children."

Rice described the hospital as "one promising part of a larger and hopeful picture." She praised Laura Bush, saying that her support "has been and continues to be absolutely essential." When the first lady rose to speak, the audience gave her a standing ovation. She told them that their contributions were helping make a brighter future in Iraq. "Every country's success depends upon the health and well-being of its children," Mrs. Bush said. "By working together, we can help future generations of Iraqi children grow up strong and healthy."

But Richard Garfield, the Columbia University doctor, said it was too late for some Iraqi children. He feared the hospital would meet the fate of many such ambitious projects in the Third World, with the Iraqis unable to maintain it after the United States and Project HOPE departed. "Many deaths would have been averted if this money had gone into setting up clinics for diarrhea and respiratory illness," he said. "It was a stupid thing."

OIL AND AIR

One case in particular demonstrated how political favors, money, and corporate avarice strangled the reconstruction process from the start. It began in March 2003, when a lobbyist named Jonas Neihardt paid a visit to the offices of Representative Darrell Issa, a Republican congressman from California. Neihardt represented Qualcomm, the San Diego telecommunications company in Issa's backyard. He wanted to talk business.[9]

USAID was proposing to award a contract to build a cellular phone network in Baghdad after Saddam was deposed. Neihardt told Issa's staff that he was worried by rumors that the proposal favored a European cellular phone technology called the Global System for Mobile Communications, or GSM. Qualcomm had patented a competing technology called Code Division Multiple Access, known as CDMA. The two telecom standards were locked in a global battle for dominance, a modern-day version of Microsoft versus Apple. Neihardt's point was simple: If the United States was going to the trouble of invading Iraq, shouldn't American companies reap the rewards?

Issa, a Republican car alarm dealer whose district is filled with Qualcomm employees, agreed. "The U.S. government will soon hand U.S. taxpayer dollars over to French, German, and other European cell phone equipment companies to build the new Iraqi cell phone system. This is not acceptable," Issa wrote in a letter to Defense Secretary Don Rumsfeld. On March 26, with soldiers charging toward Baghdad, Issa introduced a bill on the floor of the House that demanded that the U.S. government give preference to American companies in awarding contracts in Iraq. It specifically required that any cellular phone contracts use CDMA technology — guaranteeing that Qualcomm would make money off the war. Issa's bill failed, but House Resolution 1441 was the first sign that Iraq was open for business to American firms, courtesy of their friends in Congress.

The race to build the first mobile phone system in Iraq eventually erupted into one of the biggest scandals of the reconstruction. It destroyed the careers of two American civil servants who blew the whistle, led to an FBI investigation, the cancellation of a portion of a lucrative contract, the resignation of a senior Republican political appointee, and a congressional inquiry into the Defense Department's inspector general. The players included the Senate's longest-serving Republican, Ted Stevens, of Alaska; a former elevator engineer turned Iraqi minister of communications; a dashing young Irish Internet entrepreneur; an international financier suspected of ties to Saddam Hussein; and a tribe of Alaska Natives. The action played out from Iraq to the Pentagon's E-ring to the Arctic Circle. It was, without question, the strangest chapter of the reconstruction.

The story turned not on Iraq's most famous natural resource, oil, but on its most unexploited: air. Afraid of the threat the mobile devices represented, Saddam had blocked the formation of a cellular phone system during the long years of his dictatorship. On the eve of the war, Iraq was the last major untapped market in the world — a nation with 26 million people and no cellular phones. Analysts guessed the country was worth between $500 million and $1 billion in revenue per year to the company that built out and ran a network. That was big money by any standards — a siren's call that could not go unheeded in Washington.

The untrammeled airwaves represented a particular attraction for Qualcomm, whose technology had struggled to gain a foothold outside the United States. Qualcomm's technology had many advantages — it required fewer cellular phone towers and was also more advanced in its ability to move large chunks of data. But the European technology, developed in France, was more widespread, in use throughout Europe and the United States, where it was employed by companies such as T-Mobile, Cingular, and AT&T. In the Middle East, GSM was completely dominant, the standard in every country. That gave Qualcomm little chance to penetrate the market, since the two systems are incompatible. (Most phones using European technology cannot access a CDMA-based network and vice versa.) But if Iraq chose Qualcomm's technology for its network, every Arab businessman who traveled to Iraq would have to purchase a new cellular phone, one to use in Iraq and another for use in his home country. As a result its technology seemed almost certain to lose out — unless the U.S. government was willing to help.

JACK SHAW

Qualcomm's first two efforts to break into the Iraqi market failed. In late May 2003, the Defense Department, on behalf of the Coalition Provisional Authority, awarded a small cellular phone contract worth $45 million to MCI — a boost to the fortunes of another U.S. company. MCI, formerly WorldCom, had entered bankruptcy in 2002 to recover from an accounting scandal that resulted in a $500 million fine from the Securities and Exchange Commission. Despite its suspect history, MCI established a functioning, if unreliable, Iraqi cellular phone system by June 2003, using the European GSM technology.

Qualcomm's second shot came in the summer, when the coalition announced a competition to award three cellular phone licenses to operate in Iraq. Qualcomm joined a consortium called Liberty Mobile led by a mysterious Irish entrepreneur named Declan Ganley. A multimillionaire, Ganley alternately drove a Rolls-Royce and a Mercedes, traveled around Europe in a helicopter that he parked by his lavish mansion in Galway, and threw legendary parties. In interviews with reporters, he declined to provide many details about his wealth, but it was clear he knew how to operate in emerging markets, places with chaotic conditions and flexible rules. He made his fortune in the Russian timber business after the collapse of the Soviet Union, then invested in a series of Internet, telecom, and other ventures in places like Latvia, Bulgaria, and Albania. Iraq was the latest frontier to promise great riches for great risk.

When the final winners of the cellular phone contest were announced on October 7 by the Iraqi minister of communications, Haider al Abadi,

Liberty Mobile was not among them. Instead the three licenses went to GSM operators with proven track records of operations in the Middle East: Orascom, a group based in Egypt; Asia Cell Telecommunications, an existing Kurdish GSM operator; and Atheer Group, an Iraqi consortium including a Kuwaiti GSM operator, MTC. Liberty Mobile's proposal didn't even finish in the top ten.[10]

With that, Qualcomm's technology appeared shut out of Iraq. Luckily for Qualcomm, it had picked up an especially well connected backer: Jack Shaw, a deputy undersecretary in the Department of Defense.

Shaw could have been a caricature of the Beltway insider. He was a garrulous, rumor-mongering partisan who saw Washington's bureaucracy as a sort of Fight Club for political appointees. He had come from money, frittered away a considerable amount of it living in France as a young man, and then married into a wealthy Houston family, friends said.[11] In Washington he was an established member of the social set, enjoying long dinners at the exclusive Metropolitan Club, just across the street from the White House. He was balding, overweight, and intensely loyal to his patrons, who ensured him jobs whenever a Republican administration came to power. Shaw had held midlevel positions as a political appointee under Gerald Ford, Ronald Reagan, and Bush senior, when he was appointed an assistant secretary at the Department of Commerce. In between Republicans, he had worked in the private sector. He had helped build industrial oil cities in Saudi Arabia for Booz Allen Hamilton, one of Washington's power consulting firms, and was also a senior fellow at the Center for Strategic and International Studies, a think tank.[12]

The Clinton years had been lean ones, however. After a few years doing consulting work, Shaw became president in 1998 of a company called American Overseas Clinics, a medical company, but had trouble making money. In a disclosure form at the Pentagon in October 2001, he listed no assets. He mentioned that he was in arbitration with the clinic and that he had received "no income" the previous year. He also mentioned a credit card debt worth between $10,000 and $15,000 at 19 percent interest.[13]

With the election of George W. Bush, Shaw's fortunes reversed. Rumsfeld appointed him the Department of Defense's deputy undersecretary for international technology security in October 2001. On paper Shaw was responsible for monitoring the transfer of sensitive technologies to foreign countries, similar to work he had done at the Commerce Department. But another deputy undersecretary held similar responsibilities. Shaw's new job brought him a title, a small staff, and an office in the E-ring with a "me-wall" filled with pictures of him and dignitaries — but not much work.

Then came Iraq. Although he had no background in either defense contracting or telecommunications, the White House designated Shaw as the Pentagon's liaison to Iraq on telecommunications issues. Appointed to support the coalition senior adviser in Iraq who was working with the Iraqi minister of communications, Shaw was on the front lines when the mobile phone fight first came up. Both Issa and Senator Conrad Burns, a Montana Republican who also had close ties to Qualcomm, urged Shaw to make sure the company's technology had a shot in Iraq. There were, they argued, national security reasons to do so: Qualcomm's technology is harder to tap than the European standard, which potentially meant that U.S. intelligence agencies — but not our enemies — could listen in.

Unknown to anyone else, Shaw also had a personal reason to aid the Qualcomm effort. One of the members of the Liberty Mobile consortium, a suave, silver-haired businessman named Don DeMarino, was one of Shaw's oldest friends. DeMarino had worked under Shaw at the Department of Commerce before becoming the president of the U.S.-Arab Chamber of Commerce. In April or early May, DeMarino introduced Shaw and Declan Ganley. DeMarino and Ganley convinced Shaw that Qualcomm's technology was best suited for Iraq's business needs — though Shaw later said he was unclear as to the exact nature of his friend's role in the consortium. "There's been a long gray line of people coming through my office," Shaw admitted. After Liberty Mobile got shut out of Iraq, Shaw was in a quandary: How could he get his friend's company a piece of the action?

That's when he thought of the Eskimos.

UNCLE TED

Fierce, irascible, and given to histrionics, Senator Ted Stevens has become famous for his ability to deliver federal dollars to his home state. Tiny wilderness outposts throughout Alaska have roads and bridges leading to them thanks to "Uncle Ted," a nickname reflecting the deference and admiration paid to the slight, cantankerous World War II pilot. But the roads and bridges are just the tip of the iceberg. On a per capita basis, Alaska gets twice as many federal tax dollars as any other state. A government watchdog group called Citizens Against Government Waste named Stevens the number one pork provider for six years running.[14] If there was money in the pot, Stevens wanted a piece of it for his people — and Iraq was a big, big pot.

Thus Stevens was acting at his avuncular finest when he inserted a last-minute provision into the Iraq reconstruction bill that Bush signed in November 2003. The language guaranteed special contracting privileges for a group of constituents that supplied Stevens not only with votes, but also with a portion of his personal income: the Alaska Native Corporations.

Alaska Native Corporations, or ANCs as they are known, were created with Stevens's help in the 1970s as a way to settle outstanding territorial claims from tribal Alaskans. Thirteen regional corporations and scores of smaller village corporations were formed, with tribal members as the shareholders. The idea was that the corporations would be able to use oil, mining, and timber rights to provide impoverished tribal natives with income and jobs. By the 1980s, however, many corporations had plunged into debt or were verging on bankruptcy. To save them during the 1990s, Stevens crafted a series of special designations in federal contracting law. The most lucrative of those benefits was that the federal government could award unlimited, no-bid contracts to small businesses run by native corporations. These contracting privileges were extraordinary, not available to any other minority group.

The logic behind the special designations was that the no-bid contracts would promote the growth of the corporations, which in turn would provide benefits to impoverished natives, many of whom lived in remote villages without running water or decent schools. In that regard the special contracting rules had a mixed record. While the percentage of Alaska Natives living in poverty dropped by half since 1970, they continued to economically lag behind other groups. In 2000 the per capita income of Alaska Natives was $12,500, compared with $26,418 for whites.

But in another regard the special rules were an unquestioned success. They created a tremendous loophole for defense contractors. Alaska Native firms don't have to hire tribal members, nor do the firms have to actually do all of the work. An Alaska Native firm could win a no-bid contract, then subcontract most of the work to a giant defense contractor with no connection to the tribe. Lobbyists "packaged" Fortune 500 firms like Lockheed Martin and Bechtel with Alaska Native Corporations. The native corporations provided the guaranteed contract; the contractor provided the work.

By the time the Iraq reconstruction rolled around, the Alaska Native Corporations had become a boom business. In 2002 U.S. Small Business

Administration records showed that Alaska Native firms made up less than 2 percent of all small businesses but accounted for 12 percent of government contracts awarded to small businesses.

A final beneficiary of the success of the Alaska Native Corporations was Stevens himself. In 1997 Stevens invested $50,000 with an Anchorage developer named Jonathan B. Rubini, who used the money to form a partnership called JLS Properties. JLS, in turn, helped to finance a $35 million office tower in downtown Anchorage. Centerpointe I, as the tower was known, became headquarters for Arctic Slope Regional Corporation, the largest of the Alaska Native firms. Arctic Slope paid a whopping $6 million a year for a twenty-year lease on the building. In short, Stevens created legislative benefits for Arctic Slope, which in turn paid money to Stevens's investment partnership.

Naturally, neither Arctic Slope nor Stevens saw it that way. Arctic Slope maintained that it did not know of Stevens's involvement in signing the lease. Stevens was unapologetic when confronted by two of my colleagues who were looking into the senator's sudden accumulation of wealth. He denied knowing the details of the lease signing, saying that he did not deal directly with Arctic Slope. He unapologetically vowed to continue pushing legislation that would benefit Alaska Native firms. When Stevens sold his interest in JLS in 2004, citing the controversy generated by the deal, he made a tidy profit: $822,000.[15]

ESKIMOS IN IRAQ

Democrats and Republicans alike had been angered by the first round of reconstruction contracts, many of which had been awarded in secret or without competitive bidding. With $18.4 billion in new spending proposed, Congress wanted to improve transparency. Senators Susan Collins, a moderate Republican from Maine, and Ron Wyden, a Democrat from Oregon, inserted special language into the reconstruction bill that required full and open competition for any contracts except those that involved matters of national security. Wyden wanted to restore order: "My view is that right now the contracting process looks a little like Dodge City before the marshal showed up."[16]

The senators' insistence on full and open competition set off alarms within the Washington microindustry that nurtured the Alaska Native loophole. Iraq was, after all, the new contracting frontier and the Alaska

Native Corporations wanted in on the action. An Anchorage-based company called NANA Pacific was the most aggressive. NANA Pacific was a subsidiary of NANA Regional Corporation, whose shareholders were some 7,200 Inupiaq living in a dozen communities straddling the Arctic Circle in far northwest Alaska. NANA was a large corporation, including major mining and oil drilling operations, with NANA Pacific as its small business arm, focused on sewer and water system engineering. As the bill was being debated, Janet Reiser, the non-Inupiaq president of NANA Pacific, told Stevens and other members of the Alaska delegation that the Alaskan firms wanted to be part of the gold rush in Iraq. Her pitch was that Alaskan firms, paired with U.S. companies, could speed up the contracting process because no time would be wasted in gathering competitive bids. In the final meetings between the House and Senate to hammer out details of the reconstruction bill, Stevens took advantage of his rank and the urgency of the moment to quietly slip in language that protected the Alaska Native firms. Reiser ignored the snickers on the Hill over the notion that Eskimos would go to work in Iraq. "If you exchange snow for sand, work in Iraq is similar to the work we've done in Alaska," Reiser told me. "We know how to do logistics in remote areas." And a few months after the reconstruction bill passed, Reiser's company was on its way to winning a contract in Iraq — thanks to Shaw.

CONCOCTING A PLAN

In the fall of 2003 Shaw received a visit from another old friend, a lobbyist named Dick Powers, who was representing NANA Pacific. At the time, NANA was interested in winning a contract to dredge the harbor of Umm Qasr in southern Iraq by partnering with a Seattle stevedoring company called SSA Marine. Shaw, however, realized that NANA could just as easily partner with Liberty Mobile and Qualcomm — and without competitive bidding, the deal would be theirs. There was only one problem: the coalition had no plans to issue a new cellular phone contract.

Shaw saw the chance he needed in a program to create a new police radio system in Iraq to link together Iraqi security forces. Shaw realized that the police contract could be modified to allow Liberty Mobile to erect a nationwide series of cellular phone towers using Qualcomm's CDMA technology — in effect granting his friends the foothold they had long sought. In November 2003 he described his plan in an e-mail: "Believe we could concoct a new configuration of Liberty CDMA bid with emergency system grafted on top of it. . . . We would have an essentially American contractor which is all ready to move and which we could bring aboard with little or no fee to build out a system." In another e-mail, he said that the United States could "graft" a CDMA system onto the police contract that could then "morph into a commercial service with our having total control over it."

To effect his plan, Shaw arranged for Reiser to call Ganley and discuss the cellular phone proposal. Over four months, the two negotiated an alliance, Reiser even visiting Ganley in Ireland to finalize terms. By January they agreed to work together. NANA would get the police contract using the firm's special no-bid abilities. It would then subcontract the actual work to Ganley, who formed a new company called Guardian Net for the job. Its board of directors was nearly identical to Liberty Mobile's. Ganley and DeMarino served on both boards, as did Paul Fiskness, a senior vice president for Qualcomm.[17]

On January 12, 2004, Shaw held a meeting in his office at the Pentagon. In attendance were Ganley, Shaw, and representatives from NANA and Qualcomm. In a handout Ganley made clear that his long-term vision for the police network — also called the first responder network — was a commercial cellular license using Qualcomm's technology. "NANA Pacific and Guardian Net will have the right to provide nationwide commercial cellular coverage in a manner that will enhance the overall security of Iraq," the handout said. One of those present recalled that Shaw was emphatic in promoting the NANA–Guardian Net combination. "He says, 'This is a done deal.' It's always been, 'I want NANA Pacific and I want CDMA. This is our solution,'" the attendee told me. "There was almost a thuggy quality to it. You can't do anything, here's the solution. Get out of the way."

But if that was the message, there were two people who didn't get it: Dan Sudnick and Bonnie Carroll.

THE WIDOW AND THE EAGLE SCOUT

Daniel Sudnick worked in telecommunications for nearly three decades before going to Iraq to work as the senior adviser to the Ministry of Communications. Tall and broad-shouldered, with icy blue eyes, he was an Eagle Scout, a retired military officer, and a defense contractor. He was pure military brat, the son of a career Marine Corps major and a World War II navy nurse. As a small boy, his mother took him to see Dwight Eisenhower's inauguration. He grew up at a series of bases, mostly in Southern California. He attended college at the University of California in Santa Cruz and at Berkeley. At two of the most liberal campuses in the country, in the middle of the social upheaval of the late 1960s, Sudnick was the straightest of arrows. He majored in engineering and chemistry, and went to naval officer training school during the summers. The protest kids were from another planet. "It went without saying that unless there was something precluding me from going into the military, that I would do that. That was my ethos from my youth," he said.

After graduation Sudnick began a lifelong balancing act. A restless, probing intellect made him too academic for the military; but his roots in military life made him too practical for academia. The navy paid for him to get his physical chemistry PhD at Pennsylvania State University, where he used lasers and magnets to pick apart the secrets of esoteric rare earth elements like europium and terbium. Instead of remaining in academia, Sudnick took a job at AT&T's Bell Laboratories. His twenty-year career was heavy on the development side of R&D. He built machines to check circuit boards for errors and designed networks to move medical data across the ocean. When AT&T broke apart for the first time in 1984, he was a manager, overseeing business units with $50 million a year in revenue. By 1997, when AT&T split itself again, he decided that he had seen enough of Ma Bell and its offspring and went into business for himself.

By the time the war in Iraq broke out, Sudnick had spent several years kicking around the world of management and defense consulting. One of his business partners was Jerry Jones, the man the White House charged with hiring key personnel for Iraq. Jones called him while Sudnick tended to his terminally ill father over the July Fourth weekend. He wanted Sudnick to join the CPA to oversee Iraq's Ministry of Communications. Sudnick said yes. Here was a challenge that he had been long awaiting, a task that combined intellect, experience, and patriotism. "They've got this big stack of résumés of twenty-something Georgetown wannabes who want to become the next secretary of state by age thirty-eight. They got a lot of those. For this senior job, they wanted a guy who knew telecom and military. They wanted a guy who knew how to manage big programs. I was their guy."

Sudnick spent the weekend at his computer doing one Google search after another, turning up some old United Nations studies on Iraq's prewar phone network. He drafted his plan and presented it to the Pentagon over the weekend. Two weeks later, he was on his way to Iraq.

That summer Sudnick ran the cellular phone licensing competition. It was a brutal, exhausting process. The coalition received thirty-five formal proposals to establish cellular service. Sudnick personally reviewed the selection of the winners. All the while, Ganley's group continued complaining about bias against American technology. Burns, the Montana senator, had even gone over to Baghdad for a personal briefing, declaring himself "satisfied" when he returned to Washington.

After the winners were announced in October, more controversy broke out. One loser filed a protest. Stories began appearing in the *Financial Times* and other publications about corruption, each more ominous than the last. Though Sudnick did not know it at the time, the stories were planted by Shaw, who hoped to discredit the process so that the United States would scratch the awards and announce a new competition. In addition Shaw contacted the Defense Department's inspector general to complain. The investigation, which took time and money and found no evidence of wrongdoing, further clouded America's efforts in Iraq. Thanks to Shaw's planted stories, the United States appeared to be wallowing in the same stew of corruption and graft that had marked Saddam's rule. "A process of enormous symbolic and economic importance has become what many involved agree is a mess," declared one *Financial Times* story.[18]

Unaware of what was going on, Sudnick called upon Shaw for support. In response Shaw assigned in December one of his most valuable assets to help out in Iraq: Bonnie Carroll. A loyal Republican and Washington veteran, Carroll was a vivacious redheaded army widow who managed to mix Beltway cynicism with a bracingly pure sense of public duty. She had worked in the White House for both Reagan and the senior Bush before marrying Tom Carroll, a brigadier general who headed the Alaska National Guard. When Carroll was killed in a 1992 military plane crash with several other guard members, Bonnie embraced a new mission. She founded a nonprofit veterans service organization dedicated to helping all those who had been affected by a death in the military. The Tragedy Assistance Program for Survivors, or TAPS, helped survivors cope with their loss, including those who slipped through the cracks of the Pentagon's benefits programs: the army sergeant's child by a mistress, for instance, or the widow whose Marine Corps husband committed suicide. Carroll took pride in raising hell to get benefits for her surviving families, and to see that the system worked as it should. She was steeped in patriotism but had a front-line soldier's skepticism of Pentagon bureaucracy.

When the war in Iraq broke out, Carroll was the White House's liaison to the Department of Veterans Affairs, a reward for her efforts to win veterans' votes for Bush's 2000 campaign. She volunteered to help in Iraq and was assigned to work in Shaw's office. Knowing she was an Alaskan, Shaw was eager to introduce her to Reiser, the head of NANA Pacific, and her assistant, Ed Cronick. It turned out Carroll had met Reiser before, in Anchorage, her hometown. Both Sudnick and Carroll were aware of Shaw's support for Qualcomm's technology. He extolled its virtues constantly, though he appeared to know very little about it. He frequently got confused, mixing up the letters of the abbreviation. Sudnick and Carroll also knew that Shaw wanted the Qualcomm consortium to pair with the Native Alaskans and gain the "sole source advantage" that would allow them to win the police contract. Carroll told me that Shaw was almost gleeful about the plan, apparently pleased at the idea of using the Alaskans' contracting shortcut. "He was like a little kid. He was so excited," she said. Neither Carroll nor Sudnick knew about Shaw's friend on the Liberty Mobile board; nor did they take seriously his plans to expand the police radio system into a cellular phone network. After all, Sudnick had sent Shaw memos explaining that the two projects were entirely separate.

In December, Carroll accompanied Shaw on a special investigatory trip to Iraq, a haphazard affair during which Shaw bizarrely dressed up as a Halliburton worker to sneak across the Iraqi border from Kuwait to inspect the port at Umm Qasr. Carroll was horrified by Shaw's antics but impressed by the mission in Iraq, so much so that she volunteered to go to work for Sudnick in Baghdad. The two formed a fast, close friendship. Sudnick was the guy with the vision for Iraq's future communications network; Bonnie was putting it to work. He admired her knowledge of Washington. She admired his devotion and his knowledge deeply: "He was one of the best people that Bremer had in Iraq."

CONTRACTING MINUET

Just days after the January 12, 2004, meeting in Shaw's office in Washington, NANA Pacific sent a letter to Baghdad requesting a no-bid contract to create the police radio network. Pressure to get moving on the network was growing at the highest levels in Washington. The insurgency was getting worse, and the police network was seen as an important component to improving Iraq's security forces. On February 24 Sudnick flew back to Washington to give a briefing to the National Security Council. Cheney was there, along with Powell, Rice, Wolfowitz, and Armitage. They listened intently as Sudnick told them how the three companies that had won the cellular phone networks — all of them based on the European technology — were racing to set up communications towers. Cellular phone use among average Iraqis was growing by leaps and bounds. He emphasized that U.S. intelligence agencies would be able to monitor traffic on the cellular phone networks. (With concurrence of the Iraqis and the cell phone licensees, the coalition had inserted "lawful intercept" language into the respective licensing agreements.) The police system was the next big telecommunications project, and Sudnick estimated that key pieces of it could be running before the United States departed Iraq that summer.

Sudnick felt cheered after the meeting. He had initially been given ten minutes to talk but was allowed to continue for nearly an hour. Cheney had said nothing, and Wolfowitz had seemed hostile, but Powell, Rice, and the others had thanked him warmly. Afterward, Cheney, Rice, and the others agreed that the police system was "the single highest communications priority for the [U.S. government] in Iraq," according to a cable sent from Powell to Bremer a short while after the meeting.[19]

The cable also contained a series of anxious queries from the State Department to Bremer. One referred to rumors about an "odd" scheme of using tribal Alaskans to install the network. Sudnick was unsure about the origin of the question, but someone in the State Department had gotten wind of Shaw's plan. On March 4 Shaw sent his most explicit instruction yet, ordering Sudnick to make sure that NANA got the contract, installed the American technology, and allowed Declan Ganley's Guardian Net to build out the system. "The continuing contracting minuet has obscured what must be part of the NANA/Guardian rollout. . . . This first step is the foundation for the build out of a truly national [police network] using CDMA," said one e-mail, sent on March 3. "NANA, by getting this first contract is assured by law of being the vehicle for all the add-on contracts necessary to build out the national system."

On March 7 NANA sent a proposal for the contract back to Baghdad. It contained language similar to Shaw's e-mail. The new proposal said that NANA and Guardian Net's police network "shall be designed so that the operators of the network shall be able to offer nationwide commercial cellular service on a nationwide basis throughout Iraq." Carroll was befuddled. Where had this new language come from? Why was NANA talking about creating a nationwide commercial cellular phone network? Sudnick had made it clear that the only thing the coalition wanted was a police system.

Carroll called Reiser, who told her that Ganley had suggested the change. Carroll then called Ganley, reaching him on his cell phone at Stansted airport in London. As he ate a breakfast of sausage and scrambled eggs, Ganley explained to Carroll that he had decided to put in the language allowing a new, commercial cellular phone network. It would guarantee that the future operators of the network — "whoever they would be" — had a commercial option available to them. He told Carroll that when he noticed that no such language was included in the contract, it was in the middle of the night in Baghdad, so he had called Shaw to ask for permission to include it. Shaw, he told Carroll, told him to insert the offending paragraph. Carroll's accusatory questions struck him as strange, he would later tell Shaw. "My thoughts were, so what, we're talking about an option, no big deal," he wrote in an e-mail to Shaw. "I was of the opinion that any real opposition to the idea was illogical anyway."[20]

Spooked by Ganley's response, Sudnick and Carroll pored over all the documents they had accumulated during the cellular phone licensing process. Slowly they began to piece together Shaw's scheme. For the first time they realized that Guardian Net was essentially the same company as Liberty Mobile, the cellular phone license loser, and that the police contract was a back door for Qualcomm to set up its own cell phone network. That night in Baghdad, Carroll and Sudnick figured that Shaw had been manipulating them and the entire process. Furious, they talked with coalition officials and urged them to yank NANA off the contract. It was a risky move. They knew they were taking on powerful forces, including a Pentagon deputy with influential friends and a major American corporation. Once that was done, Carroll turned to Sudnick. "Our careers are over," she said. As instructed, the coalition canceled the part of the NANA contract that dealt with the police radios (though the company continued work to dredge the port of Umm Qasr). And Carroll's intuition proved right.

2 A.M. PHONE CALL

At 2 a.m. on March 9, Carroll was working at her office in the Republican Palace when Shaw called. The hour was not unusual for those working for the coalition, and four other colleagues were toiling away, hunched over their computers. Carroll waved at them frantically as she held the phone away from her ear, then punched the speaker phone button. Shaw was screaming. He ordered her to keep the new language in the contract. "There will be hell to pay. You don't know how big this thing is," he shouted. Then he hung up.

Later in the day, Carroll got a surprise visit from a Sunni tribal sheik named Sami Majoun. Earlier Shaw had unsuccessfully promoted Majoun as Iraq's minister of communications. Although nobody but Shaw and his cronies knew it at the time, Majoun was a board member of Liberty Mobile. Majoun asked Carroll to accompany him outside the Republican Palace to "go for a ride." Simultaneously unnerved and amused by the mafioso-style invitation, Carroll went next door to find a military officer with a sidearm before refusing the offer. (When a reporter from *Mother Jones* interviewed Majoun at his home in summer 2004, he denied that he had any stake in the Qualcomm consortium. Apparently oblivious of the reporter's translator, Majoun then turned to another person in the room and said in Arabic, "Of course I am involved in contracts, but I'm not going to talk about any of it.")

A day later Shaw focused his fury on Sudnick. He wrote that the "Qualcomm folks" were concerned by the canceled contract, the military was "frustrated," and Senator Stevens was "not pleased," and that the canceled contract would "threaten the Eskimos." Shaw threatened to remove Carroll and suggested that Sudnick resign. On March 11 Shaw sent Sudnick a rambling e-mail full of invective and the locker-room language of the Pentagon bureaucracy.

Your silence is deafening. You complained months ago that you would not allow yourself to "be set up for failure." In the end you have set yourself up for failure. As your principal supporter at [the Department of Defense] let me suggest that you step aside and become part of an immediate solution rather than a continuing part of the problem. You are close to receiving a unanimous vote of no confidence in your ability to manage. With the cellular license award in shambles the [police network] is the last opportunity to install a viable cellular network that is responsive to our needs and requirements. Your continuing unresponsiveness and calculated delays in its implementation have nearly killed the projected plan, which may have been what you had in mind. But if you can't lead or follow, get the hell out of the way.[21]

In Washington, Shaw worked full-time to undermine Sudnick, and the Pentagon's corridors filled with "hallway talk" that Sudnick was corrupt. Wolfowitz's office sent letters demanding to see copies of the cellular licenses. NANA wrote the coalition to threaten legal action if their contract was canceled, further delaying the first responder network. Not surprisingly, Shaw had far more clout at the Pentagon than Sudnick. On March 23 retired U.S. Navy vice admiral Scott Redd, who was newly appointed as Bremer's deputy for operations, called Sudnick to his office and demanded his resignation. Bitter and feeling betrayed, Sudnick agreed. Carroll's resignation followed shortly after.

As Sudnick sat in the departure lounge of the Baghdad airport, he reviewed the whirlwind. He could not make sense of what had happened, how he had lost the confidence of so many people. "I had been misled. I felt violated. I was being set up as a dupe," he concluded. "People were dying because of the delays over this contract." Just before he got on the plane to leave Iraq, he saw Redd, who was also at the airport. Bremer's deputy strode up to him and, seemingly disturbed, made a cryptic comment: "On the Shaw situation, you were on the side of right." Then he walked off. It was the only time that Sudnick ever heard anything close to an apology.

EXPLOSION

Upon his return Sudnick reported his concerns to the Pentagon's inspector general, a Bush appointee named Joseph Schmitz. But in another strange twist, Schmitz had approved an unusual agreement that deputized Shaw as a kind of adviser to the inspector general. As a result Schmitz transferred the case to the FBI, citing the potential conflict of interest. Sending the case to the FBI was the kiss of death. The bureau was far more interested in terrorism than in official corruption. Schmitz's own senior investigators objected to the transfer, seeing the decision as a calculated move to help a fellow political appointee. Predictably, the FBI investigation never went anywhere, and it was eventually dropped. Although the bureau never confirmed or denied the final disposition of the case, one senior official in the inspector general's office who maintained contact with the agency told me the case had been put in the "too hard to do pile." Schmitz himself would later become the target of an inquiry led by Senator Charles Grassley, a Republican from Iowa, who accused Schmitz of stonewalling investigations into Shaw and other top Republicans for political reasons.[22]

For his part Shaw continued to heap accusations on Sudnick, each elaboration feeding into an increasingly bizarre alibi. He eventually produced a 118-page report that was a fantastic story of international intrigue. In Shaw's version, a suspected Saddam financier named Nadhmi Auchi secretly rigged the cellular phone licensing process to ensure that he controlled the entire network in Iraq through a shadowy business alliance. Shaw based his report on anonymous e-mails, information from Ganley and DeMarino, and rumors on the "Arab street." His theory knit together the Oil-for-Food scandal, a French version of the Tri-Lateral Commission called Le Cercle, and an obscure Luxembourg telecommunications company.[23] In subsequent iterations, the octopus grew ever more tentacles. By the end, Shaw believed that the scheme included Doug Feith, the undersecretary of defense, Ahmed Chalabi, and Larry DiRita, Rumsfeld's chief of staff.[24] It was John le Carré and Joseph Heller mixed into one. Shaw told me he had "huge circumstantial evidence that we're dealing with the most sophisticated money laundering operation and ruthless group, as ruthless and sophisticated as you'll find in the world."

Shaw would remain in office until the fall of 2004, when his penchant for conspiracy theories erupted again. This time it was in the closing days of the presidential campaign. On October 25, the *New York Times* published a damning front-page story about the Pentagon's failure to secure a weapons depot in Iraq during the invasion. More than 380 tons of explosives had vanished from the Al Qaqaa facility south of Baghdad.[25] Senator John Kerry seized on it as evidence of "one of the greatest blunders" in the Iraq war. In the closing days of a hard-fought race, the vanished explosives exploded into a major campaign issue.

Ever the soldier, Shaw waddled into the chaos. He called friendly reporters at the *Washington Times* and the *Financial Times*. His office, Shaw claimed, had obtained "reliable" information from two unnamed European intelligence sources that Russian commandos had slipped into Iraq just before the U.S. invasion to spirit away the explosives. For twenty-four hours the story changed course. Conservative commentators and television networks trumpeted the news that a senior Pentagon official had an explanation that lifted blame from Bush. It was, of course, preposterous, and even if it did help the president, one Bush official after another was forced to deny Shaw's report. Richard Armitage, deputy secretary of state, said he had "never seen any such information." Rumsfeld himself issued a blanket denial: "I have no information on that at all, and cannot validate that even slightly."[26]

The fictitious Russian commando story was the final straw. No longer able to countenance Shaw's antics, the Pentagon asked him to resign. Instead of going quietly, Shaw fought back, threatening to reveal unspecified, embarrassing details about senior Defense Department officials that would unleash "Iran-Contra II." "I think you . . . are aware of how flexible I have been to prevent any embarrassment to this administration," he wrote in one e-mail.[27] He even appealed directly to Rumsfeld, explaining that his comments were an effort to protect Bush. ("I was probably the only person in the country who could disprove the story" of the missing munitions, he wrote — either an indication of megalomania, or a dramatic new condemnation of U.S intelligence agency abilities.) He said he was being persecuted because of what he had discovered in investigating the cellular phone licenses. "I cannot submit my resignation to you until it is clear that the well-orchestrated campaign to obstruct justice and suppress the findings of my office has been properly addressed and stopped," Shaw wrote. On December 6 — with the election safely over — Shaw turned down a final opportunity to resign. Instead he was fired.

Shaw's ouster did little to clear up the mysteries of the cellular phone scandal. Shaw never faced charges, nor did he appear to make any money from the deal. Shaw's friends and allies claimed repeatedly that Shaw was not interested in money. He was a patriot on a mission and his pursuit of business for his friend's company was a zealous, if misguided and eccentric, effort to do what he believed was right: protect American business and intelligence interests in Iraq. "Hey, we won the war. Is it not in our interests to have the most advanced system that we possibly can that can then become the dominant standard in the region?" he once told me. Shaw flatly denied that he had any monetary interests or promises of employment with any of the companies involved. He acknowledged that others in the Pentagon questioned his sanity, telling a "privately-sponsored" intelligence summit in February 2006 that DiRita "whispered sotto voce to journalists that there was no substance to my information and that it was the product of an unbalanced mind."[28]

Shaw's departure from the Pentagon did nothing to vindicate Sudnick. He had once been considered for a job as a Pentagon deputy himself. Now he found himself in career limbo, unable to get work anywhere. Shaw's accusations of corruption lingered about him like a stench. His status as a whistle-blower made him suspect. He was an untouchable. Instead Sudnick began working with Carroll, who had returned to her nonprofit veterans group. Together the two have made a special effort to orient TAPS's work toward Iraq. They wanted the group to be a bridge between the countries, to connect war widows in the United States with their counterparts in Iraq. It was, Sudnick said, the best satisfaction he could draw from his experience.

After Sudnick's departure the United States had to begin the entire police radio process again. It would take two more years before a functioning police system, called the advanced first responder network, was fully operational. The final technology, installed by Lucent, used a specialized European standard for emergency communications. During that time thousands of American soldiers and Iraqi police officers were killed, at least some of whom could have been saved had they been able to pick up a phone and call for help. The whole episode was a shameful victory of narrow business interests over a vital strategic policy. Much the same could be said in the case of Iraq's oil industry.

4

The Halliburton Gang

No company in American history has ever been as tied to a war as Halliburton Company was to Iraq. But then, no war in this country's history has ever been as dependent on a single company. From reveille to lights out, the American military depended on Halliburton for its existence. The company fed, housed, and cleaned for most soldiers in Iraq. It built dozens of military bases across the country, small cities housing thousands of people, complete with restaurants, movie theaters, power stations, and water treatment plants. Its trucks moved the military's meals, mail, spare parts, electrical generators, tires, refrigerators, and other equipment. Iraqis were equally reliant on the company. Halliburton made sure the country's petroleum flowed. It delivered the gas that Iraqis needed to heat their homes and cook their food and run their cars. Halliburton was everywhere in Iraq, a corporate fairy godmother that promised to deliver anything a commander wanted at the snap of his fingers.

This was not the first time that Washington and corporate partners had allied during wartime, but the connection to Halliburton was unlike any other thanks to Dick Cheney. Indeed the vice president and the company were as tightly interwoven as the fibers in a 300-count bedsheet. As defense secretary in the early 1990s, Cheney had directed an increase in outsourcing military functions to private companies. Halliburton was one of the biggest contract winners. As the company's chief executive officer from 1995 to 2000, Cheney oversaw a massive expansion in Halliburton's government contracts and overseas business. And as vice president, he pushed forward the war that brought the company billions in new revenue. The federal government awarded Halliburton half the value of all contracts issued in Iraq, an astonishing sum potentially worth nearly $22 billion.[1] The company's stock price rose from $20 to $83 a share over the Iraq war — a stunning 300 percent increase. Its Iraq contracts were not the only reason, of course. Like all energy companies, Halliburton benefited from rising oil prices. But it certainly paid to have friends in high places.

Democrats and antiwar protesters turned the connection into a political weapon during the 2004 presidential campaign. They alleged that Cheney and Halliburton were proof that the war in Iraq was about profit, not democracy, a taxpayer-financed bit of corporate welfare to benefit Republicans and their cronies in the oil business. Representative Henry Waxman from California and Senator Frank Lautenberg from New Jersey led the charge. In reports, congressional hearings, and press conferences, they accused Halliburton of wasting billions in Iraq. Among the things they noted was that Cheney's retirement package — stock options and a delayed paycheck — meant that the vice president had a continuing "financial interest" in the company's performance.[2] "Halliburton is gouging the taxpayer, and the Bush administration doesn't seem to care," Waxman said. The message was clear: every dollar misspent by Halliburton meant more money in the pocket of the vice president.

Democrats also charged that Cheney lied about his knowledge of the company's lucrative contracts in Iraq, which were awarded in secret and without competition. Cheney said he had "absolutely no influence on, involvement of, knowledge of in any way, shape or form of contracts let by the Corps of Engineers or anybody else in the federal government."[3] Waxman disagreed, pointing out that the Department of Defense revealed to his staff that Cheney had been told about Halliburton's contracts before they were issued. In an interview with me, Doug Feith confirmed Waxman's version. To spare the vice president possible political embarrassment, Feith said, his office made sure to alert Cheney about the Pentagon's intention to award a contract to Halliburton. The answer came back: the vice president wanted the Defense Department to do whatever was proper to accomplish the mission, Cheney would take whatever political flack arose. Feith told me that it was "ironic and sad" that Cheney's attitude was distorted into the allegations about Halliburton, whose KBR subsidiary actually won the Iraq contract. "The vice president's former connection made people in the government reluctant to award the contract, not eager to do it, even though awarding it to KBR was the right thing to do," Feith said.

But while there was never any hard evidence that Cheney personally intervened to enrich himself or his former company, the Democrats' dogged investigations did reveal that the federal government was grossly negligent in controlling its chief contractor in Iraq. Ultimately Halliburton was a business. Its goal was profit. If Halliburton wasted money, the United States let it. Federal officials repeatedly broke the rules or looked the other way as Halliburton racked up more than a billion dollars in questionable costs. Government audits accused Halliburton of wasting money, or being unable to track how much it spent. The Pentagon paid the company anyway. Government employees who raised questions were overruled, ignored, or punished. Top military officials waived regulations designed to ensure accountability. The Pentagon covered up the release of embarrassing information in public records at the company's request. Whistle-blowers were dismissed as ignorant or ill-informed. And the evidence certainly suggested that the vice president's shadow, at least, played a role in the company's treatment. Commanders in the Army Corps of Engineers, in particular, were hesitant to challenge the company or embarrass the vice president. In one instance they demoted one of the company's highest-profile critics after she insisted on contract terms that were less advantageous than those Halliburton was proposing. In another instance a high-level Army Corps attorney confessed in an e-mail to sending paperwork about Halliburton to higher levels for approval. "If it had been any other firm, we would have done this and moved forward without further consideration," he wrote.[4]

Halliburton's treatment was different from that of other contractors because the company *was* different from other contractors. Halliburton had two large missions in Iraq that made it indispensable. The first and biggest had as its primary goal the housing and feeding of the 200,000 U.S. and coalition troops and civilians in Iraq. The other crucial job was to restore the country's oil infrastructure. The United States couldn't afford to crack down on Halliburton. Its role was too big, too important, too vital to the American mission. The issue was not so much that Halliburton profited from the United States. It was that America could not profit in Iraq without Halliburton.

CONTRACTORS ON THE BATTLEFIELD

The U.S. military has always depended on contractors for help. Halliburton officials were fond of pointing out that a private company supplied bullets to the Continental Army during the American Revolution.[5] During the Civil War contractors supplied food and tents and set up telegraph communications. In World War II contractors built the airfields that the marines used as they island-hopped toward Japan. In one incident hundreds of contractors building an airstrip were captured or killed by the Japanese. The reliance on contractors grew unevenly: There was one civilian worker for every twenty soldiers in World War I, one for every seven in World War II, and one for every six soldiers by the Vietnam War.[6] The end of the cold war saw a dramatic increase, however. As the American military downsized, contractors filled the gap, and by the first Gulf War defense contractors were edging their way onto the battlefield, mostly to maintain weapons systems like M1 Abrams tanks and Patriot missile batteries.[7]

The increasing reliance on contractors produced unease in the military. The biggest issue concerned combat. Contractors were employees, not soldiers. If things got hot they could simply walk off the job. (Such an incident occurred in South Korea in the 1970s, when army contractors evacuated in the face of a possible attack from North Korea.[8]) A related question was protection: Who was supposed to defend contractors during fighting? And did local commanders have enough troops to do it?

Contractors in war also presented murky legal problems. Under the Geneva Conventions and the Law of The Hague, contractors were defined as noncombatants, putting them off-limits as targets and providing them prisoner-of-war protections in case of capture. But as contractors took over jobs once done by soldiers, it became difficult to maintain that status. Contractors made sure that tanks ran properly. They analyzed and suggested military targets. They conducted interrogations on captured enemies. The questions grew especially blurry around private security companies, who deployed heavily armed guards to protect U.S. officials. The companies claimed to maintain their noncombatant status by engaging in only "defensive" operations. But in Iraq such companies fought hours-long battles with insurgents, protected vital targets like American and Iraqi leaders, and routinely fired at vehicles suspected of being car bombs. Was that offensive or defensive? And did it make the private military contractors legitimate targets?

Contractors accused of committing crimes while working for the government posed another complex legal problem. Soldiers are always subject to the Uniform Code of Military Justice anywhere in the world. But contractors are not, except in cases of war declared by Congress. Theoretically, a contractor accused of wrongdoing could face prosecution in a host country. But in practice the cases fell into a legal netherworld. Sometimes American officials were reluctant to turn over a contractor to face justice before foreign courts. In other cases foreign prosecutors were hesitant to insert themselves into crimes that didn't involve their own nationals. The Military Extraterritorial Jurisdiction Act of 2000 was supposed to fix the problem by making contractors responsible to U.S. courts. But by the time the war in Iraq broke out, most of the legal questions about who was responsible for contractor behavior were unresolved.

Col. Steven Zamparelli of the U.S. Air Force wrote a seminal essay in the late 1990s that captured the rising alarm within the ranks. Written for the Air War College, the essay caused a stir by its blunt portrayal of the military's dependence on uncertain partners for victory. It criticized the Defense Department for failing to develop any cohesive strategy for contractors on the battlefield. "I believe this puts our field commanders at risk," Zamparelli said.[9]

Iraq was the culmination of the outsourcing effort. With 50,000 contractors supporting 130,000 troops, there was more than one civilian worker for every 2.6 American soldiers in Iraq, a ratio matched only once before, during the Korean War. But unlike that war, with its battle lines defined by latitude, Iraq had no clear front — the fighting was everywhere. Contractors, for the first time in U.S. military history, were not only supporting the war, they were in the middle of it, fighting and dying alongside soldiers. "The enemy does not distinguish whether you're in uniform or not," Col. Joe Schweitzer of the U.S. Army told me during a visit to a bunker in the Green Zone filled with television screens to track contractor activity. "This is combat reconstruction." And that effort had Halliburton written all over it.

BIG RED

Halliburton's march to the front lines in Iraq was the result of a business plan that had long mixed politics, the military, and federal contracts. The company traced its roots back to two companies that took remarkably different paths to success. The first was founded in the Oklahoma oil fields in 1919 by Erle P. Halliburton, a cantankerous entrepreneur who despised big government.[10] He built the company as an oil services firm, helping wildcatters maintain and boost the production of their wells. Nicknamed Big

Red, Halliburton earned a can-do reputation for its engineers' willingness to go anywhere and take any job.

Halliburton's aversion to the government was cast aside in 1962, when the company bought out Brown & Root, a Texas engineering and construction firm with a political past. Brothers George and Herman Brown had built their company through government contracting, thanks in large part to their connections to a young Texas Democrat named Lyndon Johnson. Johnson played a critical role in shuttling legislation through the House of Representatives to guarantee Brown & Root's first big project, a dam in the Texas Hill Country. And Brown & Root's contributions played a critical role in Johnson's first big political triumph. In his tumultuous run for Senate in 1948, which resulted in a razor-edge victory, Brown & Root made sure that several grocery bags filled with thousands of dollars quietly made their way to Johnson's campaign.[11] As Johnson rose politically, Brown & Root rose financially. The company won an impressive list of federal contracts, from military bases abroad to shipbuilding during World War II to the Johnson Space Center in Houston. By 1969 Brown & Root had become the largest construction company in the nation, with sales of $1.6 billion.[12]

The Vietnam War gave Brown & Root its final boost to the top. After being bought out by Halliburton, Brown & Root joined a consortium of four companies in Vietnam that built $2 billion worth of airfields, hospitals, and military bases between 1965 and 1972.[13] By 1967 the General Accounting Office (GAO) had faulted the "Vietnam builders" for massive accounting lapses and allowing thefts of materials. Brown & Root became a target for antiwar protesters, who dubbed the company Burn and Loot. The controversy even prompted a denunciation from a young Republican congressman from Illinois, an exact echo of the remarks that Democrats would make about the same company forty years later. "Why this huge contract has not been and is not now being adequately audited is beyond me," he said. "The potential for waste and profiteering under such a contract is substantial."[14] The congressman's name was Donald Rumsfeld.

LOGISTICS

Halliburton cemented its importance to the American military in the 1990s, thanks to the end of the cold war and the ascendancy of Dick Cheney. Cheney, then defense secretary for the first President Bush, cut military spending by $10 billion and reduced troop strength from 2.2 million to 1.6 million.[15] To accomplish these cuts, Cheney embraced the idea of outsourcing to the private sector. He commissioned a study to examine whether the military could let private firms handle some of its support functions. Brown & Root won the contract to do it.

Brown & Root's study led to the creation of the Logistics Civilian Augmentation Program — LOGCAP for short. LOGCAP essentially turned over the military's quartermaster functions to a private company. It was a daunting task: the contractor had to be ready at a moment's notice to set up food and housing for 20,000 troops in a variety of potential global hot spots for up to 180 days.[16] The first company to win the contract? Halliburton. In 1992 the company beat out thirty-six other bidders to win a five-year contract — not surprising perhaps, given that it was the company that drew up the plans.

The logistics contract was "cost plus" — an ugly phrase but a simple idea. Cost-plus contracts essentially guarantee profit. The government pays for any expenses incurred by the contractor with a small profit margin on top. The rationale is that such contracts remove financial risk that might otherwise discourage qualified companies from bidding.

Cost-plus agreements are supposed to have limited use, only in situations with great uncertainty — for instance, when a contractor can't be sure how much money is needed to accomplish a task — since both the government and watchdog groups consider the contracts an invitation to abuse. Rather than place responsibility to hold down costs on the businessman who wins the contract, as in a contract for a fixed amount, the practice places the responsibility wholly with the government.

Halliburton's first logistics contract had a profit margin of just 1 percent, but if the company did well, and held down costs, the army could increase the percentage up to 9 percent. All through the 1990s the army turned to Halliburton for help. It had to: by the time Defense Secretary Cheney left office in 1993, the military was at its smallest size since Korea. Halliburton built camps and delivered food and water for troops in Somalia, Haiti, Rwanda, Kuwait, and the Balkans. The program turned out to be immensely popular. It allowed commanders to increase the "tooth-to-tail" ratio, freeing more soldiers for fighting rather than food preparation. Soldiers also liked it. Tents, meals in a bag, and cold buckets of water were replaced by air-conditioned trailers, cafeterias, and hot showers. Halliburton was happy with the arrangement too. The Balkans deployment generated

$2.2 billion in revenues through 2000, and Halliburton always received at least 98 percent of the contracted bonus.

Not everyone was pleased. Government auditors and Army Corps officials complained about waste. The GAO said some military commanders wondered whether the level of services "may be above and beyond what is really needed." There were reports that Halliburton was so overstaffed in the Balkans that offices were cleaned four times a day. But the complaints had little effect on Halliburton's fortunes. In 1997, when the logistics contract came up for renewal, Halliburton lost to DynCorp, but it was only a temporary setback, with the army carving out an exception to allow the company to continue work in the Balkans. When the logistics contract came up for renewal a second time, in 2001, Halliburton won again, through its subsidiary KBR, created by the merger of Brown & Root and M. W. Kellogg.

The contract was for ten years, but the profit margins were even slimmer. KBR was guaranteed a profit of 1 percent, but this time the company could only gain an additional 2 percent for good performance. It was an indefinite delivery, indefinite quantity contract — meaning that KBR had to be prepared to provide almost anything the government wanted for as long as it wanted in whatever amount it wanted.[17]

The September 11 attacks and the war in Iraq put the company — and the military's entire philosophy — to the test in an unprecedented way.

BAPTISMS AND BURGER KING

Neither the U.S. government nor Halliburton had planned on a lengthy occupation involving more than 200,000 troops spread across a country the size of California. When the magnitude of the task became apparent, the U.S. military began placing enormous, constantly changing demands on KBR. Not surprisingly, KBR struggled to keep up. The prewar priorities contributed to the chaos. For example, the GAO found that the Pentagon did not order KBR to begin planning for housing and feeding troops in Iraq until May 2003 — nearly seven months after it ordered the company to begin planning for the care of Iraq's oil fields.

KBR's initial task called for six camps in Kuwait with a maximum of 50,000 soldiers. Within months of the U.S. invasion, that job grew rapidly. In June 2003 the United States gave KBR just three weeks to set up twenty-four camps and serve meals to 120,000 soldiers in the U.S. Army's Fifth

Corps. The orders kept coming, one after another. Slowly KBR began to catch up with the demands. A year after the invasion, KBR had built the equivalent of five dozen American towns, under gunfire and in hostile wastelands, spread throughout locations in Iraq. The camps held 211,000 U.S. and coalition soldiers. By then the company had served 60 million meals, hauled off 3 million cubic meters of trash, cleaned 1 million portable toilets, and washed 1.5 million bundles of laundry.[18]

Whenever I went to Iraq, I never had any doubts that KBR was delivering for American soldiers. From Kirkuk to Basra, the company did an astonishing job of housing, feeding, and caring for the military. Camp Liberty, the U.S. military headquarters in Iraq, was a prime example. Located next to the Baghdad airport, the camp was a small city. Soldiers indulged at KBR's dining facilities, or "D-facs." The mess halls held burrito bars with nachos, fry cook stands where hot dogs and hamburgers were made to order, and Baskin-Robbins ice-cream sundae booths. KBR provided support for other restaurants too: Subway occupied a rickety booth by the military airstrip and Burger King had a dusty white trailer on wheels that was hauled around the grounds. Air-conditioned lounges with leather couches had satellite televisions, usually tuned to Fox. Unlucky soldiers slept in KBR's air-conditioned tents; luckier ones slept two to a trailer and shared a single bathroom.

KBR helped the military mount a PX on base that was the size of an airplane hangar. It sold everything from CDs by Fatboy Slim, Dave Matthews, and Beyoncé to barbecued pork rinds to Red Bull to Game Boys. Liberty had workout rooms, salsa dancing, and rows of computers connected to the Internet. Buses driven by Pakistanis made regular rounds of the base, their speakers cranking out hypnotic Middle Eastern synthopop. Churches were filled on Sundays and did a brisk business. At one long, low canvas tent at Camp Stryker, which adjoined Liberty, there was even a wooden crate lined with plastic for a full-body, Southern Baptist baptism. It was one camp, but there were dozens of others just like it all across Iraq. KBR had scooped up slices of suburban America and scattered them across a desert land 6,000 miles away.

Providing the comforts of home was not cheap. And from the ground, many of the company's actions appeared mind-boggling and wasteful. A series of whistle-blowers came forward to describe a chaotic environment where employees had to process more than a hundred purchase orders daily, working twelve to fourteen hours a day, seven days a week. In the rush to complete the tasks at hand, employees frequently cut corners, resulting in costly mistakes, the whistle-blowers said. John Mancini, a procurement supervisor, described to me an incident in which Halliburton bought a $750,000 fire engine that was useless because the threads on hoses on the engine didn't match Kuwaiti fire hydrants. In another incident, Halliburton purchased twenty-five tons of nails that were too long. The nails were dumped in a fenced enclosure in the middle of nowhere. The waste wasn't entirely accidental: Henry Bunting, who worked as a field buyer in Kuwait, said the company purchased bright yellow towels monogrammed with the KBR logo for $7.50 apiece, when ordinary bath towels could be purchased for $2.50. Senator Byron Dorgan of North Dakota held aloft one of the offending towels at a hearing, turning it into an image of KBR's waste. Afterward the company stripped its logo off all equipment purchased in Iraq. Monograms or not, Halliburton still came out ahead.

Marie deYoung was a dark-haired former military chaplain who joined Halliburton in the hopes of going to Iraq, but got assigned to Kuwait instead. During her six months of work for Halliburton, she said, she was overwhelmed by the chaos and waste she saw every day. She told me that she had tried to negotiate lower prices several times but was repeatedly rebuffed by higher-ups, who showed no interest in bringing down costs. In one instance, deYoung said, Halliburton was paying a company called La Nouvelle up to $1.2 million a month to do about twelve thousand bags of laundry — a cost of $100 per bag. (A La Nouvelle employee was later indicted with a Halliburton manager in an alleged $5.5 million kickback scheme on a contract for fuel storage.) "There was this whole thought process that we can spend whatever we want to because the government won't crack down in the first year of a war," said deYoung, who had resigned in disgust in May 2004 and gone back to school to get her doctorate in education and public policy analysis. "They have no incentive whatsoever to be prudent. It's cost plus."

QUESTIONABLE COSTS

KBR's spending generated concerns at the top as well. The Defense Contract Audit Agency, the Pentagon's primary audit office, examined Halliburton's accounting system closely as its contracts inflated. The auditors came to conclude that the company's internal systems simply weren't sufficient to track all the money coming in and going out, especially in regard to its tens of thousands of subcontractors. In one case the company told the government it was spending $70 million for food services when it had actually canceled the relevant agreements. KBR blamed the problem on the huge volume of contracts it was processing.[19]

The auditing agency also grew concerned that KBR was charging as much as $200 million for meals that had never been served to soldiers. The auditors said KBR should bill only for each soldier actually served. The company argued that it was acting like a wedding caterer. If the military told the company to serve 4,000 soldiers but only 3,500 showed up, the military still had to pay. The dispute was eventually resolved, with KBR keeping all but $55 million of the disputed amount.[20] Month after month the amounts snowballed. By May 2005 Halliburton had staggeringly racked up more than $1 billion worth of questionable costs.[21] Even Halliburton acknowledged that the mission turned out to be far more than it could handle initially. "No one at KBR would presume to say that our operation was flawless under these circumstances," Alfred Neffgen, KBR's chief operating officer for government operations, told Congress in July 2004. "While we have undoubtedly made some mistakes, we are confident that KBR has delivered and accomplished its mission at a fair and reasonable cost."

In essence KBR's troubles with the mission to support the troops mostly concerned accounting problems, not performance. The company delivered, but wasted a lot of money doing it. Much has been written about the fact that the United States did not have enough troops to secure Iraq. The same applied to contract officers, who are supposed to be looking out for the taxpayers as they oversee private firms working for the federal government. The military simply did not have enough people, knowledge, or time to clamp down on ballooning expenses. The problem was especially bad on the ground. For an entire year, the 101st Airborne Division did not have a contracting officer in Iraq to deal with Halliburton, although military commanders continually placed orders for supplies and equipment with the company.[22] Inexperienced reservists with less than two weeks' training were ineffectively rushed in to fill the gap.

The result was that the military essentially cut Halliburton a blank check. Halliburton set its price and the army paid it. Rules and terms became details that the military had no time or inclination to investigate, let alone dispute. A November 2004 Army Audit Agency report chronicled the mess. In one case the army told Halliburton to provide a camp superintendent for a year — but then drew up the contract to provide the superintendent with two years' pay. In another case Halliburton charged the government $617,000 for soda pop for 2,500 soldiers — an amount equal to $247 of soda per soldier. The audit agency totaled up $40 million of questionable costs by Halliburton during an eighteen-month period ending in October 2004. "The perceived performance shortfall was primarily caused by government actions or inaction," the report said.

After its own in-depth review of the logistics contract, the GAO reached a similar conclusion. David Walker, the head of the nonpartisan agency, told Congress in June 2004 that neither KBR nor the military seemed particularly interested in holding down costs on the logistics contract. The army did not issue specific orders to commanders telling them to economize on the contract until December 2003, nine months after the war's start. Though the Pentagon blamed mistakes on the pressure of the war's early days, Walker said his investigators had found ongoing waste a year after the invasion. "We saw very little concern for cost considerations," he said.[23] After the hearing he told a clutch of reporters that the total waste involved could be in the "billions" of dollars. Suffice it to say, a billion here and there added up to real money.

SOMEONE NAMED MOBBS

KBR's logistics contract was the origin of its second and most controversial deal: the restoration of Iraq's oil industry. As Feith, the defense undersecretary, wrestled with postwar planning in the fall of 2002, he turned to his top aide, Michael Mobbs, to handle Iraq's oil. A Russian-speaking lawyer, Mobbs was a sort of neoconservative Zelig, starring in a series of minor controversies. (Perhaps most memorably, he at one point submitted the famous "Mobbs declaration," a sworn statement arguing that the government could indefinitely detain a suspected terrorist without charges. The judge in the case rejected the argument: "Due process requires something other than a basic assertion by someone named Mobbs," he said.[24]) The reconstruction of Iraq's oil industry was another temp job in the war on terror.

Mobbs concluded that Iraq's oil industry was in bad shape — worse than anybody in the administration would publicly admit until long after the invasion had begun. Mobbs got "informal input" from former oil company executives, the military, and government agencies to determine who could deal with the myriad of problems in the industry. Iraq's aging system of wells, pipelines, and refineries needed serious help. One company's name came up over and over: Halliburton, which specialized in oil services — repairs, maintenance, and other tasks associated with extraction of petroleum from the ground. The company had one additional distinct advantage over other companies that could also do the job: Halliburton's subsidiary, KBR, already held the logistics contract, meaning that it was currently working closely with the military to plan for the invasion of Iraq.[25]

On November 11, 2002, at Mobbs's urging, the U.S. Army officially awarded a $1.9 million contract to KBR to carry out a planning study for the repair of Iraq's oil infrastructure. Government contract officers — who actually sign the contracts on behalf of the U.S. government — are supposed to be free from any influence in making their decisions. But in this case Mobbs, a political appointee, was steering the award of the contract to the company that he thought best. It was the first example of the United States breaking the rules for Halliburton.

Second, Mobbs used KBR's logistics contract to commission the planning job. Under the logistics contract, government officials would assign KBR jobs — called task orders — that the company would then perform. Mobbs decided that he would make planning for the war into a task order. Two army lawyers objected: the logistics contract was supposed to be used for feeding soldiers, not planning oil contracts. Mobbs went to a lawyer working in Rumsfeld's office. There he found the approval he was seeking. The GAO determined in June 2004 that Mobbs's use of the logistics contract was inappropriate. But by then it was too late. Nothing could be done. "Rumsfeld's political lawyers steamrollered the career guys to push through Halliburton's secret deal," Charles Tiefer, a law professor at the University of Baltimore, told me. "It creates a disturbing appearance of influence."

Finally, everyone involved realized that the short time line of the march to war meant that the company that drew up the plans would also carry them out.[26] That was a violation of contracting guidelines that discouraged companies from bidding on jobs that they helped to create. KBR was essentially writing its own job description.

BUNNY HOPS IN

During the winter, the Pentagon's efforts to cut corners in awarding the oil contract to Halliburton hit a roadblock: Bunnatine Greenhouse. Greenhouse was a tall, broad-shouldered black woman who had worked her way through a mostly white, mostly male hierarchy to become the most senior contracting official in the U.S. Army Corps of Engineers. She had an inspiring, by-the-bootstraps story. She grew up poor in Rayville, Louisiana, a segregated cotton town. Her father, who never passed third grade, operated the town cotton press. Her mother made sure that all her children were educated, and proud. "Nothing was going to stop me at being the best at what I could. I wasn't going to stand for the vision of Rayville, Louisiana. There had to be another life," Greenhouse told me. Most of Greenhouse's siblings went on to earn advanced degrees. Her brother, Elvin Hayes, became a Hall of Fame basketball player for the Houston Rockets. Her sister was one of the first black professors at Louisiana State University, an expert in Chaucerian literature, and Greenhouse can today recite the opening stanzas of *Canterbury Tales* in Middle English.

Greenhouse found a home in the world of government contracting. She married her childhood sweetheart in 1965, Aloysius Greenhouse, and accompanied him as he moved through a series of army posts. She eventually followed him into his career as a procurement officer, earning three master's degrees on the way. She thrived in a profession that rewarded mastery of and strict adherence to the Federal Acquisition Regulations, the 1,923-page rule book for government contracting. Greenhouse was tough, no-nonsense, and a stickler for rules. A deeply religious woman, she believed in right and wrong. The contracting regulations had been written to make sure that every company — big and small, rich and poor — got a fair shake from the government. She believed deeply in that vision. And she was troubled by what she saw as the Army Corps of Engineers' overly close relationship with Halliburton.

In February 2003, less than three weeks before the war's start, Greenhouse went to a meeting at the Pentagon with the major players in the reconstruction effort: the Department of State, the Pentagon, USAID. The topic was the oil contract. The Army Corps of Engineers wanted to hand it to KBR. The whole idea made Greenhouse uneasy. She didn't understand why the corps was being given the job of overseeing Iraq's oil industry. The agency had no experience in the oil business. The Army Corps built dams, bridges, and waterways, not oil wells. Second, she was worried about the regulations that discouraged the government from awarding a job to the same company that drew up the blueprints for it. Why was KBR even being considered?

Greenhouse was even more startled by the presence of people at the meeting who were actually from KBR. The company was at the table, helping decide its own contract terms. And the contract proposal seemed unreasonable to Greenhouse. The Army Corps was suggesting that KBR be awarded a cost-plus contract — giving KBR a guaranteed 2 percent profit, plus an additional 5 percent bonus fee. Worse, the contract was being issued in secret, without competitive bidding, for a five-year period. Greenhouse could understand the secrecy; it was a war. She could also see some justification for doing it without bidding, since time was running short. But she didn't understand the reason for such a lengthy contract. Why not make it for one year, and then extend it later if necessary?

Greenhouse walked up to Gen. Carl Strock, who was chairing the meeting and would later become commander of the Army Corps. She whispered in his ear to ask the KBR representatives to leave. After they did, Strock and everyone else in the room continued to insist that KBR get the contract. Given the late date, they were the only company that had the ability to do the job, he told her. "I'm saying, 'Red Flag!'" Greenhouse told me. "If they developed the contingency plan, they shouldn't be qualified to participate in it. That's a conflict of interest. . . . Nobody wanted to hear it."

Greenhouse did not know it at the time, but Strock was acting under orders from the secretary of defense. Rumsfeld had determined that putting the oil restoration contract out to bid would be a waste of time, at least with the war so imminent. Instead he wanted the Army Corps to be ready to sign the contract with KBR at a moment's notice. In a memorandum on January 22, 2003, he had directed the army to "negotiate, but not award, a contract for execution with the developer of the plan [KBR] that can be awarded as soon as the Army receives direction to execute the plan." The Army Corps added its own justification: "No delay can be tolerated."[27]

When the contract came to Greenhouse for approval four days later, it reflected none of her suggestions. It was still for five years. Filled with misgivings, Greenhouse felt she had no choice but to sign off. In a final act of defiance, she decided to write her objections directly onto the contract. It was the only way that she felt she could ensure she was respecting her oath to protect taxpayers from the potential for waste, fraud, and abuse. "I caution that extending this sole source effort beyond a one year period could convey an invalid perception that there is not strong intent for a limited competition," she wrote in cramped handwriting beneath her signature.

Three weeks later U.S. and coalition ground troops rushed into Iraq from Kuwait. KBR engineers followed the next day. Greenhouse had lost the first round in Greenhouse v. Halliburton. There would be more to come.

FUEL TO THE FIRE

A month after the invasion, Halliburton had finished its primary task under the oil contract. The feared oil field fires — which during the first Gulf War had raged for months — never materialized. In the meantime another crisis had erupted, one that took the United States by complete surprise. Iraq's aging refineries had long ago stopped being able to supply all the kerosene, diesel, and gasoline that Iraqis needed to light kitchen stoves and fill up their cars. Looting had shut them down completely, and the war disrupted imports. By May 2003, oil-rich Iraq was running out of gas. Long lines formed at gas stations, and Iraqis who considered gasoline a birthright reacted with anger. At least one U.S. soldier was killed trying to quell a near riot inspired by the gas shortage. The U.S. Central Command decided it had to begin trucking in fuel or face a serious crisis.

In a panic the military turned to Halliburton. The $7 billion oil contract was intended to put out oil fires and rebuild the country's oil infrastructure. But it was broadly written enough so that gasoline delivery could be added. The Army Corps of Engineers objected: sending in fuel to Iraq would hamper the original goal of getting oil flowing.[28] Central Command overruled them. On May 3 the Army Corps ordered KBR to begin importing fuel into Iraq within ninety-six hours.

The snap decision turned into one of Halliburton's biggest jobs — and its biggest headache. Over the next eleven months, the company delivered 463 million gallons of gasoline a month. It built up a fuel tanker fleet that was the equivalent of the fourth largest trucking company in the United States. It bought up every available tanker truck in Kuwait, and imported hundreds more from Saudi Arabia, Jordan, and Turkey. It imported thousands of truck drivers from India, Pakistan, and the Philippines, and built camps to house and feed them. The company averted a humanitarian fuel crisis. But it did so at an enormous cost. By fall 2003 Waxman's staff had unearthed figures showing that Halliburton was charging the United States $2.64 per gallon to import fuel to Iraq. The Pentagon's own fuel agency, the Defense Energy Support Center, had a contract to import the military's fuel that was half that, about $1.08 per gallon.

Over the next few months, the news worsened. Waxman's attacks were dismissed as politics, but on December 11, the Defense Contract Audit Agency hastily called a press conference that essentially confirmed his findings. The agency had conducted an emergency audit that found Halliburton had overcharged taxpayers by $61 million in fuel costs, repeatedly failing to get lower bids from other gasoline suppliers. The next day the president weighed in. "We're going to watch, we're going to make sure that as we spend the money in Iraq, that it's spent well and spent wisely," Bush said in response to a reporter's question. "If there's an overcharge, like we think there is, we expect that money to be repaid."

THE KUWAITIS

Once again, however, it would turn out that the company was responding to frantic and confused orders from the U.S. government. In the days after the initial order to buy gas, Halliburton had turned to a company called Altanmia, a Kuwaiti company with no previous experience in supplying fuel. Altanmia's backers were mysterious, but they were believed to be related to the Kuwaiti oil minister and other members of the royal family.[29] Kuwaiti officials told the U.S. embassy that Altanmia was the only company in Kuwait certified to sell fuel to a private company.[30] But by summer 2003, the two companies had gotten into a dispute over whether Altanmia had fulfilled its end of the bargain, and Halliburton was shopping for other fuel suppliers.

The business dispute soon became political. The Kuwaitis called the U.S. embassy and demanded that it step in, accusing Halliburton of reneging on deals and demanding kickbacks, though they provided no proof. An embassy official quoted Altanmia general manager Waleed Humaidhi as saying that "it was [Altanmia's] assumption that 'political' or 'kickback' considerations must be behind KBR's complaint" about the company's performance.[31] Altanmia also accused a Halliburton executive of demanding a Cartier watch for his wife from a subcontractor. A Halliburton spokeswoman confirmed that a $2,600 watch had been stolen from a hotel housing Halliburton employees, but said that the executive, Thomas Crum, had asked the hotel, not a subcontractor, to replace it.[32]

As Halliburton tried to find other fuel suppliers at a cheaper cost, Kuwait urged the U.S. embassy to force Halliburton to close a deal. Kuwait's undersecretary of foreign affairs, Khaled Jarallah, called the embassy on instructions of the prime minister to say that Kuwait felt "betrayed and tricked" by Halliburton's refusal to sign a contract with Altanmia. U.S. officials worried that angering Kuwait would threaten other U.S. initiatives, including a pledge from Kuwait for hundreds of millions of dollars to help out in Iraq.[33] As a result, on December 2, 2003, Richard H. Jones, the U.S. ambassador to Kuwait and simultaneously Bremer's top deputy, stepped in. A brusque career foreign service officer with long experience in the Middle East, Jones ordered the purchase of additional fuel from Altanmia. "Please tell KBR to get off their butts and conclude deals with Kuwait NOW!" Jones wrote in an e-mail to an unidentified U.S. official. "Tell them we want a deal done with Altanmia within 24 hours and don't take any excuses."[34]

Even then some in the government tried to stand up. On December 6, an Army Corps contracting official at the Palestine Hotel in Baghdad wrote to Halliburton, which had asked for a waiver to buy fuel from Altanmia at higher prices. She said she had located at least two other companies that could supply the fuel, potentially allowing for better prices. She could not approve the higher prices for fuel, she told the company. "Since the U.S. government is paying for these services, I will not succumb to the political pressure from the [Kuwaiti government] or the U.S. Embassy to go against my integrity and pay a higher price for fuel than necessary," wrote Mary Robertson, an Army Corps contracting officer. "If I am directed by a higher command to do this, then the [U.S. Army Corps of Engineers] will have to find another [contract officer] for this mission."[35]

Two weeks later, as the controversy over the high fuel prices exploded back home, the U.S. Army Corps of Engineers gave Halliburton the out it was seeking. Gen. Robert Flowers, head of the Army Corps, issued a highly unusual waiver excusing the company from providing "certified cost and pricing" data on the fuel contract. Flowers's order essentially blocked the Pentagon's audit agency from conducting further investigations of Halliburton's or Altanmia's books. Flowers said he issued the waiver because Iraq was in the middle of a fuel crisis. "If I didn't do that there would be no way you could come close to meeting demand," Flowers explained. "Bad things would happen."[36] The auditors eventually recommended that the United States withhold $263 million in payment to KBR for the fuel purchases and other equipment. The Defense Department ignored the recommendation and paid KBR all but $10 million of the bill.[37]

BUNNY AGAIN

In giving Halliburton a pass, Flowers had to run over Greenhouse again. As the highest-ranking Army Corps contract official, Greenhouse had to approve any such waiver. She was working at home when the waiver was hurriedly rushed through on December 19, 2003. To get all the necessary signatures, the documents had to be flown from San Antonio, where the Army Corps stationed its senior oil contract administrators, to Washington, where they were signed by Flowers. Although Greenhouse signed other documents that day for the Army Corps, she was never called to weigh in on the waiver. Instead her deputy, Lt. Col. Albert Castaldo, signed in her place. In an internal memorandum for the record, Castaldo described his role as essentially a yes-man to allow top corps officials to go behind Greenhouse's back. "It was fully understood that I would have to exercise the 'Just Do It' card to accomplish my mission for the command," Castaldo wrote.[38] It was one of the more damning pieces of evidence to show how far the U.S. government would go to cover up the mess it created with Halliburton.

Greenhouse was now a target. She began to be cut out of all meetings involving Halliburton. She had one more clash over the company. In the summer of 2004 she objected to an Army Corps decision to award a sole source contract to Halliburton for another logistics contract to maintain troops in the Balkans. She again scrawled over the paperwork, objecting to what she saw as fatuous reasoning. "I cannot approve this," Greenhouse wrote on one version of the proposal. "Incorrect!"; "No! How!"; and "Not a valid reason." It was the last straw. On October 7 she was called in and demoted. In short order her salary was cut, her staff was removed, and she was put into a junior position.

Greenhouse has spent many hours thinking about her stance. Unlike many whistle-blowers, she is not given to conspiracy theories. She does not think that Cheney or anyone from Halliburton ordered her downfall. Rather she imagines that top Army Corps officials acted in a misguided effort to keep the vice president happy. The idea that they could save the Bush administration from embarrassment during an election year was enough for senior Army Corps officials to come after her, she said. "I want someone to tell me what I did. I want them to. I was just doing my job. And that's all," she told me.

Greenhouse's bruising treatment was typical when it came to the government's dealing with Halliburton. Like a sheriff in a town where the rustlers have taken over, the United States let Halliburton run wild. If Dick Cheney had wanted to, he could have used his bully pulpit to demand better accountability. But the vice president showed little interest in cracking down on his former employer. Throughout the U.S. invasion and occupation of Iraq, the company became a law unto itself, racking up charges while escaping punishment. The American military rewarded the behavior by handing more and more work to Halliburton, each job another deposit in the corporate bank account. Nor did the company disappoint. Most soldiers in Iraq were well fed and well housed. Halliburton got the job done, albeit at sky-high prices. When it came to the oil business, though, it was an entirely different story.

5

The Mother Lode

An hour and a half outside of Basra, surrounded by nothing but the flat, empty desert of southern Iraq, lies a small crossroads called Berjesiya. There a sudden oasis blossoms, a small compound of concrete walls and shady trees where foreigners have long been forbidden: the Iraq Drilling Company, the keeper of the secrets of Iraq's 2,300 oil wells. The company is headquartered in a long, low structure with louvered windows that resembles an elementary school building. It was built in the 1950s by a British petroleum company as a drilling camp and shows its age. Paint flakes from the walls. Bare wires hang down from flickering fluorescent lamps. The building's dark interior smells of sewage that bubbles up from squat toilets just off the main corridor.

On the day I paid a visit with my translator, in the middle of a weeklong tour of Iraq's petroleum industry, we caught glimpses into rooms filled with intrigue: sheiks in long robes and headdresses arguing loudly with bureaucrats in dark suits. We were escorted into the manager's office, where we met Kadem Oush, a tanned, smiling Iraqi who served as senior consultant to the state-owned company. I had mistaken him for an American when I first entered, assuming him to be a U.S. adviser. Oush was wearing a Kansas City Royals cap, a checked short-sleeved shirt, blue jeans, and sneakers. He had spent most of his life immersed in Iraq's oil business, starting as a young boy laying mortar for the building in which we were sitting. He first went to work for the Kuwaitis, then private oil companies, and even for an American president, he joked. (Oush was a Santa Fe International employee when Gerald Ford was on its board in the 1980s.) He eventually took a job at Iraq's state oil company, overseeing the drilling of wells in Kirkuk in the north and Rumaila in the south. Now in his sixties, he had few peers when it came to expertise on Iraq's oil fields. He combined international experience with on-the-ground knowledge. And he was particularly displeased with KBR.

Engineers from KBR had come out a few months after the invasion to take stock. As was the case everywhere else, looters had descended upon the drilling company headquarters. Compressors, engines, cables vanished. Even pieces of the drilling rigs needed to do oil well maintenance jobs called workovers had been stolen. "Only we had the skeleton left and the pieces of this structure," Oush said. In a series of visits, KBR had promised to right things: to bring equipment to fix the drilling rigs, even to replace the furniture. But it never happened. "They say, but they didn't do. They tell us we're going to give you, we're going to give you and give you, but they didn't do anything," Oush said. He settled back in an overstuffed leather sofa and patted the arms. "KBR came out here many, many times. We made a list of requirements. We didn't receive nothing."

Oush's story was repeated again and again as we crisscrossed southern Iraq to reach different Iraq state oil company sites during the summer of 2005. When it came to restoring Iraq's oil infrastructure, neither the United States nor its chief contractor, Halliburton, delivered. Numbers told the story. Right before the war, Iraq's oil production was running around 2.5 million barrels per day, depending on who was making the estimate.[1] After two years and more than $2 billion in spending, oil production hovered at just under 2 million barrels per day. That was well below the American goal of up to 3 million barrels per day by December 2004. And it was well below what Iraq needed to pay for its own reconstruction. The shortfall meant $8 billion a year less that Iraq had for schools, health clinics, and its military.

The United States' inability to boost production was stunning given the importance of oil to Iraq and its reconstruction. From the start the Pentagon's most senior officials counted on oil to fund the rebuilding program. They believed that Iraq's oil industry could generate up to $100 billion over a three-year period, an average of $30 billion per year. Oil revenues were supposed to pay down Iraq's foreign debt, provide raises for government bureaucrats, and fund the reconstruction. The country's oil revenue accounted for 98 percent of Iraq's export earnings and 90 percent of the government's budget. The U.S. view was simple: "Oil is the lifeblood of Iraq," said Lt. Gen. John Vines of the U.S. Army, the commander of U.S. forces in Iraq.[2]

Indeed, with proven reserves of 115 billion barrels, Iraq had the potential to be a new Saudi Arabia. Even more enticing, most of the country had never even been explored. Estimates varied widely, but Iraq contained possibly 45 billion to 214 billion potential barrels of oil. The failure to restart the oil industry put that potential in doubt. Oil experts that I interviewed in Washington, London, Amman, and Baghdad worried that Iraq's reserves, the third largest in the world, had suffered permanent damage because of the botched rehabilitation efforts by the United States and its chief partner, KBR. It was a grim, and stunning, possibility: America not only failed to boost Iraq's oil flow, but wrecked the productivity of its most important resource.

Contrary to popular belief, insurgent violence had less impact on oil production than on other areas of the reconstruction program, though its effect was by no means insignificant. Iraq had two oil-producing regions — one up north around Kirkuk and a second, larger set of oil fields in the south near Basra that accounted for more than two-thirds of the country's production. Insurgents continually bombed the pipelines around Kirkuk, which ran through areas dominated by hard-line Sunnis; the majority of the nearly three hundred attacks recorded against Iraq's pipelines between April 2003 and October 2005 happened in the north.[3] As a result, flow in the north was only about 200,000 barrels a day, crippling production.

But southern Iraq, where KBR did most of its work and which had Iraq's largest petroleum reserves, had far fewer problems. The Rumaila oil fields and their pipeline system experienced little violence, especially after the United States reached a peace deal in August 2004 with Muqtada Sadr, the rebellious Shiite cleric who had a large following in Basra. As a result the southern fields were the one place in Iraq where the U.S. reconstruction program could have made a difference. But the results were disastrous. "We had the worst quality of U.S. service, staff, and companies," said Jaafar Altaie, who was a senior planner at the Oil Ministry before becoming a consultant with Amman-based Tabouk Energy Group. "We had maximum rhetoric and minimum results on the ground." For its part, Halliburton pointed toward Washington. KBR, company officials said, was just carrying out the orders it was given. "KBR can't emphasize enough that it performs all work at the direction of the U.S. government," said Melissa Norcross, a company spokeswoman. "We only do what we are tasked to do."

LIFEBLOOD

The modern nation of Iraq was literally born from oil. After World War I, the French and the British were jostling for control of three provinces of the former Ottoman Empire that today make up modern Iraq. Premier Georges Clemenceau of France went to London ten days after the armistice was signed on November 11, 1918, to meet with Prime Minister David Lloyd George. France had claim to an area north of Mosul. Britain wanted it. At the French embassy in London, the two men came to a casual agreement: Britain would recognize France's control of Syria, and France would recognize Britain's dominance of Iraq — so long as France received a share of the potential oil production from Mosul. Lloyd George agreed.[4]

Although Iraq wasn't producing oil at the time, there were few doubts the country had reserves. In an area north of Kirkuk called Baba Gurgur, about two dozen holes had supposedly been spewing flames of natural gas since biblical times. The Dutch, English, Germans, and Turks had been scheming for drilling concessions in the region a decade before the war. Finally, at 3 a.m. on October 15, 1927, a drilling rig hit oil. A roar filled the air and oil gushed out fifty feet above the derrick, spewing at the rate of 95,000 barrels a day — an enormous amount. Almost immediately the town of Kirkuk was threatened by the flood of oil and the spread of poisonous gases. Some seven hundred tribesman were enlisted to build dikes and dams to contain the oil.[5]

Iraq's oil production grew slowly until 1971, when the country nationalized the final part of its concession with the Iraq Petroleum Company, a conglomerate of American companies, state oil companies, and private capital. The Iraqi state oil company that took over helped to usher in an era of rising prosperity for Iraq, and many Iraqis fondly recall the 1970s as a time when Iraq was on the cusp of joining the modern world. It had the Arab world's best hospitals and colleges, a booming economy, and an exchange rate of three U.S. dollars for one Iraqi dinar. But the oil boom also provided the money that Saddam Hussein needed to finance his territorial ambitions. "Had it not been for oil wealth, this regime could not have launched three wars, could not have invaded Kuwait, could not have used resources to purchase weaponry," said Mahmoud Othman, a silver-haired Kurd who ran a think tank in Baghdad, more than a hint of sadness in his voice.

After reaching a peak in 1979 of 3.7 million barrels per day, Iraq's oil production began a long, uneven descent. The war with Iran and the Gulf

War brought devastation. The American-led bombing campaign destroyed storage facilities, pumping stations, and the Al Bakr oil export terminal on the Shaat Al Arab. Oil production in the south was cut from around 2 million to 75,000 barrels per day.[6] Recovery was hampered by United Nations sanctions and the Oil-for-Food program that followed. Under the UN program, which began in 1996, Saddam was supposed to sell oil in exchange for humanitarian goods. During the program's seven-year history, Iraq deposited nearly $70 billion in revenue into a United Nations bank account, which was overseen by a UN committee that was supposed to make sure the money was used to purchase humanitarian supplies, like food and medicine, and block the sale of materials that could be used to manufacture weapons of mass destruction. But American and British representatives on the committee delayed the purchase of spare parts and equipment needed for oil production. The sanctions also blocked desperately needed foreign investment. Iraq had to turn to a seedy chain of second- and third-rate suppliers for used equipment, or simply put off purchases. By 1998 the United Nations described the state of Iraq's industry as "deplorable."[7]

The Oil-for-Food program also resulted in the destruction of the human infrastructure of Iraq's oil industry. Under corrupt UN officials and the Saddam government, Oil-for-Food became a giant criminal enterprise. Through a variety of kickback schemes, Saddam evaded sanctions and raked in an estimated $1.8 billion in bribes, paid by more than two thousand foreign companies selling humanitarian goods or trading oil with the regime.[8] In order to maintain oversight of the corruption, Saddam purged the Western-educated technocrats on whom he had long relied to run the Oil Ministry. The Saddam cronies who took over contracted out exploration and management functions to Russian and Chinese companies. But the projects never got off the ground, and Iraq's oil infrastructure degenerated further.

By Saddam's last months in office, Iraq's oil industry was in an advanced state of decay. The U.S. invasion was the final push. U.S. Air Force bombers largely spared oil targets, but the looting that followed the hostility was devastating, accounting for nearly 80 percent of the damage to the system.[9] A coalition assessment in 2003 found that looters stole or damaged more than $900 million in equipment at Iraqi oil facilities.[10] Much of the looting, American officials came to believe, appeared to be an inside job: looters took specific equipment and instruments, and had access to the most sensitive locations. In one case they managed to penetrate the country's largest gas refinery complex, make their way to a command room hidden deep inside, and smash control panels — hardly spontaneous behavior. The looting was the functional equivalent of the oil well fires that Iraqi commandos ignited when retreating from Kuwait in 1991. It crippled oil production, made repairs difficult, and caused a debilitating loss of oil revenue.

Issam Chalabi had served as the oil minister before Saddam appointed his brother, Kamal, a month after the Iraq invasion of Kuwait in August 1990. After the Gulf War, Chalabi, who had once lectured in engineering at London University, relocated to Amman. He watched as Saddam slowly ran the ministry, and the country, into the ground. "Oil could have been the solution for all of Iraq's problems, and still is," Chalabi told me over lunch at a restaurant in Amman, where he worked as an oil consultant. "We would not have needed these handouts."

COMING AND GOING

Oil's importance to Iraq's history, economy, and psyche demanded the United States' full attention. It lingered in the shadows of every debate the country faced after the invasion, a constant, menacing roar, like the sound of churning sea. Iraq's economic problems? Oil production shortfalls were to blame. Iraq's insurgency? Financed by oil smuggling. Iraq's ethnic split? Oil fired internal divisions by providing an economic foundation for dreams of independent existence. When talks bogged down over the Iraqi constitution in August 2005, the main sticking point was how to split up the oil revenue. The Kurds wanted to keep 65 percent of the oil revenue generated in their territories in the north. The Shiites wanted the same ability for the provinces in the south. The Sunnis rejected the plan since the Sunni-dominated provinces did not produce oil. In the end the resolution was put off for a future government.

In the face of such a vital task, America failed to exert strong, centralized leadership. U.S.-appointed senior advisers, mostly retired oil company executives, were supposed to be the main link between the Iraqis and the U.S. government. But they came and went every three to six months, the short rotations making it difficult to embark upon sustained initiatives, understand the complexities of the oil industry's problems, or acclimate to the Iraqi way of doing business. One senior adviser told me he was stunned by

hours-long meetings that drifted without any apparent direction or purpose. Iraqi managers chatted on cellular phones and walked in and out of
gatherings. "To a Westerner's eye, this seemed very chaotic and at first very
inefficient," he said. In one twenty-four-month stretch, the United States
appointed five separate senior advisers to the oil ministry. The constant
shifts dismayed the Iraqis. "There were so many changes of leaders. They
would appear and disappear every three months," said Thamour Ghadban,
Iraq's ex–oil minister.

Some advisers had backgrounds that raised eyebrows. Robert W. Haugen, a senior adviser in 2004, had been an executive for Coastal Corporation, a company with a long, controversial history in Iraq. Coastal's CEO
was Oscar Wyatt, a flamboyant Texas oilman who had been buying Iraqi
crude since the 1970s. Right before the outbreak of the first Gulf War in
1991, Wyatt won fame by flying his company plane to personally rescue
American expats being held hostage in the Rasheed Hotel. Haugen was
never linked to any wrongdoing, but Wyatt was indicted in 2005 on
charges that he paid Saddam kickbacks as part of the Oil-for-Food scandal. Another senior adviser was Bob Todor, a former executive for Unocal
International, which drew fire after negotiating with the Taliban to build a
pipeline through Afghanistan.[11]

American instability was matched on the Iraqi side — though again this
was mostly the fault of the United States. Ibrahim Bahr al-Uloum was the
first U.S.-appointed oil minister, an oil field analyst with a PhD in petroleum engineering from the University of New Mexico. Short and squat,
with a thatch of unruly black hair, he had little hands-on experience in the
industry, but solid ties to the Shiites as the son of a cleric active in the exile
movement. His appointment was essentially a political move. After the
June 2004 handover to the Iraqis, Uloum was replaced by Ghadban, a
competent technocrat and ally of Ayad Allawi, Iraq's interim prime minister. Ghadban was a tall, thin man who had spent thirty years in Iraq's oil
ministry. Urbane and blunt, he was a favorite among American advisers
because he was seen as a pragmatist. The Shiite sweep in the January 2005
elections resulted in Uloum's return to power in April. But the December
2005 elections saw Uloum resign, to be replaced temporarily by Ahmed
Chalabi, the former Pentagon favorite who by then had few friends left in
the 202 area code.

Constantly shifting leadership postponed resolution of any of the most
difficult issues facing Iraq's petroleum industry. One example was the best

use of the country's natural gas resources. Iraq had an estimated 110 trillion cubic feet of natural gas. Most was a by-product of oil exploration, emerging from the ground at the same time as liquid crude. In most modern oil-producing countries, the natural gas is captured as it escapes and put to use, often in firing electrical generators. But the Iraqis simply burned it away. Iraq's southern desert was lit at night by giant candles that burned uninterrupted in the darkness — towering flares of natural gas. Americans could not decide what to do about the wasted resource. Some wanted the Iraqis to build new pipelines and facilities to use the gas. Other advisers advocated delaying natural gas projects in favor of quickly boosting crude production to earn more revenue. In the meantime the gas wasted away.

The biggest, most politically sensitive issue was the privatization of the industry. Iraq's crumbling oil infrastructure needed up to $35 billion in investment to boost production to 5 million barrels of oil per day. In that context the American investment of $2 billion was merely a down payment; private industry would have to contribute the rest. American senior advisers believed that outside companies were necessary to bring in the money and expertise needed to fix the system. But even knowing this, they were exceedingly cautious in pushing the Iraqis to allow in foreign companies. When Jerry Bremer unveiled his plans to sell off Iraq's state-owned companies to private bidders, he specifically exempted the most important of all: the state oil company. After the United States turned over sovereignty to the Iraqis in June 2004, the American oil advisers became consultants and took even more of a backseat role. "We tried to bring information or suggestions on how you do this. We were really trying hard to concentrate on that as opposed to more active involvement in decisions," one senior adviser told me.

Iraqis were themselves divided. Some believed that outside firms were needed for their expertise and their capital. However, there was a general consensus that such deals would be limited, involving upstream activities like oil refining or transportation instead of production. "We can't really rely on foreign assistance," Ghadban told me. "Iraq must depend on itself and its ways and means." Other Iraqis, however, were against any foreign involvement, most notably Iraq's newly emergent unions. Saddam had banned all labor unions in a famous nationwide television address in 1987, but a month after the March 2003 invasion, a handful of Iraqi oil workers banded together to announce the rebirth of the labor movement. Two years later, the General Union for Oil Employees claimed to have twenty-five thousand members. "No to privatization" became one of the union's principal planks. Its first battles were with KBR. When word leaked out in the summer of 2003 that KBR was importing thousands of Filipinos to work as cheap labor instead of hiring Iraqis, union members staged a hasty protest by using a fifty-ton crane to block a route to a gas-oil separation plant. By August 20 the union issued a demand that KBR abandon its work in the oil sector. When the company refused to talk with them, they shut down oil exports for two days.

The man responsible for the protests was Hassan Jumaa, a squat, bull-necked oil worker who was union president. With thick hands, a square head, and short white hair, Jumaa could have been a Cleveland union boss except for the blue turquoise prayer beads that he constantly fingered. Over a long meal of kebabs, roast tomatoes, and sweet tea in a hotel restaurant, he laid out his vision. The union was pro-Iraq. It would not, for instance, hold a strike that would completely shut down the oil industry, because that would be too damaging to the country. But the union had no intention of allowing foreign companies any part of Iraq's oil business. The experience with KBR had convinced them that American companies were proxies for the American occupation. "The company is connected to the Pentagon and it's financed by the Pentagon," Jumaa said. "KBR did nothing to help the oil sector. They were a burden."

OIL AND WATER

KBR began its operations in Iraq forty-eight hours after the invasion began on March 19. The company's engineers were startled by the disrepair they found. At one plant they found compressor pumps held together by leather straps.[12] There were only two working drilling rigs in the entire country. "We faced mines, unexploded ordnance, booby traps, roving bands of looters," said Charles "Stoney" Cox, KBR's vice president of operations.[13]

Nevertheless Iraq started flowing oil through pipelines on April 22, 2003, just five weeks after the war. By June 2003 the state oil company started selling oil again.[14] Each month brought slightly higher output. By December 2003, for the first time since the invasion, Iraq's oil production hit 2.4 million barrels a day. Optimistic coalition planners set a new target of reaching between 2.8 and 3 million barrels of oil a day by the end of 2004. The Bush

administration predictions of boosting Iraq's oil pumping to 3 million barrels a day — and of an Iraq that could fund its own reconstruction —
seemed in reach. "The oil is in fact flowing extraordinarily well," Mike
Wynn, the acting undersecretary of defense for acquisition and the Pentagon's top contracting official, told Congress in June 2004. The reason? "All
the folks at Halliburton."[15]

The recovery would not last. After reaching a monthly high in September 2004, production began a long, steady decline. By December 2004,
when Washington hoped Iraq would be pumping close to 3 million barrels
per day, the country was producing only 2.2 million barrels daily. Two
months later, with output declining by another 100,000 barrels a day, the
United States officially lowered its sights. A new goal was set of reaching
2.5 million barrels per day. By early 2006 Iraq's oil pumping had slipped to
1.5 million barrels per day — a decline from the postwar peak that cost the
Iraqi government and its U.S. backer some $54 million daily in potential
revenue at 2006 market prices — enough to build a new hospital for Laura
Bush every day of the week. The Department of Energy declared that the
Iraqi invasion ranked as the third largest cumulative oil disruption since
World War II, behind the nationalization of Iran's oil fields in the early
1950s and the Iranian revolution in 1979.[16] "Just about everything that
could have gone wrong has," said Jamal Qureshi, an oil analyst with PFC
Energy in Washington.[17]

Three botched projects contributed to the decline, each a chronicle of
poor leadership by the United States and poor execution by KBR. One of
the first jobs that the United States gave KBR was the repair of the Qarmat
Ali water treatment plant, a complex of twisting pipes and rusting metal
that sits in the middle of drab, flat nothingness a few miles north of Basra,
in southern Iraq. Both the United States and Iraq considered the water
treatment plant a high priority. Oil rises from the ground in southern Iraq
because of natural pressure in the sands. As the oil surges out, the pressure
declines, making extraction more difficult. To counter the problem, the
Iraqis inject water back into the earth to maintain the pressure in the oil
field and assure continued pumping. That water, however, must first be
cleaned at Qarmat Ali so that particles or bacteria don't plug up the holes
in the soil that allow the oil to rise.

By August 2004 KBR had completed most repairs at the plant, which
had badly deteriorated during sanctions and the looting that followed the
invasion. KBR rebuilt motors, refurbished pumps, and installed electrical

generators and chlorination and anticorrosion systems. But when KBR opened the taps to send the treated water rushing through buried pipelines toward Iraq's legendary Rumaila oil field, the deteriorated pipes were unable to handle the increased pressure. The pipeline burst repeatedly, delaying work for weeks on end. In a five-month period in fall 2004, KBR managed to send water through the pipes for only twenty-nine days. To make matters worse, farmers tapped into the pipeline, using it to irrigate their fields. KBR found one local who was watering his entire tomato crop courtesy of the Qarmat Ali pipeline. As of August 2005 the plant was delivering only about a third of its capacity.

Despite the problems reconstruction officials never assigned KBR the task of repairing the aging lines. Bob Todor, the U.S. senior oil adviser to the Iraqis, told me that by the time the problem became apparent, most of the money available in the south had already been committed to other projects. The United States was squeezing the Iraqis to pay for the repairs without luck. The Iraqis were themselves facing a budget deficit, partly because of oil revenue shortfalls. Their money was already dedicated to paying for government salaries and state subsidies of fuel, electricity, and food. "The Iraqis have not had the money to do the work," Todor told me.

When I visited the sprawling, decades-old complex in August 2005, the decay was obvious. The walls were cracked; motors, valves, and pipes were rusted. Dirt and mud covered the floors. Only two of the five pumps that KBR fixed were operating. An Iraqi engineer said a machine to add cleaning chemicals to the water was unusable. Another system to protect the interior of the pipelines from rust was not being used for fear that the anticorrosion additive would damage the oil fields. Neither the United States nor KBR provided additional maintenance or operating funds to the plant after turning it over to the Iraqis. For their part the Iraqis said KBR had installed substandard equipment and had not provided sufficient training.

The plant had the ragged feel of an industrial neighborhood a long way from urban revival. In one corner a sullen group of Iraqis was gathered around a single welding torch, fixing a water pipeline that carried drinking water for the workers at the plant. Inside the main office a group of Russian businessmen was negotiating with the plant manager to supply chlorine. The cavernous pump stations were the size of airplane hangars. Inside, a few pumps hummed while most were silent. The plant's assistant manager was a young Iraqi with a bare command of English and a sad smile. "It's useless. We have material from KBR, but we don't have documents on how to use it," said the Iraqi engineer, who requested anonymity because of security concerns.

The end result of the U.S. investment was that Qarmat Ali did not produce enough water to safely ensure maximum production, nor could the water reliably be delivered to the injection stations, which also were in need of repair. Every day the water shortage meant that Iraq was giving up production on 200,000 barrels of oil — about $12 million a day. "This is a vital project to us," Ibrahim Bahr al-Uloum, Iraq's oil minister, told me in August 2005. "We need to hit the targets as soon as possible." In 2005 reconstruction officials removed KBR from the project and replaced it with a joint venture between WorleyParsons, an Australian firm, and Parsons, a California company, which had won a contract to restore Iraq's northern oil fields. Officially the United States said the decision had nothing to do with the quality of KBR's work. The Iraqis were less guarded. KBR had simply moved too slowly.

The lack of reliable water injection led to a debate about whether the U.S.-directed reconstruction effort permanently damaged Iraq's southern oil fields. Although nobody was sure, some oil experts feared that America's failure to fix the problems had worsened damage that began during Saddam Hussein's rule. United Nations oil experts told the U.S. government that some oil reservoirs in southern Iraq were so badly managed that the Iraqis will be able to recover only 15 percent to 25 percent of the oil, well below the industry standard of 35 percent to 60 percent, according to a Department of Energy report. Norm Szydlowski, a former Chevron executive who served as a U.S. senior adviser to the Oil Ministry, called the possibility of permanent damage a "significant concern."

"The extent of the potential damage is really unknown," he told me.

The status of reservoirs in northern Iraq led to other worries. Once an oil well begins production, it is difficult to shut it down. But attacks on pipelines in the north occurred so frequently that the Iraqis could neither export oil nor store it. As a result, when oil production backed up the Iraqis were forced to pump the oil back into the ground — a practice widely condemned in the industry because the reinjected oil, which is thicker, can plug fissures through which the petroleum flows. In 2005 Iraq was pumping almost 200,000 barrels of oil per day back into the ground, further lowering the actual production figures. "Once you have damaged the fields, there is almost nothing you can do about it. I have a great worry that we are not too far from it," said Farouk Kasim, an Iraqi oil expert, at a 2005 conference in London. "The last two years have been a nightmare."

THE BRIDGE

The second botched project involved the pipelines at the Al Fathah bridge. A squat concrete-and-steel structure over the Tigris River in northern Iraq, the bridge was bombed by U.S. jets during the 2003 invasion. The attack knocked out a stretch of the span, destroying a network of oil and gas pipelines that ran underneath the bridge. The sixteen pipelines were a crucial part of Iraq's deteriorating oil infrastructure, moving crude and other petroleum products from northern wells around Kirkuk to Bayji, a dusty refinery town south of the bridge. The United States decided that fixing the pipelines was one of the most important steps toward restoring oil flow in the north.

In the summer of 2003 U.S. government officials and contractors surveyed the bridge site, an arid moonscape of dirt hills surrounding a dull green ribbon of river. At first USAID planned to fix the bridge using Bechtel, which held a contract to repair infrastructure. Bechtel predicted a $4.3 million price tag and three-month completion time, according to USAID documents. Instead the U.S. Army Corps of Engineers, which was in charge of the oil effort, decided to use KBR to run the pipelines under the riverbed, a distance of more than eight hundred yards. Army Corps and KBR believed that it would be the quickest fix.

In the fall of 2003, according to one Army Corps official with knowledge of the project, the corps paid for a study that raised serious questions about soil stability under the riverbed. The Army Corps ignored the warning and ordered KBR to go ahead with the drilling plan. The official — who had described the project as "placing a pipe in a large box of marbles" — got sent back home. When I tried to contact him after being given a copy of e-mails that he had sent describing the problems, he refused to talk. Instead he sent me an e-mail that said simply, "Too scared."

Trouble began soon after the project started in January 2004. As predicted, the soil was unstable and a borehole drilled to hold the pipes collapsed. The project, originally envisioned to take ten weeks, turned into a nearly yearlong job. As the months went by, the cost soared. KBR warned about the increases, but the Army Corps told them to continue, approving ever more spending on the flailing project. In the end KBR managed to install six of the sixteen pipelines originally planned. The final price tag for the incomplete job was $76 million — almost $50 million over the original budget. "In hindsight, maybe you would have done things differently," said Todor, the adviser to the Oil Ministry. In November 2004 reconstruction officials reassigned the pipeline crossing, again to the joint venture between WorleyParsons and Parsons. American officials insisted that it was no reflection on KBR's abilities. The WorleyParsons joint venture spent another year on the project, and an additional $62 million. The firm wrapped up work in 2006, with the project two years and almost $150 million over original estimates.

A government investigation concluded that the whistle-blower had been right: both the Army Corps and KBR had ignored the warning signs in the assessment. "The geological complexities that caused the project to fail were not only foreseeable but predicted," according to a report released in January 2006 by the special inspector general for the reconstruction of Iraq. The report estimated conservatively that the delay in repairing the pipeline had cost the Iraqi government $1.5 billion dollars,[18] money that could have built several new power plants, hundreds of clinics and hospitals, and weapons and equipment that the Iraqi army needed to move U.S. soldiers out of harm's way. Under the Al Fathah bridge, millions of American taxpayer dollars simply washed away.

The third KBR project that resulted in delays involved well workovers — cleanup jobs that can improve the productivity of oil wells. The Project and Contracting Office, a government reconstruction agency, wanted KBR to perform thirty workovers on wells in southern Iraq for $37 million. At stake: an estimated increase of 300,000 barrels of oil per day. According to a senior U.S. official, negotiations got bogged down over KBR's demand that the United States indemnify it in case of lawsuits arising from the work. KBR insisted on the guarantee, saying that such indemnity was provided by governments worldwide. The United States' position was that only the Iraqi government, as a sovereign nation, could give such protection. In July 2005 the two sides reached an impasse and American officials terminated the project. Instead they decided to turn the work over to the Iraqis.

This kind of dispute was common. Since arriving in Iraq, KBR had constantly quarreled with Iraqi oil company officials, Iraqi oil workers unions, and American oil advisers. "I want to follow this path, and they choose a different path. This isn't good," said Jabbar Ueibi, the general manager for

South Oil Company, the largest oil producer in Iraq. KBR engineers installed modern, high-end equipment like gas-fired electric generators that the Iraqis didn't know how to use and were unable to keep running. KBR lawyers got into lengthy contract disputes with the United States that delayed important projects. KBR buyers had trouble obtaining spare parts and refinery equipment on a hot world market. Project deadlines slipped.

Ueibi, seemed uncertain of the prospects for success during an interview in his office, filled with bouquets of artificial flowers. He said Iraqi engineers and workers had "mainly" restored the oil sector, with "some" help from KBR. He said KBR's refusal to do the workovers had left him scrambling. "It's difficult. It's a challenge. But we'll succeed," he said. "We need every bit of help that we can get."

He didn't sound like a man who was sure of himself.

EMPIRE OF STEEL

The last stop I made on a tour of Iraq's oil facilities was at the Southern Gas Company. The plant took associated gas — the natural gas that comes out of the ground along with oil — and turned it into liquid petroleum gas for power plants, and butane and other gases for cooking and home heating. The complex, located in the middle of brown, searing desert, sprawled across the equivalent of six football fields. It resembled an Escher drawing — an industrial maze of enormous steel spheres and pipes that twisted off into infinity. It was eerily quiet. Only one small corner of the complex was working, emitting a faint hum that filled the blistering 110-degree heat like a ceaseless cicada.

Inside in a darkened office, Abdul Raof Ibraheen presided over the empire of silent steel by himself. The plant's workers came every morning but left by the early afternoon. There was not much for them to do. Before the war the plant, the largest in Iraq, had pumped out about 3,000 metric tons of gas a day — almost enough to satisfy Iraq's internal demand. Now, more than a year after the invasion, the plant limped along, producing at most 1,000 metric tons a day. The shortfall was made up by importing fuel — gasoline, diesel, and kerosene — from other countries. The imports cost Iraq some $400 million per month. In essence Iraq was selling its oil to other countries and then buying it back, in refined form, because the United States had been unable to get refineries like the Southern Gas Company running again. It was a Middle East version of coals to Newcastle.

And the uncertainty surrounding Iraq's oil industry ensured that the world's largest oil companies continued to stay away. More than three years after the invasion, Iraq didn't even have a hydrocarbons law to govern the terms of transactions with foreign companies. By 2005 the only agreements that Iraq had signed with major oil companies were deals designed to build up future business relationships. Chevron, for instance, signed a deal to provide free training to Iraqi engineers. Beyond such symbolic partnerships, the majors were reluctant to commit money or manpower. When Royal Dutch/Shell won a contract to help analyze the country's oil reserves, the company decided against a tender to develop a field near Kirkuk: "We would welcome the opportunity to help Iraq rebuild its energy industry once the security situation allows and once an internationally recognized Iraqi government is established," the company said in a statement.[19]

Ibraheen was a short, rumpled man whose hair was slowly turning gray. He had met with KBR representatives every time they visited his lonely outpost, which was not often. They had brought him forklifts, cranes, and air-conditioning units, but most of it came from the state oil company's own warehouses, he said. KBR had not brought him control panels to replace the ones that had been smashed by looters or helped run a new pipeline to bring more gas. "This is not our plan," he said. "This is their plan, and we're forced to do it." KBR engineers had recently told Ibraheen that a worldwide spending boom in oil infrastructure had made it hard to purchase the needed equipment. The last word Ibraheen had was that the parts would arrive in twelve months or so. A frown creased over his tired face. He looked over at the Army Corps of Engineers supervisor who had accompanied me to the site and hesitated. The American engineer encouraged Ibraheen to speak freely. Ibraheen took a deep breath.

"Frankly speaking, I am not satisfied with KBR's work. What I saw from KBR, their performance is not what we had expected," he said. "We heard a lot about KBR, but we're not satisfied. The results have meant nothing for us." While the Iraqis may not have gotten much out of Halliburton, the company got plenty from Iraq. Halliburton made more than $2.5 billion off the oil contract, some of it paid by U.S. taxpayers, and some of it paid by the Iraqis themselves. It didn't matter that the company that built the Johnson Space Center couldn't run eight hundred yards of pipe under a river.

During that first long, crazed summer of 2003, the United States paid heavily for its failure to plan to build a new democracy. Bush administration officials like Donald Rumsfeld and Condoleezza Rice had counted on an Iraqi government to stand up and do the work. When that didn't happen, the White House deputized a motley posse of amateur nation builders who were neither well trained nor properly equipped for the task that lay ahead. Contractors ran the show, racking up costs with little concern over whether their projects accomplished anything. Eskimos were going to build a cellular phone network and the president's wife was ramming through a pet hospital. America had contracted out nation building but neglected to send in a supervisor. In many cases money and morals, rules and regulations, commonsense and caution, flew out the door. By the end of the summer, the pendulum was swinging back. Congress, the public, even the White House wanted order. The shift was so extreme that it impaired the rebuilding for almost a year.

Part II
Turning Dirt

6

The Builder

On a chilly morning a few weeks before Thanksgiving in November 2003, thousands of federal contractors, lobbyists, and government types in dark suits and overcoats streamed into a cavernous ballroom in the Crystal Gateway Marriott just down the street from the Pentagon. They overflowed the room and spilled into the hallways outside, which were already jammed with businessmen waving flyers. "Body armor," called out one man as people jostled past. "Hope you land a big contract."[1]

Inside the dim ballroom, large white projector screens showed images of soldiers from the 101st Airborne Division in Iraq. Bagpipes played "Amazing Grace." Then, as the lights came on, a thin, rangy man stepped onto the stage, his white hair and oversized glasses giving him the look of a grandfather. Earlier that summer, David Nash had left a job at an engineering firm to set foot in Iraq for the first time. In the four months that followed, he designed the structure for the largest U.S. foreign aid program since the Marshall Plan. Now it was time to sell it to the world.

Nash explained to the crowd that Congress had just approved $18.4 billion for the rebuilding of Iraq. Most of that money would be given to the companies the audience represented, big multinational firms from the United States and coalition allies. The United States would issue contracts to do reconstruction work in six separate sectors: oil, electricity, water, security, transportation and communications, and housing and health. The companies that won these contracts would be the ground troops of the rebuilding, the men and women who would wear the hard hats and do hard work.

Above them would be two more layers of contractors, each helping

Nash and his staff manage the work. These contractors became, in essence, the bureaucracy of the reconstruction, the managers and file clerks and secretaries. Nash was the ringmaster. He would coordinate the other groups at work on the reconstruction: the U.S. Army Corps of Engineers, USAID, and the military; two dozen Iraqi ministries with their own pot of money to spend; and then the international donors, led by the World Bank, which had pledged yet more funds at a conference in Madrid a month earlier.

The whole business would move at light speed but with maximum transparency, Nash told the audience. Congress had made clear it wanted this round of contracting to be open and competitive. No more no-bid deals, awarded in secret to favorite companies. The companies would have to compete for every contract, according to the regulations spelled out in federal guidelines. As Nash spoke the coalition was in the last stages of planning for more than two thousand individual projects, a number that would eventually grow beyond three thousand. A final list would go to Jerry Bremer in Iraq for approval, then to Congress. Companies would submit their bids for the work sometime in December. Teams of contracting officers would sort through the proposals and make a final decision to award work by February 1. That was seventy-four days away.

Nash unveiled a PowerPoint slide that attempted to explain the process. It looked like a plate of spaghetti, with reporting lines and boxes flowing everywhere. The diagram barely fit on the screen. It was complicated, Nash acknowledged. But this was the plan for the reconstruction of Iraq. "It counts on you, our industry, to help me get all this done," he said. "It's my personal opinion that there's only a few people, a few entities in the world, that can do something of this magnitude. So we want your very best."

The plan that Nash laid out was a radical departure from the careful, controlled world of government contracting. He was trying to marry the ponderous federal procurement system with the urgent demands of a country in the middle of a war. He was proposing to award twenty-five contracts in two months in a system where a single contract in ninety days was considered a rush job. He was turning the government's normal two-year budget review into a two-month process. And he was hiring contractors to do work that in the United States would normally be done by government employees. Nash called it a "unique" and "highly leveraged" approach.

In the United States, the Army Corps of Engineers had thirty thousand people and a budget of about $12 billion to do the same kind of work that

Nash was contemplating. Nash never had more than fifty government employees and a budget of $18.4 billion.

Afterward Nash held a hasty press conference in a small meeting room off the main lobby of the hotel. He didn't have many details. He wasn't sure about the final list of projects. He didn't know for certain yet whether companies from noncoalition partners such as France or Germany would be allowed to bid on the contracts. He wasn't even sure about his organization's name. "We're still looking that over," he said ruefully. In fact the Iraq Infrastructure Reconstruction Office would change its name two more times, to Program Management Office and then finally to the Project and Contracting Office.

Nash was tired. He had a hacking cough that he blamed on a dust storm that blanketed Baghdad before his departure. He looked worn, harried, and exhausted. And it was only the beginning. He would spend the better part of the next year enmeshed in bitter bureaucratic infighting, chaos, and bloodshed.

KING BEE

David Nash spent most of his adult life in the intersection of the military and private industry. He grew up without much money in Mount Vernon, a small town in central Ohio where his father worked as a clerk in a factory that made engines for power plants. After graduating from Indiana Institute of Technology in Fort Wayne, he entered the navy as an engineer during the height of the Vietnam War. He got his first taste of government contracting there, working with the building consortium that included Brown & Root in building roads, bridges, and ports.

Nash moved up through the navy's construction ranks to become "King Bee," the head of the Seabees made famous by the John Wayne movie.[2] The Seabees are an elite corps of military engineers, rushed in with troops to build airstrips, housing, and other facilities under combat conditions. Nash was promoted to rear admiral in 1993 — nominated by Defense Secretary Dick Cheney on the last full day of the first Bush administration.[3] By the time Nash retired in 1998, he was head of the navy's entire construction program, overseeing a budget of $8 billion, twenty thousand sailors, and nine thousand engineers. He was responsible for everything from environmental cleanup at navy bases to upgrading ports and harbors to overseeing the Seabees' disaster relief efforts. There were few people in the U.S. government who had more experience in contractors and construction work.

Once out of the government, Nash took a job in the private sector, doing what he knew: building things. He went to work as an executive for Parsons Brinkerhoff, an engineering firm that specialized in transportation and public sector work — in Nash's case, overseeing the renovation of a massive General Motors campus in Warren, Michigan, where engineers designed new automobiles. Soon thereafter came an offer to head up a new group at BE&K, a privately owned engineering firm based in Birmingham that was interested in beefing up its work with the federal government. Nash had just accepted the job in June 2003 when he was tracked down by an old friend. Vald Heiberg, a retired general, had been the head of the U.S. Army Corps of Engineers, a position similar to the one that Nash held in the navy. Nash was sitting in a coffeehouse in Buffalo, finishing up some work before starting his new job, when he got the call on his cellular phone. Heiberg was helping the small circle of Nixon-era Republican friends in the Pentagon who were scrambling to fill jobs in Iraq. Nash told Heiberg he'd be happy to join. "I thought it was something I could do to help," Nash told me in an interview in January 2006. "When the fire horse stops pulling the wagon, he still runs to the fire every time the bell rings."

When Nash arrived in Iraq on July 19, 2003, the Bush administration was just coming to understand that the short-term occupation was going to cost more and take longer than anybody had planned. During the first few weeks in Iraq, Nash had been working as a deputy senior adviser in charge of communications and transportation. But by August, Nash was working for Bremer's budget director, Dave Oliver. The two men were acquaintances from their navy days, and Oliver thought Nash's program management skills would come in handy. In one of the snap hiring decisions common in the coalition's scramble for manpower, Nash became the head of what would turn out to be the largest nation-building program since World War II.

Nash's selection shaped the entire course of the reconstruction. Other than his experience in managing large construction programs, there was nothing in his background to suggest that he was particularly qualified for the job of nation building. He had not played a major role in any of the seven postconflict rebuilding programs that the United States had launched since World War II.[4] He had no expertise in the political or economic theory of developing countries. He had no expertise in the complexities of doing construction work in the Middle East. He was, as one State Department official told me later, "a guy they picked out of the hallway because there was nobody else around."

THE NASH PLAN

Ever the optimist, Nash put it another way: "I was the only one that was willing to give it a try who had program management experience." Nash brought confidence in his own ability to the job. "I thrive on responsibility," he said. He was an engineer, a manager, a careful watchdog of the public's money. He had spent his life building big things by hiring big companies. Iraq would be no different.

Working with a small staff in two rooms the size of a kitchen on the ground floor of the Republican Palace, Nash came up with a blueprint. Under Nash the rebuilding program developed into what was essentially a giant construction project. Nash was not sure how much money he would get, or where, exactly, it would go — that was up to Congress and the U.S. Army, which would actually issue the contracts. But he believed that the best use of the money would be to provide the Iraqis with solid, up-to-date infrastructure. New power plants would provide electricity for factories. Paving roads to small villages would encourage commerce. Water treatment plants and health clinics would better the lives of ordinary Iraqis. The work would go on all across Iraq, at the same time, in many different areas. It was up to Nash to figure out how to get it done. "We started basically with a blank sheet of paper," Nash said.[5]

Nash made two crucial decisions. First, he believed that large, multinational corporations should do the work. These powerhouse design-build engineering companies — the same ones he had worked with in Vietnam, the same ones he had relied upon for years in the navy — had the resources necessary to juggle multiple complex construction projects. Firms like Parsons and Bechtel and Washington Group International might not be household names, but they had the experts who could design and build a bridge or a dam in the most unforgiving conditions. They were also accountable, with experience in the complicated world of government contracting. In addition, Nash thought, the big companies could provide a real-world university to the Iraqis, who had been isolated by sanctions. The engineering firms would hire as many Iraqis as possible, and teach them cutting-edge techniques in modern engineering and design. It would be win-win.

Nash's second decision was to create a brand-new government agency to oversee the reconstruction. Nash saw his Project and Contracting Office, or PCO, as the switchboard of the rebuilding. There was no other agency, he believed, that could do the job. USAID, with years of experience in building democracy and liberal institutions in developing nations, was a natural choice, but it had never handled anything the size of rebuilding Iraq. The U.S. Army Corps of Engineers was expert at managing giant building contracts in the United States, but the corps was still scrambling to establish a presence in Iraq. Nash's PCO would fill the gap.

The PCO would coordinate the flow of all the reconstruction money: funds from Congress, international donors, and Iraqi state oil revenues. All other government agencies would be "executing agencies," charged with implementing the plans and policies of the reconstruction agency. PCO would get its own staff by borrowing from other agencies and hiring subject-matter experts — basically private-sector executives and retirees who had worked in the oil or electricity business — but Nash and his organization would respond only to Bremer, who in turn reported directly to Rumsfeld. "It sounds military, but it's not. You have to have clean lines of authority or things get all hosed up. There was great concern over bureaucratic autonomy. You can't have that," one senior reconstruction official told me, in defending the decision. Nash was obsessed with maintaining control over a program in which Rumsfeld and the rest of the Defense Department seemed uninterested.

In choosing how to proceed, Nash ruled out several alternatives. Iraq, of course, had its own engineering and construction firms, which had built the country's highway system, its oil network, and its power stations. Most of those, however, were companies owned by the state, controlled by Saddam and his cronies. They had operated in a command-driven, subsidized economy, and on a practical level they were falling apart. A coalition survey found that none of the approximately two hundred state-owned companies had turned a profit in years. Their material, technique, and skills were years out of date. Worse still, many of the companies had been looted. They simply didn't have equipment anymore; the looters had stolen cranes, bulldozers, and construction supplies. Thus Nash decided to hire American firms instead of contracting directly with their Iraqi counterparts.

Nash was also worried about issues like leadership and corruption if he dealt with Iraqi companies. Most of the Baathists who ran the state-owned companies had lost their jobs in Bremer's purge. They had been replaced by junior directors with a fear of action acquired from the Saddam days. There were a handful of large, private construction firms in Iraq, mostly conglomerates owned by families like the Khudhairys, Janabis, Dulaimis, and Kubbas, but they were widely assumed to have worked closely with Saddam — how else would they have thrived in a dictatorship? Graft was standard operating procedure during Saddam's regime, for both the state-owned companies and the privately held construction firms. Nash believed there was no way to ensure that money poured into an Iraqi company would reach the ground. Nash was spending U.S. taxpayer dollars, and he knew he had to report back. "I knew that someday accountability would be more important than speed," he said.

ROADBLOCKS

Only a month after Nash spoke to the contractors in Crystal City, his rebuilding plan ran into trouble. On December 5, 2003, Wolfowitz issued an unusual memorandum blocking any countries that were not part of the coalition that invaded Iraq from receiving the prime reconstruction contracts. Although it was not a surprise, the ban immediately caused a backlash in media and political circles. Here was proof, it was said, that rather than being a multinational effort of nations, the war in Iraq was a payoff for American firms. Secretary-General Kofi Annan of the UN branded the U.S. policy "unfortunate." German chancellor Gerhard Schröder suggested it might violate international trade law. Bush had to place a personal call to Canada's prime minister, Jean Chrétien, to assure him that his nation's firms would indeed be eligible.[6]

Behind the scenes another conflict broke out that further delayed the contracting process. The State Department and USAID wanted more money for their projects. Only a tiny slice of the $18.4 billion rebuilding bill was dedicated to education, refugees, human rights, and governance. No money was devoted to agriculture, even though it was the second largest source of employment in Iraq, especially in the rural areas where the insurgency had flared. As State, USAID, and the Pentagon fought over the distribution of money, the dispute brought a sudden halt to the contracting process. Back home for Christmas, Nash viewed the money fight with dread. He thought that spreading the reconstruction money among different agencies was a recipe for disaster. He wanted his agency to control everything. Nash threatened to resign. He sent an e-mail to a Bremer aide on December 16: "I personally feel that we are setting ourselves up for failure."[7]

By early January the dispute was resolved through a compromise. The Pentagon agreed to withhold $4 billion in spending until after the United States turned over power to the Iraqis in June 2004. The withheld money would serve as a carrot to convince a new Iraqi government to continue cooperating with the Americans. But it also gave the State Department more of a say in how the money would be spent, since State was going to replace the coalition as the official diplomatic (and financial) channel after the handover of sovereignty. Nash was not exactly happy — he had planned on having far more money to spend — but he accepted the change. Nash wrapped up his visit to the Pentagon by meeting with Rumsfeld for an hour and a half to present his vision of the rebuilding. At the end, the secretary exhorted him to get moving. "You got a plan, go get it," Nash recalled Rumsfeld's telling him.

The next few months were a whir of activity as Nash struggled to get moving. He used a preexisting air force construction contract to immediately begin refurbishing Iraqi military bases, which had been looted during the war. He boasted of "turning dirt" — a favorite phrase — by February. A month later the army, working with Nash's agency, began awarding a series of big contracts with the new reconstruction money. By the end of March nearly $12 billion — almost two-thirds of the money available for reconstruction — had been handed out. The contracts were massive, some of them for more than $500 million dollars. Most went to a handful of large American firms: Parsons, based in Pasadena; Washington Group, based in Idaho; Perini International, based in Massachusetts; and Fluor Group, based in Aliso Viejo, California. "It won't be long until you find a lot of satisfied customers in Iraq," Nash predicted in March 2004.[8]

Unfortunately Nash had been closer to the mark in that December e-mail. Ignorant of the past, the United States had set itself up for failure.

THE MARSHALL PLAN

The Marshall Plan was unveiled to the public on Harvard's commencement day, June 7, 1947. Secretary of State George C. Marshall, the legendary general-turned-statesman, announced that the United States needed to act to counter a complete breakdown in Europe's economy. Cities, factories, and railroads across the continent had been destroyed by the war. Bad harvests had followed an especially cold winter in 1946, and Europeans were facing starvation. The Soviet Union was a growing threat, and communist parties were on the rise across Europe. A rebuilding plan was necessary, Marshall said, to help both Europe and the United States. The Americans would provide the money, the Europeans the plan. "It would be neither fitting nor efficacious for this government to undertake to draw up unilaterally a program designed to place Europe on its feet economically. This is the business of the Europeans. The initiative, I think, must come from Europe," Marshall said.

The European Recovery Plan, as the Marshall Plan was formally known, was itself a response to a disastrous recovery effort. In the years immediately following the German surrender in May 1945, the United States pumped $10.5 billion into Europe, mostly in the form of emergency food, shelter, and other basic necessities. The scattershot, uncoordinated aid had done little to alleviate the deeper economic and political misery on the continent, however. Allen W. Dulles, a diplomat and former CIA station chief who lobbied heavily for passage of the Marshall Plan, pointed to the paucity of results as reason to spend billions more on a new rehabilitation effort. "The United States has lent or given money and goods to individual countries without any overall plan. It is useless to do this any longer," he said, in a remark that remained relevant many decades later.

As the Marshall Plan developed over the next several years, Europe, the Truman administration, and the U.S. Congress constantly discussed the program's size, goals, and management. Marshall's challenge resulted in a lengthy, multilateral debate between the United States and Europe. For both political and military reasons, the Americans were interested in creating a more united Europe. Britain, France, and other countries were reluctant to drop nationalistic goals that focused on protecting their own industries. They were not eager to model their economy on the American system. "We cannot ask that Europe be rebuilt in the American image," said Henry Stimson, the secretary of war during World War II.[9] In the end neither side got what it wanted. The Marshall Plan didn't unite Europe, but it laid the groundwork for the formation of the European Union decades later by loosening tariffs and fostering international cooperation. The Europeans did not exercise complete control over the funding, but rather shared it with the Americans. "Marshall planners made occasional mistakes and offended local sensibilities, but overall they did not impose policy in detail," wrote James Cronin, a Boston College history professor.[10]

In selling the restoration of Iraq, the Bush administration used the Marshall Plan as the model for what the reconstruction could accomplish. The administration spoke of a "generational commitment" to Iraq. "Like the transformation of Europe, the transformation of the Middle East will require a commitment of many years," Condoleezza Rice told a convention of journalists. President Bush himself made the comparison explicit in his national television address on September 7, 2003, when he announced his $20 billion rebuilding plan. "America has done this kind of work before. Following World War II, we lifted up the defeated nations of Japan and Germany, and stood with them as they built representative governments," Bush said. The investment had been "repaid many times" since the 1940s. As a political candidate, Bush had disdained nation building. At a speech at the Citadel in South Carolina in 1999, he laid out his vision for pulling the United States out of extended rebuilding efforts in the Balkans. "We will not be permanent peacekeepers, dividing warring parties. This is not our strength or our calling."[11] But now Bush embraced America's obligations in Iraq. He issued a stirring call to action: "We will do what is necessary, we will spend what is necessary, to achieve this essential victory in the war on terror," he said.

The reconstruction of Iraq, however, was not the Marshall Plan. Nor was it very similar to any of the other recent rebuilding efforts that America had engaged in, from Somalia to Kosovo to Bosnia. Historic parallels are always dangerous, of course, and each of the different nation-building scenarios was different. But in crafting its reconstruction vision, the Bush administration ignored many of the most important lessons of past efforts, ones that had cost American lives and treasure.

Perhaps the most crucial was the need to provide security. A few months before the invasion, a Marine Corps major working for the National Security Council created a briefing to spell out the number of forces required in past American nation-building endeavors. Major Jeff Kojac told the council that the United States needed 480,000 troops in Iraq in order to maintain a peacekeepers-to-population ratio similar to the level in Kosovo. If Afghanistan was the basis for comparison, only 13,900 troops would be needed. But Iraq, Kojac's slides indicated, was more like the Balkans, where more of the population lived in urban centers that were difficult to police. The briefing made no apparent impact on the White House.[12]

Nor did the Pentagon respond a few months later, when Bremer provided Rumsfeld a copy of a RAND Corporation study led by James Dobbins, a veteran diplomat who headed reconstruction efforts in Afghanistan. The study compared the reconstruction programs of every major postconflict operation since World War II, from Japan and Germany through Somalia, Kosovo, and Afghanistan. The three most important factors in determining success were troop levels, funding, and the length of time committed to the effort — a minimum of five years in most cases.

Like Kojac's study, the RAND analysis showed that Iraq's per capita troop levels were glaringly out of place when compared to postconflict situations in places like Germany and Japan, where reconstruction efforts had been able to take place in relative calm. Bremer told Rumsfeld that the data showed a successful reconstruction needed twenty occupying troops for every thousand people in the country. By that comparison, Iraq needed 500,000 troops — more than double the number in the country. Bremer got only a cursory response from Rumsfeld.[13]

Getting the Marshall Plan through Congress had taken an enormous political investment by the Truman administration. It required a year of debate and an intensive public relations and lobbying campaign by a bipartisan coalition of Democrats and Republicans, business leaders and union bosses, think tanks and trade groups. The far left, led by presidential candidate Henry Wallace, decried the plan as commercial-style American imperialism, designed to benefit "Wall Street wolves."[14] The right, mostly conservative, isolationist Republicans from the Midwest, dubbed the plan Operation Rathole, a giveaway to support Europe's socialist democracies.[15] The State Department wrangled endlessly with a skeptical Congress, led by Michigan senator Arthur H. Vandenberg, the chair of the Foreign Affairs Committee. By the time the allocation passed in April 1948, the plan was a compromise: less money than requested by the Truman administration, but still greater than the combined sum of all foreign aid previously donated by the U.S. government.

The political process surrounding the formation of the Iraq restoration plan could not have been more different. Rather than a cooperative, deliberative process with foreign partners, the reconstruction plan was put together by Oliver and Nash in a matter of weeks. Iraqi input amounted to a hasty poll of the Iraqi exiles whom the coalition government had appointed as ministers, and third-tier bureaucrats who survived the purge of the Baathists. Rather than a long debate in Congress, passage of Bush's proposal took all of two months. (The only congressional effort to shape or change Bush's proposal was embarrassingly selfish. Republicans wanted the money provided as a loan, demanding that the Iraqis pay it back with oil revenues. The Bush administration blocked the proposal after intense lobbying.) The reconstruction was essentially created without serious debate, with no buy-in from the American public or participation by ordinary Iraqis, the people it was supposed to serve.

BEST BRAINS

The Marshall Plan was also structured differently than the rebuilding in Iraq, with an attempt made to carefully balance American business interests with political concerns. Vandenberg had wanted to make the Marshall Plan probusiness in order to win the support of U.S. corporations and ease fears that the plan was a waste of taxpayer money. His insistence resulted in the Economic Cooperation Agency, an ad hoc agency headed by a presidential appointee with cabinet-level rank — a level of importance and prestige never granted to any of the U.S. officials charged with overseeing Iraq's reconstruction. The ECA was the single government organization used to coordinate aid in Europe, and many of its top staff were captains of industry, beginning with Paul Hoffman, the administrator. Hoffman, who had been the CEO of Studebaker prior to taking over the agency, saw his role as that of an "investment banker."[16] As a result he focused on getting the "best brains" of the business world to participate in the rebuilding program.[17] His staff ultimately resembled a who's who of American business, including Averell Harriman, a senior partner at the Wall Street firm of Brown Bros., Harriman; George W. Perkins, a partner at Merck and Company; and Cecil Burrill, an executive at Standard Oil of New Jersey.[18] Hoffman remained in charge of the new agency for almost two and a half years — far longer than any American official served as head of the different U.S. agencies responsible for rebuilding Iraq.

The business influence was deliberately tempered by design. The Marshall Plan did not rely upon contracts with American businesses to do the bulk of the reconstruction. Instead the plan was based on cooperation between American and European governments. The U.S. government purchased commodities from American companies: surplus food, fuel, steel, coal, farm equipment, and other materials. The material was then shipped to the European governments, which provided it through credits or loans to European businesses. The politicians acted as a buffer between the business interests — not a particularly efficient system, perhaps, but one which guaranteed that policy, not profit, dictated actions. As a result the Marshall Plan was hardly a boon to American businessmen. U.S. exports to Europe actually plunged during the Marshall Plan, declining by a third between 1946 and 1950. The program imposed quotas that hampered U.S. shipping firms from expanding their business. "Few American firms captured any real benefits from the European economic recovery programs," wrote Jacqueline McGlade, a history professor at Monmouth University.[19]

Finally, the type of aid delivered by the two plans was different. In many ways Europe emerged from conflict worse off than Iraq — its cities and infrastructure leveled, its political, social, and economic structures destroyed by a genocide and two horrific wars in the span of three decades. The Marshall planners focused on short- and medium-term aid — emergency fuel, for instance, or farm equipment so that European farmers could boost harvests. They also embarked upon structural reforms, trying to convince the Europeans to create the economic conditions needed to stimulate longer-term investment. The Marshall planners specifically discouraged large infrastructure projects. Although railroads, power plants, and factories were destroyed throughout Europe, the planners believed that private corporations would contribute the capital and expertise to build them faster and more efficiently than governments. The Marshall planners also put a premium on training the Europeans in the most modern techniques in manufacturing, management, and farming. France alone sent three hundred missions with 2,700 business, union, and government officials to visit American factories and institutions.[20]

The Bush Iraqi reconstruction plan basically inverted the Marshall Plan's structure. The reconstruction paid mostly for large, big-ticket infrastructure like power plants, oil facilities, and water treatment stations — large, long-term private investments that the U.S. government had no particular experience in managing. (Economic reforms were an afterthought. Bremer issued a series of measures by fiat, such as lowering corporate tax rates, which were never successfully implemented by the Iraqis.) The Iraqi plan paid so little attention to training that American-built power plants and water stations began to collapse soon after they were turned over to the Iraqis for operation.

When the Marshall Plan came to an end three years after its creation in 1948, America had provided $12.6 billion in aid to seventeen nations in Europe and elsewhere in the West, an amount in today's dollars equivalent to $130 billion. The biggest benefactors were Britain, followed by France,

Germany, and Italy. Over three years the plan provided $3.4 billion for raw materials and semimanufactured products; $3.2 billion for food, feed, and fertilizers; $1.8 billion for machines, vehicles, and equipment; and $1.6 billion in fuel. During that time Western Europe's GNP jumped 32 percent, from $120 billion to $159 billion, agricultural production increased by 11 percent, and industrial output by 40 percent. Scholars today dispute the exact value of the Marshall Plan, with some contending that Europe would have recovered without the money, albeit more slowly. But the bottom line is this: Europe was well on its way to recovery within three years of the passage of the Marshall Plan. Michael Hogan, the author of the definitive work on the Marshall Plan, wrote that the plan ushered in "an era of social peace and prosperity more durable than any other in modern European history."[21] The Bush administration's modern-day Marshall Plan seemed unlikely to do the same for the Middle East.

NOUR

The flaws inherent in the rebuilding program that developed during the fall of 2003 did not take long to surface. The new, $18.4 billion reconstruction package was directed first at what the Bush administration considered to be the most important task: arming and equipping Iraqi security forces. The initiative quickly bogged down in accusations of cronyism, profiteering, and fraud, a case study in the dangers of relying too heavily on corporate America and the government's peacetime contracting system to restore a nation.

That fall the coalition decided to outfit Iraq's new security forces. Rather than rely upon state-to-state military sales, or donations from the United States or an ally, the coalition decided to hold a competition to award the work to a private business. Coalition officers issued a shopping list for one (1) new army in a box: 3,000 heavy trucks and jeeps (painted "Desert Tan"); 16,000 AK-47 machine guns for troops ("only new items considered"); 1,350 9 mm pistols for officers; 20,000 uniforms, complete with dust goggles, body armor, and helmets; sleeping bags (rated to 3 degrees Celsius); tents and field kitchens and even shovels ("entrenching tools," in military lingo).[22] The U.S. military would provide the training; the contractor would equip the forces. A half-dozen firms from around the world entered, including some of the most experienced in the arms industry: General Dynamics, Raytheon, Lockheed Martin, the Polish state-owned weapons manufacturer, and a consortium of Spanish arms dealers. When the winner of the competition was announced in January 2004, it caused an uproar. An obscure company from Virginia called Nour USA had won a contract worth $327 million. Most of the other firms had established histories of supplying their nations' militaries. Nour USA, on the other hand, had no history in the weapons business. In fact it didn't have much of a history at all: the partnership was created in May 2003 by a Jordanian-born U.S. citizen named A. Huda Farouki.

Farouki may not have had much of a past in the arms business, but his political connections were among the finest in Washington. To be his lobbyist, he had hired the Cohen Group, founded by former defense secretary William S. Cohen. Farouki was a fixture on the Washington social scene and society pages and a heavy donor to political causes, especially Democratic ones. Most important, in the eyes of those protesting, was his close relationship with the controversial Ahmed Chalabi, now a member of the Governing Council of Iraq.

Farouki had known Chalabi since the 1980s, when the Virginia businessman was running American Export Group International Services, Inc., a holding group that he founded as a young engineer in 1971. Operating through subsidiaries, AEGIS developed into a company that specialized in procurement and construction. (One of its jobs was helping to furnish King Saud University in Saudi Arabia.) By the early 1980s the company was taking in $85 million a year. In 1987, however, AEGIS collapsed financially. It subsequently entered into a prolonged bankruptcy fight, seeking protection from two banks that were threatening to take possession of Farouki's Watergate condo in Washington and his home in wealthy McLean, Virginia. In court papers the banks blamed Farouki for AEGIS's problems. Attorneys for the creditor banks, National Bank of Washington and First American Bank, accused Farouki of "mismanagement, inattention to contract cash flows and financing requirements, and lack of timely reduction in overhead." The attorneys included a memo documenting complaints from company employees about low morale and management problems at AEGIS. The memo described a company on the edge of collapse, facing $2 million in debts and only a few hundred thousand dollars in revenue. Bank officers complained about the exorbitant overhead: $9 million annually for a staff of one hundred people.[23]

To stave off his creditors, Farouki turned to Chalabi, who ran a bank in Jordan. Farouki got a $12 million loan from a U.S.-based branch of Chalabi's

Petra Bank even as that institution struggled with its own financial problem. AEGIS eventually emerged from bankruptcy, but it shut its doors in 1991. Petra's own collapse, in 1989, led to Chalabi's conviction on bank fraud charges in Jordan in 1992. Chalabi fled the country rather than face a twenty-year jail term.

Farouki and Chalabi remained in contact over the years, connected by a web of social and economic ties. In 1995, for instance, Farouki's wife entered into a business venture with Chalabi's nephew, Mohammed Chalabi.[24] And in August 2003, Farouki joined up with a security company called Erinys Iraq to win a controversial $80 million contract to patrol Iraq's oil pipelines. One of the partners in that deal was Faisal Daghastani, the son of Tamara Daghastani, the aide who reportedly smuggled Chalabi out of Jordan in the trunk of her car in 1992 after his bank fraud conviction.

GRASPING AT STRAWS

Aside from Farouki's connections to Chalabi, questions emerged about Nour itself.[25] Bidding documents submitted to win the contract inflated the company's size, experience, and connections. In its proposal Nour said it was the lead company of a consortium called DES Group, but DES appeared to be nothing more than a web of interrelated companies controlled or financed by Farouki. Consortium members included Virginia-based American International Services and UniTrans International, both partly owned by Farouki. American International Services claimed to have twenty-five years of business experience, but the company had been formed only thirteen years earlier, in 1991, according to corporate records in Virginia. The consortium also included four Iraqi companies with which Farouki had agreements to provide financial and commercial support. Farouki acknowledged financial ties, or what he described as a "contractual relationship," with seven of the nine members of the DES consortium.

There were also questions about the remaining members of DES. One partner was a Polish arms company called Ostrowski Arms — a strange situation, since the Polish government said the company had no license to export weapons. Nour itself was an alliance between a U.S. financial firm, HAIFinance, headed by Farouki's wife, and a Jordanian pharmaceutical and construction consortium called Munir Sukhtian Group. The Sukhtian Group was crucial to the bid, an established construction and communications firm whose long history of business in the Middle East helped establish Nour's credentials overseas. But several Jordanian business sources told me that the Sukhtian Group, which was jointly owned by three brothers of Palestinian descent, was not a full participant in the bid. Instead they described an internal feud in which one of the brothers, Ghiath Sukhtian, had unilaterally pledged the company to the deal with Nour without the approval of the other brothers. Ghiath Sukhtian acknowledged a "small tiff" among the brothers but said it would be worked out soon. The company eventually issued a statement saying it was a "strong supporter" of Nour USA.

At least Sukhtian promised support. Questions about the partnership remained. Others listed by Nour as partners denied links to the company. For instance, Nour said it had paired up with Booz Allen Hamilton, a well-regarded Washington consulting firm whose participation would have lent credibility to the newly formed company. But Booz Allen officials denied such a relationship, saying they had only a small contract with Nour to help in planning the execution of the contract. Moreover, a source with knowledge of the negotiations said the $50,000 contract with Booz Allen was signed nearly a week after Nour won the award — meaning that Nour had no formal link with Booz Allen during the proposal phase. "We don't have a teaming arrangement," said George Farrar, a Booz Allen spokesman.

Nour also boasted an impressive advisory board of retired high-ranking military officers. Several of the officers, however, denied any involvement with Nour. "Our résumés were used in the competitive bid process, but we never met nor were we ever consulted or paid," Dave Richwine, a retired Marine Corps major general, told me. Another person listed as an advisory board member, Vice Adm. Joe Dyer, U.S. Navy (retired), said that a friend had sent his résumé to Nour but that he had never had any contact with the firm. "I was pretty dumbfounded when I heard that I had been listed. I am not related in any way to this company," Dyer told me.

Farouki and Chalabi fiercely fought the accusations, especially those concerning their relationship. Both men acknowledged their friendship, but both denied that it played a role in Nour's winning any contracts. Chalabi said he had severed his business relationships to concentrate on politics. In any case, he said, he played no role in awarding contracts as a member of the Governing Council. "I have no financial relationship with Farouki," he declared.[26]

For his part, the voluble and aggressive Farouki denounced the attacks against him as "sour grapes" by losing bidders. Farouki noted that the $327 million contract was awarded in an open contest with eighteen other companies. No favoritism was involved. "There's absolutely no commercial or business relationship between Ahmed Chalabi and Nour USA, or with me personally," Farouki told me.

Farouki also denied that he had inflated Nour's résumé. He was, Farouki claimed, able to beat out the established companies by hundreds of millions of dollars because he was a savvy businessman who had cut good deals with Ukrainian and Polish companies. Ostrowski was nothing more than an "adviser," not an arms dealer. "This is all nonsense. There's no credibility to their allegations," Farouki said. "They are grasping and grabbing at straws." Farouki denied any misrepresentations in his bid. His corporate relationships had been revealed to coalition officials. The claims of decades of experience were based on his personal involvement in the business. "Not one fact in that proposal is incorrect," he said. He also said that his personal lack of experience in the arms dealing business was not important. The contract was essentially a shopping list. Any company with experience buying in the world market could fulfill it. No special expertise was needed.

CARS WITHOUT ENGINES

By February, Bumar, the Polish entry, and another company, Cemex Global, had filed formal protests with the government over the bid. Bumar, whose price was $200 million higher than Nour's, accused the company of lowballing, a contracting practice whereby a bidder submits an unrealistically low price in hopes of increasing it once he's won the deal. Cemex produced e-mails which suggested that the bidding process was sloppy; in one, a contracting official acknowledged that she had overlooked a packet of documents submitted as part of the firm's bid. "This protest is one hundred percent justified," Bumar Group chairman Roman Baczynski said during a news conference in the Polish capital, noting that it was the first the company had filed in its thirty-year history. "We are questioning [Nour's] credibility."

Two weeks later the Pentagon acknowledged it had made a mistake. The protests from Bumar and Cemex "although not clearly meritorious, raise questions concerning the evaluation," according to a coalition statement. The decision to reevaluate the proposals of Bumar, Cemex, and Nour only drew more protests: other companies that lost out to Nour also wanted to be reconsidered. By March five companies had filed protests. The arms contract was in danger of becoming tied up in legal wrangling for months.

Then, in a rushed conference call with reporters on March 5, 2004, the Pentagon announced that it was canceling the entire award because of "irregularities" in the contracting process. The Department of Defense took all the blame. A senior U.S. Army official described the contracting office in Baghdad as overwhelmed by the task of sifting through complex bid proposals. The official said the office had a staff of only five people, who were issuing as many as fifteen contracts a day. The contracting officer who initiated the bidding process had rotated out in the middle, a function of quick duty tours in Iraq. (The personnel shortfalls would persist more than a year later. In 2005 an army expert testified that the military "required ten times the oversight personnel to properly oversee current contracts."[27])

Nobody in the coalition had bothered to visit any of Nour's locations, nor checked up on its consortium members or advisory board. The specifications for the bid were too vaguely written: the difference between the high and low bids was almost $700 million — an extraordinarily high differential. "We frankly found some procedural irregularities in the contract filing," the army official said. He said questions about Nour's ability to fulfill the contract played no role in the decision.

Over the next eleven weeks the Pentagon conducted the entire bidding process a second time. This time the bidding was conducted out of the army's Tank-Automotive and Armaments Command in Warren, Michigan, the experts in the kind of vehicles that made up the largest single dollar value in the contract. The army held a bidders' conference, where it answered questions, and produced an exhaustive 131-page list of equipment, as opposed to the 21-page list in the original proposal. And then, on May 25, it announced the new winner. Once again it was Nour, this time reconfigured as a consortium called ANHAM. With the new specs, the company had reduced its price to $259 million. Farouki had stopped talking to the press, but a spokesman described the company as "very pleased." Competitors were stunned a second time. "We were shocked," said one. Army officials denied that favoritism had played any role. They insisted that Nour offered the best deal at the best price. "We checked this very carefully," one army official told me. The Nour contract was pushed through as quickly as possible. But the bidding, the confusion, and the protests had turned a planned three-month process into a seven-month ordeal.

The whole experience created deep resentment in the military and among senior Bush officials about the pace of rebuilding. At a press conference in

March 2004, Maj. Gen. Charles H. Swannack Jr., commander of the Eighty-second Airborne Division, pointed up the disastrous effects of the protracted contracting process. Iraqi forces didn't have the body armor, radios, or vehicles they needed to restore order in Al Anbar, the restive province west of Baghdad. Iraq's border forces had no more than five buses and only a couple of small trucks to patrol the country's entire 2,260 miles of frontier. Insurgents were slipping in daily. Iraqi commanders were constantly asking: When will the U.S. deliver? "I would tell them that I would get body armor in soon, that I would get radios in soon, and I had to keep on postponing that," Swannack said. "I could not get the quantities of equipment that I needed." Testifying before Congress a month later, Wolfowitz blasted Washington "bureaucracy" for the Iraqis' lack of firepower. "A lot of the equipment problems, frankly, are an embarrassment to the United States of America. Our red tape, our regulations, our slowness," he said.

When the equipment finally began arriving in the summer of 2004, the Iraqis disparaged it. Defense Minister Hazim Shaalan, a moderate Shiite appointed by the United States in June 2004, said the vehicles that Nour delivered were in poor shape. Some of them, he said, were refurbished ambulances that bore marks indicating they had been built in Russia — in 1954. Spare parts, not surprisingly, were difficult to find. Shaalan refused to accept delivery of some of the cars, which began stacking up at the ports and parking lots. Ziad Cattan, Shaalan's military procurement chief, said that the AK-47s delivered by Nour were low-quality models made in the Czech Republic. Some of them seized up when Iraqi forces attempted to use them against forces of Muqtada Sadr, a rebel cleric. Armored vehicles supplied by Nour broke down in the field, leading the Americans to burn them to keep them out of the hands of insurgents.[28]

Both Shaalan and Cattan were later enmeshed in scandal, accused of corruption in connection with weapons deals that they negotiated with Bumar, the Polish firm, so it was possible that in their comments the Iraqis were denigrating a competitor. But U.S. military officials were also hesitant about endorsing Nour. One U.S. military official described, in essence, the classic problem of relying upon the low bidder: "The heavy trucks provided by [Nour] were good," the military official said. "The light trucks were not as good, but they met the requirements." Nour's aim had been to clear the bar by the slightest possible margin — and it did. But those who had to live with the consequences had a hard time not feeling they'd been taken for a ride.

The failure to get weapons and equipment to the Iraqis came back to haunt the United States. The concerns over the equipment were serious enough that Gen. David Petraeus, who headed the training mission in Iraq after June 2004, ordered the coalition to rely less on Nour and begin purchasing more equipment through another contract with the Defense Logistics Agency. But by then it was too late. As the Pentagon fumbled through the weapons contract in the spring of 2004, Iraq exploded in fighting, with simultaneous uprisings in Fallujah and Najaf. The violence permanently changed the face of the reconstruction.

7

The Shooting Starts

On the morning of April 9, 2004, two dozen truck drivers working for KBR clumped together beside a long, dusty row of dark green fuel tankers at a U.S. military base north of Baghdad. They were dressed in work boots and blue jeans, in lumberjack shirts and bulletproof vests. Some wore cowboy hats, others had on Kevlar helmets. They were getting ready to haul 125,000 gallons of military jet fuel to the Baghdad airport. They would be accompanied by army reservists in armored Humvees and Mad Max–style gun trucks with .50 caliber machine guns. Several of the drivers were new to the job. They had never been off the base or even driven the fuel tankers.

As they all stood nervously, waiting for the mission to start, a Humvee pulled up. A soldier jumped out and called the men over. The route had changed. They were going to the airport's north entrance. Grumbling followed. Only two or three of the veteran truckers had been to the airport, none through the rarely used north entrance. None of the soldiers guiding the convoy knew the route either. A hasty search produced a sergeant first class from another company who was familiar with the trip, but even he wasn't sure of the exact way. He called his headquarters to get the number of the highway exit, then knelt as the truckers circled around. He drew a crude map in the dust with his boot, what he called a sand table overview. It was the only map the men would have to guide them across forty miles of hostile country.

Steve Fisher called his wife back home in Virginia Beach. Ingrid was there with the three kids, exhausted from another day of work at the day care center. Back in the states, Fisher had put in fourteen-hour days hauling trash. A former marine with a bushy mustache and a wide smile, he had gone to Iraq in hopes of making enough money to put his oldest daughter through college. The pay was good, no doubt: truck drivers could make more than $80,000 a year, tax free if they stayed overseas for a year. But his tone that morning made Ingrid worried. It was the first anniversary of the toppling of Saddam Hussein's statue by the marines in Baghdad. Perhaps Iraqi insurgents would mark the occasion with an attack against the convoys or U.S. troops.

"It's the worst day to go out," he said.

"Why are you going, then?" she asked.

"I don't want to go," he said. "But I have to."

CUP OF WATER

Many of the men in the convoy shared Fisher's unease. It had been a bad few weeks in Iraq. Earlier, in March, the first civilians working for the coalition had been killed. Fern Holland, thirty-three, a civil rights lawyer, her translator, Salwa Ourmashi, thirty-seven, and Bob Zangas, forty-four, a public affairs specialist, had been slain while driving toward the coalition's regional headquarters in Hillah in southern Iraq. Holland insisted on driving around by herself, refusing a security escort because she was afraid it would impede her job of establishing women's and human rights centers. About twenty miles outside of town, a white pickup truck had pulled alongside Holland's Daewoo sedan. The men inside the pickup unleashed a fusillade on the unarmored car. Everyone inside was killed, though Holland in particular seemed to have been the target of the attack: the gunmen had pumped more than thirty bullets into her body.[1]

The reasons for the assassination were unclear. Some believed it was revenge for Holland's work in Hillah and Karbala, two traditionally conservative towns. The centers she had established had attracted the attention of Jerry Bremer, who paid a splashy visit to Hillah in October 2003. But they also stirred resentment toward Holland, especially among the followers of Muqtada Sadr, a young, radical preacher opposed to the U.S. invasion. Some complained to Sadr-allied clerics that the centers were an affront to Islam. "We told them, no, we cannot approve [violence against the centers]," said Sheik Hamza Taie, the deputy director of Sadr's office in Karbala. "But it's the duty of any honorable Muslim to take care of anything harming the name of Islam."[2]

But others, including the FBI, came to suspect that Holland was targeted for a specific incident. Shortly before her death, Holland met with two elderly Iraqi widows clad in black head-to-toe abayas. The women told her they had been unfairly expelled from their land by a powerful local leader with ties to Saddam Hussein. They showed Holland the paperwork and a judicial writ from a local court ordering the man's home destroyed. Holland agreed to help. The morning of her death, Holland had hired a bulldozer and traveled to the small farming town of Kifl. Accompanied by the judge and a contingent of police officers, the bulldozer plowed the home into the ground. The women got their land back.

It was classic Holland, aggressive and audacious. A colleague had warned her: a bulldozer smacked of the tactics the Israelis used against the Palestinians. And in the conservative, tribal culture of southern Iraq, it would be humiliating to have an American woman carrying out such justice. Holland had ignored the advice. She was a committed champion of social justice, a Peace Corps activist who had done pro bono legal work in Guinea on behalf of sexually exploited women. She had given up a six-figure income in a DC law firm to come to Iraq. She was not an ideologue; she simply believed that American democracy could make life better for poor, long-oppressed Iraqis. Bulldozing the house was a way of making a point: in the new Iraq, everybody would play by the rules, no matter how powerful. "Nobody will move the guy. Everyone's afraid of him. So much for the rule of law," she wrote in an e-mail to a friend of hers in Oklahoma, where she grew up.[3]

Zangas, too, believed deeply that America had something to offer Iraq. A lieutenant colonel in the Marine Corps Reserve, he had served in the first Gulf War and did a second six-month stint in Desert Storm as a civil affairs specialist based in Kut in southern Iraq. There he had worked with local Iraqis on basic infrastructure, trying to get power and clean water flowing. He left the military to return to his wife, three kids, and a job as a salesman in Pittsburgh. But he wanted to do more: "As much as he had done — which is a lot — he still felt it wasn't enough," his wife, Brenda, said.[4] Zangas decided to return to Iraq to take a job with the coalition, helping to build a free press.

Zangas's Iraq was a place of small triumphs and stubborn problems, where success was rarely clear-cut and frustration constant. Nevertheless, in the blog he kept, he remained guardedly optimistic. His last entry, dated the week of March 6, 2004, was titled "Working for the Man." It told of a trip that he made to bring new media equipment to a center promoting press freedom in Hillah. The Iraqis had thanked him, but then asked for more. "It is like pouring a cup of water out in a dry desert. The water disappears and you are left with the feeling of 'did it do any good?' Sometimes the answer is 'yes.' Sometimes the answer is 'no,' " he wrote.[5] On the day of his murder, it appeared that he was simply in the wrong place at the wrong time, coincidentally in Karbala at the same time as Holland, and deciding to hitch a ride with her to get back to the coalition base in Hillah.

EXTREME UNPROFESSIONALISM

Holland's and Zangas's deaths struck fear into coalition workers, who found their movement more restricted than ever. But it was an incident a few weeks later that unsettled the KBR drivers waiting to head to the Baghdad airport. On March 31, four security contractors were escorting a truck caravan on a mission to pick up some kitchen equipment from a military base outside Fallujah called Camp Ridgeway. During twelve years in the military, Scott Helvenston, thirty-eight, had risen to become an instructor for the SEALs, the navy's most elite special forces. Wesley Batalona, forty-eight, Jerry Zovko, thirty-two, and Michael Teague, thirty-eight, had all been Army Rangers. After their military service, the four men had joined Blackwater USA, a North Carolina–based private security company founded by a rich and secretive former SEAL, Erik Prince.[6]

Prince's father, Edgar Prince, had made a fortune selling car visors with lighted mirrors. His company had sold for $1.35 billion in 1996, and Prince had inherited his father's wealth and devotion to Republican causes. A conservative Christian, Prince made his first political contribution at nineteen, giving $15,000 to the Republican Party. He had an internship at the conservative Family Research Council and worked for Representative Dana Rohrabacher of California, an Orange County Republican. He interned in the White House for President George H. W. Bush, but left in 1992 to campaign for presidential candidate Pat Buchanan. (Bush senior's brand of conservatism had apparently been too tepid for Prince: "I saw a lot of things I didn't agree with — homosexual groups being invited in, the budget agreement, the Clean Air Act, those kind of bills. I think the administration has been indifferent to a lot of conservative concerns," he said in a 1992 interview.[7]) When he joined the navy, the rumor in the Pentagon was that he was the richest person ever to enlist.

After he left the service in 1996, Prince capitalized on his military experience by opening Blackwater on six thousand acres in rural Moyock, North Carolina. The estate quickly established a reputation as the largest training ground in the country dedicated to the private security industry, providing sniper ranges, a mock town for urban combat drills, and even a small air fleet with helicopters. When the war in Iraq broke out, Blackwater won the highest-profile security contract in Iraq: a deal worth $21 million to protect Bremer. The company would later make a selling point of the fact that Bremer left Iraq alive.

Prince's riches did not stop his company from being cheap in Iraq, according to a lawsuit against the firm. Blackwater had inked a security deal with a Cyprus-registered company called ESS just days before the March mission. Though no company officials would confirm it, ESS appeared to be a Halliburton subcontractor under the Texas company's contract to feed and house U.S. troops.[8] Under the terms of the contract between Blackwater and ESS, there were supposed to be six men on each security mission. The men were supposed to travel in armored cars. To save money, Blackwater entered into a secondary contract with a middleman that called only for a lesser "protection kit" on the vehicles. The deal, according to the lawsuit, resulted in a $1.5 million savings for Blackwater.[9] In Iraq, nobody knew the path to stability, but everyone seemed able to cut corners.

One of Blackwater's first jobs under its new contract was to pick up the kitchen equipment from Camp Ridgeway, just west of Fallujah. Under pressure to perform, Blackwater hurriedly dispatched Scotty Helvenston and his crew on March 30, 2004, from Baghdad to rendezvous with three ESS flatbed trucks at Taji, a nearby military base. The convoy then proceeded toward Camp Ridgeway to pick up the kitchen supplies, lacking any of the preparation or equipment called for in the contract, the lawsuit said. Instead of armored SUVs, the men were traveling in two small Mitsubishi Pajeros with a metal plate welded in back. With four instead of six men per vehicle, there was nobody in the back of the cars to provide protection from the rear. The men had no maps, and no clear idea of where they were going. They got lost on the way, spending the night in another military base just east of Fallujah. It was typical poor planning by Blackwater. In an e-mail sent shortly before the mission, Helvenston accused some company officials of "extreme unprofessionalism."[10]

The next day, on March 31, Helvenston, Batalona, Zovko, and Teague resumed their journey, heading for Ridgeway by driving straight through the middle of Fallujah, a dangerous, unsettled area that the U.S. Marines had yet to enter. When the men got stuck in traffic, they were ambushed. Helvenston and his team were attacked, shot, and dragged from their vehicles. Their bodies were hacked and burned. The mob hung two of them from a metal bridge spanning the Euphrates. Arabic television stations quickly showed up. The image of the blackened corpses dangling grotesquely became one of the most indelible of the war.

Following classic counterinsurgency doctrine, the marines favored a measured response to the deaths. Lt. Gen. James T. Conway of the First Marine Expeditionary Force, in charge of Fallujah, didn't want to risk civilian casualties that would inflame Iraqis and strengthen the insurgency. "We felt . . . that we ought to let the situation settle before we appeared to be attacking out of revenge," Conway said later. But the Bush administration took a more aggressive approach. In Baghdad, Bremer promised retribution: "Their deaths will not go unpunished," he said. In Washington, Rumsfeld and Gen. John P. Abizaid, U.S. Army, the commander of forces in the Middle East, recommended "a specific and overwhelming attack." Bush approved immediately. By April 4 the marines were on the march.[11]

The resulting attack set off a chain reaction. As the marines fought their way to the center of Fallujah, Arab news channels broadcast scenes of devastation, smoking mosques and hospitals filled with blood-covered Iraqis. Iraqi politicians began resigning in protest from the U.S.-appointed Governing Council. In Baghdad's slums and in the Shia heartland, Iraqis loyal to Muqtada Sadr rose up to attack American and coalition forces. Iraq was exploding, and Blackwater was saving money.

THE FRONT LINES

KBR's two thousand truck drivers were the unsung heroes of the war in Iraq. They delivered everything the U.S. military needed to survive: fuel, water, food. KBR had seven hundred trucks on the road on any given day in Iraq, each of the vital convoys accompanied by a military escort. Each convoy was essentially a military mission, an easy target for insurgents intent on disrupting supply lines. Perhaps not surprisingly, more than half of all convoys in Iraq got hit — and in dangerous areas, nearly *every* KBR convoy was attacked in one way or another. Sometimes it was just kids throwing rocks, but often it was a roadside bomb, some so powerful that they could blast a semi off the road. "The front lines are no longer what we think of,"

Capt. Catherine Wilkinson, a spokeswoman for the army's Thirteenth Corps Support Command, told me when I visited Balad to meet and travel with a convoy of KBR's truckers in August 2004. "The front lines are the convoys." (One of the clearest signs of the fusion in Iraq between private contractors and the U.S. government was that the U.S. Army protected KBR, while private contractors protected the U.S. ambassadors.)

The truckers whom I rode with were mostly blue-collar Americans trying to get ahead. Edie Hair, a thirty-four-year-old from Fort Hood, Texas, was the rare female driver. Big and broad with thin blond hair, she had five windshields replaced in a month, each of them shattered by rocks or bullets. She had come to Iraq because she needed money to get her children braces. "I'm also supporting our troops," she hastened to add; her husband had just finished a yearlong rotation in Iraq with the army. Clay Henderson, thirty-four, was the convoy commander, a veteran driver who had put in nearly a year in Iraq. He had skinny legs and a big chest, a combination that gave him the pectoral proportions of a comic book superhero. A big man with a beard and long hair, he had nine horses back home, and he dreamed of owning a ranch in the Louisiana countryside. "I want to mess around and do something fun instead of getting up at three a.m. and working until midnight and have nothing to show for it at the end of the year," he said.

Iraq, ironically, was perhaps the only place where a truck driver could still earn enough money to realize the American dream.

Driving on a convoy was a real-life version of *Road Warrior*. Typically about two dozen drivers and their trucks would roll out with an equal number of soldiers stuffed into five to seven Humvees. When stretched out, the convoys were up to two miles long, but the truckers often ran "tight" — bunched together about one hundred yards apart to make it more difficult for a suicide bomber to squeeze in. The distance demanded intense concentration: at fifty miles per hour, a driver had less than four seconds to react if something went wrong. And things were always going wrong. The truckers endured sniper fire, car bombs, roadside explosions, and rocket-propelled grenades. Insurgents mounted ambushes to pick off trucks from behind. They threw bricks and dropped eight-foot-long steel pipes from overpasses into the cabs. KBR lost more contractors than anyone else in Iraq. Many of them were truck drivers. By August 2004 eleven of the eighteen U.S. civilians killed working for KBR were truckers.

The danger was partly KBR's fault. None of the trucks the company brought in immediately after the invasion, when Iraq was still relatively calm, were bulletproofed. As attacks worsened, KBR attempted to upgrade by purchasing armor kits, but it had trouble installing them because of their weight. U.S. soldiers' vehicles also lacked armor, of course. But the soldiers' plight generated outrage in Congress and eventually forced the Pentagon to act. The contractors, on the other hand, had only KBR to appeal to. The trucks' windshields posed another problem — they were constantly being shattered. Company mechanics tried wiring on metal cages, but the drivers complained of headaches from straining to see through the mesh. During my visit in August 2004, most KBR drivers were racing through clouds of bullets and flying shards of metal with no more protection than a seat belt, a helmet, and a bulletproof vest. All the truckers could do was hit the gas and pray for the best. "If you don't get nervous, you're stupid," said Billy Lee Tripp, forty-four, a La Vernia, Texas, native who was wiry as a stray cat. "If you don't get nervous, it's time to go home."

Living conditions were hard. Unlike KBR managers, who stayed in four-star resorts in Kuwait, KBR drivers were stationed alongside troops. At Balad, the fifteen-square-mile air base that was the U.S. military's primary logistics hub in Iraq, KBR's facilities had the air of a company town. Balad seemed like an industrial park set in a baking, monochromatic landscape of arid flatland and low bushes. KBR's white trailers sat like piano keys on one side of the base, stretching for miles. The air was filled with the constant buzz of C-131s and Chinook helicopters coming and going. Meals were eaten cafeteria-style, the air conditioners blasting, the Indian servers dishing out heaping plates of french fries, Salisbury steak, and battered fish sticks. Drivers' shifts were long — twelve hours a day, seven days a week. The newly arrived stayed in a tent divided by low plywood walls into twenty cubicles, each with a bunk. Veterans got a trailer the size of a shipping container. The trailers were stacked two high, row after row, only a few feet apart. Just outside sat concrete bunkers for shelter during mortar attacks, which came so often that the truckers' nickname for Balad was Mortaritaville.

THE WIRE

For my run with KBR, I rode with Melvin Winter, a lanky driver with metal glasses and a paunch sticking over his blue jeans.[12] Winter's face was wide and flat as the Texas prairie, honest and open. He wanted to build a house to replace his double-wide trailer back home in Greenville, Texas. "One year over here, it's equal to two to three years working in the U.S. You can advance considerably," he told me. Sgt. Hosea Lark, the military commander for the run, passed out chemical light sticks to the truckers before the convoy rolled out. He told them to toss the sticks out the window if they got hit by rocks. "If you see a rock thrower, blast [him] away," Lark said. He told his men from the Army National Guard's 1171st Transportation Company to take no chances. "The risk is extremely high."

As Winter and I climbed into the cab of his white flatbed Mercedes, he pointed to a hole in his door surrounded by jagged shards of metal like the petals of a flower. He called it his "lucky bullet hole," since the shot had not harmed him. Winter's truck, like those of the other drivers, had no armor. He compensated by finding a piece of steel to weld onto the side of his cab. It would do little against a high-velocity round, however, so he kept a pack of tampons stuffed into a cubbyhole on the dashboard. They were to stanch gunshot wounds.

As we rumbled into place to head out of the base, Winter strapped on his helmet and sealed the Velcro on his bulletproof vest. I did the same, wondering what it would feel like if the windshield glass shattered and sent shards into my face and hands. Winter eased the truck into gear, and drove across "the wire," as the base entrance was called.

"Put your game face on," he said. "It's time to put on the gloves."

Over the next four hours, from blood-red dusk to pitch-black midnight, Winter and his convoy sped through a landscape of fire, fear, and danger. The route took them first down a four-lane stretch of highway nicknamed IED Alley for the constant explosions of roadside bombs — called improvised explosive devices in military jargon. Truth was, though, on any road in Iraq, endless piles of rocks and trash by the side of the road were potential hiding places for bombs. Nor were the routes closed to other traffic: Iraqis motored alongside the convoy in both directions. Was the battered white Daewoo pickup ahead loaded with vegetables or explosives? "If you roll out thinking that everybody is trying to kill you, you're better off," said Winter, a veteran of the 1991 Persian Gulf War.

After thirty minutes of driving, we encountered fires burning in clumps by the side of the road. Huge clouds of black smoke rolled across the highway, maybe from trash burning, maybe from recent combat. The cab was hot, acrid. Like all the drivers, Winter had the cab's windows down to keep them from being shattered by explosive concussions.

"Mash the gas. Drive it like it's stolen," came a voice across the radio. It was Clay Henderson, the convoy commander. He sounded nervous. The convoy bolted up onto an elevated highway that ran over marshland, providing a hellish view of fires, billowing smoke, and haze. After a while the trucks descended to make a slow turn to join another highway. Suddenly the radio crackled again.

"AK-47. Right side. It's hitting your truck," a KBR driver called out to the military escort in front of him. Ahead in the convoy, perhaps a thousand yards, red tracers lit up the sky as a military truck packed with soldiers in back returned fire. Radio calls reported fire from the left and the right.

"It's pretty bad," one driver called out. "You got bullets flying from both sides."

And then, just as suddenly as it began, the shooting stopped. Henderson called on the radio for injuries. Silence.

"It didn't hit nobody," Henderson announced. "Keep rolling. Keep rolling."

The trucks sped up briefly but then slowed again. Ahead, brake lights from another convoy filled the road. Like the rest, Winter's truck slowed to a halt. The highway was a parking lot, surrounded by high walls and darkened homes. There were no cars coming from the other direction. The Iraqis had abandoned the highway — a sign of a possible ambush. Truckers grew agitated. Chatter filled the radio: "There's not enough traffic. Be advised of it," one called out. Gunners in the military escorts trained their weapons on the moonlit fields and low, two-story homes around them. The truckers didn't know what was happening. Neither did the military. The convoy had stopped in the middle of one of the most dangerous places in Iraq. Their best defense, speed, had been stripped away.

Some of the men got out and crouched in the shadows of their trucks, children hiding from a nightmare. The air was tense, brittle. You could feel the beat of your heart, the breath in your body. "Let's go, let's go," Winter said quietly. "This is not a nice neighborhood."

After twenty minutes of waiting, the convoy ahead began to move. Truckers scrambled back into their cabs. The soldiers eased up on their guns. Winter put his truck in gear and edged ahead. The scare was over. Half an hour later, the convoy hit the exit for the Baghdad airport, where the truckers were dropping off their load. The trucks crossed an overpass, trundled down a short section of highway, and found themselves at the gate of the airport. A soldier with a clipboard lifted up the metal arm blocking the route, and the trucks joggled along a bumpy, rutted dirt road and into a dusty parking lot. The drivers climbed down and dropped their trailers. The trucks' headlights cut strips of light in the dust. The truckers' faces were tired and sallow. They talked quickly among themselves. In an hour they'd hit the road again to brave the same stretch of gunfire and smoke. But for now jokes and shared bravado filled the air.

"It was a good run," Winter said. "It was only small-arms fire. That's a good run."

Their buddies on April 9 hadn't been so lucky.

BLACK FLAGS

The KBR truckers who headed out of Balad on April 9 knew they were surrounded by danger. A picture of the men taken in the morning shows them gathered in a clump. Some have on helmets, others bulletproof vests. Only a few are smiling.[13]

Several of the men approached Tommy Hamill, the convoy commander, who was the highest-ranking KBR official in the group. It was his job to work with the military to plan the route. He could also turn down the run. KBR men were contractors, not soldiers, and they could back out if they wanted to. Eddie Sanchez, one of the drivers, told Hamill it was too dangerous. During a trucking run the night before, some of the drivers had watched the marines turn the sky above Fallujah into a fireworks show as they attacked the rebel city with rockets and tracer rounds. "It was just different than other days. It was in the air. The molecules in the air were really heavy. It was there from the very beginning," Sanchez told me.

Hamill turned him down. The airport was in urgent need of fuel. "They lead, we follow," he would say.

At 9:54 a.m., a soldier working for the logistics command relayed a final change to the route by e-mail to the transportation company's headquarters. The convoy would head for the north entrance of the airport, though it was never clear why. About fifteen minutes later, the convoy rolled out Balad's main gate. In the interim, however, the same soldier sent a second e-mail to the command center. There was fighting raging along the final portion of the route, where First Cavalry Division was taking fire from 200 to 300 fighters in Sadr's Mahdi Army. "Sorry, it looks like [the route to the north gate] is closed until further notice."

Doug Feith led the Pentagon's planning efforts for postwar Iraq. Like many other neoconservatives, he believed that the United States would be able to quickly pull out troops after turning over responsibility for governing to Iraqis. The miscalculation resulted in a chaotic period after the invasion in which Iraqis lost patience with the occupation and insurgents began attacking American forces. AP/WIDE WORLD PHOTOS

Frank Willis, left, and Darrell Trent hold shrink-wrapped packs of $100 bills worth $2 million at an office in the Republican Palace, the center of the U.S. occupation government in Iraq. The two men, officials in the Coalition Provisional Authority, gave the money to a security firm called Custer Battles for payment on a contract. Custer Battles was later found guilty of multimillion-dollar fraud, and the picture became one of the icons of Iraq's Wild West atmosphere during the first summer after the invasion. INTRODUCED AS EVIDENCE AT PUBLIC CONGRESSIONAL HEARING

Jack Shaw, the Pentagon's deputy undersecretary for international technology security, poses in a helicopter during a visit to Iraq in December 2005. Shaw was investigated by the FBI after accusations that he attempted to direct a contract to a cellular phone company that included a personal friend. The case was closed with no charges filed.
PHOTO BY BONNIE CARROLL

Bonnie Carroll and Daniel Sudnick oversaw the creation of Iraq's cellular phone network—later recognized as one of the single most successful reconstruction efforts—as the top advisers to the Iraqi Ministry of Communications. But they ran into trouble when they exposed a Rumsfeld appointee in the Pentagon for trying to steer a contract to a friend's company. The whistle-blowers were asked to resign and sent home. COURTESY OF BONNIE CARROLL

Bunnatine "Bunny" Greenhouse was the most senior contracting official in the U.S. Army Corps of Engineers. When she protested a sweetheart deal for Halliburton Company to rebuild Iraq's oil industry, she was demoted and ostracized. She called the Halliburton deal "the most blatant and improper contract abuse I have witnessed during the course of my professional career." AP/WIDE WORLD PHOTOS

A photo taken in August 2005 shows two Iraqi workers attempting to fix a pump at Qarmat Ali, a water pumping plant important to Iraq's oil pumping infrastructure. Halliburton subsidiary KBR tried to repair the plant under a multibillion dollar contract with the Army Corps of Engineers but failed to get the plant fully operational. AUTHOR'S COLLECTION

David Nash was a retired admiral appointed to head the reconstruction of Iraq shortly after the U.S. invasion. He relied heavily on American engineering companies to build large infrastructure projects. The State Department objected to his plan as costly and ineffective. AP/WIDE WORLD PHOTOS

Sgt. Hosea Lark, of the Army National Guard's 1171st Transportation Company, briefs truck drivers hired by Halliburton subsidiary KBR before a run in August 2004. The drivers were blue-collar men and women who braved gunfire and roadside bombs to deliver food, fuel, and other equipment for U.S. soldiers. AUTHOR'S COLLECTION

A group of truck drivers for contractor KBR are shown standing at a military base in Balad, Iraq, on the morning of April 9, 2004. Several of the men in the photo died later that day in the single worst incident of violence for American contractors in Iraq. Six drivers and two soldiers were killed in a deadly, five-mile-long ambush by Iraqi insurgents. U.S. military and KBR officials sent the men into an active combat zone without adequate protection or communication. Keith Stanley, left, survived. Stephen Hulett, in checked lumberjack shirt, was killed, as was Steve Fisher, center, in glasses and bulletproof vest. In the background are Jeffrey Parker and Jack Montague, who also died. COURTESY OF THE FAMILY OF TONY D. JOHNSON, RECOVERED FROM HIS EFFECTS

A Texas attorney, Stuart Bowen, right, was one of President Bush's most ardent supporters, helping him win the Florida recount in 2000 and working at the White House. His critics expected a whitewash when Bowen was made the inspector general overseeing the reconstruction of Iraq. Instead Bowen used the post to become one of the most persistent critics of waste, fraud, and abuse in Iraq. Bowen is talking with Judge Rahdi Rahdi, the head of Iraq's anticorruption forces.
COURTESY OF THE SPECIAL INSPECTOR GENERAL OF IRAQ

James "Spike" Stephenson was the director of USAID in Iraq in 2004 and 2005. A veteran of postconflict situations in places like Kosovo and Lebanon, he clashed with the Pentagon over how to rebuild Iraq, favoring smaller projects in focused areas and macroeconomic and political reforms. By fall 2004, the State Department had begun to implement many of his ideas. COURTESY OF USAID

Lt. Col. Jamie Gayton talks with an Iraqi family outside a sewer pumping station in Sadr City, a notoriously poor slum in eastern Baghdad. The American military launched an intensive, coordinated rebuilding effort in Sadr City which helped reduce attacks against U.S. soldiers and produced noticeable improvements to residents' lives.
AUTHOR'S COLLECTION

Sadr City is a poor Shiite slum on the eastern edge of Baghdad. Traditionally neglected by Saddam Hussein, the neighborhood had raw sewage running in the streets and a haphazard power supply. An intensive U.S. reconstruction campaign there helped relieve tensions between U.S. troops and locals. Iraqis could see improvements coming and greeted soldiers with waves rather than hostile stares. AUTHOR'S COLLECTION

Col. Ted Westhusing, third from right, was appointed to head the training of an elite Iraqi police unit. In June 2005, a month after receiving a letter accusing a security company of human rights violations and fraud, Westhusing was found dead in his trailer. At the time, Westhusing was the highest-ranking military officer to die in Iraq. The army labeled his death a suicide, though some in his family suspected foul play. In this photo, Colonel Westhusing and his commanding officer, Gen. Joseph Fil, review newly trained Iraqi police. COURTESY OF THE FAMILY OF TED WESTHUSING

Dale Stoffel (with President Bush) was an American businessman who went to Iraq with dreams of patriotism and profit. An arms broker, he was killed in December 2004 by an unknown assailant after blowing the whistle on what he believed was a corrupt deal by Iraqi defense officials. His case remains unsolved. PHOTO POSTED ON INTERNET BY IRAQI TERRORIST GROUP

Jit Bahadur Khadka sits with his family outside their home in Lele, an impoverished village south of Kathmandu, Nepal. Khadka's son, Ramesh, was one of a dozen Nepalese workers who were brutally slaughtered in the desert in Iraq in August 2004. Halliburton subsidiary KBR and other American contractors hired thousands of poor immigrant workers for menial labor in Iraq, relying upon a shadowy network of labor traffickers. AUTHOR'S COLLECTION

Hayder Kharalla was working as a translator for U.S. troops with the Eighty-second Airborne Division when his leg was shot off in a street battle in August 2003. He spent more than a year fighting with his employer, Titan, and its insurance company, AIG, to get a prosthetic leg. Thousands of contractors—Americans and Iraqis—found themselves trapped in a private health insurance system poorly designed to handle the demands of a war zone. Kharalla was most regretful about being unable to walk around with his newborn son, Ali, shown in the picture. COURTESY OF SAAD KHALEF

Mark Oviatt, USAID's energetic director for water projects, explains the workings of a newly refurbished water treatment plant to Abdulkader Muhammad Ameen, chief of the Iraqi water system in Kirkuk. Oviatt was one of the first to sound the alarm about the United States' failure to train Iraqis to maintain and operate the expensive infrastructure projects that the United States was building in Iraq. Many of them collapsed after being turned over to the Iraqis. AUTHOR'S COLLECTION

A photo in August 2004 shows the Bayji power complex, spewing polluted smoke into the air. Bechtel was in charge of repairing the plant under a contract with USAID. Almost a year and a half after the invasion, the plant was producing at less than half capacity. AUTHOR'S COLLECTION

Nobody ever saw the message. An army report concluded later that the soldier had accidentally sent the e-mail to himself.

On a clear, hot morning, the convoy started south on the broad, four-lane highway that leads from Balad to Baghdad. There were twenty-six vehicles — nineteen KBR trucks, each carrying about 5,000 gallons of jet fuel, interspersed with seven armored military vehicles. Some of the soldiers — newly arrived reservists from Bartonville, Illinois — rode along with the truckers in the passenger's seats; others drove in Humvees and customized five-ton transport trucks. Steel plates had been welded together in their beds, squat walls rising up where the gunners crouched with the .50 caliber machine guns. The KBR trucks also had a distinctly military look. Normally KBR drove white Mercedes trucks to emphasize their civilian status to potential enemies. But Halliburton was short on trucks that month, and the military had deeded over some of its unarmored vehicles to the company. Thus the convoy that rolled out of Balad that morning appeared to be a long green line of military vehicles.

The first hour of the run passed without incident, a convoy passing down a freeway like any in America. But then, after turning west onto the highway leading toward the airport about ten miles distant, the first drivers were greeted by an odd sight: two M1A1 Abrams tanks blasting away at the neighborhood south of the highway. Up ahead they saw black flags hanging from overpasses. Even more ominous, a few trucks that appeared to be from an earlier convoy were ahead, burning in the highway. Nelson Howell, a forty-four-year-old trucker from Huntsville, Alabama, was in the lead KBR truck. Next to him sat Hamill, the KBR convoy commander.

"This doesn't look right," Howell said, looking around worriedly. The men were in a long, narrow canyon in the urban landscape. High walls ran on each side of the highway, with homes peeking over the top. It was the same place my convoy would stall in months later.

"Keep following the military," Hamill replied.

Just then gunfire ripped into the Humvees directly in front of Howell and Hamill. A roadside bomb burst on the left, then the right. Two rounds struck the convoy's military commander, 1st Lt. Matt Brown, in the head, knocking him out and blinding him in the left eye. The convoy had lost its leader. The radio came alive with screams of panic.

"I'm taking fire, I'm taking fire," screamed one driver. One of the military Humvees swerved off the road and onto a frontage road in an apparent attempt to dodge blockades in the highway. Howell swerved to follow.

Then bullets suddenly shredded the cab, blasting a chunk out of Hamill's arm. Bleeding profusely, Hamill grabbed a pair of socks in his bag and stuffed them into the wound. The truck began to slow, its air brakes locked up by the gunfire. Howell pulled over to the side of the road, unable to go on. He could not believe the amount of gunfire that filled the air. Soldiers later told investigators it was unlike anything they had seen before. "Hell broke loose," one said.

Suddenly a soldier appeared, jumped on the hood of the crippled truck, and opened fire at the houses that loomed on either side of the trucks. Howell and Hamill were crouched inside the cab, which was pierced with so many holes that it reminded Howell of a spaghetti strainer. Just then another Humvee sped into view. Howell, Hamill, and the soldier jumped from the truck and ran for safety. The Humvee slowed down just long enough to pick up Howell and the soldier, but for some reason the driver raced off, leaving Hamill behind. Insurgents seized him moments later as he lay by the truck, trying desperately to call for help. Hamill spent the next twenty-four days in captivity, being moved from shack to shack through the Iraqi countryside. He would be rescued on May 2, when he saw a U.S. military patrol passing by and broke out of his makeshift prison to flag it down. A dairy farmer from Mississippi, Hamill was given a hero's welcome when he returned to the United States. KBR gave him a job as a recruiter giving speeches to prospective drivers; his chilling story was supposed to frighten away those unwilling to face the dangers of Iraq. But the tactic didn't deter them, which was a measure of the desperation for work in middle America. "So far, nobody has got up and left," he told me months after the incident.

WE DELIVER

As Hamill's captors were driving him away, the rest of his convoy was getting bogged down in gunfire and flames. As the jet fuel spilled out from shot-through tankers, the roads became as slippery as ice. The trucks struggled to negotiate a hairpin turn on an exit ramp leading to the airport. Some trucks jackknifed and flipped, catching fire. Damaged trucks began to lose power and slowed to less than ten miles per hour as drivers frantically stamped on gas pedals. Insurgent roadblocks and the burning tankers made maneuvering difficult.

As the stricken convoy limped ahead, truck-to-truck communications were sporadic. Even when the radios worked, soldiers and truckers couldn't hear over the gunfire. Those who could hear later described a horrible sound track of pleas from burned and wounded truckers and soldiers. The truck cabs — without any armor — were being sliced open. Eddie Sanchez heard one panicked trucker's voice break through the din. It was Bill Bradley, calling out that he was taking fire.

"Oh God, please don't let me die in Iraq," yelled Bradley, a Vietnam vet, who was ahead of Sanchez.

"Then he yelped like bullets were hitting him. Then he stopped. It was kind of a relief," Sanchez said.

The first few fuel tankers struggled ahead. But the soldiers and truckers in the middle of the convoy, like Bradley, were cut to pieces by bullets and rocket-propelled grenades (RPGs). Tony Johnson's truck flipped over and burst into flames. A masonry worker for twenty years, Johnson had gone to Iraq in hopes of earning enough money to buy his own big rig. Jeffrey Parker, forty-five, of Lake Charles, Louisiana, pulled off to the side of the road to help and was hit with an RPG. Steve Hulett died on the same stretch of road. A forty-eight-year-old from Michigan, he was in Iraq to help pull his family out of bankruptcy. Jack Montague, fifty-two, a trucker from Pittsburg, Illinois, was seen by one driver screaming into a handheld radio. Another trucker saw him a few minutes later, dead, flat on his back staring at the sky, his helmet and vest apparently stripped off his body by looters. Sgt. Elmer Kraus, forty, of North Carolina, was driving with Montague. Later his body would be found in a shallow grave near the highway.

"We just kept driving. More and more of us were disappearing. I could see the damage in my truck. My cab was littered with gunfire. I had been hit. I was bleeding. The only thing I could do was keep going. If you stopped you were dead," Keith Stanley told me. Stanley was a fifty-six-year-old driver from Fayetteville, North Carolina. An air force vet, he had signed up with KBR after watching his wife fight a losing battle against cancer for five years. Emotionally drained, he thought the work in Iraq would take his mind off his loss. "I didn't even know I was hit. The only thing I knew was that it felt like somebody had thrown a handful of sand in my face. It was extremely small pieces of metal hitting me, penetrating me, and I didn't know it. I felt something wet on my left arm. It was blood. I saw the holes in me. I felt the burning. We were in a chainsaw."

Stanley coaxed his crippled truck forward, now deaf in one ear, his left arm bleeding heavily, his Kevlar vest in shreds. His helmet, he later learned, had a three-inch tear where a round struck. He was unsure of where he was going or what he was doing. Finally he saw concertina wire stretched in front of an opening in a wall in front of him. It was the north entrance to the airport. He guided the truck inside, reaching an outpost that the First Cavalry had set up just inside the gate. As Stanley climbed down from the cab, an officer came up screaming. They had no idea that a convoy was on its way.

"What the fuck are you people doing here?" the officer yelled at Stanley. "This road is closed. This is a combat zone!"

Rick Tollison, a heavy equipment operator from Texas with a wife and four kids, rolled into the airport a few minutes later. He was one of the truckers who had never driven in Iraq before the morning of April 9. He had been pulled into the convoy mission at the last minute when convoy commander Hamill turned up short a driver. Tollison remembered weaving through burning trucks and concrete hunks in the road. He was riding with a sergeant who got hit by gunfire. Tollison suddenly found himself splattered with blood. The soldier handed Tollison his rifle. Tollison fired the M16 out the window with one hand while using the other to steer through smoke, flames, and insurgent barricades.

"You'll do anything when you're getting shot at," Tollison said. "We were just creeping around like snails, trying to keep going on. You could hear them shooting us, plus hitting the truck. It was boom, boom, boom, and you could hear the hits: thunk, thunk, thunk."

Those bringing up the rear of the convoy were greeted with a hellish scene of fire, flying bullets, and dying men. But there were no options. The highway had become a gauntlet of death. Enemy fighters darted out of bushes and from roadside berms, and popped out of houses. Some took cover behind women veiled in black. Children fired AK-47s.

"It was just like something you would see in the movies," one soldier, Jarob Walsh, wrote later in his report for investigators. He recounted with regret shooting a boy about seven years old in the throat after the youngster and his brother opened fire on him.

We kept going, and came upon five or six . . . tanker trucks that had been blown up and were on fire; there was black smoke everywhere. We drove right through it, praying that we would not hit any debris in the fire; we couldn't see anything. It was extremely hot in the fire and there was so much black smoke everywhere that I couldn't breathe. It was phenomenal — there is no way to exaggerate what was happening and what it looked like. The most horrible thing you could imagine is what it looked like. Bodies everywhere, trucks on fire and exploding, so much weapons fire.[14]

A handful of soldiers and drivers who survived the onslaught huddled near the ruins of their crippled vehicles and prayed for rescue. Months later, the intensity of the fright was terribly present. As trucker Jackie Lester remembered the moment, he seemed transformed. A heavy, balding man with white hair and a ruddy face, his eyes grew big, the trucker in a John Deere baseball cap and open-necked shirt suddenly seeming more like a little boy recounting a nightmare. "I was scared. I was like this: uhhh, uhhh," he said, keening and clenching his fists as he spoke. "The fear was set in. We were all scared. I was scared to death. All I saw was burning. I said, 'I'll try to find the end of the rainbow.' I was in the kill zone." Lester was one of two drivers bringing up the rear in bobtails, trucks without trailers specifically designated to pick up stragglers. Lester rescued one driver, then broke down and had to be rescued himself. He was haunted by one voice, screaming at him to come back. Lester had no idea where the man was or how to get to him, he said. "I could hear him saying, 'Jack, you bastard, come back!' " said Lester. "I couldn't handle that. I didn't want to answer. I didn't want to tell him, 'I can't help you.' "

Sgt. Robert Goff's Humvee, which was in the middle of the convoy, stopped first to pick up Howell and the other soldier (accidentally leaving Hamill behind). Then Goff stopped to gather up Steve Fisher, the trash hauler from Virginia Beach who drove a second bobtail. Fisher had tried to help a driver stranded at the top of an overpass but was hit in the process. He bled to death in Goff's Humvee, calling out the names of his wife and children. Goff stopped a third time, surrounded by flaming trucks and rattling gunfire, to pick up Eddie Sanchez, two other truckers, and a soldier Sanchez had rescued before his truck broke down. The Humvee, which normally held five occupants, now had ten.

With the airport entrance in sight in the distance about a mile away, the Humvee's engine suddenly shuddered to a halt. The men were stranded on open highway, bullets and RPGs flying all around. The gunner estimated that he had already fired between eight hundred and a thousand rounds from the large-caliber machine gun mounted on the Humvee's top, and his ammunition was almost out. There was nothing to do but fight, and pray that someone would rescue them. The barriers between soldier and trucker vanished. Soldiers began bandaging wounds, while the drivers began firing weapons. One soldier, Pfc. Gregory Goodrich, thirty-seven, was killed when a bullet hit him through an open window in the Humvee. "Everybody was working together. The panic went by us," said Ray Stannard, a trucker from New Mexico, who was crammed into the Humvee.

Just as desperation set in the men heard a screeching noise. Off in the distance, they saw three tanks and two armored Humvees rolling in their direction. The First Cavalry had arrived. "It was like an old John Ford–John Wayne cavalry movie," one of the soldiers would later write. The tanks pulled up around the Humvee, allowing the soldiers and truckers to evacuate their crippled vehicle. Then the tanks and Humvees returned to the airport, still firing at the insurgents. The last of the living had been saved.

At the airport base, the soldiers and truckers took stock. The convoy had fought 200 to 300 insurgents through a five-mile-long zone of nearly constant fire. Of forty-three men in the convoy, there were twenty-five casualties, a rate equivalent to that suffered by the first American paratrooper units in Normandy. Six KBR drivers and two soldiers were dead. Two more men, driver Tim Bell and Spc. Keith "Matt" Maupin, were missing and are today presumed dead. Six of the seven military vehicles had survived, thanks to their armorproofing. Only a third of KBR's nineteen trucks had managed the same feat. The highway behind them was an inferno, littered with burning trucks, black smoke, and dead Americans.

For their part in the combat, eight soldiers in the 724th Transportation Company were awarded Purple Hearts. Spc. Jeremy Church was awarded the Silver Star for driving through fire to safety and then returning with the First Cavalry soldiers to rescue Goff's crippled Humvee. He was credited with saving the lives of five soldiers and four KBR drivers. "Even though this was a tragic event, the soldiers did what they were supposed to do. There was never any hesitation," said Capt. Jeff Smith, the company commander. "We executed what we were supposed to do." Surviving KBR employees were treated to dinner at a hotel in Kuwait and gold coins from KBR inscribed with the company's motto in Iraq: "We deliver."

A WATERSHED IN IRAQ

Back in the United States, the families of the drivers had seen clips of the aftermath of the attack on CNN, but they didn't know their loved ones were involved until they started getting phone calls from KBR. The company was unsure of what had happened, representatives told family members. Neither the military nor KBR had a clear idea of who had been on the convoy, which truckers were killed, and which were missing. The company sent out grief counselors but had few answers.

The families were at a loss, unsure of where to turn. They wanted answers: What had happened to the convoy? Unlike the military, with both formal counseling services and the informal community of military families, the contractor families had to rely solely on KBR. They had only a vague idea of who their loved ones worked with and no idea of how to get in touch with the other families. They didn't fit into the categories usually associated with war dead. The men killed were not soldiers, and their wives were not war widows. The families felt alone and abandoned.

Two of those family members were Kim Johnson and her daughter April. Johnson was the ex-wife of Tony Johnson, the former masonry contractor. The days following the attacks were filled with nightmarish uncertainty. First came news that the military had recovered three bodies in shallow graves. Kim and April had to give DNA samples. Finally, two weeks after the incident, a KBR representative called Kim from a pay phone at the supermarket down the street. He asked if he could come visit. Kim knew that Tony was dead. "It's him," she told the KBR man. He said, "Yes." "It was the worst week of our whole lives," Johnson said. "It was absolutely life-changing."

Tim Bell's family took the lead in demanding explanations. They were a close-knit group, a middle-class family of five brothers and sisters raised in Mobile, Alabama. Bell was the oldest of the five, a natural-born leader with an outsized personality. He would walk into a room of people and just start shaking hands: "I'm Tim Bell, someone you should know," he'd say. A former marine, Bell had been working at a paper mill outside Mobile when he heard about the money that could be made in Iraq. He decided to go, but only after KBR officials told him that he'd be safe. He wound up working in the mailroom in Balad but was assigned to drive a truck only a few days before the run down to the airport. The last time that Bell spoke with his family, he told them he was scared. He had been in Iraq almost a year and was scheduled to return home, hopefully for his mother's birthday in late April. Then the Bells got a call from KBR on April 9: Tim was missing.

The Bells spent weeks in agony, calling constantly. After months of pestering, they convinced KBR to set up a briefing for them at the Pentagon. The whole family flew up in July. There, at the Ritz Carlton in Pentagon

City, they met at a long table with a dozen Pentagon officials. They got two brochures on grief, and no answers. "We were still in the dark. I feel like they knew what was going on but hadn't told us," said Tim's sister Debora. "They stopped me after I asked eight or nine questions. They said, 'A lot of questions, we aren't prepared to answer.'"

As the months passed, the Bells and other family members continued their battle for answers with KBR and the Pentagon. Slowly they began making contact with each other. Finally, in February 2005, the Pentagon made an unusual gesture. It sent out the head of the military unit that had been guarding the truckers to reveal the results of the army's own investigation into the attack. Col. Gary Bunch, commander of the 172nd Corps Support Group, had the rare distinction of briefing civilians on the internal workings of the military — yet another acknowledgment of the close relationship between KBR and the army.

The military's 280-page report was a document of disaster. Battlefield commanders with the First Cavalry Division had been fighting along the airport highway for two days prior to the convoy run. Such fighting is supposed to automatically close a route, but the word had never reached all parts of the logistics command that oversaw transport missions. The military ordered stepped-up security for the mission but failed to follow through. The convoy was supposed to have a minimum ratio of one army soldier sitting with a driver in every two Halliburton trucks. The April 9 convoy had six soldiers spread among nineteen trucks. The soldiers had only rough maps of their final destination, and the truck drivers had none.

The military report's most revealing conclusion was how the army had failed to work closely with its supposed partner in the war, KBR. Unwilling to issue its classified radios to contractors for fear they could fall into the wrong hands, the army had a makeshift system of handheld radios to talk to Hamill, the KBR commander. Hamill, in turn, had a radio system that he used to relay information to his drivers, and yet another system to communicate with KBR headquarters at Balad. The different systems were incompatible. The result was a breakdown. "Once engagement began there was a complete lack of ability to communicate under intense enemy fire," the report concluded.

In his visits with the families, Bunch downplayed the more critical elements of the report. He described the April 9 massacre as an extraordinary incident that could not have been foreseen. We "had not been attacked like this before. It was a wholly singular event and it was a watershed in Iraq," he said, according to a tape recording of one of the meetings. "Were they in the right place doing the right thing? The answer is yes."

For their part, KBR officials said that they had taken steps in the days after the attacks to improve security, though they declined to reveal what they had done. They also noted that the company was dependent on the military for protection. KBR had to balance the safety of its drivers with the importance of its mission. "Lives depend on our work, as does the military's ability to carry out its missions," said Beverly Scippa, a Halliburton spokeswoman. "KBR employees and subcontractors working in Iraq understand the dangers and difficult conditions involved in working in a war zone and have made courageous decisions to deliver the services necessary to support the troops."

But the families and the surviving drivers by then had their doubts about the version of events they had been given by the government and KBR. Several truckers recalled KBR's own internal security advisers warning about trouble on the route before the convoy departed. Another convoy sent out seconds earlier had been turned back, apparently because of worries of what lay ahead. Yet another convoy traveling the route was hit earlier the same day, losing several vehicles. The leader of that convoy told colleagues that he e-mailed his superiors about the danger. To the drivers and their families, it appeared that the convoy attack was not only foreseeable but avoidable.

When I met the Bells a month after Bunch's visit, they sat in the front room with CNN on, as it always was, just in case there was news from Iraq. Outside their modest brick home in a pine-filled neighborhood, the azaleas and dogwoods were bursting into bloom. Inside the family grieved. The Pentagon had recently received a letter that Tim's truck had been found, melted into slag. No insurgent group had ever surfaced to ask for a ransom. "We don't want a flag. We just want to know where he is. They can keep all the other stuff," his sixty-eight-year-old mother, Marjorie Bell Smith, told me. "We don't want medals. We want the truth."

Across the country, in a neat subdivision of ranch homes outside Riverside, California, Kim Johnson shared the Bells' determination to get answers. Johnson had spoken to Tony, her former husband, the night before the convoy. Johnson was excited because he had finally left a tent for the air-conditioned comfort of his own trailer. He had sent her pictures of his new quarters, showing him smiling in front of the wall unit, and tears filled Kim's eyes when she leafed through the photos. Johnson's adult daughter,

April, had received a $50,000 payment from KBR, the standard life insurance policy on each driver. KBR had kicked in another $50,000 to help pay college bills. But Kim had come to feel that her daughter needed more than money. She needed answers too. In making war a for-profit enterprise, the army and KBR had made mistakes. Somebody had to make sure they were not repeated. "They can't just walk away from this," she said, her eyes tearing. "This man will not have died in vain. He will not. He will not."

In April 2005 the Bells, the Johnsons, and other family members filed suit against KBR, claiming that the company had knowingly sent the men to their deaths to meet the terms of their contract. The suit was filed on behalf of Ingrid Fisher, the day care worker whose husband had called her just before pulling out. Fisher said that the suit was important to her because she wanted some recognition of what her husband had done. He hadn't been a soldier, she acknowledged. But he had served. "If it wasn't for these guys, the soldiers wouldn't have fuel. They wouldn't have food," she said. "Nobody cares about the civilians. Nobody thinks about them."

Fisher was wrong in one respect. At least one set of people was thinking hard about the civilians: the Iraqi insurgents. Under David Nash, the reconstruction program was hiring thousands of Americans and Iraqis to carry out the work of the rebuilding. But the Bush administration — once again not paying attention to its multibillion-dollar rebuilding program — had given little thought to how to protect them. When the insurgents started hitting the relatively easy targets represented by the contractors, the Pentagon was again caught without a plan. There were not enough troops to secure Iraq, much less safeguard American businessmen and their Iraqi hires. So the Defense Department turned to its favorite solution. It had contracted out nation building. It had contracted out the oversight. Now it was time to contract out an army.

8

Private Armies

The world headquarters of the Parsons Corporation hunkers at the far western edge of Pasadena's fashionable Old Town shopping district, an octagonal block of concrete squatting above the strip's expensive restaurants and shoebox boutiques. Inside its dull brown shell, engineers and project managers, secretaries and computer technicians, shush through hallways of gray carpet and beige walls. They have turned Parsons into the largest employee-owned engineering and construction firm in the world. Parsons dug the subway tunnels beneath Washington and Los Angeles. It conjured an oil port city of fifty thousand on the desolate coast of Saudi Arabia. The company has erected airports in Greece and China; highways in the Arab capitals of Abu Dhabi and Doha; and bridges throughout America. It restored an entire island in Hawaii once used as a navy firing range, and helped decommission chemical weapons in Russia. The company's mission is as simple and plain as the headquarters facade: it builds big, important things that cost a lot of money, and it makes a lot of money doing so.

Like many major American engineering firms interested in lowering their insurance bills, Parsons obsesses about the safety of its workers. The first thing employees see upon walking into the main lobby is an electronic screen broadcasting the company's "safety message of the day." There is a corporate vice president whose only role is overseeing safety programs throughout Parsons operations worldwide. When the company's CEO, Jim McNulty, one day jaywalked to a favorite restaurant across the street from company headquarters, he got a chastening e-mail from an employee who spotted him. Subsequently, McNulty had an orange sign posted on the light post directly across from the restaurant. It directs employees to the nearest crosswalk, some one hundred yards away. "Safety is our number one priority" is a McNulty mantra.

Given that focus, Parsons's decision in the fall of 2003 to enthusiastically pursue work in Iraq might seem odd. At the time, however, the insurgency was only simmering and Iraq was seen as an important business opportunity. In Iraq the company could gain a foothold in the lucrative market for overseas federal contracts, a practice in which Parsons was not well established. Moreover it was not the company's first foray into Iraq. Parsons had done water surveys in the country in the 1950s and designed part of a subway for Baghdad in the 1980s that was never built.[1] Still, the company's plan to work with the United States to rebuild Iraq was clearly more ambitious than anything it had done previously.

The board hired Earnie Robbins, a retired two-star air force general, to guide the new effort. Robbins plunged into the assignment, working with Parsons's engineers as they crafted proposals to respond to the plans David Nash announced at the November business conference. As the months went by, Parsons honed its strategies, seeking partners in other coalition countries to improve its chances. When the final awards were announced in March 2004, Parsons ended up among the biggest winners. The company won eight separate contracts valued at up to $2.8 billion. Overnight, Parsons vaulted into becoming the second largest contractor in Iraq, its total trailing only the much larger Halliburton.

Parsons's two biggest projects involved health and security. The company won the job of building scores of new health clinics and refurbishing hospitals throughout Iraq. It also won the task of constructing border forts, walled outposts along the Iran-Iraq frontier that stretched from the deserts in the south to cold, inhospitable mountain passes in the Kurdish north. Parsons also became a minority partner in a joint venture to repair Iraq's northern oil fields, worked under Bechtel to do water and sewer line installations in Sadr City, and even had a job building camps for the demolition of Iraqi missiles, bombs, and other munitions found by coalition soldiers. Despite the range, the jobs were more or less standard engineering and construction work. But Iraq turned out to be anything but typical.

When Parsons sent employees to Iraq, Robbins would often personally brief them in a conference room at company headquarters. Robbins liked to begin his talks about what lay ahead by showing the workers a fifty-three-second clip from a U.S. Air Force video shot in Iraq. In it a mass of about thirty suspected insurgents clad in black can be seen gathering near the wall of a building in Fallujah. A voice orders an F-16 pilot to "take them out." The plane launches a five-hundred-pound bomb from eight miles away. Ten seconds later an enormous black cloud erupts across the screen. All thirty men simply vanish. The pilot's voice can be heard in the background: "Oh, dude." Robbins, a thin, intense man who incessantly twisted his wedding ring, spoke in a precise, military clip, a former general used to making recommendations and having them followed. The video, he told the workers during a session I attended in February 2005, made a point. "The war in Iraq was instant gratification," he said. "I will assure you that the reconstruction of Iraq has not been an instant gratification sort of thing."

Parsons got word on winning its final contract in Iraq on March 24, 2004. A week later the four Blackwater contractors were ambushed and mutilated in Fallujah. A week after that, the KBR convoy was wiped out. By the time Larry Hartman arrived in Iraq in April, the company was scrambling to cope with the violent new reality. Hartman was the project manager for Parsons's health contract. A former Army Corps engineer, he was a blunt-speaking man with square glasses, thinning hair, and a brusque manner that let you know he did not suffer fools. Hartman had initially planned on renting out a villa in Mansour or another of Baghdad's upscale neighborhoods. Now he found himself scanning aerial maps of the fortified Green Zone, looking desperately for an open patch of land to set up trailers for the company's headquarters. And that was just the beginning. Soon Parsons engineers bound for Iraq had to go through detailed security briefings. They were taught how to wear bulletproof vests (the Velcro fastens around the front, to prevent shrapnel from entering the seams of the vest); how to apply a tourniquet (use a marker to write the time of application near the injury so doctors will know how long blood flow has been cut); and how to handle the corkscrew landing at Baghdad airport (tighten your seat belt). Each Parsons employee in Iraq had to pass a physical that included running four hundred yards with forty pounds. It was designed to simulate fleeing a potential kidnapper while wearing a bulletproof vest.

Parsons's reactions to the violence mirrored those of every other American company working in Iraq. They fled behind the walls of the Green Zone, abandoning daily contact with Iraq and its people. They stopped taking trips to construction sites, relied heavily on their Iraqi staff, and hired extra security guards. They were companies under siege.

THE FORTRESS

Parsons's Green Zone compound contrasted starkly with the company's Pasadena headquarters. It seemed more like a frontier outpost than an engineering firm. The entrance was a battered metal gate, pockmarked by ragged, rusted shrapnel holes. Parsons employees lived in pairs in small white trailers surrounded by stacks of sandbags. Each worker got a bedroom about twice the size of a garden shed, with false wood paneling, television set, DVD player, and minifridge. Bathrooms were shared, and came with a twelve-gallon water heater — just enough for a few minutes of hot water. Parsons's security guards lived in bunk beds stacked in garages that once held Saddam's luxury vehicle fleet. American tanks stood guard outside. Blackhawk helicopters thundered overhead, shaking the trailers. The faint smell of sewage filled the air.

Commuting was not a problem. The main Parsons office was ten yards from the sleeping quarters. It rambled across a half-dozen construction trailers wired together. Inside, cheap carpet covered the floors and a buzz filled the air. Iraqis and Americans stood in groups, reviewing projects. Desks were jammed side by side, stacked with blueprints and contract documents. People hustled in and out of the narrow aisles. Every computer seemed to have a webcam and taped pictures from home: family photos and bright notes in crayon from the kids. Engineers rarely left the compound, much less the Green Zone. They worked seven days a week, twelve hours a day, for ninety days in a row, a routine broken by two-week vacations, often to Dubai, the Arab Las Vegas.

The threat of violence was never far away. Mortars whistled overhead about three times a month. Most missed, though one incoming round had knocked a jagged hole into the wall of a building that loomed above the trailers. In recognition of the danger, a long, low, spinelike row of concrete bomb shelters ran through the center of the camp. When engineers did go out, each trip was a pseudomilitary operation led by the company's security guards, clad in bulletproof armor and with machine guns ready, who barreled through the streets at top speed in SUVs. To get to the airport, engineers sometimes had to travel by helicopter.

For most of the workers, the only relief came from a small trailer at the end of the compound that had been turned into a makeshift bar — which, in true engineering style, had been given the resolutely drab name The MWR, for morale, welfare, and recreation. When I visited, the bar was crammed with a half-dozen black-topped tables, red chairs, and worn leather couches. Security contractors with shaved heads played darts. A CNN fashion special showed scantily clad models. Mosquitoes flitted through the air. A handful of engineers sat around the fake wood bar, drinking beer. One of them was Doug Zwissler, a burly, white-haired man who had been in Iraq for nearly a year.

Zwissler was between engineering jobs, doing fund-raising for his church back home in the States, when the war broke out. Like many Parsons employees, he came mostly for the pay. A typical Parsons engineer earned about $150,000 a year in Iraq, roughly double normal pay in the United States. Almost $90,000 of it was tax free. The money meant that Parsons never had much trouble staffing: when the company began recruiting to fill positions for its new contracts in Iraq, it got twenty-seven thousand applicants for three hundred spots. Even during the height of the violence, applications continued to roll in, abetted by the weak economy at home.

Zwissler was Hartman's deputy, in charge of overseeing the construction of the new health clinics and hospitals that Parsons was building. He found himself chained to a desk, rarely able to get out to work sites. "I'm in the cradle of civilization," Zwissler said. "I've read about it since I was in grade school. And I can't go anywhere. That's a major frustration." Not being able to visit made it difficult to envision what needed to be done. Consultations were done through digital photos taken by Iraqi employees who went to the sites and supervised construction. As a result it was hard to anticipate problems before they happened. And they happened all the time.

AN AMERICAN PROJECT

Zwissler's job was made more difficult by his many, many bosses: the five different U.S. agencies involved in improving Iraq's health and water. In a single year, Zwissler worked for seven different contract officers — the U.S. government representatives directly responsible for assigning and monitoring Parsons. Some had stayed for as little as two months. Zwissler couldn't even remember their names. (One was simply "the Philadelphia guy.") Each new officer, typically an air force or Army Corps captain on temporary duty, had to adjust to the country, learn about a specific project, and get to know the relevant Iraqi and American counterparts. Then he would leave. An inspector general report on the reconstruction found that some personnel had stayed as little as two days for temporary assignments.[2] The constant turnover was a nightmare in terms of tracking progress. Contracts were stuffed in drawers and stacked on filing cabinets. Files were incomplete; a sample of thirty-seven contracts worth $184 million found that barely half had complete documentation. Ten other contract files couldn't even be found.[3] How could the government enforce the terms of its contracts when the documents were missing?

The churn led to conflicting, constantly shifting mandates. Parsons spent $1 million rebuilding Iraq's looted Education Ministry. Then a new contract officer decided it would cost too much to complete. Midway through, the project was abandoned, and the buildings sat useless and vacant. Though neglect was the order of the day, the pendulum sometimes swung the other way. Auditors sporadically swarmed projects, insisting on elaborate documentation in a place where deals were often sealed with a handshake. "The government wants all this work done quickly, and they want it done with the least expense, and they want it done in total compliance" with federal regulations, said Earnie Robbins, Parsons's Iraq operations chief. "Sometimes those goals are mutually exclusive." In one case Parsons proposed using bulldozers to clear a site for a landfill. The military, however, wanted day laborers to do the work by hand; that way it would provide more jobs to young Iraqi males who might otherwise be tempted to join the insurgency. Parsons insisted on a letter documenting the order, fearing that federal auditors would later criticize the company for spending too much money on workers instead of the cheaper bulldozer. Parsons got the letter, and Iraqis got the jobs. But the landfill was later closed down because of violence, a junkyard junked.

The United States also made demands that Zwissler felt endangered Parsons's employees, especially their Iraqi hires. There was, for example, intense pressure to demonstrate the success of the reconstruction to Iraqis. But to reduce risks, Parsons, like other contractors in Iraq, stripped its projects of any signs of Western involvement. On a hospital in Sadr City, for instance, a Parsons subcontractor posted a sign with a portrait of Muqtada Sadr, the rebellious Shiite Muslim cleric, suggesting that he was paying for the renovations. The effort was designed to appease Sadr's militia and avoid violence, but Parsons knew the military would object, and so it reluctantly ordered that the sign be taken down. The company insisted that its laborers don safety goggles and hard hats. The workers rarely wore them, however, since they were a sure sign that the project was being funded by the Americans. No Iraqi contractor would use safety gear for his employees. At one project U.S. troops in Humvees showed up at a construction site where Parsons was trying to operate under cover. A soldier took out a bullhorn and announced: "This is a U.S. project!"

Finally, Zwissler and Hartman had to work with the Iraqis, who provided their own input on projects. The men frequently felt like they should be wearing wires. In one case in southern Iraq, Parsons was called in to clean up a hospital after a fierce battle with insurgents. Corpses were floating in the flooded basement. The hospital's top official ordered Parsons to hire a specific firm. Concerned about a possible kickback scheme, Parsons refused and sent over its own crew of subcontractors. The hospital official called the local police and had the entire crew arrested. In the end, Parsons allowed the U.S. Army Corps of Engineers to take over the task. "I don't want to spend five years sitting in a cell because I got the job done," Zwissler said.

THE IRAQIS

Zwissler's primary contact with the Iraqis was through Parsons's local employees. Parsons hired more than five thousand Iraqis, from laborers to engineers. This was partly a necessity — Parsons simply couldn't have done the work without them — but also a requirement of the original contract. The United States wanted Parsons to train and provide jobs to as many Iraqis as possible. As a result, Iraqi engineers were introduced to a whole new world of technology. Under the Saddam regime, there were no three-dimensional engineering software programs, no fax machines, not even cellular phones. The Iraqis also had peculiar skills that required retraining. Iraqi architects were accustomed to using Saddam's height (six feet two inches) as a unit of measure. Another particular talent — building the octagonal structures favored by the dictator, whose name contained eight letters in Arabic — was no longer in demand.

The Iraqis I spoke to seemed inspired by their work with the company. Parsons had opened their eyes to new possibilities. Bosses didn't demand bribes. Work was efficient and focused. Employees were allowed to speak their mind. They also felt as if they were taking part in something larger than themselves: the rebuilding of their country. That sense of mission helped dispel the considerable risks of working with an American firm. Parsons's locals were followed, threatened, shot at, and kidnapped. They stood in hours-long lines to enter the Green Zone, exposing themselves to suicide bombers. Every one of the more than a dozen Iraqi workers I interviewed had relatives or coworkers who had been killed. One Iraqi engineer had personal reasons to work on a project to clean up pumping stations that carry waste to treatment plants. His relatives lived on streets where raw sewage oozed up in reeking pools. Every time he walked home, he passed a section of his neighborhood where grieving families hung the black banners that serve as Iraq's obituary pages, announcing the deaths of loved ones killed by insurgents. Many of the dead were engineers. It was a daily reminder of the value that he held as a target for the militants. "It's not easy for us," he said. "I won't lie. I'm afraid. But if we don't do it, who will?"[4]

Parsons's work did produce some results. The firm constructed scores of forts along the Iraq-Iran border, some of them almost whimsical, straight from *A Thousand and One Nights,* with crenellated walls and sturdy block towers. It completely refurbished several hospitals and administrative offices for two Iraq ministries. But Parsons did not turn dirt quickly enough to satisfy either the Americans or the Iraqis. The company wound up doing far less than either it had planned or the U.S. government wanted. The company that built entire cities in the sand became a poster boy for the trouble that American firms had in rebuilding Iraq.

A major police academy that Parsons refurbished in Mosul burned to the ground after an insurgent attack. An inspector general's audit found that some of the border forts and fire stations were shoddily built, with structural stability problems. Most egregious of all, Parsons was paid almost $186 million but finished only 20 of 150 health clinics that were originally planned, citing overruns caused by higher than expected security costs. The rest of the clinics were only partially completed, many of them walled up with cement and left for a future Iraqi government to pay to finish off. Millions of dollars' worth of health equipment purchased for the clinics was crated up and stored in a warehouse. The news only got worse. In June 2006 the U.S. Army Corps of Engineers terminated Parsons's $99 million contract to build a jail north of Baghdad — the largest single project canceled in the reconstruction of Iraq. In the United States' efforts to build a free Iraq, its chosen contractor couldn't even complete a prison.[5]

As I spent time with Parsons, it seemed to me that fear and confusion were better reasons than greed for explaining why the company acted the way it did. Parsons tried to carry out the tasks assigned by the United States, but it was most interested in protecting its workers and the company's bottom line. The slow pace of the work was the result of a paralysis brought on by the violence, the mercurial demands of U.S. overseers, and the permanent threat of public relations disasters at the hands of auditors and the press. Like most American companies in Iraq, Parsons found out that the rebuilding of Iraq was its own kind of war, the company caught in a crossfire between customer satisfaction, profit, and death.

PULL OUT

Parsons was hardly the only company affected by the outbreak in violence in April 2004. Iraq had been a violent place for months. But the bloodletting in the spring of 2004 was so shattering that U.S. and foreign companies pulled out employees, limited movement, or suspended work. General Electric and Bechtel both evacuated workers, halting the rehabilitation of more than two dozen power plants. Washington International locked down its workers at two electricity plant sites hit with small arms fire and mortars. Fluor began sending workers home early to avoid travel after nightfall, resulting in fewer hours of work per day. A subcontractor for CH2M Hill, a Colorado-based construction and consulting company, simply refused to show up.[6] The United Nations and nonprofit groups also withdrew or relocated employees, including Mercy Corps, which was distributing food, and the North Carolina–based RTI, which was doing voter education.[7] Several countries, including Germany, Russia, Portugal, Poland, and France, urged their citizens to evacuate. Siemens AG pulled out contractors from the Doura power plant, one of the country's largest. Russia's main contractor in Iraq, state-owned Tekhpromexport, said it decided to evacuate 370 Russian staff members because of the rising violence.

Iraqi workers hired by U.S. firms also stopped showing up for work. As many as one-third of about 5,300 Iraqis working at various construction sites throughout Baghdad failed to turn up after the April attacks, delaying the opening of new military bases designed for Iraqi army forces. In particularly dangerous areas, nearly half of the workers abandoned their jobs.

Perhaps most seriously, KBR temporarily suspended its convoys. KBR employees who wanted to go home — and dozens did after the April attacks — were free to leave. As the violence spread across Iraq in early April, Don Kerbow, a manager in KBR's truck transportation program, wrote to his coworkers involved in shipping food and other supplies across Iraq. The army, Kerbow wrote, had told KBR that "we are officially back at war." "It is going to be extremely hard to get equipment to sites due [to] the extent of the situations [sic] that is going on as we speak. . . . I know that each of you will do your part to make this thing work," Kerbow wrote. "All I ask is that we keep safety in mind in the process." Then he added: "No job is too important as to do it unsafely."[8]

Military analysts had long worried about depending too heavily on contractors. What would happen if a company ceased work in the face of violence? KBR's hiatus gave a glimpse: starvation. Although the company ceased work for less than two weeks, the coalition faced immediate problems in supplying food and water. U.S. Marines in Al Anbar province west of Baghdad issued rationing orders two days after the April 9 attack on the KBR convoy. A week later, marines at some outposts were down to a single hot meal a day, relying otherwise on prepackaged MREs, or meals ready to eat.[9] By April 17 the situation had grown so bad that Bremer considered ordering food rationing for the CPA itself.[10]

There was little the United States could do. Peter W. Singer, a scholar at the Brookings Institution in Washington and an expert on military contractors, noted that American contracting officers could threaten to impose financial penalties on a company for failing to perform, but there was no immediate recourse to force a civilian worker to do a job. "There is no legal jurisdiction over these personnel to order them the way the military does a soldier," Singer told me. "These gaps in service are quite dangerous." The heavy reliance on contractors now threatened American troops — indeed, the entire reconstruction project. Outsourcing to save money appeared to have costs of its own.

HIRED GUNS

While Iraq's spiraling violence chased some companies away, it created a boom, literally, for one industry: private security firms. Private security companies swarmed into Iraq from across the globe. Ex–Delta Force and Navy SEALs from the United States. British-trained Gurkhas from Nepal. Elite SAS (Special Air Service) forces from the United Kingdom. Former South African police commandos. American-trained Colombian and El Salvadoran soldiers. The Pentagon — as always, caught off guard in the reconstruction — had no real idea how many men at arms were under contract in Iraq. It estimated that there were eventually sixty firms with about twenty thousand employees, while other estimates ran as high as eighty to one hundred firms, with perhaps twenty-five thousand armed men.[11] Taken together, the tens of thousands working for private companies were the second largest armed contingent in the country, ahead of the British and Polish armies. Never before had so many private security companies gathered in the same place. Nor had they ever played such a crucial role on the world stage. Iraq became the Silicon Valley of hired guns: a place that rewarded risk and nurtured explosive growth. If you wanted to compete, you had to be there.

The American government paid handsomely for the services. Security contractors with special forces backgrounds easily commanded salaries of between $100,000 and $200,000 per year. Sending a squad of five men to protect a single engineer to conduct an inspection at a power plant cost $5,000 per day. Security costs ate up an average of 22 percent on reconstruction contracts. Security firms were awarded at least $766 million in contracts in Iraq, according to a Government Accountability Office report. "The impact of security costs on the rebuilding of Iraq cannot be overestimated," said Stuart Bowen, the inspector general. One Defense Department official declared it "clearly unprecedented."[12]

The private security industry could trace its roots back thousands of years. For almost as long as there has been war, there have been people paid to fight. The Egyptian pharaoh Ramses II hired Numians for the battle of Kadesh in 1294 B.C. The Carthaginians were so dependent on hired help that the first Punic War with Rome is also known as the Mercenary War. From the Middle Ages through the 1700s, European warfare was dominated by mercenaries, hired bands of roving soldiers who sold their services to the highest bidder.[13]

By the early twentieth century, however, paid warriors had nearly disappeared from the scene. The use of mercenaries declined as national governments sought to monopolize the use of force. Patriotism took the place of profit as the chief, or at least the idealized, motive for war. The Geneva Conventions created formal, narrowly drawn definitions that essentially outlawed mercenaries by stripping them of wartime protections. The cold war sapped the economic rationale for hired armies. The United States and the Soviet Union funneled billions of dollars to client states to support their militaries. Why pay to hire an army when the superpowers would fund your own?[14]

The end of the cold war reversed the long decline in the practice of privatized warfare. All through the 1990s, nations in Latin America, Africa, and Asia began hiring private military companies to supplement, or sometimes even replace, state armies that had once been propped up by foreign aid. The private firms were hired to fight in a series of squalid wars in Africa, often involving clashes over resources like diamonds or oil. Executive Outcomes was one of the most famous. Its fighters, drawn largely from the ranks of elite squads from the apartheid-era South African Defense Forces, were hired by the Angolan government to retake an oil town seized in 1993 by Jonas Savimbi's UNITA rebels, backed by the United States during the cold war. A commando assault with eighty men returned the port city of Soyo to government control and proved the effectiveness of highly trained, well-equipped mercenaries versus a rebel army, even one as experienced as UNITA.[15]

Some international experts began to see the private firms as a solution to the small, vicious wars that dominated the post–cold war period. The international community was reluctant to commit troops to peacekeeping operations, and local governments were too weak to mount their own military operations. The private military companies filled the gap. They were often more disciplined than the armies that they sought to replace, and with better equipment and experience, they often did a better job in fighting. In Sierra Leone, Executive Outcomes defeated a guerrilla group, the Revolutionary United Front, infamous for press-ganging children into military service and amputating limbs from its civilian victims. In Afghanistan, private aid groups like CARE could not have safely operated without help from gun-toting contractors. At least one estimate put the annual revenue of the industry at $100 billion.[16]

In Iraq the private security companies took on their biggest role yet: they supplied the missing division that many military experts believed the U.S. Army needed in Iraq. Critics complained that the contractors were modern-day mercenaries, men with shadowy pasts hired to kill Iraqis for profit. But the United States could not have functioned in Iraq without the private companies. The military did not have troops to patrol vital strategic sites such as oil pipelines, electrical towers, or government ministries and buildings. It lacked the forces needed to protect the American officials and private contractors dedicated to restoring the country. Established private security groups like DynCorp and Armor Group, Global Risk and Hart, made up the difference. But so too did groups that materialized seemingly overnight to take advantage of the booming market for security: Custer Battles, Triple Canopy, and the aptly named Meteoric Tactical Solutions. The United States would pay more than it imagined for the army of private warriors that it helped to create.

PRIVATE BATTLES

On several occasions, private companies fought fierce, hours-long battles with Iraqi insurgents, especially in the days following the April uprising. In Kut, four contractors from Hart Security spent fourteen hours on the roof of their local headquarters building, fighting off ten times as many insurgents as coalition forces failed to respond to their pleas for help. One Hart worker was killed in the assault, his body later dismembered by the mob.[17] Across town at the same time, four Triple Canopy contractors and some three dozen Ukrainian soldiers battled a siege of the coalition's local headquarters by the Mahdi Army, guerrilla fighters loyal to the rebel cleric Muqtada Sadr, armed with rocket-propelled grenades and mortars. The Triple Canopy guards fired, by one estimate, 2,500 rounds of ammunition.[18]

The most publicized battle between private forces and insurgents took place the same week in Najaf, a religious center west of Kut, when eight Blackwater employees repelled an attack by the Mahdi Army to seize the local headquarters of the Coalition Provisional Authority. Trapped on the roof of the building, the men repelled snipers, RPGs, and gunfire during a harrowing firefight that saw three Blackwater employees wounded. As the hours passed and none of the local coalition forces responded to pleas for help, company executives sent in the firm's own helicopters to evacuate the wounded and resupply the contractors. (Bremer's staff approved dispatching the helicopters, which were normally used to ferry the ambassador and other VIPs around Iraq.) The men were down to tens of rounds of ammunition by the time help reached them.[19]

The private security companies strenuously rejected the term "mercenary" or even a reference to them as an army. The companies were limited — by U.S. military regulations, by contract, and by international law — to engaging only in defensive operations. They were supposed to respond to attacks, not initiate them. Nor were the private companies supposed to carry anything other than light weapons — machine guns, assault rifles, grenades. The contractors did shoot and kill Iraqis — but Iraq was a war zone. Insurgents frequently drove explosives-packed cars into convoys transporting officials. A security contractor had only seconds to decide whether an approaching vehicle was being driven by an insurgent or an innocent Iraqi.

The security companies claimed that several safeguards prevented abuses. Above all else, the companies argued that market forces checked bad behavior. A private firm that wanted to win more contracts had to uphold high standards. Each company set up strict rules of engagement for firing weapons. Cowboy employees were terminated at the first sign of poor discipline. Bad companies would be forced out as employers sought firms with records of outstanding service. That was the theory, at least. But Iraq was no ordinary market. Demand for security services was so high that companies with questionable reputations survived and some, such as Custer Battles, even prospered.

Beyond the market, several security companies banded together to lobby for better oversight — a rare instance of an industry seeking *increased* governmental regulation. In the United States, a security trade group with the Orwellian name International Peace Operations Association helped draft Defense Department guidelines for security contractors — more than two years into the war, the Pentagon still had no formalized procedures for regulating private military contractors. Rumsfeld was anxious to outsource the war but showed little interest in the details. In Iraq scores of companies had joined the Private Security Company Association of Iraq, a trade group whose creation was testimony to the boom in security business. The group's primary purpose was to share information on attacks with each other and the U.S. military — a sort of private intelligence network. But it also worked with Iraq's Ministry of the Interior to come up with a licensing system. Security contractors "don't want to shoot innocent people," said Lawrence Peters, the director of the Private Security Company Association. "But it's a war zone, and mistakes do happen."

I rode on SUV convoys with contractors from DynCorp, AKE, Erinys, and many others. In every case the men were serious, professional, and restrained. In Basra contractors from AEGIS Defense Services had even established their own hearts-and-minds operation. As we traveled down one back road toward an electrical plant, the convoy stopped in front of a squat cinder block house with a dirty curtain for a door. The convoy leader hopped out and brought a package of water bottles to an elderly woman who hobbled out of the home, surrounded by children. "We stop and give them a little something every now and again," the AEGIS contractor told me. "We want them to know there's a benefit to having us keep coming by."

ACCOUNTABILITY

Even though some contractors adeptly walked the line, their presence was a constant complication. They were neither dogs of war nor disciplined warriors checked by the market's invisible hand. They were instead a third force on the battlefield that the American government was ill prepared to control. The private contractors introduced problems of coordination, discipline, and transparency. "The contractors are making the mission of the U.S. military in Iraq more difficult," Joshua Schwartz, codirector of George Washington University's government procurement program, told a contracting symposium in the fall of 2005. The most notorious scandals of the reconstruction centered on private security companies. Some had killed innocent Iraqis or even shot at American soldiers. Others ripped off American taxpayers.

Marine colonel Thomas X. Hammes put his finger on the crux of the problem at a January 2005 conference in Washington about contractors on the battlefield. Simply put, the military and the private security contractors didn't have the same goals. The military's chief aim was to win the war; the contractors' goal was to make money. The two ends were not always in harmony. Hammes, an expert on insurgent warfare, pointed to the protection provided to Bremer by contractors from Blackwater as an example. Blackwater executives boasted that the company succeeded in performing its contract: the ambassador had survived. But in doing so, Blackwater alienated ordinary Iraqis, habitually pointing guns at Iraqi men, women, and children to keep them at bay, and speeding in convoys that blithely ran Iraqis off the road. Blackwater had protected the ambassador, but the military lost an opportunity to win hearts and minds that could have benefited thousands of U.S. soldiers. For Hammes, it was an uneven trade. "We can always get another ambassador," Hammes joked grimly.

Although on paper the contractors were regulated by the U.S. and Iraqi governments, in practice they answered to no one. By March 2006 not a single private security contractor had been convicted of any type of criminal wrongdoing by either the United States or Iraq. The spotless record was absurd on its face: either twenty thousand armed men in a hostile environment had conducted themselves as angels for three years, or someone in authority was not paying attention. "Any time you get a large group of people together in one place, bad things are going to happen," said one official disappointed by the United States' inability to crack down on contractors. The single biggest problem in Iraq surrounding the private security contractors was lack of accountability. They followed their own law.

Although the United States had no formal system in place to police the security contractors, I found out that the U.S. Army Corps of Engineers was asking the companies to voluntarily report insurgent attacks and other serious incidents in order to compile a daily intelligence briefing. After I filed a Freedom of Information Act request, the Army Corps gave me hundreds of pages of reports. The government blacked out names of companies and individuals. Still the documents were revealing. They showed that private security contractors played a leading role in the daily violence of Iraq.

About 11 percent of the nearly two hundred reports involved contractors firing toward civilian vehicles. In most cases the contractors received no fire from the Iraqi cars. Instead the contractors shot first to protect themselves from what they deemed a potential car bomb. Usually the contractors justified their decision to open fire by noting that the drivers failed to heed warning signs such as a clenched fist. In February 2004, for instance, a contractor reported opening fire on a black Opel after the driver did not respond to hand signals and a warning shot. The contractors fired twenty-three rounds from a Russian-made PKM machine gun and nine more shots from an AK-47 into the car. "We had to open fire directly into that car," wrote the contractor, adding with evident amazement: "Driver of that black Opel survived." The reports also provided numerous examples of lawlessness on the roads. In several cases they detailed traffic accidents involving Iraqis who either did not see or ignored security convoys. In one case a contractor with "very little warning" forced a car with an Iraqi man, woman, and child off the road. It slammed into a tree. It was "an example of unprofessional operating standards."

Another 20 percent of the reports provided evidence of communication failures between the security contractors and American forces. The reports documented what the military called "blue on blue" attacks — essentially friendly fire in which U.S. troops mistakenly shot at contractors. Contractors in Iraq frequently traveled in unmarked vehicles and did not always have reliable communications with military units. The rest of the reports were harrowing accounts of insurgent attacks on contractors that involved roadside bombs, ambushes, rocket-propelled grenades, mortar rounds, and machine-gun fire. It was clear that the private security contractors were very much involved in the war in Iraq.

The reports could have provided a starting point for investigation. But the contractors escaped scrutiny because they functioned in a legally sanctioned gray area. Under an order issued by the Coalition Provisional Authority, which stayed in effect under successive Iraqi governments, contractors accused of wrongdoing were supposed to be tried in their home countries. The order essentially gave the contractors immunity from Iraqi courts, but it did not obligate the United States or any other country to carry out prosecutions. Nor were there civil remedies in the case of property damage or wrongful death. Some security contractors had informal compensation programs which paid out cash to aggrieved parties, but such payments were entirely voluntarily and haphazard. In effect the Iraqis had no recourse to seek justice in either criminal or civil courts for wrongful actions by the contractors. The result was deep resentment among Iraqis that often transferred over to Americans in general.

The legal ambiguity surrounding contractors was markedly different from the system for the U.S. military. The army set up a formal commission, with offices in the Green Zone, which reviewed damages claims and made payments when troops were determined to have erred in opening fire on property or people. American troops suspected of shooting at Iraqis also faced trial in military tribunals. More than twenty U.S. service members were accused of crimes leading to the deaths of Iraqis, and at least ten were convicted. The military system wasn't perfect, of course. But it provided at least a path to justice. With the contractors, there was nothing but a dead end.

NO WARNING

The tragic killing of a nineteen-year-old Iraqi newlywed by security guards was a case in point.[20] Robert J. Callahan was the spokesman for the U.S. embassy in Iraq. In May 2004 he was wrapping up his tour of duty by saying farewell to reporters at different American newspapers and television stations, many of which were housed in walled, guarded compounds outside the Green Zone. As was typical for State Department officials, Callahan relied on Blackwater for transport around Baghdad. Callahan was returning from visiting friends at one media compound when his five-vehicle convoy turned onto a broad thoroughfare running through Baghdad's Masbah neighborhood, an area of five-story office buildings and ground-level shops.

At the same moment, Mohammed Nouri Hattab, thirty-two, was headed north on the road in his Opel. A truck driver for the state oil company, Hattab was moonlighting as a taxi driver, transporting two passengers he had picked up moments earlier. Hattab looked up and saw Callahan's five-car convoy speed out of a side street in front of him. He was slowing to a stop about fifty feet from the convoy when he heard a burst of gunfire ring out, he said. Bullets shot through the hood of his Opel, cut into his shoulder, and pierced the chest of nineteen-year-old Yas Ali Mohammed Yassiri, who was in the backseat, killing him. The second passenger escaped without serious injury. The convoy roared on, leaving chaos in its wake. "There was no warning. It was a sudden attack," Hattab told me. On background, one U.S. official said that embassy officials had reviewed the shooting and determined that two Blackwater employees in the convoy that day had not followed proper procedures to warn Hattab to stay back; instead they opened fire prematurely. The two employees were fired, the U.S. official said, and shipped home. The workers were never prosecuted, and it was not clear whether the State Department even bothered to inform the Justice Department of the findings of their investigation. Blackwater declined to comment.

I met with Hattab in the restaurant in the shabby lobby of the Al Hamra Hotel and journeyed with him to the scene of the shooting. His descriptions of the incident matched with the account that I received from the U.S. official. A slight man who was no longer able to move his right arm, Hattab said he had been shot at by Americans three times since the U.S. invasion in 2003. Once he had been watching the American invasion from the rooftop of his home in Najaf when soldiers saw him and opened fire. On the second occasion, he was driving a truck when an American military convoy passed by and fired rubber bullets into his windshield, shattering it. On both occasions, he said, the U.S. troops later apologized when he complained about his treatment.

But in this incident, Hattab described an endless legal fight for compensation. Like many Iraqis, Hattab had only a hazy notion of the difference between the military and the contractors. To him they were all agents for the same government, and so he had first gone to the U.S. military compensation board. After the army informed him that they had no patrols in the area on that day, Hattab had gone to the Iraqi courts. There a judge told him he needed to return to the Americans. He had bounced around for months while on disability leave from his job, his pay cut in half to $51 a month.

The family of his passenger, Yassiri, fared no better. A Shiite from an impoverished neighborhood in Najaf, the newlywed was on a trip to Baghdad when he got into the taxi with Hattab near the Palestine Hotel. Sitting in their two-room home on a dusty, unpaved street, family members said it was a reporter who told them that Yassiri had been killed by private guards and not U.S. soldiers, as they had earlier been told. "What was my innocent son's crime?" asked Zahra Ridha, Yassiri's mother.

The poor Shiites of Najaf were among those who welcomed American troops as liberators, having suffered badly under Saddam's regime. But the occupation and constant bloodshed, the confusion and violence, turned the welcome into a wellspring of resentment. Blackwater's execution of one poor Shiite teenager created another pocket of anger. "We lived in poverty and oppression during the time of Saddam, and we were expecting the opposite when he left," said Adil Jasim, twenty-six, a family friend. "I say that the situation is the same and even worse. American forces came to occupy and to achieve their goals. They don't care about Iraqis."

If the Iraqis suffered at the hands of private contractors, so too did the American taxpayer. The private security contractors were often cowboys, turning potential friends into enemies. Many of the biggest scandals in the reconstruction revolved around fly-by-night security companies that appeared out of nowhere — sometimes with support from U.S. officials. Security guards from a company called Zapata were arrested by the U.S. Marine Corps in Fallujah after allegedly shooting at soldiers and Iraqis on a wild ride through town. The contractors were released and kicked out of Iraq, but some later came back with other security companies. Erinys International was a South African company that had allied with A. Huda Farouki, Chalabi's friend, to win an $80 million contract to provide security guards for Iraq's oil pipeline. An audit by the inspector general found that the government managed the contract poorly, leaving the pipeline vulnerable to attacks that crippled oil production. Even Jay Garner's military aide got caught up in the stampede. Col. Kim Olson was reprimanded and had to resign from the air force after she admitted to opening the U.S. branch of a South African security firm while she was working for the Coalition Provisional Authority in the summer of 2003.

One private security company came to be synonymous with corruption and lawlessness in Iraq. The firm's very name evoked the Wild West: Custer Battles. The connotation was unsettlingly accurate.

WILD WEST

Baghdad International Airport is where the city begins its surrender to the hard, spare country around it. To the east the Tigris River slips through the capital's heart, past the crowded old city that gave rise to a civilization, past the dusty groves of date palms and the marbled riverside mansions of Saddam Hussein. Just to the west, on the other side of the airport's gray apron of runway, the urban sprawl vanishes into the onion fields and irrigation ditches of poor farmers. Farther out, the green patches give way to the barbed wire walls of Abu Ghraib prison, violent towns huddled along the Euphrates River, and finally the stark, blistering nothing of Iraq's western desert. The airport is a sort of frontier, Baghdad's last outpost between the city and the wastelands beyond it.

In April 2003 that outpost had been overrun by an invading army, a churning mass of steel, cat track, and cannon. The Third Infantry Division's Abrams M1A1 tanks punched holes in the perimeter walls. Its gunners pounded the grounds with artillery rounds, reducing to rubble buildings that housed the Iraqi army's Republican Guard.[21] Air force bombs pitted the two main runways with craters the size of minivans. The French-built terminal, a five-story tan-and-white structure that looked vaguely like a radiator grille, was reduced to a dark shell. The building was left with neither power nor running water. The employees fled. Inside, the windows were shattered and wires dangled from the ceiling. The walls were inexplicably smeared with shit.[22]

The man picked to clean up the mess was Frank Hatfield, a gray-haired cop who ran security for the Federal Aviation Administration back in Washington. Hatfield had volunteered to come to Baghdad to get the airport working, but he was running out of time. Jerry Bremer wanted the airport open fast. In a show that Iraq was returning to normal, Prime Minister Tony Blair was planning to fly in on July 15 on a British Airways flight. The airport had to be ready by then.

Working in Iraq was like tying your shoes in quicksand. Even simple tasks took forever. There were no phones. No computers. No Internet. Nobody was coming to work. One of Hatfield's pressing needs was finding someone to play sheriff at the airport: screen passengers, check baggage, patrol the grounds. Lt. Gen. Ricardo Sanchez, the commander of coalition forces, had told Bremer that his troops were already stretched too thin to guard government buildings and property. Bremer had reported the concern to Rumsfeld as well, but there were no more soldiers coming — not now, not ever. As a result the coalition would have to hire private security companies to do the job. A blue-collar cop at heart, Hatfield did not have any expertise in government contracting, but he put together a committee to select a company, drew up a crude job description, and posted a notice on a bulletin board at the Republican Palace, where the newly formed American-led Coalition Provisional Authority had set up headquarters. Custer Battles was one of the first companies to answer the call.

At the time, Custer Battles was essentially two people: Scott Custer and Mike Battles, two army buddies looking to make some cash in Iraq. Battles had taken a taxi from Amman to Baghdad in May, arriving with $450 in his pocket. Baby-faced and soft-spoken, he heard about the need for airport police while prowling the crowded black-and-white marble corridors of the palace, a sprawling compound on the banks of the Tigris. When Battles found out about the possible job offer, he called Custer, who was working back in the United States. In two frenzied days, they put together an ambitious proposal to deploy guards, hire baggage screeners, and set up a checkpoint with dogs and bomb-sniffing devices, all in two weeks — faster than the two established security companies competing against them.

It was a plan that mixed adrenaline, audacity, and blind ambition. At the time, Custer and Battles were broke. The men had maxed out their credit cards, taken out home equity loans, and raided their IRAs, plummeting themselves $50,000 in debt.[23] Custer even bummed cash from a friend to pay for his airplane ticket to fly to Baghdad.[24] Custer Battles had neither weapons nor accountants. Neither man had any experience in airport security. They were competing against companies that did security business all over the world, like DynCorp International and Armor Group International Ltd, a British firm.[25] Custer Battles had never even held a government contract before.[26]

None of that made a difference. Hatfield was desperate, and Custer and Battles were promising to do the job faster than anybody else. If Hatfield had doubts about their qualifications, he didn't let them show. On July 1 he signed a $16.8 million contract with Custer Battles. Nor did he lose faith when Battles revealed days later that the company's supposed loan guarantee had fallen through. Indeed, with the deadline ticking to Blair's flight, Hatfield promised to help.

"Give me an idea of what you need to spend and why. I'll try to get you paid. Please move as fast as you can," Hatfield told Battles as they stood outside the Republican Palace in 100-degree heat. Hatfield nervously smoked a cigarette. "I promise I won't fuck you."

"That was as technical a contracting term as I had been exposed to at that time," said Battles, laughing as he recalled the incident later.[27]

A few days later Hatfield descended to a vault in the palace that held millions of dollars in shrink-wrapped stacks of hundred-dollar bills. He stuffed some of the cash into old cardboard boxes that had once held military rations. He then handed the money to Battles.[28] Battles later expressed astonishment that he was given a handwritten receipt by Hatfield's colleague Doug Gould and told not to worry about the informality. "The contracting process would catch up" later, Gould told Battles.[29]

Hatfield had given Battles $2 million.

Over the next year, Custer Battles became the business success story of Iraq. Scott Custer and Mike Battles were the golden boys, two hard-charging thirty-somethings who risked big and hit big. They won a deal to help replace dinars bearing Saddam's portrait with new currency, another deal to guard electrical towers, and yet another to secure shipments of uniforms for the new Iraqi army. The duo even opened an airline called the Flying Carpet to move passengers and cash in and out of Iraq.

Their plans were endless, tumbling out like a fevered business-school brainstorming session. They wanted to get into shrimp farming, home loans, and a skin care company that specialized in cosmetics made without pig fat or alcohol to respect Muslim customs. The CIA even hired the two men, paying Custer Battles under a clandestine "black contract" to purchase ordinary-looking Iraqi cars and secretly equip them with bulletproof armor. The black Mercedeses, BMWs, and taxis that Custer Battles procured were used by the agency to discreetly move around the country in the hunt for Saddam Hussein.[30] Battles even started writing a book, a business plan for the upside of peril called "Blood in the Streets: Seizing Opportunity in Crises."

Quickly Custer and Battles grew rich. The company's revenue rose from just under $200,000 in the first six months of 2003 to $32 million by the second half, a growth rate faster than the early days of Google, Inc.[31] By 2004 the firm was claiming $100 million in contracts and had plans to bring in twice that by the following year. Battles said he made $3 million in salary. Media favorites, the partners would talk about the private security business on national TV; nobody else in that secretive world would even return a phone call. Battles made regular appearances as a security expert on the Fox network. The men were profiled on the front page of the *Wall Street Journal*.[32]

What made the company's rise so astonishing was not the fast pace, but that it occurred at all. Custer and Battles won government deals even as an ever-growing number of coalition officials believed the company was in-competent, inept, or criminal. During their first six months of business in Iraq, more than a half-dozen senior U.S. government officials or consul-tants came to suspect wrongdoing. In at least one case, a retired general thought that Custer Battles's service was so bad that it put soldiers' lives at risk. "They never could accomplish the mission," said Gen. Hugh Tant, who had to bring in army trucks and soldiers to replace the bald-tired lemons that Custer Battles provided to move currency around Iraq.[33] But their mission had never been to save the troops or stabilize Iraq. Their mis-sion had been to make as much money for themselves as possible, and on that front Custer and Battles were heroes.

COMMANDO RAID

Custer and Battles slipped easily into the frenzy of the first summer of the occupation. Battles was a failed Republican congressional candidate from Rhode Island. Within a month of his 2002 campaign loss, he brought his political connections to a partnership with Custer, his old army buddy and a distant relative to the infamous general. Undeterred by the memories of Little Bighorn, the men named their new venture Custer Battles. Private se-curity was an occupation filled with mercenaries and soldiers of fortune who had served in the world's dark corners. But Custer and Battles saw themselves as something different. Theirs was a clinical approach to the messy business of hired guns. They were not cowboys. They were "Green Berets with MBAs," Battles boasted.[34] They aimed at becoming the masters of chaos.

The two men appeared to personify the melding of the boardroom and bloodshed. Battles was the smooth, outgoing public face, responsible for using his political contacts to win public contracts. He had spent six years in the army, rising to the rank of captain before joining the CIA, where he had worked overseas to recruit covert agents. Afterward he had kicked around in a series of jobs, once even working as a professional bull rider.[35] He eventually returned to his home in Rhode Island and decided to run for Congress in 2002.

Battles ran on a vow to restore honor to the government. His staff were former aides to Senator Lincoln Chafee, and he attracted high-level Repub-lican interest. Mississippi governor and former Republican National Com-mittee chair Haley Barbour sent money. Arizona senator John McCain endorsed him. Battles's campaign events were apple-pie Americana: red, white, and blue helium balloons, hot dogs for the crowd, clowns for the kids. Custer helped coordinate Battles's biggest campaign stunt, when he walked fifty-five miles across the length of Rhode Island's First Congressional District. Even in punishing heat, the slim, bespectacled West Point grad wore khakis and a blue jacket.[36] But despite being the local Republican Party's officially endorsed candidate, he lost in the primary to a more conservative Republican, 41 percent to 25 percent.

Custer was the brains of the outfit, more cerebral and reserved. He spent a decade in the army before leaving to go to school at Georgetown University. There he got a master's degree in international relations. Custer, with narrow eyes and an upturned nose, grew chubby in postmilitary life. He dabbled in security consulting for a nonprofit group called Relief Solutions and another firm called Blue Sky Strategies Consulting, both of which worked with humanitarian groups in places like Afghanistan. He also advised utility companies on how to protect water sources from terrorist attack. Although he was a Democrat, he liked to brag about Battles's political connections. He once told a criminal investigator that Battles had close ties to the White House.

One of the first to suspect problems with Custer Battles and the airport security contract was Col. Richard Ballard of the U.S. Army. A thin man with a pale face and dark, penetrating eyes, Ballard was the inspector general for the army's Fifth Corps. Ballard had crossed the LD, or line of departure, into Iraq on the second day of the U.S. invasion. He was the designated watchdog for the entire coalition, the U.S. military's top investigator in Iraq. Pentagon brass wanted Ballard's early entry into the war zone to serve as a warning to troops to be on their best behavior.

Once Jay Garner's mission had collapsed and the United States geared up for a longer, larger occupation, Ballard's job expanded dramatically. Ballard went from overseeing some 43,000 soldiers in the Fifth Corps to overseeing 196,000 soldiers serving in the Coalition Joint Task Force Seven, as the combined forces from different countries were known. Overnight the budget that Ballard had to watch soared from $65 million to $2.5 billion. He had eight people to do the work. Throughout May and June, there was a frenzy of contracting. Concerned about the possibility of abuse, Lieutenant General Sanchez, the U.S. ground forces commander, issued a specific directive to Ballard to investigate a dozen contracts that had been issued to private security companies. Ballard's attention soon fixed on Custer Battles. In a matter of days after Battles signed the $16 million contract with Hatfield, conditions at the airport had changed drastically for the worse. In early July insurgents had attacked the airport with mortar rounds and AK-47 fire. The hope of quickly opening the airport evaporated. With it so did the necessity for much of the work called for in the contract with Custer Battles, which included things like hiring screeners to check bags.

Ballard's first step was to review the contract itself. What he found surprised him. It was all of two pages long. Attached to the back was the original proposal written by the company and a reference to an Annex A that he could not find. "My fifth-grade son or daughter could have written the contract. It was the most cursory, boilerplate, joke of a contract that I had ever seen," Ballard told me. Of course Hatfield, who had issued the original contract, had no background in contracting, and the army captain who was in charge of overseeing payments to Custer Battles had never held such a responsibility before. Battles would later say that the company itself had simply written an initial version of the contract, sending a copy for signing to the Coalition Provisional Authority.

Ballard's worries grew when he saw the company in action. Custer Battles had set up a checkpoint outside the airport, which sprawls across thirty-two thousand acres. Hard against the airport was a neighborhood of two-story, dun-colored homes housing former officers in Saddam's army. During an inspection in July, Ballard heard gunfire from the neighborhood. He assumed it was the sort of celebratory shooting that frequently filled the air in Baghdad, perhaps teenagers firing toward the airport in a show of bravado.

As Ballard approached the checkpoint, he saw two Custer Battles employees creeping along a fence toward the homes where the gunfire had originated. The two men had on black fatigues, bandoliers of ammunition, and camouflage face paint. At the checkpoint, another Custer Battles employee was casually firing an M16 into the air in an apparent attempt to keep the shooting from resuming. Ballard realized he was witnessing a commando raid by the private guards on a handful of Iraqi teenagers. He ordered an immediate halt to the attack, since it was illegal under international law for private military companies to conduct offensive military operations.

"I thought this was an extremely grave situation," Ballard said. "I told them, 'You are jeopardizing all of us.'" The Custer Battles crew responded with a shrug.

RED FLAGS

After the airport checkpoint incident, Ballard paid even closer attention to Custer Battles, which had taken over Terminal D at the airport and turned it into its headquarters.[37] At a time when U.S. soldiers were still living in tents, Custer Battles had built a pool, installed air-conditioning, and set up a wireless Internet connection for themselves. They could afford to, with the government shoveling money at them.

During one inspection Ballard talked with about a dozen Custer Battles guys who were inspecting incoming vehicles. All the men present, he said, told him that they had no training before arriving in Iraq, neither on their weapons nor on the legal standards they were supposed to follow as private contractors. Some of the men were Gurkhas, Nepalese guards trained by the British Army, that Custer Battles was luring away from another security company hired to protect the Green Zone. None spoke Arabic and no translators were present to quiz drivers, most of them Iraqis who spoke no English — or, for that matter, Nepalese.

In twenty separate inspections, there were never any dog teams present to hunt for possible explosives. Once, Ballard told me, he saw Custer Battles employees simply waving trucks into the airport without bothering to check the trunks. When he asked what was going on, a Custer Battles employee told them that Bremer had personally ordered them to speed trucks through after the ambassador had witnessed a long backup. Bremer told Ballard that he had never issued such an order. "I went berserk. They were doing it on their own," Ballard said.

Furious, Ballard demanded the opportunity to inspect Custer Battles headquarters. Employees refused him permission to enter. He asked to inspect the company's dog kennels. He was blocked by armed Custer Battles guards. Ballard went to Sanchez, the commanding officer, and got a special directive to access the Custer Battles compound. Still Custer refused, telling Ballard that he did not have the authority to investigate since he worked for the military while the firm's contract was signed by the Coalition Provisional Authority.

"If I don't have the authority to review your contract, who does?" Ballard asked.

"Nobody," Custer told him.

By October 2003 Ballard recommended terminating Custer Battles's contract. But before he could follow up, the Abu Ghraib prison scandal broke out. Although it would not become public for several months, all of Ballard's time was devoted to investigating reports of prisoner abuse. By November, Ballard had developed medical problems and was sent to Germany for treatment. In the end he took no action against the company. Custer Battles had escaped.

Custer Battles continued to guard the airport until June 2004, when the coalition awarded a new contract to a different company. By that time Doug Gould, who had served on the committee that originally selected Custer Battles, had returned for another tour of duty at the airport. Although the company had been repeatedly criticized, Gould delivered a glowing letter of recommendation to a Department of Defense official who was considering awarding the firm yet another contract. "Custer Battles is one of the best firms I have dealt with in my 34 years of government service," he wrote. A U.S. official said Gould, who has never spoken publicly about the case, was aware of "rumors" about problems with Custer Battles, but had no definitive information. "Nothing was raised as a red flag," the U.S. official said.

When I visited Ballard in his suburban Virginia home on a snowy day in January 2005, he had just retired from service. He said that he regretted that he had not been able to do more. Like any good military officer, he had developed a list of "lessons learned" from his time in Iraq. "This was a unique environment that developed on the fly without adequate planning, preparation, or what-iffing," Ballard said. "The military was required to conduct significant postconflict missions that it had not anticipated, had not rehearsed, and was not equipped to conduct."

As for Custer and Battles, he simply concluded that they were "rip-off artists."

"In my opinion, they went to Baghdad to see if they could get a piece of the action. They perceived it as an open door — no checks, no balances." And they were right.

OPERABLE TRUCKS

Soon after Custer Battles won the airport deal, it landed a second job to help destroy Iraq's old currency, stamped with Saddam's face, and replace it with newly minted money. Once again the two men found themselves in the middle of one of the biggest jobs in Iraq. Logistically the task called for visiting the two hundred or so banks in Iraq and collecting every single dinar in circulation — 13,000 tons of paper that, stretched end to end, would have circled the earth thirty-two times.[38] At the same time, the coalition had to fly in 2,400 tons' worth of new dinars and redistribute them throughout Iraq. All of it had to take place in three months, in the middle of an increasingly dangerous war zone.

Custer Battles was supposed to build camps to house workers at the project's three main hubs in Mosul, Basra, and the Baghdad airport. And they were supposed to bring in the five-ton trucks needed to haul the money around Iraq. Custer Battles signed a contract with the coalition government for $9.8 million on August 27, 2003. By the next month, however, the coalition team heading the project was growing frustrated. Custer Battles had missed deadlines to set up the camps. The food was substandard. More than half of the trucks they supplied had broken down. Subcontractors that supplied Internet and other services to the camps complained that they were not being paid.[39] Cabins to house workers were so overcrowded that the coalition began to worry about health problems.[40]

Coalition officials called Custer and Battles in for a meeting on October 18 to explain the delays. It was stormy. Battles rightly pointed out that the size of the mission had expanded, requiring more people and more supplies. He accused the coalition of changing the terms of the contract and then not paying for the inevitable increases. Custer Battles had gone "out on a limb" for the government, he argued, and wanted a formal letter of apology for criticizing the firm's performance.[41]

For their part, the coalition officials accused Custer and Battles of falling down on the job. At one point, Hugh Tant, the retired white-haired general in charge of the money exchange, told Custer and Battles that the trucks the company had imported from Syria were breaking down. They were too small to get the job done. The brakes didn't work. The tires were bald. Tant found the whole situation "appalling." To replace Custer Battles's broken vehicles, he had been forced to call generals in Iraq that he knew from his army days and beg them to loan him military trucks. The convoys were taking fire all over the country, and he thought that U.S. soldiers were being needlessly put in harm's way because Custer Battles was providing lousy trucks.

Custer and Battles stood up in response and threatened to walk out of the room and off the job — a potentially crippling delay.

"I have to have operable trucks," Tant told the men.

"You asked for trucks. Whether they are operable or not doesn't matter," one of the men roared back.[42]

After the meeting ended, Jeff Ottenbreit, a consultant at work on the project, noticed that Custer and Battles had left behind a printout of an Excel spreadsheet on the table. The spreadsheet appeared to show that Custer Battles was artificially boosting profits. It indicated that the company had invoiced the government $2.1 million for $913,000 worth of work — doubling its profit on a contract that was supposed to have a 25 percent profit cap. Custer Battles bought a digital camera for $100, then charged the coalition $400 for it. A printer that cost $365 was reimbursed at $1,000. A flatbed truck bought for $18,000 wound up costing the government $80,000.[43] Ottenbreit, an accountant for BearingPoint, would turn this information over to criminal investigators. The document was inescapably damning, and a few weeks later, William "Pete" Baldwin, the Custer Battles employee in charge of the money exchange project, resigned after a meeting with coalition officials and walked down the hallway of the Republican Palace to the warren of cubicles where the Pentagon's inspector general had a desk. There he began to describe a complex scheme to defraud the government.

According to Baldwin, who had spent twenty years in the construction industry, Custer had talked repeatedly about wanting to make more than the 25 percent profit cap built into the money exchange contract. Under pressure from the coalition to show receipts for their purchases, Custer and Battles created a series of offshore companies in the Grand Cayman Islands, including one called the MT Holding Corporation. Employees were instructed not to disclose the ownership of the companies to the coalition. Custer Battles used the companies to write up fake leases and bills with artificially high prices. Custer Battles then submitted the faked invoices to the coalition for reimbursement, thereby boosting its profit. An investigating agent found that the address of one of the companies was an abandoned building in Baghdad.

Baldwin's accusations were backed up by his friend, a former FBI agent named Robert Isakson, who had briefly worked for Custer Battles in setting up the camps at Baghdad airport. Isakson described overhearing similar discussions about setting up fake companies. Together the two men filed a False Claims Act lawsuit against Custer Battles, charging that the company had defrauded the government. Such suits are one of the federal government's primary anticorruption tools. The act encourages contractor employees to report fraud by promising them a cut of any money returned to the government.

Baldwin's account was further bolstered by Custer Battles's own internal investigation, undertaken in response to the growing coalition concerns over abuse. Custer and Battles hired a former government fraud investigator to review the contract. Pete Miscovich's report in January 2004 contained no good news. It found at least $2 million in fraudulent invoices. In a memo Miscovich said that "a clear criminal act had occurred" and that he had "no doubt . . . that elements of money laundering [were] evident."[44] His report concluded: "The documents are prima facie evidence of a course of conduct consistent with criminal activity and intent."[45] Subsequently Custer and Battles fired the man who signed the money exchange contract, a West Point graduate and former Proctor & Gamble executive named Joe Morris. They accused Morris of stealing thousands of dollars from the company's petty cash fund, using it to buy a Mercedes-Benz and taking a mistress on a shopping trip to Paris.[46] Morris would deny those charges, but acknowledged paying bribes to help the company move goods into Iraq. He called Custer and Battles "two assholes who were in over their heads."[47]

WAR PROFITEERS

Despite it all, Custer and Battles remained brash and defiant, insisting that they had done no wrong and attacking their accusers as unreliable. Isakson, they claimed, was a disgruntled employee who left Custer Battles on bad terms. In addition his trustworthiness was in question: one of Isakson's companies was being sued by USAID on fraud charges. (Isakson denied wrongdoing.) Baldwin was also suspect. After quitting Custer Battles he had gone on to form his own security firm in Iraq, AISG, and Custer Battles attorneys portrayed Baldwin's complaint as an attack by a competitor. Miscovich, who continued to work as the company's internal fraud investigator, later distanced himself from his conclusions, saying they were only preliminary. Certainly, Custer and Battles acknowledged, it was possible that the company had made mistakes in submitting paperwork to the government. But Custer and Battles themselves had nothing to do with such details. Nor had there ever been an intention to cheat anyone. The company had fulfilled all the work required by its contracts in the middle of a war zone — a task that required ingenuity, hard work, and flexibility. Their reward had been to witness the destruction of their reputations. "The rules were nightmarish. They didn't really exist. Radar O'Reilly from

M*A*S*H would clearly go to jail under these rules," said Jack Boese, one of Custer Battles's attorneys, referring to the television character famous for maneuvering through military bureaucracy.[48]

Despite the suspicions of fraud both inside and outside the company, the CPA continued to pay Custer Battles. Even after the Pentagon's criminal investigators formally opened a case in October 2003, coalition officials approved $5.6 million in additional payments. In their internal discussions, they noted that the contract was being paid from Iraqi oil revenues that the Americans controlled during the occupation, not with U.S. taxpayer dollars. If any investigation turned up fraud, they could always try to recover the money later.[49] "Termination of work by Custer Battles . . . would have a disastrous impact on the success of the currency exchange program," Al Runnels, then the chief financial officer for the Coalition Provisional Authority, wrote in a memo in November 2003.[50] Action was more important than accountability.

The Bush administration never made any serious attempt to recoup the money. Pentagon auditors' efforts to examine the company's books ended in failure when Custer Battles attorneys blocked the inquiry. The coalition official who wrote the contract forgot to include standard language that permitted such audits. The Justice Department refused to join the lawsuit filed by Baldwin and Isakson, apparently concluding that there were too many fuzzy legal issues: Was the allegedly pilfered money actually U.S. funds? Since the contracting officers were working for the coalition, did U.S. law even apply? The FBI's criminal investigation dragged on, without charges being filed. The only action the government ever took against the company was to issue an order barring Custer Battles from receiving more contracts — nearly a year after the first signs of fraud surfaced. In the interim, new contracts and millions of dollars continued to flow toward Custer Battles.

For their part, Baldwin and Isakson continued to pursue their False Claims suit with the help of their lawyer, a crusading antifraud attorney named Alan Grayson. Grayson, a tall man with a fondness for cowboy boots and fine tailored suits, had made a small fortune in a telecom start-up and moved to Florida, where he continued to run a small law firm back in DC. He was a fiery liberal, outraged by the war in Iraq and convinced that the Bush administration let Custer and Battles off the hook because of their Republican connections. He called the two men "war whores." After investing more than two years' work and nearly a million dollars of his firm's own money, Grayson was vindicated in March 2006 — almost three years after Custer and Battles had made their way to Iraq in search of a fortune. A jury found that Custer Battles had bilked the CPA out of millions of dollars. They had to pay fines and penalties totaling more than $10 million. "There is an orgy of greed among contractors in Iraq, and the Bush administration is for all practical purposes participating in it," Grayson said after the verdict, the first of its kind. "They have done nothing to get the taxpayers' money back. They've done nothing to punish the wrongdoers."

Frank Willis was another in the long line of coalition officials suspicious about Custer Battles. A retired Transportation Department official, he spent six months in Iraq working as a deputy adviser to the Transportation Ministry. After his return to the United States, Willis became one of the most vocal critics of the government's oversight of the reconstruction effort, with the Custer Battles deal as Exhibit One. At a congressional panel sponsored by Democrats — Republicans refused to allow a formal hearing — Willis testified about his concerns. He brought with him a photograph that became one of the more memorable images of Iraq's fast and loose environment. It was a picture of Willis and Darrell Trent, his boss, standing at a table stacked with $2 million in cash — a payment for Custer Battles. Willis said he and Trent had played football with the money, tossing about bricks of cash worth $100,000 each. When he had called Battles to pick up the payment, he told him: "Bring a bag."[51]

Such free and easy handouts from the government were common for Custer Battles. They never encountered any significant resistance to their schemes. They blocked the few government employees who raised questions and waited out the rest. They knew that the coalition was rotating people in and out of Iraq every few months. They knew there was too much to be done and too few people to do it. It didn't matter if they provided trucks that didn't work; or if their men conducted commando raids; or if they submitted fake signatures and backdated documents. They knew that they were working on a schedule that permitted no delays, no second thoughts, no time-outs. It was a system ripe for abuse. And they worked it.

"They are what I call war profiteers," Willis told me. "It's called playing the chaos, and they were masters at it."

The private security companies played an important role in Iraq. Their presence meant fewer soldiers on the ground — and, not coincidentally, allowed the Bush administration to keep down both troop counts and fatalities. If that had been their only part, the firms would have been a strategic and political success. But the Pentagon was not in any position to police their private police. As a result, as the numbers of private contractors sky-rocketed after the outbreak of violence in the spring of 2004, many of the private contractors ran wild, alienating Iraqis and possibly making Iraq more dangerous with their violent and sometimes lawless behavior. The companies ripped off U.S. taxpayers too — but as American investigators were beginning to find out, the firms were only the tip of the spear when it came to fraud, waste, and abuse.

9

Blind Mice

Nervous about the reports of fraud and corruption streaming out of Iraq all through the summer and fall of 2003, Congress demanded oversight. The Bush administration finally responded by choosing a scholarly, guitar-picking attorney named Stuart Bowen as its watchdog. Nearly a year after work had begun, with billions already spent, the new inspector general for the reconstruction of Iraq made his first trip to Baghdad in February 2004. It did not take long for signs of trouble to emerge. Bowen had talked to Jerry Bremer, David Nash, and some other senior officials, but his face was unknown in the Republican Palace. As he walked through the marbled hallways one morning, he passed two men talking in guarded tones. One said to the other: "We can't do it that way anymore. The inspector general is here."

The two were among the few people in either Baghdad or Washington who actually worried about Bowen. Democrats had greeted the news of his appointment with derision. Senator Hillary Clinton accused the Republicans of creating a "fake inspector general."[1] Representative Henry Waxman said Bowen had a conflict of interest. There was, in fact, every reason to think that Bowen would not be particularly aggressive in exposing corruption in Iraq that might embarrass the Bush administration. He was, after all, one of George W. Bush's most loyal allies, one of only a handful of lawyers that Bush brought with him to the White House from Texas, a man who once threatened elections officials in Florida with arrest to force them to count ballots presumed favorable to the president. Worse yet, Bowen had no experience as an inspector general. He had never worked as an auditor, nor had he ever been to Iraq. When he met with Paul Wolfowitz, then Secretary

Rumsfeld, both men asked with apparent amazement why he had taken the job. Rumsfeld called the position "extremely difficult and politically problematic." "I started to wonder, what have I gotten myself into?" Bowen later told me.

The answer came soon after, as Bowen began making monthly trips to Baghdad in the spring of 2004. During a stay at the Hilton Hotel in Kuwait City, he noticed that contractors were splurging on the free laundry service and lunchtime buffet offered to government executives headed to and from Iraq. He dinged KBR, the contractor, for allowing unauthorized personnel access and for putting its employees up in expensive hotel rooms. Savings: $3.6 million per year. He got furtive visits from contractors working in the comptroller's office, who worried about the free and easy access to money in a vault in the palace basement. Bowen's auditor discovered that the key to the safe through which $600 million flowed was kept in an open backpack sitting out in the comptroller's office.

Bowen also found out how murky the contracting system had become. He got a tip that one coalition official was scheming to cut private deals with Iraqi and American construction companies. The official was fired over the allegations, but shortly before leaving, he convinced Bremer to sign a $6 million, no-bid contract with a security firm. When Bowen found out, he ordered the contract canceled. The security firm's owner had already received $3 million and left the country. The experience taught Bowen that money was moving out of the coalition far too quickly, with far too few controls. "It didn't take much to get some money out of the vault," he said.

Bowen would surprise the skeptics. He became the most credible critic of the reconstruction and the most vocal advocate for its reform. He pushed hard for the arrest of U.S. military officers and contractors suspected of corruption and embezzlement. He also had a flair for the creative, using satellite images to check on the pace of work at construction sites and hiring engineers to accompany his investigators. He did what he called "real time auditing." Unlike most government investigators, who deliver their findings months and even more than a year after an inspection, Bowen turned his reports around in weeks. Bowen wanted to fix problems as they happened — and there were plenty of problems. As he began picking them apart during the spring of 2004, he found a common thread: a pot of gold that seemed to be little more than a coalition slush fund. It was called the Development Fund for Iraq.

EASY MONEY

The Development Fund was created after the invasion by United Nations Resolution 1483, which spelled out the guidelines for the U.S.-led coalition's occupation of Iraq. The fund was essentially a bank account for Iraq's oil revenue. It was also designed to hold the nearly $1 billion in cash that American soldiers had found hidden away in homes and offices controlled by Saddam and his cronies. Finally, the account had so-called vested funds, mostly money frozen in Iraqi bank accounts held abroad in the United States. All told, the fund held more than $20 billion. The resolution required the coalition to use the money in "a transparent manner to meet the humanitarian needs of the Iraqi people." It was Iraqi money, but the United States was responsible for safeguarding it.

During the first summer of the occupation, Bremer decided to set up an ad hoc mechanism to spend money from the fund. First he created the Program Review Board, a council consisting of ten coalition officials who would jointly review proposals and award contracts. In keeping with the UN resolution requiring "consultation" with the Iraqi interim government, the board had a single Iraqi representative, but he had little power and didn't show up often. (Finance Minister Kamil Mubdir Gailani attended just one session of the board's twenty meetings in fall 2003.)[2] The board immediately established itself as a rubber stamp that approved nearly any contracts that the occupation government wanted to issue.

A second order made it easier to spend Iraqi cash than American reconstruction dollars approved by Congress. Coalition Provisional Authority Memorandum No. 4 set out contracting guidelines that ran for 31 pages, as opposed to the 1,923-page-long U.S. regulations. Proposals could be posted and awarded in a single day. Contracts did not have to be competitively bid. Protests were limited. Contracts bigger than a half million were supposed to be reviewed by at least three people, but the requirement could be waived. Waste, fraud, or abuse had to be disclosed to unspecified "appropriate authorities."

The guidelines, in short, turned the Iraqi funds into easy money, and the coalition wasted no time spending it. The biggest single beneficiary was, not surprisingly, Halliburton.

Back home in Washington, Representative Henry Waxman was complaining about the high prices the United States was paying to the Houston company to import fuel into Iraq. American taxpayers were paying Halliburton prices that were double what it cost the Pentagon's own fuel agency to import gas. Rather than force the price down, the coalition stuck the Iraqis with the bill. That fall the American-controlled Program Review Board began paying Halliburton's contracts with money from the Development Fund for Iraq instead of taxpayer dollars, directing $1.64 billion to the company to cover the sky-high fuel prices.[3]

Halliburton was not the only company to benefit, of course. When it came to dishing out the Iraqis' money, the coalition was hardly a discerning shopper. Custer Battles, the security company found guilty of ripping off the government, got a $16.8 million contract to guard the airport using Iraqi money. Florida-based AirScan Inc., a private aerial surveillance firm being sued for human rights violations in the United States, won a $10 million deal to patrol Iraq's oil pipelines. All told, the coalition issued thirty-seven large contracts worth more than $5 million each. Of those, 85 percent of the value went to U.S. companies.[4]

Iraqi companies won contracts too, but it was hard to tell who got the money, since the names were kept secret to prevent them from becoming insurgent targets. Meeting minutes showed that the review board approved $120 million for printing and distributing currency, $36 million for renovating police stations, $15 million for a national micro credit program, and $4 million for creating a radio system for the railroad network. The board also signed off on scores of smaller projects, including $3,500 to start a Baghdad theater festival, $50,000 to pay two zookeepers, and $79,245 to reestablish the Baghdad stock exchange.[5] In all cases, it was difficult to determine how much the money achieved, or whether it just greased palms of well-connected Iraqis.

The Development Fund also came to be a petty cash drawer for the CPA. It was a way to get quick approval for reconstruction projects without the hassle of burdensome contracting regulations. Several CPA officials whom I interviewed over the course of the coalition's existence said they believed that the money was used to pay bribes or buy favors for allies and family members. "It's just like anybody who wanted something would get it [through the Development Fund] and then the money would go out," one former CPA official told me. "Some people were working the system, trying to figure out how to get their hands on a lot of loose cash lying around." But it didn't matter: it was Iraqi money, not U.S. funds.

The procedures were so fast and loose that USAID refused to use the fund for fear that the funds could be abused. "With the [Development

Fund for Iraq], you could make up the rules as you went along," said James "Spike" Stephenson, the USAID director in Iraq during 2004. There was simply no telling what would happen with the Iraqi money. It vanished into a black hole.

CASH DUMP

As the deadline to turn over power to a new Iraqi government approached in July 2004, Nash's reconstruction was sputtering. The violent outbreaks in Najaf and Fallujah had caused American companies to suspend many operations. The slow-paced contracting process also meant that little was getting done. It was taking forever to get money flowing. Bremer worried that the Americans risked becoming "the worst of all things — an ineffective occupier."[6]

Bremer decided that the coalition had to boost spending as fast as possible. The easiest way to do that was the Development Fund for Iraq, which had fewer restrictions, less oversight, and, as a bonus, less scrutiny from the press and the Congress. Bremer's decision was helped along by a second development. In March 2004 the United Nations suddenly deposited $2.5 billion into the account. The money was the final transfer from the UN-controlled Oil-for-Food account. The cash dump caught Bremer and his budget directors by surprise. Nobody at the United Nations had told them that the Oil-for-Food account contained such a large surplus. The result was an intense internal debate. Should the coalition spend the cash or leave it for the new Iraqi government to manage?

Over a few hurried weeks of debate in April 2004, the United States and its coalition partners decided that Iraq's needs were too urgent to wait. The windfall "was kind of a curse," one senior coalition official who was involved in the decision making told me. He said that the United States was worried that the transition to the new, Iraqi-controlled government would delay desperately needed work. The Iraqis would be too inexperienced, too busy forming a new government to make spending decisions on multimillion-dollar projects. "Either we work with the Iraqis to determine spending priorities or we sit on it. Neither option was attractive." The senior official said the coalition worried about misspending the money, but Bremer and his senior directors decided that wartime circumstances demanded a focus on action, not accounting principles. "There was no way in the world to have a system that would have satisfied [American auditing] standards . . . that would have also resulted in significant money being provided to the Iraqis," the former senior CPA official said. The coalition decided to spend $2.5 billion in less than three months.

So the spree began. Contracting officers on the ground tried desperately to come up with new projects. In early May, U.S. and Iraqi officials proposed billions in new spending for oil, security, and electricity. Representatives from the United Kingdom and Australia asked the coalition comptroller, a senior U.S. Treasury official named George Wolfe, to allow more time to consider the new proposals. Wolfe gave them three days. On a single day, May 15, the Program Review Board approved $1.9 billion in new projects to be contracted out competitively in six weeks.

As the clock ticked down toward the handover of power to the Iraqis, the rush to spend money turned manic. June 2004 became a month when both money and accountability were thrown out the window. It was like a Barneys sale in the Wild West, with the United States playing the role of frenzied shopper and the Iraqis stuck with the bill. More than one thousand contracts were issued by American officials in June, about double the usual number. Of those, seven hundred were issued without following standard procedures, according to one of Bowen's audits. One U.S. official in Hillah, in southern Iraq, was given $6.75 million on June 21 and told to hand it out by the end of the month. "There was definitely a rush to get money out the door. We were sitting on this big pile of resources that we could make up the rules for," one midlevel official in the coalition told me. He joked that he had become a multimillionaire for forty-five minutes, when he had to carry $3.5 million across the Republican Palace to his office without once having to sign any piece of paper that he had possession of the money. "It became a head-over-heels exercise. Proper accounting was the victim."

POCKET CHANGE

In the final days of the American occupation, the United States blasted money across Iraq like a leaf blower. The Development Fund money was actually held in an account maintained by the Federal Reserve Bank of New York. On June 11, the coalition asked the federal bank for a $2.4 billion delivery. ("Just when you think you've seen it all," read one e-mail from an exasperated Fed official.) Federal officials scrambled to line up U.S. Air Force C-130 cargo planes to hold the money. On June 22, 2004, the reserve shipped $2,401,600,000 in pallets of shrink-wrapped $100 U.S. bills called cashpaks. The shipment weighed twenty-eight tons and took up as much room as seventy-four washing machines. It was the largest one-time cash transfer in the history of the Federal Reserve Bank.[7]

Even then the coalition was not done moving money. The day after the federal reserve transfer, the coalition loaded fifteen tons of the cash onto three military helicopters bound for Irbil, the largest city in Kurdistan. The $1.4 billion was a payoff to the Kurds, who insisted that they had been shortchanged by Saddam during the Oil-for-Food program. The coalition flew the money to the central bank for the Kurds, who had an autonomous region in northern Iraq. They left without providing any receipts to show where the money had come from or where it was going; nor did they get any acknowledgment from the Kurds that they had actually received the money.[8]

Five days later, at 10:26 a.m. on June 28, 2004, Jerry Bremer handed a blue Morocco leather folder to the Iraqi chief justice, Medhat Mahmoud. It placed control of Iraq into the hands of an interim Iraqi government handpicked by the United States and the United Nations. It was a surprise ceremony, held two days ahead of the scheduled handover to catch off guard any insurgents who had been planning attacks. In Turkey, where they were attending a NATO meeting, National Security Adviser Condoleezza Rice passed President Bush a note. "Iraq is sovereign," she wrote. Bush scrawled on the note, then showed it to Prime Minister Tony Blair, who was sitting next to him. "Let Freedom Reign!" it read.[9]

A few days later Bremer issued a final "historic review of CPA accomplishments." At the top of the list was the creation of a new, free Iraq with an interim constitution that established the rule of law and respect for human rights. Second was the development of Iraq's new security forces. All told, the coalition had established a police force with 176,000 officers and a military that would have 75,000 trained soldiers by March 2005. The coalition had refurbished 2,600 schools, shepherded into existence a cellular phone system with 340,000 subscribers, boosted electricity to 4,900 megawatts, and returned oil production to 2.5 million barrels per day.

But most of the figures that Bremer reeled off were just numbers, with little meaning for those living in Iraq. The police force was corrupt, outgunned by insurgents, and undermanned. The new Iraqi military forces had crumbled during the violence in April and May, with many units abandoning their posts. Even a year later, the Pentagon determined that in the entire country, only a single unit was capable of independent operation. Power production may have briefly reached 4,900 megawatts during the coalition's final month of operation, but it could not maintain such output. And even then it was not nearly enough to satisfy the demand for electricity, guaranteeing long blackouts in Iraq's cities and towns.

As for the claim that the coalition had returned oil production to the prewar level of 2.5 million barrels per day — well, it was a crude lie. The Bush administration's own Department of Energy estimated production at 1.7 million barrels per day in June 2004.

Bremer's decision to rush reconstruction spending was another example of the pendulum's swinging too far. Congress had tried to clamp down on the Wild West atmosphere of the first summer after the invasion by insisting that David Nash's U.S.-funded Project Contracting Office follow cumbersome contracting rules designed for peacetime. But rather than go back before Congress, or even make use of built-in exceptions in contracting laws, the Bush administration and Bremer did nothing as Nash's plan stalled. Instead they seized upon the one stash of money with no strings attached — the Development Fund for Iraq — and started pushing it out the door with no plan. The results — or lack of them — were a foregone conclusion.

Bill Keller was one of those in the coalition who wondered what the United States had really accomplished during the fourteen-month occupation. Keller was a Naval Academy graduate and MBA assigned to advise the Iraqi Communications Ministry in the final few months of the coalition's existence. A telecommunications executive, he had spent a decade in the Navy Reserve working in contracting and military construction. Keller had come to Iraq believing that he could make a difference. But what he found upon arriving was that the Americans in charge seemed far more interested in spending money than in accounting for it. The attitude, he told me, was that the Development Fund for Iraq money "was somebody else's. It wasn't our tax money. So spend it first."

Keller, who was the second-highest-ranking American at the Communications Ministry, had come to believe that the Iraqi leaders he worked with were corrupt. One of his first tasks had been to write up a memo for Bremer recommending the firing of the U.S.-appointed minister of communications on corruption charges. Keller had also seen a memo from BearingPoint, an American financial consulting firm hired to work in the Communications Ministry, that questioned the ministry's cash flows. A BearingPoint consultant found that the ministry's process for disbursing

Development Fund money was "open to fraud, kickbacks, and misappropriation of funds." Despite the warnings, higher-ups kept pushing Keller to spend more money to improve Iraq's phone system.

As the handover date approached, Keller told me, senior coalition officials brushed aside concerns about accountability. In an e-mail in April 2004, one Washington official noted that an article in a British newspaper had warned of "corruption in contracting for Iraq reconstruction." The official wrote to one of Keller's colleagues: "I expect this to heat up in coming days and weeks. This could bring the entire process to a screeching halt, so time is of the essence." The official ordered a BearingPoint contractor working at the ministry to "force projects through quickly."[10] To Keller it was clear that the United States wanted to boost statistics to show the world that the occupation was a success. It was much less interested in doing the hard, careful work needed to actually produce results. "We were squandering the money we were entrusted to handle," Keller said. "We were a blind mouse with money."

NEW SHERIFF

Stuart Bowen is tall, slender, and pale, with thinning hair and metal-rimmed glasses that give him the look of the academic that he once considered becoming. In person he is a mix of professor, political junkie, and prosecutor. He enthuses over the poetry of Reynolds Price and the Agrarian philosophy of Andrew Lytle, both men giants in the world of Southern literature, but he is equally adept at the intricacies of White House politics and obscure legal concepts. His approach toward Iraq mirrored his personality, a blend of pragmatism and public interest.

Descended from a long line of military veterans, Bowen relished his contribution to the war in Iraq. It was dangerous, complicated, and ultimately rewarding. "If you are dealing with a government in chaos, you ought to have more controls, not fewer. You ought to have more assurances, not fewer, because the likelihood of fraud or misapplication of funds is high," he told me during interviews in his office overlooking the Potomac River in Crystal City. "You're dealing with a government in chaos."

There were few clues in Bowen's background that he was anything other than a fierce partisan. Bowen came from an old Washington family that traced its roots to Supreme Court Justice John C. Marshall, the founding father who promoted the court's authority in the young republic. Bowen's grandfather fought in the Pacific during World War II. His father was an air force pilot, flying one hundred combat missions over Vietnam in an F-4. Bowen's family was steeped in bedrock American values, filled with warriors and Republicans, their accomplishments never far from Bowen's mind.

With some hesitancy, Bowen followed their path, taking a route through the aristocracy of the modern-day South. He graduated from Sewanee, where he studied under Lytle, drinking bourbon out of Jefferson cups on the front porch of his house. From there he entered the air force, becoming a military intelligence officer before deciding to pursue a career in law. He bounced around schools — briefly considering a PhD in English that would allow him to specialize in Southern literature — before landing in Texas at St. Mary's University in San Antonio. He was on the law review, made the dean's list, and clerked at the Texas Supreme Court. Graduation produced a job at the Texas attorney general's office.

It was at a meet-and-greet lunch for Republican lawyers in Austin where he first met George W. Bush, then running for Texas governor in a long-shot race against the favored Democratic incumbent, Ann Richards. They spoke briefly, no more than ten minutes. Bush asked him some questions about an obscure case that Bowen was then working on involving a Texas firefighting commission. His knowledge impressed Bowen, who declared his support for Bush, then fifteen points behind in the polls. "I said, 'When you win, I'd like to come work for you.' I went home and I remember having dinner with my wife and my father-in-law. I told them that I'd met our next governor," Bowen said.

That early devotion apparently made an impression on Bush. A month after Bush won the bitterly contested race in 1994, Bowen went to work for Alberto Gonzalez, the future U.S. attorney general who was then Bush's general counsel. Bowen worked on a series of high-profile, red-meat conservative issues: Indian gambling, faith-based initiatives, and death penalty cases. Bowen's work burnished Bush's conservative credentials, preparing him for his run for presidency in 2000.

Bowen worked on Bush's presidential campaign only in the final days. When the Florida election results came into dispute, he took leave from his job in the counsel's office to join the army of lawyers swarming into Florida. Bowen's key contribution was delivering scores of votes to Bush in the northern Florida panhandle. The Escambia County elections commission didn't want to count some 250 military ballots because they lacked postmarks indicating they had been cast before the election. Bowen knew that the military ballots had been tending strongly Republican. He glowered at the commissioners sitting on the other side of four or five tables overflowing with the ballots, threatening to have them arrested. "I said, Wait, time out. I'm going to put you on notice now that a knowing deprivation of a military member's voting rights is a criminal offense. I'm putting you on notice," Bowen said. "They came back and said we're opening them."

Once again Bush showed his appreciation. Bowen followed Gonzalez to the White House general counsel's office, eventually going to work for Harriet Miers, Bush's staff secretary and future failed Supreme Court nominee. (He was one of those in the West Wing who had to flee the White House on September 11 when the order came to evacuate.) The seven-day weeks wore him down, however, and after a stretch, Bowen decided to take a job with Patton Boggs, the powerful Washington law firm. The war in Iraq broke out, and Bowen was hired to lobby for a contractor. He was part of a three-man team that helped to set up a meeting between USAID and URS Group, Inc., a San Francisco–based company specializing in international construction planning. URS didn't win any USAID contracts as a result of that meeting, but it was part of a joint venture that won a contract with Nash's agency to oversee reconstruction projects worth nearly $30 million. Bowen's connection with the company would become a point of minor controversy after his appointment as inspector general, but Bowen denied any conflict of interest, saying that his involvement with the firm had been insignificant.

The corporate realm left Bowen cold, however — he often declared his goal was "public service" — and within months of leaving the White House he was asking to return. In December 2003 he got his chance. During the debate over the $18.4 billion reconstruction package, Democrats had insisted on creating an inspector general, a government watchdog to oversee the Coalition Provisional Authority. The Bush administration had pushed back, imposing unusual limits. Inspectors general are not the sexiest cops; they conduct audits and do reports, mostly, with an occasional arrest. They are the public's eyes and ears into the inner workings of the federal bureaucracy, designed to operate with complete independence. But the administration insisted that the Pentagon have the right to quash any reports deemed to endanger national security. The restriction had spooked the administration's first candidate, a NASA inspector general who turned the post down. But when the White House personnel director called

Bowen, he had no problems with the design of the new position. Bowen later said that neither the Pentagon nor the White House had ever attempted to interfere in his publishing a report. In fact, Bowen told me, he had never heard directly from Bush or any other White House official regarding his work in Iraq.

"It's just silence," he said.

UNREALISTIC STANDARD

As Bowen began to piece together the story of the Development Fund for Iraq, he came to believe the United States had violated its duty to hold the Iraqis' money in trust, spending it with little restraint or accountability. He ordered an audit of the entire $20 billion fund. The billions were gone, but he insisted on finding out what had happened. It was not a pretty story.

Bowen's investigators discovered that the coalition could not account for nearly $9 billion shipped from Iraq's central bank to Iraq's two dozen ministries. In the dry terminology of the audit report, the coalition had "less than adequate" controls over the money; there was "no assurance" that the money had actually been used as intended, to pay for budget expenses like government salaries and reconstruction projects sponsored by the ministries. Some of the money appeared to have been paid to ghost employees who existed only to collect paychecks. At one ministry supposedly protected by 8,206 security officers, only 602 guards were actually showing up for work.[11] Bowen was cautious; he did not say the money had been wasted. He said that neither the coalition nor anyone else would ever be able to show what happened to the funds. One did not have to be an expert in nation building to know that $9 billion was a staggering amount of money.

A quick look at the audit revealed a catalog of chaos that had allowed those billions to vanish into accounting Neverland. The United States had appointed senior advisers to most of Iraq's ministries. The Iraqis called them "shadow ministers" — a reflection of the power that they held. The advisers' job was to serve as the liaison between Bremer and the ministers, to provide advice on how to run an effective and transparent agency in the new Iraq. But the report found that the advisers had either failed or were unable to exercise adequate oversight of the money. In one case the coalition's main budget office had twelve of the fifty-five staff members that were needed, and most of them were "inexperienced recent college graduates." In another case the coalition awarded a $1.4 million contract to a company called Northstar Consultants to review controls over the Development Fund — but the firm had no certified public accountant and did not perform the review. The report also chronicled the desperation of the advisers, many of them retired executives who stuck around for only months before returning to the United States. Some of them tried to ignore the money flowing into the ministries they were supposed to be helping.

Bowen's audit provoked a strong response throughout the U.S. government. The State Department tried to block the report, arguing that Bowen's mandate did not extend to investigating Iraqi money. They convinced Bowen to hold off on releasing the results until January 2005, for fear of upsetting the Iraqi elections scheduled to take place.

Bremer himself offered a scathing, condescending response, the battlefield commander excoriating the pencil pusher back home. The report, he wrote Bowen, "does not meet the standards Americans have come to expect of the Inspector General." It was filled with "misconceptions and inaccuracies." The coalition knew that Iraq's ministries had problems with their payroll system, but decided to go ahead with salary payments anyway: "There was a war going on in Iraq, and it would have been dangerous for our security — ours and Iraq's — to stop paying armed young men." Bremer accused Bowen of not giving the coalition credit for its efforts to ensure accountability. Bowen, he argued, was demanding unrealistic accounting principles in the middle of Iraq's chaos. The "auditors presume that the coalition could achieve a standard of budgetary transparency and execution which even peaceful Western nations would have trouble meeting within a year, especially in the midst of war," Bremer wrote. "Given the situation the CPA found in Iraq at liberation, this is an unrealistic standard."[12]

Bremer may have been right. It would have cost the Bush administration a lot to demand accountability in Iraq: more people, more time, more money, and better planning. But not having the standards carried a price tag too, as Bowen's investigators discovered. At the coalition's outpost in Hillah, in southern Iraq, it amounted to at least $8,641,375.

I LOVE TO GIVE YOU MONEY

Robert J. Stein was the comptroller of the coalition's headquarters in Hillah in southern Iraq, an old hotel surrounded by coils of razor wire and concrete blast walls on the banks of the Euphrates. He was an odd character, remote, surly, with unkempt hair, and heavy metal glasses. He wore black, even in Iraq's withering summer heat.[13] During the nine months he spent in Iraq with the Coalition Provisional Authority, Stein controlled $82 million in reconstruction money, most of it cash from the Development Fund for Iraq. A good chunk, he later admitted to authorities, he put in his own pocket.[14]

As Bowen and federal investigators described it, Stein was the lead actor in a wide-ranging conspiracy that involved five Army Reserve officers and an aging American contractor who had lived for many years in Romania named Philip H. Bloom. Stein admitted to directing $8.6 million worth of reconstruction contracts in southern Iraq to Bloom and his companies between January and June 2004. In return Bloom provided Stein and the officers with first-class plane tickets, real estate lots, an RV, brand-new SUVs, cigars, Breitling watches, jewelry, alcohol, sexual favors from prostitutes, and cash bribes.

Stein's personal share amounted to $1 million in cash and goods and another $2 million that he admitted stealing from the vault that he controlled at the Hillah outpost — a vault that Bowen's auditors determined had "no tracking system to determine how much money was on hand and who was responsible for it."[15] Adrift and unsupervised in a hostile land, Stein and Bloom turned to each other for comfort and support. "I love to give you money," Stein wrote Bloom in one e-mail exchange.[16] Bloom helped Stein launder the hot money by running it through bank accounts in Switzerland, Romania, and the Netherlands. Stein used the cash to buy a 1965 Cessna airplane, a six-carat diamond ring, a 2.54-carat sapphire necklace, a diamond tennis bracelet, and a 2004 Lexus. Stein told investigators he planned to open his own private security company in Iraq, using grenade launchers, submachine guns, and .45 caliber pistols stolen from the coalition.[17]

For some, it was a mystery that Stein had been hired at all. Court records showed that he had been convicted in 1996 on credit card fraud charges. He pleaded guilty and was sentenced to eight months in prison and three years of supervised release. He also was ordered to repay $45,000. The criminal affidavit against him said that he used $200 of the money he got from Bloom to make one of the restitution payments. His wife used another $5,821 to pay off back taxes. They thus used fraud to repay fraud.

When Stein was hired by a contractor to the coalition in October 2003 — through a no-bid contract given to a Native American firm called S&K

Technologies (the Native Americans enjoyed the same kind of no-bid benefits as Senator Ted Stevens's Native Alaskan companies)[18] — he was also in the middle of a lawsuit charging him with skimming $700,000 from a former employer. Grundy Marine Construction accused Stein of conspiring with subcontractors at a building project at Pope Air Force Base in North Carolina to overcharge on labor in exchange for kickbacks. The company dropped the suit after settling with Stein for $75,000. Grundy Marine vice president Peter Caruk said Stein had cost his company $1.5 million.[19] "This guy is a thief. He's a con artist and a crook," Caruk concluded.[20]

Lt. Col. Michael Brian Wheeler, forty-seven, of Amherst Junction, Wisconsin, was Stein's boss in Iraq. He allegedly used his military credentials to smuggle the arms and cash back into the United States. For his troubles, he kept some of the weapons and $100,000. Another of the officers, Lt. Col. Debra Harrison, forty-seven, allegedly stole $80,000 to $100,000 from the CPA to add a deck, new cabinets, and a hot tub to her home in Trenton, New Jersey. In 2004 she acquired a Cadillac Escalade, worth $50,000 to $60,000, after money was wired directly to a dealership from accounts controlled or used by Bloom. When government agents confronted Harrison, she admitted getting the car from Bloom. It was what she deserved for going to Iraq, she told the agents. Both Wheeler and Harrison were arrested and charged with conspiracy and money laundering.[21] For their misdeeds in Iraq, both Bloom and Stein pled guilty in February 2006 to bribery, money laundering, and conspiracy charges.

Bowen stumbled on the whole mess in the course of doing audits on the use of the Development Fund money at the coalition's Hillah outpost, which was responsible for six provinces in south-central Iraq that represented half the country's land mass and held much of its Shiite population. Bowen's auditors found that the work done on a regional police academy and a library was shoddy or incomplete. In some cases it was never done at all. For example, Stein awarded Bloom's company, Global Business Group, and its subsidiaries a set of contracts to build a new police academy in Hillah on the site of the old Baath Party headquarters. The academy was supposed to be the centerpiece of the coalition's efforts to create a new police force to improve security in the south. Bloom carried out some of the work: he built new classrooms and living quarters. But the rest of the project was a disaster. For starters, the police academy was constructed on illegally transferred land. Despite this Bloom's firms mysteriously were contracted to clear the same site twice. His company was then supposed to deliver three electric generators to the academy. Only one arrived, and it turned out to be a hollow shell, a box with nothing inside.[22] Bloom got at least $7.3 million in contracts to redo the academy.

Next up for Bloom was a new library. The library in Karbala was set in the middle of one of the historical centers of teaching in the Arab world. The library, a two-story building of yellowing brick with a turquoise metal arch, had been looted and its grounds trashed during the war, and the coalition decided to make renovating it a top priority. Stein awarded Bloom contracts to provide new landscaping, furniture, and computers that would grant the impoverished, mostly Shiite population of Karbala publicly available Internet access for the first time. The contracts called for basics such as ceiling fans, doors, and carpets. None were delivered. There were supposed to be bookshelves, tables, and computer desks. Bloom provided plastic chairs instead of upholstered ones, used furniture, and no computer desks. Bloom provided no Internet service at all; only fourteen of the sixty-eight computers, no servers, and no workstations. Bloom was paid nearly $500,000 for goods and services valued at $30,000.[23] Karbala's library, like its people, remained in the dark.[24]

BLOOD MONEY

As Bremer, Bloom, and Stein left Iraq — the one destined for a Presidential Medal of Freedom, the other two for jail — Nash stayed behind a few months more. At sixty-one, Nash had pushed himself harder than many of his younger colleagues in Iraq. He worked six days a week, twelve hours a day, and traveled to all eighteen of Iraq's provinces in the course of a year — a feat very few others accomplished. He spent fourteen months in Iraq — longer than Bremer; longer than the generals on yearlong tours; certainly longer than the senior advisers, who rotated every few months. He singlehandedly created a new agency to carry out the largest rebuilding plan that the United States had embarked on since the Marshall Plan. His staff was rabidly loyal to him. Amy Burns, his press aide, called him a "genius." His effort was heartfelt, a reflection of one man's deep-seated faith in American industry and his own know-how. But it was also a guarantee for controversy that permanently impeded the rebuilding.

Nash's Project Contracting Office, an amalgamation of officials from the State Department, the Defense Department, other government agencies, and private contractors, had no champions — and plenty of enemies — in Washington and Baghdad. Rumsfeld himself had publicly disavowed U.S. responsibility for rebuilding Iraq. State Department officials thought the agency was cumbersome, ineffective, and poorly organized. They viewed Nash and his organization as an interloper. Some senior officials were convinced that the PCO and the reconstruction program were nothing more than Pentagon payback to American firms for supporting the war.

Nash was puzzled by the attacks. Everybody up the line had approved the idea of building big projects: first Bremer, then the Bush administration, and finally Congress. Only a handful of firms, most of them American, had the ability to do the work. Nash had no staff, so he had to create an agency. What other alternatives were there? Nash felt like he carried out the job that he was given. He called it "the art of the possible." In return he had been criticized, pushed aside. In his memoirs, Bremer failed even to mention Nash.

"I personally, deep down in my heart, never had any desire to do anything other than help the Iraqis rebuild their country. I never said I was the expert on how to do that. I can build things. I can manage programs. I can get contractors to work. But I was not controlling where the money went. Congress set that up with a lot of rules. We were just trying to abide by the rules," Nash told me in one of a series of interviews. "I'm not the enemy. I was just there to execute the program that I was given. I wasn't trying to be a development program. I was trying to be a public servant. . . . All I ever wanted to do was get the job done," he said.

In August 2004, a month before his final departure, I accompanied Nash on a helicopter tour of southern Iraq. It was a bittersweet trip. New and refurbished power stations were coming on line — the month turned out to be a record since the invasion for the generation of electricity. Private contractors were finishing plans for restoring thousands of schools, clinics, and other infrastructure. The rebuilding projects were now employing 88,000 Iraqis, up from just 5,300 a few months earlier.

But the progress was not widespread. Nash heard nothing but complaints throughout a long, hot day. Where's the money to rebuild Iraq? The jobs for broke Iraqis? The promised health clinics and schools, bridges and dams, electricity and clean water? Many of the people that Nash visited on his trip said they were bitter and no better off materially than they were under Saddam Hussein. "You need to put more people to work to make them happy," said Muthina Hussein, twenty-seven, an engineer who found a $250-a-week job on a U.S. reconstruction project on a military base. "The bad guys are saying America lies. They say it's just like what Saddam did."

Nash's first stop was a conference room in Hillah. It had been converted into a consulate of the U.S. embassy after the handover. There Nash ran smack into the new man in charge of the reconstruction effort in south-central Iraq: Anton Smith. Smith did not yet know about Stein's criminal activities, but he already knew that the U.S. efforts had produced almost nothing in the troubled region. As Nash was visiting, Muqtada Sadr's followers were battling U.S. and Iraqi forces at the Imam Ali Shrine in Najaf.

"It's important that we raise some earth," Smith pleaded with Nash. "Najaf's need is immediate. It's big. We need to move quickly to make sure we don't lose them again. It's in our national interest to win their hearts and minds."

Smith, an intense State Department official, was most concerned that Nash give more autonomy in decision making to local U.S. officials with more direct contact with regional needs and conditions. Smith felt that he was in a better position to say where money needed to flow.

Nash dismissed Smith. As always, he insisted on being in charge. It was his program and he was going to have ultimate control.

"Autonomy scares me. . . . Nobody has autonomy," he told Smith as they huddled together over a long, gray cafeteria table. "There's some boundaries we have to live with whether we like it or not."

Next on his visit was a fifteen-minute drive in armored cars across dusty roads to Camp Babylon, headquarters for the Polish soldiers who controlled south-central Iraq as part of the U.S.-led coalition. There, in an ornate high-ceilinged room with air conditioners blasting, Polish officers made a plea to Nash for help. They had no money for the coming year. The recent pullout of Thai and Philippine soldiers had left them without engineers or public health specialists. They seemed confused as to where to turn. Where could they get money? Where could they propose projects? The final slide of the Polish presentation consisted of four question marks — Could Nash help? Suddenly a muffled boom shook the room. A nearby car bomb had just exploded, killing one Polish soldier and injuring six others. Col. Mariusz Saltera, the head of the Polish contingent's public outreach efforts, shook his head. Last year, he'd traveled six thousand miles throughout Iraq. This year security concerns kept him confined to base. "I can't say this is really working," Saltera said.

Nash and his security team mounted two Black Hawk helicopters to ride to Numaniya, a sprawling, six-square-mile military base that private American contractors built for the Iraqi army with $115 million in U.S. taxpayer money. The helicopter thundered low and fast over a barren landscape of scrub, mud huts, and camel herders. The featureless terrain wavered in 115-degree heat.

Minutes after Nash landed, a pack of cars rumbled up in a cloud of dust. Nash's security guards, men in dark glasses and bulletproof vests, tensed. Out jumped a score of Iraqi men, many with AK-47s. A man in a gray suit and top-buttoned white shirt strode forward and offered his hand. The local governor and tribal leader had come for a visit accompanied by his security detail. Governor Mohammed Jayshami exchanged pleasantries for thirty seconds, then got down to business. "The assistance we have received so far is minimal. I'd like to see more," he said, smiling.

Nash responded with what by now had become pat. "It's taken a little while to get things going, but we're really getting going." Surrounded by their entourages, the two men strode into a newly refurbished barracks. They stopped under a whirring fan and then the electricity cut out. The air instantly became stifling and the smell of fresh paint overwhelming. One of Jayshami's men appeared with a box of pink tissues. He handed one to Nash. Sweating in his dark jacket, black pants, and desert boots, Nash dabbed his forehead. Jayshami acknowledged that members of his tribe had benefited from the project's 1,200 jobs. But he said the word had not filtered down to most Iraqis.

"So far, everything you have done, nobody knows about," he said. "If only the U.S. would promise the poor to take care of them . . . half the insurgents would drop their weapons."

Nash nodded. "One of my biggest problems is getting the information out," he said.

Jayshami then made a dramatic announcement. He declared that seventy-five families in his tribe had loved ones who had been mistakenly killed by Americans during the war. Jayshami ordered everyone out of the room so he could speak privately with Nash. He wanted to talk *diyat* — blood money.

Blood money — the payment of compensation by an attacker to the family members of a dead or injured loved one — is one of the most ancient forms of justice in the Arab world. According to legend, the Prophet Mohammed's grandfather participated in the tradition. After agreeing to sacrifice one of his sons, Abdul-Muttalib instead settled his debt with God with a payment of one hundred camels.[25] The tradition was well documented in the pre-Islamic poetry of the incessantly warring tribes of Saudi Arabia. The payment of blood money was an adequate alternative to revenge killings, so long as the family agreed to accept the compensation.

The tradition of diyat was later enshrined in both the Quran and the Hadith, the sayings of Mohammed. The Quran is clear: "A believer should not kill a believer except by mistake. He who kills a believer by mistake must free a believing slave, and pay the blood money to the family of the victim unless they remit it as a charity" (4:92). Mohammed sent a letter to Yemen spelling out the exact number of camels demanded by death and injury. One life — as well as a completely severed nose, testicle, or penis — demanded one hundred camels as payment. A single missing foot or hand was fifty camels; a finger, ten camels; and a tooth, five camels. Those without camels had to pay 1,000 dinars in gold.

Islamic societies incorporated the tradition into their legal codes, although most had dropped it by the twentieth century. However, a few countries, such as Saudi Arabia, Iran, and Pakistan, incorporated diyat into their formalized legal system. In Saudi Arabia, for instance, the compensation was fixed by religious authorities according to gender and religion. The death of a Muslim man cost 100,000 riyals, or almost $27,000 U.S. A Muslim woman or a Christian man was half that. At the bottom of the scale was a Hindu woman, whose family received $888 for her death.

Blood money was not part of Saddam's secular Iraqi legal code, but it thrived as an informal system among tribal peoples. In 2004 one of my colleagues was traveling north of Baghdad when one of the cars in his convoy collided with another vehicle, killing the occupant. One of our translators spent months shuttling back and forth between Kirkuk and Baghdad to negotiate the appropriate amount to pay the family of the bereaved. He described sitting in a long tent, called a *diwan*, as he tried to reach a settlement in the delicate matter of the value of a man's life. "It's not a legal thing, but it's our custom," he told me.

Standing in the newly painted army base that the Americans were building for Iraq, Jayshami was simply doing what his ancestors had done for thousands of years. An enemy tribe had attacked and taken the lives of his people. Surely, he told Nash, that required some kind of compensation. Surely, the Americans would pay for what they had done. That was the point of the reconstruction, wasn't it? To make a shattered people whole somehow, in some way?

Nash simply shook his head no. The Americans were not going to pay Jayshami. His tribe would have to learn to live with its losses, just as Iraq would have to learn to cope with the destruction of its peace, its country, its society. There would be no American blood money forthcoming, not on that day in August, not three years later, not ever.

Late that afternoon, Nash climbed back into the Black Hawk for the ride home. He'd endured a car bomb, blistering sun, and constant pleas for money to visit a single, incomplete U.S.-funded reconstruction project. If it shook his faith, he did not show it.

"That doesn't just happen every day," said Maj. Tom Sands, Nash's military assistant.

Said Nash: "It does to me."

Part III
Hands Off

10

Boom Town

With the dissolution of the Coalition Provisional Authority on June 28, 2004, and the departure of David Nash a few months later, the State Department took over control of the rebuilding of Iraq. Secretary of State Colin Powell wanted things back to normal — as normal as they could be in Iraq, at any rate. In Baghdad the provisional authority was replaced by an American embassy — the largest in the world, to be sure, but structured like any other, with an ambassador, political and economic officers, and assorted diplomats. The new U.S. ambassador, John Negroponte, no longer sat at the head of the table during meetings, as Jerry Bremer had. He entered a room and deliberately took a seat off to one side. The senior advisers to the U.S.-appointed ministers were now called "consultants." They no longer had the power to override the wishes of the ministers with whom they worked. The United States still had ultimate power, of course, since the Iraqi government could not survive without American military and financial support. But U.S. control was now more carrot, less stick. America was no longer an occupying force. The Iraqis were supposed to be in charge of their own country again.

As part of the new order, Negroponte decided that the reconstruction needed reconstruction. The U.S.-funded part of the rebuilding was moving at a glacial pace. By July 2004 fewer than 10 percent of the 2,800 planned projects were under construction. Less than a billion dollars of the $18.4 billion approved by Congress eight months earlier had been spent. The violence and the inherent sluggishness of the federal contracting process were partly to blame. American multinationals were arriving in Iraq, setting up operations, and starting work. American engineers, or more often their Iraqi counterparts, had to visit sites, acquire land, and draw up blueprints. All of that took time.

The man chosen to carry out the reforms was Bill Taylor, a square-jawed former paratrooper and ambassador who replaced Nash as the head of the U.S. reconstruction effort. Unlike Nash, Taylor had long experience in "transformational issues" — enacting political and economic changes in societies in transition. After the fall of the Berlin Wall, Taylor coordinated U.S. aid to the former Soviet Union and Eastern Europe. After 9/11, he was in Kabul, where he oversaw America's reconstruction there. But it was Taylor's military background that attracted Negroponte, who personally appointed him to the job. A West Point graduate, Taylor had spent six years in the infantry during Vietnam. He led a company of soldiers in the 101st Airborne from 1970 to 1972, engaging in heavy fighting in northern South Vietnam. He also worked at a Defense Department think tank and as a defense adviser to NATO. Negroponte thought Taylor's experience as soldier and diplomat were critical. Both would be needed to bridge the divide between the bricks and mortar and "soft stuff" debate that had broken out between the Pentagon and State Department. Rather than being an academic, Taylor was upbeat, a motivator. "I called him the eternal optimist," said one of his colleagues.

In July and August 2004, Taylor conducted a full-scale review of the entire reconstruction plan. He concluded that Nash's plan was not working. The American contractors were costing too much money. Security needs hampered every move. The large projects were taking a long time to plan and launch. The bureaucracy of the contracting system was stifling. Faced with a manpower crunch and not much time, Nash had hired contractors to fill many positions. The result was three, four, and sometimes more layers between a U.S. government employee and the contractor who was actually doing the work on the ground. Nash had designed the system to work fast. Instead it was moving as slowly as the concrete that the contractors were supposed to be pouring.

Taylor could not radically alter the rebuilding program. The contracts were already locked in place. But he could change the focus of the funding and the priorities through what the State Department called reallocations — essentially on-the-fly fixes. Taylor's vision was a mirror image of Nash's reconstruction plan. First, he took charge of a new agency in the State Department, the Iraqi Reconstruction Management Office. It was supposed to be the coordinating body that Nash's agency never was, drawing together the different agencies to produce a unified policy. Second, the strategies for implementing the rebuilding program were upended. Taylor frowned on the enormous, cost-plus contracts awarded to U.S. multinationals. He wanted to focus on giving smaller-dollar contracts directly to Iraqi firms at a fixed price. No longer could a contractor spend wildly and expect to be reimbursed. Finally, Taylor emphasized highly visible projects that would show progress — ditch digging and democracy building were in, power plants and sewage treatment centers were out.

The biggest winner of Taylor's review was the American military. In a series of long conversations with USAID and the military, Taylor decided that the United States had to spend more money to make Iraq safer. It was costing $4 million per day simply for housing and feeding the American contractors in the Green Zone. On projects in especially volatile areas like the Sunni Triangle region west of Baghdad, fifty cents of every dollar went to security. At one point, 350 employees of Washington Group International, an Idaho construction and engineering firm, were erecting power lines around Fallujah while guarded by more than 700 security personnel. Taylor decided to spend an additional $2 billion for training Iraqi soldiers and police. "If we couldn't get security right, then we couldn't do reconstruction. We needed to have security first," Taylor told me. Taylor's decision was the first step in turning the rebuilding program into the rearming program. Nearly half of the $30 billion of total U.S. aid was spent for security — either to protect U.S. contractors or to train and equip the Iraqi army.

It had taken more than a year — a year of wasted money, dead contractors, and disenchanted Iraqis — but America had finally figured out its priorities.

Taylor's analysis of the program led him to a surprising conclusion. Bremer thought a successful rebuilding program would win over the Iraqis. He told his deputies, "Infrastructure equals security, and security equals lives saved — both Iraqi and American."[1] Taylor had a more realistic attitude. He was one of several Vietnam veterans in the upper echelons of the State Department team in Baghdad. (Negroponte had served as a young diplomat in Saigon and USAID/Iraq director Spike Stephenson as a combat engineer in central Vietnam.) The experience provided the men with a nuanced view of the possibilities of the rebuilding. It would not result in Iraqi loyalty to America, but it could perhaps provide a foundation to build a better country. In the long term, that would reward U.S. interests. In the short term, however, Taylor thought it was foolish to believe that the

U.S. aid would reduce the insurgency by buying new friends. It didn't happen in Vietnam and it wasn't going to happen in Iraq. "We were not in Iraq to win hearts and minds. We were not doing reconstruction to try to show that the Americans were good guys and that the Iraqis should like us," Taylor said. "If we were trying to win hearts and minds, we would have done a bunch of much smaller things. The principal motivation was to reconstruct so that stability, economic growth, security, and political growth could evolve."

Taylor's suspicions were confirmed during a trip to southern Iraq, where many Shiites long oppressed by Saddam had indeed greeted arriving American troops as liberators. A Shiite sheik pulled him aside and complained that the Americans should leave as soon as possible. Occupation, Taylor decided, was a bad idea, no matter who the occupier or what the motivation. "The Iraqis really did not want us there," Taylor said. "Fine, come in, build, and get the hell out was the attitude."

The changes to the rebuilding effort carried a cost. The decision to boost spending on security and other programs meant that Taylor had to cut back on some of the originally planned projects. Hundreds of health clinics and hospitals, sewage lines and bridges, electrical substations and power plants, vanished overnight. Only 300 of 425 planned electrical projects and 49 out of 136 water projects were built. Stuart Bowen called the cuts the "reconstruction gap" — the difference between what the United States had promised to build and what it did.[2] In all, Taylor set in motion changes that upended $5.6 billion in planned spending — about a sixth of the total American money available to rebuild Iraq.

Water was the hardest-hit sector. Taylor took more than $2 billion of the money that Nash had planned to spend on water treatment and sewage plants. Taylor even canceled a new water purification plant in Halabja, the town where Saddam's air force had slaughtered five thousand Kurdish men, women, and children with poison gas. The local water chief burst into tears when he found out from a reporter that his project had been canceled.[3] Taylor broke the news of the cutbacks to Iraq's minister of municipalities and public works, a young, energetic Kurdish woman named Nesreen Berwari. On several occasions, he had to tell her that he was cutting out more water and sewer plants. On his last trip, Berwari stared at him icily. "Never come back here and tell me this again. This has to be it. It cannot be any more."

Berwari worked out of a stylish glass and white brick home behind high concrete walls in the Green Zone. Outside were three military checkpoints and a narrow cordon of concrete, razor wire, and sandbags to defend against suicide bombers. Inside were high ceilings and a big whitewashed room furnished with plush red velvet chairs and a trickling fountain. Light filtered in from opaque, floor-to-ceiling windows. The Pottery Barn look was an indication of Berwari's ties to the secular Iraqi elites that the United States had appointed to run Iraq. She had worked for the UN's redevelopment program in Kurdistan during the Saddam years, was fluent in English, and had studied at Harvard's Kennedy School of Government. She wore her secularism on her finger: she was married to Ghazi Yawar, a Sunni sheik who was serving as Iraq's interim president.

When I met with her a few weeks after her confrontation with Taylor, she was still angry. Nobody had consulted her about the cuts, but she had to break the bad news to the tribal sheiks and local villagers who believed they would soon be getting clean drinking water for the first time in their lives. The cuts left her with less than half her original budget and far less than the $10 billion that she estimated was necessary to provide clean drinking water to 90 percent of Iraq's population. "I'm still amazed at how a program meant for reconstruction, that could have provided more services and could have effected stability, could be cut so dramatically. What kind of message does that send?" she asked.

Berwari was a realist. She recognized that the United States had inherited a crumbling, decrepit system that had been neglected for years. But she had trouble understanding why the reconstruction had not proceeded faster. We spoke just after the January 2005 election in which religious Shiite parties had triumphed at the polls. Berwari credited their victory partly to America's inability to show visible results. "I wanted us to start digging in the earth, putting walls up, putting water in pipes," she told me. "What has happened . . . was very disappointing."

SWEAT

The new direction for the rebuilding program was the final outcome of a dispute that had played out for months between Nash, the head of the reconstruction agency, and his counterpart at USAID, Spike Stephenson. Nash was committed to his vision of building a new Iraq with bridges, health clinics, and power plants. He thought that a top-of-the-line infrastructure was necessary to draw in new businesses that would help Iraq prosper. What company would bring jobs and money to a country without power or clean water? Nash also wanted to control money and plans through the agency that he created to direct the reconstruction, the Project and Contracting Office. Iraq needed a foreman; Nash was it. Without a rebuilding czar, he believed, the reconstruction was bound to get bogged down and confused. Agencies like the U.S. Army Corps of Engineers and USAID were there to implement the program, not invent it. "It seemed to me that people need the basics: water, health, and other things. That was what I thought I was supposed to do," Nash told me. "It's a program manager's job to get it done."

Stephenson had almost the opposite idea. A veteran of postconflict situations in Lebanon, El Salvador, and Serbia, he believed that big infrastructure projects took too long to get moving. Stephenson thought U.S. money was better spent on employing Iraqis, paying them to pick up trash or dig ditches, whatever it took to get money on the street. At a higher level, the United States could help by reforming Iraq's outdated political and economic systems. Stephenson thought Iraq needed trainers and educators to get out into villages and towns and talk about democracy. They needed economic experts to prepare the country's state-owned businesses to move into the private sector. Agricultural advisers could improve harvests for the millions of Iraqis dependent on farming. Teaching provided more long-term benefits than a cinder block building. Ultimately, with money in people's hands and new economic structures in place, big businesses would come in with private capital and build the power plants and oil wells that Iraq needed.

Stephenson's vision was widely accepted by the international development community. Decades of work around the world had shown that big public work projects usually turned into expensive eyesores. Third World countries lacked the money or expertise to run and maintain dams, hospitals, and power plants. The World Bank turned away from such work after finding that infrastructure projects encouraged corruption and stifled the growth of private industry. The United States had even helped implement a similar program in Iraq before. The so-called Point Four program was an outgrowth of the Marshall Plan in which Truman encouraged building in the Middle East. In the early 1950s USAID sent technical experts in water, highways, and dams to help out as Iraq embarked on a massive building program. "This was the dawn of foreign aid and large infrastructure programs, and we subsequently discovered that they don't work," Stephenson told me. "You tend to build white elephants. You don't necessarily build things in which people have ownership," he told me.

The philosophical differences were made worse by enmity between Nash and Stephenson. Tall and reserved, Nash could be sensitive to criticism. Many in the State Department and USAID found him thin-skinned, temperamental, and overly protective of his turf. He threatened to quit in December 2003 when it appeared that the Pentagon would direct more money to USAID and then again in May 2004, when the State Department proposed taking away some of his control over the reconstruction. "He was a good man, but he was a military engineer and he was in way over his head," said one senior U.S. reconstruction official who worked closely with Nash.

Stephenson, curt, tightly wound, and confrontational, was openly critical of Nash and his reconstruction plan. Stephenson even complained about Nash to Bremer. In January 2004 USAID issued a second infrastructure contract to Bechtel, the agency's primary contractor, following the first contract given to the company in April 2003. Nash was supposed to assign the specific jobs within the agreement to Bechtel to keep work flowing until his organization got moving with its own infrastructure contracts later that spring. Bechtel's so-called bridge contract had a theoretical cap of $1.8 billion. But by March, Nash had only farmed out $180 million worth of work. Stephenson interpreted this as an attempt by Nash to hoard reconstruction money for his own agency's contractors.

From that point on, Nash and Stephenson, the heads of the two largest agencies involved in rebuilding, barely spoke to one another. Each saw the other as an obstacle. "They didn't get along at all. They didn't have mutual respect for each other," said one U.S. official who worked with both men. "It was not a happy arrangement."

Stephenson was joined in his frustration by military commanders in Iraq. Generals like Pete Chiarelli saw the reconstruction as another way to fight the war. Better public services would convince the Iraqis that it was smarter to ally with the Americans than with the insurgents. Lt. Col. S. Jamie Gayton of the U.S. Army, who oversaw reconstruction for the Third Infantry Division's Second Brigade, joked that Iraqis needed to see "Americans' SWET" — sewer, water, electricity, and trash pickup. More jobs would cut into the recruitment pool of angry, unemployed men, and it seemed far better to have young Iraqis holding D-handled shovels than AK-47s. The generals also believed — quite correctly — that the slow pace of the reconstruction undercut the war effort by increasing distrust about America's intentions in Iraq.

Stephenson capitalized on the frustration by bypassing Nash to create a direct alliance with the military. In April 2004 he and Chiarelli began discussing reconstruction work in Sadr City, a particularly restive neighborhood in eastern Baghdad under Chiarelli's command. Chiarelli flew Stephenson and his staff by Black Hawk helicopter from the Green Zone to a meeting at Camp Victory at the Baghdad airport. (At the time, with the insurgency exploding, it was too dangerous to travel the six miles by road.) There the two men reached an agreement that Sadr City would become a sort of demonstration project — a tightly focused effort designed to provide jobs and community improvements. After Taylor arrived Sadr City would be a test of the new U.S. plan.

Stephenson and Chiarelli were odd partners. Stephenson was a short, intense former lawyer steeped in the international development philosophy of USAID. Chiarelli was a tall, angular West Point graduate who once dreamed of leading an armored charge into Baghdad.[4] But their alliance would produce the most successful example of rebuilding in Iraq.

SADR CITY

Unlike the approach prevailing elsewhere in Iraq, where the reconstruction fell under the purview of a hodgepodge of U.S. civilian agencies, Chiarelli's commitment to rebuilding provided sustained, focused leadership in a limited geographic area. Chiarelli, like all military commanders, served a one-year tour in Iraq, compared to the months-long rotations of civilian advisers. Military commanders also got to know their areas. Unlike civilians, they were able to get out on the streets, befriend community leaders, and hear firsthand about local troubles. "Your struggle is not with the occupation," Chiarelli told several dozen sheiks and local leaders at a meeting in an empty lot in Baghdad filled with garbage and uninstalled sewage pipes. "Your struggle is right before your eyes."[5]

A tank commander by training, Chiarelli took a crash course in municipal services. He sent his men to study with city planners from Austin, Texas, before coming to Baghdad. His focus was on basic services: sewers, water, electricity, and garbage. He wanted to quickly show Iraqis in Sadr City that the coalition could build projects that would benefit their lives. Chiarelli was not concerned with doing a project the most efficient way, unlike a profit-driven contractor. The more labor a project took, the better: that meant more Iraqis working, earning money, and seeing the fruits of cooperation with the coalition. Whenever possible, Chiarelli hired local Iraqi contractors, who in turn employed many of the militia members who had once battled U.S. troops.

Chiarelli was relentless in demanding results. Each Monday, he held a meeting at 2 p.m. in a building in the Green Zone that had once housed a unit of Saddam's secret police. The gatherings came to be known as the Pete Chiarelli Show. In attendance were his men, contractors, engineers, and other reconstruction officials — including the Project and Contracting Office, which also began participating in the Sadr City experiment. Chiarelli would review each project, sewer line by sewer line, to get status updates. Chiarelli showed a dazzling command of detail, knowing the port in Italy where a generator was delayed, or the type of microchip necessary for installation in a water treatment panel. Those who failed to show progress were treated to a blistering barrage of questions. "By force of his personality, he made things happen," said Bill Taylor.

Stephenson pitched in by supplying money and expertise to help guide the project. The U.S. military had access to only small amounts of reconstruction money through a program called the Commander's Emergency Response Program, which mostly paid for $10,000 and $20,000 projects like digging a new well or painting a schoolhouse. Stephenson had access to much more cash, but he saw the benefit to directing it toward smaller projects. "There's often a lot more value in the $30,000 project than there is in the $30 million project," Stephenson said. "If people see that things are changing, if you give them hope, there is an amazing wellspring of patience."

The program got off to a shaky start. In August the followers of Muqtada Sadr — whose father provided the slum its name — rose up in Sadr City, Najaf, and elsewhere in Iraq. For a month Chiarelli's men performed their routine duties: fighting insurgents. When I visited Sadr City that month, it was a ghost town. The neighborhood sits on the eastern edge of Baghdad, an eight-square-mile area that from the air appears to be an orderly town sliced into neat squares. On the ground, however, the slum presented a new definition of urban despair. The wide streets were dusty, potholed, and heaped with trash. The one- and two-story homes and shops were dirty, unpainted, and cracked. There was not a tree, not a park, just an endless hot tumble of concrete buildings. The only green in sight was in the Shiite banners that proclaimed loyalty to Sadr's cause. Raw sewage coursed down side streets in black rivulets. There were no signs at all that the American reconstruction had done anything.

I sat down one sweltering afternoon in August 2004 with Ahmed Kadhem, a forty-three-year-old Iraqi teacher and wood carver. Kadhem was among the Iraqis the Bush administration talked about when predicting a warm welcome for U.S. forces. A Shiite, Kadhem lived an impoverished life with his family just off Sadr City's main boulevard. His single-story concrete block home was barely the width of his arm span, wedged like a shoe box in a row of similar houses. Inside was a threadbare rug, a portrait of Imam Ali, a Shiite religious figure, and a low, worn red couch. He was in every way a typical Iraqi, marked by dictatorship and uncertain of the future.

Kadhem cheered the downfall of Saddam as the promise of a new beginning. But as the months passed, and life in his neighborhood grew worse, he began to doubt. The electricity, never good, now flowed to his house only a few hours a day. He could no longer moonlight as a carpenter, because he could not power his tools. The water from his tap, never clean, grew so muddy that he could not see the fish in his tank. A pool of raw sewage ten feet wide and twenty feet long sprang up in the street in front of his door, filling the home with a permanent, eye-watering stench. Worst of all, his neighborhood had become a battleground. As gunfire rattled outside, Kadhem and his family of four were trapped in their home, where the temperatures often soared to 130 degrees. By any definition, it was misery. "They said they were going to fix many things, and still nothing has happened," Kadhem said as we sat in his airless, reeking living room. "If the Americans had done well, most people would be with the Americans and we would not have these problems."

Kadhem waved his arm at the scene outside his door, homes pockmarked with bullets and streets rutted with potholes. He grew angry, his arms rising higher as he gestured. He and his friends had once had faith in America. No more, he said. A slight man with a Vandyke beard and skin the color of burnt caramel, he might have been speaking for all Iraqis — and many Americans as well. "The U.S. can do anything. They have all the billions of dollars, the firms, the companies," he said in the darkness of his living room, the light dimmed by another blackout. "But nothing has happened." As an American, I left the visit depressed — even ashamed — that the reconstruction had accomplished so little for a people so much in need.

By September, Iraqi prime minister Ayad Allawi had cut an Iraq-wide peace deal with Sadr's rebels, who had suffered the loss of hundreds of men in their unwise standoff with American forces. Chiarelli and Stephenson redoubled their efforts, devoting $805 million to Sadr City — more than $100 million per square mile. Contractors like Parsons and Bechtel began hiring local Iraqis, some of them from the Mahdi Army, to dig trenches for new sewer lines, pick up trash by hand, and string electric wires to buildings. "If you're employing from the neighborhood, [Iraqis are] out there digging the trenches for the pipes and they see the pipes arrive. It buys you a lot of time to get water running in those pipes," Stephenson said. In one particularly impressive stroke of genius, the men divided the city into four sectors, with each one receiving different kinds of basic services. In one area, contractors might begin putting up power lines. In another, the focus would be on fresh, clean drinking water. In that way each neighborhood could see progress in the others and realize what they would receive next if they cooperated with the Americans.

The focus on delivering services corrected another gaping flaw in the reconstruction strategy under Bremer's occupation government, what came to be known as "the pipes problem." The rebuilding designated billions of dollars for power plants, water and sewer treatment stations, oil industry equipment, and telephone exchanges. But it paid relatively little attention to the pipes needed to carry the fruits of those investments to ordinary Iraqis. The oil pipelines were corroded and collapsed continually. There were not enough substations or power lines to deliver electricity to local users. The water and sewer lines were in the worst shape of all. The pipes were cracked and leaking after decades of neglect. The clean water that flowed through them often leaked away or, worse, became contaminated by sewage. Rather than delivering clean water, the pipes carried poison. Chiarelli was determined to make sure that services were delivered to ordinary Iraqis. "This is the key ingredient, for the first time, clean water and electricity will get directly to the houses in Sadr City," Chiarelli said. "We are not only fixing it, we are helping them have a hope for their lives and their future."[6]

A WORKSHOP, WOOD, AND A WISP OF HOPE

When I returned to Sadr City a year later, it was clear that progress had been made — imperfect and incomplete perhaps, but progress nonetheless. The first surprise came when I made a run through Sadr City with Lieutenant Colonel Gayton and his soldiers. The Third Infantry Division had replaced General Chiarelli's First Cavalry Division but had continued his policies. We climbed into a convoy of armored Humvees bristling with weapons. As we rolled into Sadr City, we were not met by the usual sullen or fearful looks that I had seen elsewhere when American military convoys drove past. Instead men stood and waved. Women smiled. Children flashed thumbs-up signs as the convoy rumbled across the potholed streets. It was a far more welcoming scene than my earlier experience of an urban war zone. "We're making a huge impact," Gayton said as his men pulled up to a sewer station newly repaired with U.S. funds. "It has been incredibly safe, incredibly quiet, and incredibly secure."

After the August 2004 outbreak, Sadr City had continued to suffer car bomb attacks and violent demonstrations against U.S. forces. But overall the city had remained calm, especially when compared with other parts of Baghdad. Only one U.S. soldier had been killed in Sadr City during Gayton's year in Iraq. A tour through the city only backed up the sense that the American military had actually made inroads. At the newly repaired sewer station, the local family guarding it greeted Gayton like an old friend; he had visited several times before. Haita Zamel showed Gayton how the local sewer authority was fixing a problem that had developed in one pump. She proudly showed off the small home that had been built on the site to replace a dilapidated trailer where her family of six once lived. She even asked Gayton for computer software to teach English to her children. "When you tell me something, I know you'll do it," she said, clutching tightly at the white scarf covering her head. "To the last day of our life, we are with you. Us and all of our neighbors."

Gayton and his men clambered back into the Humvees and moved on. A few minutes later he ordered his driver to make a random stop in front of a group of stores where water lines had been installed. He wanted to make sure the water was flowing. As a crowd gathered, the shop owners acknowledged better water. But they complained about electricity, saying that power lines were being installed at nearby shops but not theirs. Gayton smiled. The strategy of dividing the city up into sectors with different restoration programs was working as planned.

"Everything happens one step at a time," Gayton told the men.

It was far from a city on a hill. As Gayton and his men roared away, one soldier, fearing a possible car bomb, fired into the ground to warn a vehicle that was getting too close. Still, at each of half a dozen stops, the complaints were tempered by friendly banter and acknowledgment of improvements. At one point residents and workers praised a health clinic being built. But then they pointed in anger at a huge puddle of sickly green sewage blocking the entrance. Gayton promised to prod the Iraqis to make repairs. "We are suffering," one worker, Jabbar Abed Khalef, told Gayton. Batting away flies, Khalef held up his shoes, coated in black muck. "Our children are sick. The road is blocked. It's a disaster." But a moment later Khalef was praising the United States for working more quickly than the Iraqi government. "We know that if the Americans don't do it, the Iraqi government will take a long time," he said.

At the end of the run, Gayton appeared pleased. A fit man with an easy command of figures, he got excited whenever the convoy passed a garbage truck at work. "I love to see garbage trucks," he'd shout to me over the roar of the Humvee. He said the investment made by the United States had paid dividends. The previous year, soldiers at Gayton's base were the target of more than a thousand mortar strikes. There had been none in the past eight months, and only a handful of attacks of any sort on U.S. troops. Gayton did not claim that the reconstruction alone had led to the decrease in violence, and he acknowledged that the militia members would rise up again if commanded by Sadr. But Gayton believed that fewer people would heed the call. "Our goal is to provide them with hope so they see that tomorrow is better than today," he said. "We want them to look to the left and the right and say, 'Hey, joining hands with the [Iraqi] government and the coalition [forces] is going to help us more so than anybody else.'"

After my ride with Gayton, I returned to visit Ahmed Kadhem again. It had been almost a year since I had last seen him. But it was again clear that things had taken a turn for the better. This time he insisted that we meet in his new workshop, where he had opened a business in an upscale Baghdad neighborhood in the north, making knockoff furniture from pictures that he found in magazines. "There is some movement," he said, as we stood talking amid the smell of sawdust and the whir of an ancient buzz saw that he powered from a gas generator. "People have taken note."

True, Kadhem's own home had not seen much improvement. A year later the blackouts were more frequent and his water was still undrinkable. The pond of sewage had disappeared only after Kadhem and his neighbors took up a collection and paid a private contractor to come and clean it up. "No government has helped us," said Kadhem. "We have helped the government." Elsewhere in Sadr City, though, Kadhem noticed a difference. His four children were again playing in the streets, now free from fighting. Kadhem and his wife, also a teacher, had seen their schools painted, books and supplies donated, and new classrooms and bathrooms built.

Sadr City had calmed down. The peace pact with Sadr's rebels, intense military patrols, and the goodwill fostered by the reconstruction were turning the slum into an oasis of security in Baghdad. It wasn't perfect, but it was enough. The relative safety was what Kadhem needed to make use of the opportunity provided by the overthrow of Saddam. With Saddam gone, once-repressed Shiite Muslims like Kadhem had more freedom. And a salary hike implemented under Bremer had increased his pay tenfold.

Kadhem now spent every free moment from his teaching career at the store, a narrow garage on the first floor of a home in a middle-class neighborhood of Sunnis and Shiites. In one corner sat a graceful, curved headboard made of wood imported from Malaysia. In another sat a partially completed bedroom set, built from a picture in a catalog. As we talked, several customers stopped by to check on the progress of their orders. Kadhem's son and two other employees flitted in and out, carrying wood, sodas, and supplies. Kadhem said that for the first time, he could imagine a future for his children better than his own life. "Things are different. Before, we felt afraid. Now there is freedom and we feel there will be a solution and it will be better," he said. "At this stage we have to endure. The change from a dictatorship to a democracy is not easy."

In Sadr City the rebuilding effort appeared to have some success. It would not be widely repeated, however. That was partly due to money woes: the United States simply couldn't afford to spend nearly a billion dollars per Iraqi city. But the promise of the new program was marred by another new American strategy.

11

The Fix

After the United States handed power to the Iraqis in the summer of 2004, the country's newly appointed prime minister, Ayad Allawi, made a request. The Iraqi army, he told his American military advisers, needed two divisions of tanks. A long row of Russian-built T-55 war machines — the model made all too familiar by Saddam — grinding down Baghdad's wide boulevards would demonstrate to the Iraqi people that a firm hand was in charge. Allawi wrote President Bush, asking that two mechanized divisions be ready before the January 2005 elections. Better to have an Iraqi tank posted outside a polling place than an M1A1 Abrams.[1]

American advisers were skeptical. At the time, Iraq's battles were taking place in cities like Najaf and Fallujah against lightly armed guerrilla fighters. Tanks had no role in such urban combat. They couldn't even fit down the narrow, winding streets in some of Iraq's ancient cities. U.S.-trained Iraqi soldiers had cut and run during the violence in April. They lacked weapons, uniforms, almost everything. "Right now tanks and heavy armament are not necessary," said Fred C. Smith, the U.S. senior adviser to the Iraqi Defense Ministry. "What's needed are well-trained, disciplined troops with the proper equipment."[2]

Smith's counsel was ignored. The Iraqis "were like, 'Hey, we're a sovereign government now. . . . We'll buy what we want,'" one military adviser told me. In August 2004, with American approval, Allawi pushed forward an estimated $283 million of Iraqi funds to refurbish mothballed tanks. The United States would oversee the training and support of the new mechanized division. Donald Rumsfeld pitched in by making a plea to former

Warsaw Pact nations that had joined NATO. Would they consider donating their old tanks to the new Iraqi army?[3]

The Americans' willingness to entertain Allawi's demand reflected another of Negroponte's new strategies in rebuilding Iraq. First, the primary goal, and much of the money, shifted away from big American companies and toward paying for security. It made little sense to build electrical towers and oil pipelines when the guerrilla fighters kept blowing them up. Second, the Americans were going to step back. Negroponte was clear: if the United States wanted Iraq to be a sovereign nation, the Iraqis had to take control. It was their country now.

The flaw in that strategy became apparent all through the fall and winter of 2005. If Jerry Bremer and the Defense Department were too controlling, the State Department was not controlling enough. As Americans tried to foist responsibility onto the Iraqis, the rebuilding program stalled. After three decades of dictatorship and a dozen years of sanctions, Iraqis were not well trained in operations and maintenance procedures. Power plant turbines broke down. Sewage plants clogged. Water treatment centers functioned below capacity. Billions of dollars in U.S. investments began falling into disrepair. The effort to empower the Iraqis began to look like neglect.

Iraq's new forces became another casualty of the laissez-faire strategy. Beginning with Allawi's tank deal, American and British advisers looked on fecklessly as the new Iraqi Defense Ministry embarked on a massive spending spree. Over the next six months, Allawi and top ministry officials crisscrossed the globe to cut deals with Polish, Pakistani, and American companies. By early 2005 the Defense Ministry had committed nearly a billion dollars in Iraqi funds, much of it in secret, no-bid contracts, for everything from trucks to helicopters to AK-47s. The money flowed in bricks of cash through the hands of middlemen linked to ministry officials.

Both Americans and Iraqis suspected corruption. U.S. military commanders complained that ministry officials refused to sign contracts for urgently needed equipment, apparently angling instead to get jobs for political allies and friends. Two American contractors who complained about possible graft at the ministry wound up dead. One of Bill Taylor's advisers ordered a review of the ministry's books. It found a "high risk of fraud." Goods and services showed all the hallmarks of skim-offs. One commander told me the Iraqi army's new helmets appeared to have been purchased at a "toy store."

When the Iraqis undertook their own inquiry, they determined that much of the equipment purchased was in fact substandard: helicopters that were too old, trucks that wouldn't run, guns that wouldn't fire. In May 2005 they released an audit of Defense Ministry purchases.[4] It was a mind-boggling chronicle of waste: nearly $1.3 billion in Iraqi funds had been misspent or could not be accounted for. Arrest warrants were issued for top ministry officials. "It is possibly one of the largest thefts in history," said Ali Allawi, Iraq's finance minister. "Huge amounts of money have disappeared. In return we got nothing but scraps of metal."[5]

One man sat in the middle of the mess: a Polish Iraqi used car dealer whom the Americans turned into one of the most powerful men in Iraq. He was the chief of procurement for the Ministry of Defense. His name was Ziad Cattan.[6]

THE DOER

Cattan was broad-shouldered with a middle-aged paunch, his hair and mustache flecked with gray. He had a habit of leaning forward as he spoke, as though always trading confidences. He could be loud, blustery, and garrulous, an Iraqi version of Zorba the Greek. Born in Baghdad in 1955, Cattan left Iraq in the late 1970s to pursue an advanced degree in economics in Poland. After receiving his PhD from the Economic Academy of Krakow, Cattan held a series of jobs. He imported cars to and from Poland, opened a pizza parlor in Bonn, and worked in public affairs for Iraqi Airways — traditionally an assignment for Iraqi intelligence officers, though Cattan insisted he had no ties to the Saddam regime. He was, he claimed, a small businessman who embraced his new country, learned its language, and married a Polish woman. "Half of my life is connected to Poland," he wrote in a short autobiography. "If the homeland is where home is, then Poland is my homeland; but Iraq will always remain my family country."[7]

Cattan returned to Iraq only two days before the U.S. invasion. He wanted to rescue his father, a retired Iraqi general who refused to leave despite the gathering clouds of war. Cattan, then forty-eight, described sitting in a sleazy bar on the Syrian border, watching Bush's final ultimatum giving Saddam and his sons forty-eight hours to leave Iraq. "There are moments in a man's life when his fate is being decided. My turning point came in March 2003. . . . The people who knew I was going to Baghdad told me: 'Fool, don't go, wait.' But I did not believe that the war would break out. Besides, I had no choice."[8]

Cattan plotted the advance of American troops on a map in his father's apartment in Officer City, a Baghdad neighborhood filled with retired Iraqi officers. After the city's fall, Cattan quickly became a bridge between the Iraqis and their new occupiers, each of them struggling to understand the other. Cattan endeared himself to the marines and army officers who occupied his area. He had a passable command of English, familiarity with the West, and a mysterious ability to get things done. He bought furniture, catered lunches, even imported Coca-Cola for the soldiers. He led marine officers to weapons caches that Saddam's army had stored in local elementary schools. He testified in favor of Capt. Roger Maynulet, an army officer accused in the alleged mercy killing of an Iraqi.[9] "The thing about Ziad is he's a doer. He can make things happen," one of his American supporters told me.

The direct, take-charge manner was a refreshing change for Americans frustrated by the cagey half-answers they usually got from Iraqis battered by dictatorship, and as the occupation progressed, Cattan won ever more important jobs. He ran for local elections sponsored by the Americans, becoming head of a large neighborhood council in an area called Nine Nisan.[10] There he worked closely with coalition and military officials to dole out rebuilding contracts for new schools, parks, and other projects. Cattan proved himself adept at moving millions of dollars needed to pay the contracts through his friendships with Iraqi businessmen known as *hawalat*, or money brokers. *Hawala* is an informal way to transfer money, used for centuries throughout the Muslim world. In its most basic form, it worked like this: An Iraqi who needed to move money would give funds to a broker in Baghdad, who charged a small commission for the service. The broker would call an allied broker in another city, who would dispense the money to its final recipient. The two brokers would settle the debt between themselves later. There was no paperwork; it was all on the honor system.

With the banking system in collapse and all transactions in cash, hawala was the only practical way to do business in Iraq in the early days of the occupation, and Cattan directed millions of dollars in business to his friends. By August 2003 one friend's company was moving as much as $7 million per day. The brokers in turn gave tips about large — and thus possibly suspicious — money transfers to Cattan, who then passed them on to his American backers. "They supported me to become a big man in Iraq," Cattan said of the money brokers, whom he referred to as "my friends."

By October 2003 Cattan attracted Bremer's attention. Bremer attended a dedication ceremony for Nine Nisan's newly refurbished district hall. Children in Sunni and Shiite Kaffiyeh headdresses and Kurdish turbans danced to drums and reed flutes. A boy stood and read a poem about mass graves and Iraq's newfound freedom. Cattan was in tears. In his memoir Bremer praised Cattan as an example of the best Iraq had to offer, even including a photo of him. "Having traded a comfortable life in Europe 'to serve my country' for a minimal salary and the drudgery of rebuilding [a Baghdad neighborhood], he embodied the dedication so many Iraqis felt for their nation," Bremer wrote.[11]

AN ESTONIAN, AN AUSTRALIAN, AND A WHITE BOARD

That fall, as the United States moved toward handing sovereignty to the Iraqis, Bremer decided that the Iraqi army needed a new command structure. The creation of a new, civilian-led Defense Ministry was typical of the last-minute rush that marked coalition initiatives. Col. P. J. Dermer, an Arabic-speaking army officer with a master's degree from Georgetown, was thrown into the task just seven months before the handover. He described creating the new ministry in a matter of weeks with two other defense experts, one from Estonia and one from Australia. "We brought in a white board and markers, and the three of us printed out the research about every Western-style ministry of defense we could find. We printed out the NATO structure and the EU structure, I think, and several other structures of organizations around the world today. We studied those for a couple days, and then we got to drawing on the white board the Iraqi Ministry of Defense, and that's literally how it started," he said. "We're paying now . . . and we'll pay forevermore, because we had to do it on the run."[12]

The coalition wanted to model the new army on Western standards, with civilians in charge. But Saddam's military had been entirely run by officers, most of them banned from public service after the invasion by Bremer's anti-Baathist order. That left no pool of experienced Iraqis from which to draw. No Iraqi civilian had ever held a leadership position in the military. Dermer began frantically recruiting candidates for the new ministry, flying around the country and relying on word of mouth to find people. The new recruits were sent to Washington for three weeks of training, a sort of crash course in how to run a defense department. Cattan was one of the first to go.

Upon his return, Cattan rose quickly through the ministry's ranks, becoming the director of military procurement after the first director's assassination. Cattan described himself as a benevolent tyrant, bent on approving every purchase to ensure accountability. "I take a lot of power over all of them," Cattan said. "And nobody can sleep if they don't ask me. If they want a pencil they have to ask me. I was more dictatorial than Saddam Hussein in Iraq — but in a positive way." Cattan also boasted about his ability to get things done. When Iraqi security forces had trouble with their weapons during the April and May attacks, Cattan said, he acquired ammunition and AK-47s on the black market. "The generals from [the American training mission] came to me and say they were very happy that [the Iraqi army] don't use old machine guns but they don't ask from where we bought them," Cattan said.

The Americans were not exactly comfortable with Cattan. But he stood out as a man willing to cut through the red tape. "He was somebody we recruited, and we were taking a chance on him just like on everybody else," Fred Smith, the American defense adviser, told me. "Ziad is not a choirboy. But he was willing to serve."

Not everyone was happy with Cattan. Shortly after taking office in June 2004, the new Iraqi defense minister, Hazim Shaalan, fired him, citing an internal workplace dispute. Smith and other coalition officials, however, convinced the ministry to hire Cattan back. Smith said he was less interested in protecting Cattan than in protecting the idea of a civil service that defends employees from arbitrary termination. Whatever the case, the incident sealed Cattan's reputation in the eyes of the Iraqis as America's man in the Defense Ministry, in charge of equipping the entire Iraqi army. "He was working in the Defense Ministry from day one with Americans," Shaalan said. "I refused to bring him back — I said to the Americans, if you want him, you hire him."

FLOWERS, SHOES, AND HELICOPTERS

Gen. David Petraeus was the U.S. military officer who oversaw the mission of training and equipping the new Iraqi forces. Petraeus was considered among the best the military had to offer, a blunt, no-nonsense leader who had spearheaded the 101st Airborne's charge through northern Iraq in 2003. Early on, Petraeus showed a better grasp than many other Americans in Iraq of the danger of the slow-moving reconstruction program. Petraeus referred to the phenomenon as the "man on the moon" problem: The Iraqis "would ask us why we could overthrow Saddam in three weeks and why we could put a man on the moon but we couldn't give them a job right then, right there," Petraeus said. "Why we couldn't throw a switch and get the entire electrical infrastructure working again."[13] As a result, Petraeus emphasized doable reconstruction projects to win hearts and minds during his time in Mosul, going so far as to reopen a closed cement factory that was a major source of employment. He was smart, telegenic, and popular among the troops. When Petraeus returned to Iraq in the summer of 2004 to begin the training mission, he was featured on the cover of *Newsweek* magazine. "Can this man save Iraq?" was the headline.

Petraeus created a task force to oversee the training called the Multi-National Security Transition Command — Iraq, or MNSTCI. One of those who felt the squeeze was Cattan, who said Petraeus encouraged him to spend Iraqi funds to supplement American spending on arms contracts that had gotten bogged down in the U.S. contracting process. At the same time, Shaalan and Allawi wanted to prove that the new Iraqi interim government could deliver results in the war against the insurgents. As a result, Cattan was given $600 million to spend, with a mandate to use it under Iraqi budgeting rules by the end of December. The new director of procurement for the Iraqi military had never before purchased arms and was bewildered by the task. "Before, I sold water, flowers, shoes, cars — but not weapons," Cattan said. "We didn't know anything about weapons."

Nevertheless, in September, Cattan signed the first of thirty-eight contracts with the Bumar Group, the Polish arms dealer that had filed a protest after losing the first U.S. contract to arm troops to Ahmed Chalabi's friends at Nour. The contracts, worth $400 million, required Bumar to supply Iraq with thirty-six Russian and Polish transport helicopters and six hundred Polish armored personnel trucks. Cattan agreed to pay for the merchandise up front, in cash — a condition imposed by Bumar to mitigate the risk of dealing with an unstable country with a bad credit history, Cattan said. To move the money, Cattan turned to one of his money broker friends, an Iraqi businessman named Naer Mohammed Jumaili. Other deals followed, and all told Cattan signed nearly $1 billion worth of contracts with Jumaili's companies. Cattan said Jumaili charged 1 percent for his services. If true — Jumaili didn't comment — Jumaili could have earned up to $10 million in fees.

Cattan described his reliance on the broker as a necessity, since Jumaili was Bumar's sole registered agent in Iraq — a claim Bumar denied. Cattan also said he used Jumaili's services because it was the only way to move money out of Iraq. That was not technically true, since the United States had set up a wire transfer system, but the American system took months to approve large cash transfers. Going through Jumaili was undoubtedly faster. Jumaili's involvement as middleman had the additional benefit of providing a way to dodge Iraq's international creditors. To the worldwide banking community, it appeared that the transactions were between the Poles and an Iraqi company, not the Iraqi state, which owed more than $120 billion in debt. The United States did nothing as this clever bit of international debt dodging went on.

Both U.S. military and State Department officials met with Cattan and Shaalan as the purchases were negotiated and paid. But they said they had only a vague knowledge of what was happening at the time. "We didn't know the numbers, we didn't know what was going on with the money," one military adviser said. "We heard rumors that Ziad was going out and buying stuff, but we had no way of confirming what it was. He would disappear for a month out to Poland and then he'd come back boasting about buying helicopters and tanks."

Then Dale Stoffel started complaining.

THE UNQUIET AMERICAN

Dale Stoffel was one of the scores of private contractors who flocked to Baghdad in search of fortune.[14] At forty-three, he had a lanky frame, a slight paunch, and a goatee that fit his self-created image as an international adventurer, a private-sector James Bond. He was roguish and sly, smart and driven. He loved Cuban cigars and exotic weaponry, George Bush and the Republican Party. His background was filled with intrigue and controversy. As a young man, he served in the navy as an intelligence officer specializing in complex weapons systems. He investigated the 1987 attack of the USS *Stark* in which thirty-seven sailors died after being struck by Iraqi missiles in the Persian Gulf. From fragments in the wreck, Stoffel determined that the ship was struck by two missiles, not one, undermining Iraqi claims of an accident.[15]

After leaving the navy, Stoffel became involved in a top-secret military program to buy arms from enemy nations to test against American weapons systems. He posed as a weapons dealer, pretending to buy arms for African nations and then turning them over to the U.S. government. Plunging into the shady world of international arms trafficking, Stoffel developed contacts across Eastern Europe, particularly in Ukraine and Bulgaria. He purchased weapons including surface-to-air missiles and antiaircraft systems. He told stories of downing expensive bottles of '61 Lafite Rothschild while drinking with high rollers in Monte Carlo.[16] At times the lines appeared to blur. The company he ran, called Miltex, was named in a 1999 Human Rights Watch Report for involvement in the illegal shipment of missiles to Africa. Stoffel said it was a case of mistaken identity, a former employee using his company's name. To prevent further confusion, he created a new company, called Wye Oak Technology, based in Monongahela, Pennsylvania, a small town fifteen miles south of Pittsburgh. The firm was essentially Stoffel and some of his closest business associates.

Wye Oak too became involved in controversy. In 2001 McDonnell Douglas, a Boeing subsidiary, contracted with Stoffel to purchase thirty-two Russian supersonic sea-skimming missiles for U.S. Navy tests. McDonnell Douglas later sued Stoffel, claiming that he delivered only a fraction of missiles ordered. Stoffel countered that the U.S. government had undercut him by hiring other companies to pursue the same missiles. The settlement was sealed, but Stoffel and his friends maintained it was in his favor, with his retaining the money paid out to him.

THE DEAL

Iraq was the perfect business opportunity for Stoffel. If he was a profiteer, he was a patriot too. Iraq's Wild West atmosphere, the ultimate free market fantasy, jazzed him, and he strolled around with a dull black Heckler & Koch MP-5 submachine gun strapped to his body and a smile on his face. "I love this shit," he would say. "This is what I was born for."[17]

Politically savvy, Stoffel hired the high-powered Washington lobbying firm BKSH, which helped him develop contacts in Iraq. BKSH was the lobbying firm that represented Ahmed Chalabi, and when Stoffel got to Iraq in early 2004, he lived for a time in Chalabi's Baghdad compound.[18] After a falling-out, Stoffel struck out on his own, but he was unable to close a deal. Frustrated, he complained to U.S. officials about corruption in the contracting process. The investigation went nowhere.

Then, in the summer of 2004, Stoffel finally struck gold. One of the people he'd met through Chalabi was a suave, urbane adviser to the Defense Ministry named Mishal Sarraf. With Prime Minister Allawi demanding a division of mechanized armor, Stoffel convinced Sarraf that his connections in the former Soviet Union could help.[19] Stoffel also hit on the idea of selling obsolete Iraqi weaponry as scrap on the international market — a deal that he estimated might bring in as much as $1 billion in revenue.

In August, Allawi's government signed a deal with Stoffel to help the Iraqis establish a mechanized division at an estimated cost of $283 million. It was the first large-scale contract issued and funded directly by the Iraqi government for military purposes. The "broker's agreement" gave Stoffel's Wye Oak Technology the exclusive right to buy tanks and other equipment for the mechanized division on the ministry's behalf. Stoffel also had to build housing and repair yards for the mechanized division at Taji, a military base fifteen miles northwest of Baghdad. Stoffel was awarded the contract without competitive bidding, and the contract was structured so that he was paid a percentage of the price of goods purchased — an arrangement barred by U.S. law but allowed in Iraq.

As part of the deal Sarraf insisted on an unusual provision, according to sources with knowledge of the contract. He required that Stoffel conduct all financial transactions through a Lebanese middleman named Raymond Zayna, who ran a company called General Investment Group.[20] Zayna would act as an escrow account. The ministry would pay Zayna, who provided a "bank guarantee" to repay the ministry in case Stoffel failed to deliver. In turn Zayna would reconcile invoices and disburse payments to Stoffel as the work progressed. In September, Stoffel signed a limited power of attorney allowing Zayna to "arrange financing and request banking guarantees."[21]

In October the Defense Ministry issued Zayna's firm $24.7 million in payments for the tank contract, money that was supposed to flow to Stoffel. The payment became the source of a bitter dispute between Zayna and Stoffel. Zayna claimed that Stoffel wasn't giving him the detailed receipts needed to disburse the funds. Stoffel believed there was another reason for Zayna's withholding money: he was refusing to pay kickbacks. In October he began complaining in Washington and Baghdad about Zayna and his relationship with Iraqi defense officials. In conversations with American military officers, Stoffel accused Zayna of charging him a 3 percent fee on financial transactions. He suspected that a portion of the fee was being kicked back to the Defense Ministry. Stoffel also said Zayna was trying to force him to use certain subcontractors that he believed were secretly controlled by Zayna and Iraqi officials.[22]

Cattan knew Stoffel from an earlier deal. He said he paid Stoffel $100,000 for some of the black market AK-47s that he purchased during the siege in Fallujah. But now he too stalled on sending out more money to Stoffel. Like Zayna, Cattan complained that he only received "vague invoices" and demanded more specifics. Americans suspected corruption. Petraeus's chief deputy on the mechanized division project was Col. David Styles. Styles believed that Cattan was deliberately blocking payments to force Stoffel to participate in a kickback scheme. "The fact that Cattan did not want money paid unless it was to a contractor he personally approved was the problem," Styles told me. In response Cattan said he believed that it was the Americans who were corrupt. Why did they keep pressuring him to pay money to Stoffel? he asked. Petraeus's task force "did everything with this contract, it did not follow the Iraqi procedures, and now we have problems," Cattan said. The task force "was outside the box, outside the procedures. We have a dirty job," he said.

Stoffel pleaded with Styles to demand better accountability. He suggested hiring an internationally recognized accounting firm brought in to handle transactions. "If we proceed down the road we are currently on, there will be serious legal issues that will land us all in jail," he wrote Styles in a November e-mail. "There is no oversight of the money and if/when something goes wrong, regardless of how clean our hands are, heads will roll and it will be the heads of those that are reachable, and the people who are supposed to know better (US citizens, military, etc.)." In another letter to a military officer involved in the tank project, Stoffel warned of consequences if the $24.7 million was not recovered. "News of it will be on the front page under the photos of President Bush, Rumsfeld, me," and Petraeus's task force, Stoffel wrote. "Jobs will be lost and congressional hearings will be held."

Stoffel also complained to contacts in Washington. Stoffel met with staff from the office of Senator Rick Santorum, his local representative. Santorum, in turn, wrote Rumsfeld on December 3, 2004, asking him to raise the issue with Shaalan. "I would appreciate comment on how the Department of Defense can assist" Wye Oak Technology in recovering payment for services provided, Santorum wrote.[23]

DISPUTE RESOLUTION

Stoffel's complaints also trickled down to Brig. Gen. David Clements of the British army, the deputy commander of the mission to train Iraqi troops. Clements called Stoffel and Zayna together to sort out the problem. Their meeting on December 5 was contentious. Stoffel and Zayna screamed at each other, calming down only when Clements stepped in to referee. Zayna eventually agreed to make an initial payment of $4.7 million to Stoffel as soon as he provided more detailed invoices. Stoffel called home afterward and sounded happy. "He left me a voicemail message," one associate said. "He was exuberant. Everything was solved."[24]

Stoffel traveled to the military base at Taji to prepare the invoices, staying for several days. On December 8, 2004, he and his friend and business partner, Joseph Wemple, forty-nine, decided to head back to the Green Zone with their Iraqi interpreter. Stoffel told Styles that he was planning to meet Zayna and review paperwork with Ministry of Defense officials the following day. "You know, I think everything is okay," he told the colonel. Stoffel and the two others got into an unarmored black BMW station wagon and headed out at dusk down a rarely used back road that ran through one of the most dangerous stretches of Iraq. When they reached a tight turn in the road, right by the Tigris River, another vehicle rammed theirs head-on. Masked men jumped out and executed Stoffel and Wemple. Stoffel was shot repeatedly in the head and upper back. Wemple was shot once through the head. Their interpreter was missing, apparently having fled the scene.

A short while later a video appeared on a website frequently used by insurgent groups. A group calling itself the Brigades of the Islamic Jihad claimed responsibility for the killings. Over the next few months another group calling itself the Rafidan Political Council of the Mujahideen Central Command unleashed five different communiqués, each filled with images and documents apparently taken from Stoffel's laptop computer. Narrated by a heavily muscled man standing behind a lectern, his face hidden by a black-and-white kaffiyeh, the videos purported to unravel a plot between the Americans and their puppets in the interim Iraqi government to sell off $40 billion worth of Iraq's prized military assets. "It is the biggest crime that has ever been committed through the ages and wars," the narrator said. "This theft was committed by an order from the United States and England and with the full agreement and acknowledgment of Allawi, Chalabi, and Shaalan." Stoffel was labeled the "CIA Shadow Manager in Iraq."

One image showed Bush and Stoffel standing together at a political rally. Another was a photo of Stoffel and Chalabi. Still another showed Zayna, labeling him a "CIA agent." There were copies of the broker's agreement contract, and letters between Stoffel and Petraeus, Shaalan, and other Defense Ministry officials.

The videos were unusual in several respects. First, the groups were unknown previous to Stoffel's killing. Neither the Brigades of the Islamic Jihad nor the Rafidan Political Council have made claims of other attacks, before or after Stoffel's killing. Second, the subtitles were in English and the documents flashed onto the screen were not translated into Arabic. The videos clearly seemed designed for an American audience. Finally, the videos didn't contain any of the bloody execution scenes typical of insurgent videos bent on terrorizing Americans. Instead the slow march of documents across the screen, complete with exhibit numbers and text breakouts highlighting incriminating sections, appeared closer to a *60 Minutes* broadcast. These were killers with the documentary fetish of investigative reporters.

The videos, and the disappearance of the translator, led some of Stoffel's friends to suspect that his killing was not simply another incident in Iraq's daily catalog of violence. They believed Stoffel was targeted by someone in the ministry upset by his whistle-blowing. It was impossible to know, of course. American contractors were killed all the time in Iraq. But even outside experts thought the suspicions had merit. "It's very strange," said Evan Kohlman, a terrorism consultant. "I really doubt they're insurgent groups. I've never seen anything like this."[25] The FBI began its own investigation but never filed any charges. The deaths of Stoffel and Wemple vanished into the daily chaos of Iraq, two more dead contractors killed by unknown hands.

A month after Stoffel's death, the most senior Iraqi and American officials in the country gathered at Taji military base to celebrate Army Day, the anniversary of the founding of the Iraqi army on January 6, 1921. There Negroponte, Gen. George Casey, U.S. Army, the highest-ranking commander in Iraq, Petraeus, Allawi, Shaalan, and other top officials presided over a military parade to show off the prowess of the new armed forces. "Together we are going to build a strong and independent Iraq, a country free of oppression and depression, a country based on the power of law, honesty, and truth," Allawi told the dignitaries and soldiers. "It's a difficult mission, but we will do it."[26] Among the vehicles to roll slowly past the parade stand were the tanks and troop carriers that Stoffel had refurbished but never been paid for.

THE AFTERMATH

Weeks after Stoffel's death, Defense Ministry workers were spotted at Baghdad International Airport loading sacks with a total of $300 million in cash into an airplane bound for Beirut. Shaalan would later say that the money was a payment for one of the Polish weapons contracts. But once Chalabi got word of the transaction, it soon appeared on the front pages of media throughout the world. The spectacle of Iraqi money vanishing into the skies dominated the final weeks of the campaign leading up to the January 30 elections.

The elections themselves were historic: the first free, fair, and open voting in the Arab world in the modern era. Millions of Iraqis defied death threats and violence to vote for a transitional government that would usher in a new constitution and a permanent new government in 2006. A Shiite religious coalition that pledged to bring an end to graft swept into power. American-appointed, secular candidates such as Allawi and Shaalan, who held power during the interim government, failed badly, shut out during the formation of the transitional government, which dragged on for months until the nomination of Ibrahim Jaafari as prime minister in April 2005.

When Jaafari's government took power, they proclaimed themselves scandalized by the corruption that had occurred on the Americans' watch. Iraq's Supreme Board of Audit completed a confidential report that documented rampant irregularities at the Defense Ministry. The report reviewed eighty-nine contracts worth $1.3 billion signed between June 28, 2004, and February 28, 2005. It was a scathing, unforgiving critique that placed Cattan at the center of scores of questionable transactions. Auditors could not find copies of contracts or payment receipts, nor could they verify that equipment had been received. The cash, pay-up-front, no-bid contracts violated nearly every facet of Iraqi contracting law. The audit criticized Cattan's cash payments as a "flagrant violation of the state monetary policy." The beneficiary on forty-three of the eighty-nine contracts was Jumaili, Cattan's friend in the money transfer business. At least $759 million in Iraqi money was deposited into Jumaili's account at a bank in Baghdad. "If one dinar is misspent, I ache for it, so just imagine how it feels for such huge sums," said Prime Minister Jaafari.[27]

At the same time, the Iraqis were raising questions about the quality of the merchandise that Cattan purchased. Much of the equipment, including guns, ammunition, and uniforms, was serviceable, if overpriced. But some of it was shoddy, useless, or simply couldn't be found. There were armored cars that couldn't stop AK-47 bullets, "German" MP-5 submachine guns that turned out to be Egyptian knockoffs, and 7.62 mm bullets that cost three times the going rate of between four and six cents.[28] Tens of thousands of bulletproof vests simply fell apart. One shipment had consisted of thousands of boxes of loose, leftover bullets, as though they had been dumped out of gun magazines. Some of the Russian-built MI-17 helicopters were twenty-five years old; the Iraqis sent to St. Petersburg wouldn't accept delivery because of their age. The Polish transport vehicles, made by Bumar, were boxy, beige trucks with metal-reinforced tires and armor sufficient to stop an AK-47 round. But at a cost of $167,000 apiece, they were vastly underpowered: designed to move ten soldiers, the trucks had 150-horsepower engines, the same as a Mazda Miata. When one of my colleagues test-drove one in Poland, he was unable to power it up a 45-degree slope. "The engine size was their decision," a Bumar executive told him. "We adjust to the client's requirements — and cost was a factor for them."

PUBLIC RELATIONS BLITZ

Allawi claimed ignorance of the details of the deals, especially Cattan's use of private intermediaries to transfer cash, and he charged that the accusations of corruption within his interim cabinet were politically motivated. "I don't think it is fair at all that we shift focus from Saddam and the corruption during Saddam's time . . . to a period of six to seven months when I was prime minister," Allawi said in an interview with one of my colleagues in which he noted that he had initiated the investigations into corruption allegations. "That is not to say that there is no corruption — there is, of course, corruption."

Shaalan vigorously declared his innocence and claimed the accusations were politically motivated. He said his longstanding opposition to Iran had turned him into a target of the religious parties that formed the heart of Jaafari's winning coalition, the Supreme Council for the Islamic Revolution in Iraq and the Dawa Party, both closely linked to Tehran. "The accusations [against me] are not true. They want to kill me politically — it is a political assassination," said Shaalan, who purchased a mansion in Amman after losing his position. Shaalan subsequently launched a public relations campaign that included a trip to Poland to hold a press conference with executives from Bumar. The executives acknowledged the helicopters' age, but said they were all in working order, waiting for delivery to the Iraqis. "There was no mistake on our side. Everything is being delivered according to specifications. Until now, I have not received any complaint, any fax, any document voicing reservations," said Roman Baczynski, Bumar's CEO.

Cattan launched his own campaign, mounting a website with stirring background music and pictures of himself posing with Bremer and other American officials. He filed libel lawsuits in Poland to clear his name. In an hours-long interview at a hotel in Warsaw, Cattan voiced pride in his accomplishments, creating an army of ten divisions and 150,000 soldiers out of the ragtag security forces inherited from Bremer's provisional authority. "I am sure that there was some mistakes in my job, but we also did a good job," Cattan said. He acknowledged shortcuts in buying weapons. But the contingencies of war demanded it, he said. "If I needed one glass, for example, I had to go through procedures," he said. "It was too much time."

All the Iraqis involved, from Cattan to Shaalan to Allawi, said that Petraeus's task force and the U.S. embassy knew what was happening. They said the Americans had encouraged them to purchase from Poland and other countries that were part of the coalition that invaded Iraq, both as a reward for participating and because it was easier to move weapons with coalition partners. Cattan said he had quarreled with the Americans about procedures, but that in the end every purchase he made eventually flowed into American military hands for distribution to the Iraqi army. "I gave [Petraeus's task force] everything, and I listed what I imported. They came and take it, everything we brought into the airport, they take it to their warehouse."

PLAUSIBLE DENIABILITY

When I first contacted Petraeus about Stoffel, his spokesman brushed me off. "We were not aware of any U.S. military working with Wye Oak," said Capt. Steve Alvarez. Besides, he claimed, the arms contract was an "MOD [Ministry of Defense] matter." Petraeus, he said, had only met Stoffel one time. "There really isn't much more to our involvement," Alvarez concluded.

Later, documents surfaced showing that Petraeus had personally endorsed Stoffel's mission. In a letter to Shaalan on July 20, 2004, Petraeus pledged to "fully support" Stoffel's proposal to refurbish the Iraqi tanks and personnel carriers and buy new equipment from Eastern European sources. A top Iraqi defense official wrote that he worked with Petraeus to arrange Stoffel's transport to different military bases to inspect Iraqi equipment. Beyond the letters, U.S. officials told me Petraeus had personally intervened several times, engaging in heated conversations with Shaalan and Cattan about the arms purchases. He had, for instance, tried without success to block the helicopter sale, thinking it a waste of money when the Iraqis did not have the capabilities to maintain such a fleet.

E-mails also turned up showing that Styles and other American officials had been in daily contact with Stoffel. They issued detailed orders regarding fixing oil leaks in the tanks, and urged Stoffel to speed up work to "get the advisers off our [backs] and ensure the uninterrupted flow of funds for the project." Petraeus did not comment, but his spokesman finally acknowledged that the general had intervened when the contract bogged down. "Quite naturally, there were contacts and communications between [the task force] and the parties to the contract in order to coordinate," Alvarez now said.

To some extent the Americans blamed each other for the scandal. The reconstruction team had advisers who were supposed to meet regularly with Shaalan and other top ministry officials to guide policy decisions. Yet they were constantly short on manpower, meaning that Petraeus's task force officers had more daily contact. But more contact or not, Petraeus's job was to train and equip soldiers, not worry about accounting procedures. "This was not the military's task," one U.S. official said.

Even if they had been able to, neither side showed a strong interest in digging into what the Iraqis were doing. The Americans wanted the Iraqis to get business done, but they didn't want to involve themselves too deeply in details. Both the military and the State Department claimed to have no prior knowledge of a contract that the Iraqis signed with Pakistan for delivering tanks, armored personnel carriers, and bullets. Was it possible that two of the United States' closest allies in the war on terror would be able to conduct a $313 million weapons deal without Uncle Sam knowing? And if so, was that a good thing?

The reluctance to meddle was partly the result of a genuine desire by the United States to respect Iraq's sovereignty. Corruption was a possible, though unfortunate, by-product of the policy. Styles, for instance, defended the strange contracting system in which a middleman stood between Stoffel and the Defense Ministry, collecting mysterious fees. "It's an Eastern, Arabic, Islamic way of business that is different than a Western, Judeo-Christian way of business," Styles said. "That does not mean it's corrupt."[29] But sovereignty provided the Americans with plausible deniability. The new system allowed the Americans to have involvement but not responsibility. The Iraqis paid for the equipment, not Americans. Iraqis signed the paperwork, not Americans. The contracts might relate to the most important American mission in Iraq, but they weren't American deals.

The hands-off approach frustrated some of the Americans who worked to help equip and train the Iraqi army. They didn't understand why the United States had not acted more forcefully. Whether American taxpayer funds or Iraqi oil revenues, money was still money — and the millions wasted on crooked or shabby arms deals were millions that could have gone to more worthwhile endeavors. "The Iraqis were screwing things up and the U.S. officials weren't doing anything about it. That should have been part of our role to oversee. Why wouldn't you just clamp down and say, 'I want to see every contract.' It's like they turned a blind eye and just let it happen under the auspices that they're a sovereign nation," one American official involved in the project told me.

But top military commanders downplayed the effects of the scandal. They estimated that much of the $1.3 billion had been spent on usable equipment. Perhaps only "hundreds of millions" were lost through Cattan's business ventures, said John Noble, senior Western adviser to Iraq's Defense Ministry.[30]

In the overall scheme of things, the $1.3 billion amounted to about one-third of the Defense Ministry's acquisition budget. U.S. taxpayer money funded the remainder. One U.S. military official said some of Iraq's battalions could have improved their combat readiness had the Iraqis focused more on buying critically needed items instead of equipment such as helicopters. They also could have benefited from better equipment. "There clearly was some impact from Ziad's practices," the military official told me. "However, it was not clear that it was all that substantial."

The facts on the ground seemed to indicate otherwise. By 2006 the training program was sending more and more Iraqi troops to the battlefield. But two years after the first equipment contracts were signed, those troops were still traveling in the same white pickup trucks that Iraqis used to take vegetables to market. And in February 2005, six months after the formation of Petraeus's training task force, the White House submitted a request for $5.7 billion to allow the Iraqi government to "begin to train, equip, operate and sustain its own security forces" because its battalions were "lightly equipped and armed, and have very limited mobility and sustainment capabilities."[31] Eight months later, long after the corruption scandals, the wasted money, and the arrest warrants, Gen. John P. Abizaid, the commander of the U.S. Central Command, acknowledged that only one of about ninety Iraqi battalions could operate without U.S. logistics support, such as transportation and feeding. Senator Susan Collins of Maine seemed taken aback. Having one ready battalion in the entire country, she said, "doesn't feel like progress."[32]

Iraqis were equally amazed. Iraqi soldiers complained that they were unable to fight effectively and were at greater risk because they lacked good-quality weapons, armored vehicles, and other supplies as a result of Cattan's shenanigans. The lack of equipment also meant that American troops had to provide support to the Iraqis longer — exposing them to more danger. "The Americans have spent two years building the Iraqi forces," said Hadi Amery, an Iraqi legislator and head of the Badr Brigade militia, the armed wing of the Supreme Council for the Islamic Revolution in Iraq, a top political party. "What have you done through these two years?" How was it, the Iraqis asked, that the United States could have allowed such slipshod execution of such an important task? "We have American experts in the Defense Ministry," said Judge Radhi Radhi, the official investigating the corruption. "When they saw such violations, why didn't they do something?"

The families of hundreds of American and Iraqi soldiers returned home in caskets had the same question. The United States had tried to foist responsibility for the reconstruction on Iraqi politicians and bureaucrats, many of whom proved unequal to the task. The United States shifted much of the actual work of the reconstruction as well: to poor foreigners and Iraqis, desperate for jobs. Their families too would see the results of the rebuilding come home to them in caskets.

12

Hired Hands

Every night scores of poor, young Nepalese men and women crowd into a small bar in a basement just off the main drag of Kathmandu's Thamel tourist district. Blue lightbulbs illuminate the long, narrow room, giving the place an eerie, otherworld feel. In front on a low stage, separated from the crowd by a white plastic chain, a group of musicians sit cross-legged with drums, flutes, and a stringed instrument called a sarangi. The music starts — high, hypnotic, droning — and the crowd takes to the floor. In leather pants and silk blouses, sandals and traditional diamond patterned saris, they move like clouds in a windy sky, wispy and twisting. *Rodi* songs are traditional to the impoverished villages of central Nepal, a kind of courtship music in which male and female singers exchange randy lyrics. "I'm going to take you home with me tonight," the man calls out in one traditional folk tune. The music stops suddenly and the crowd waits to see the woman's reaction. "You wouldn't know what to do," the woman cries, her voice keening in the sudden silence. Everyone laughs, the drums thump, and the instruments warble to life.

Modern rodi songs are often not about union but separation. The lyrics tell stories of missing lovers and absent children. "I write to my lover, but he never writes back. He's in Tokyo," one of the female singers laments in a current song. The change reflects global reality. Nepal is one of the poorest countries in the world, with a per capita income of less than $270 a year. Unemployment is worsened by a Maoist insurgency that has killed more than twelve thousand people over the past decade. The rebels frequently kidnap young men as recruits. The combination of violence and poverty has turned Nepal into a nation-sized Home Depot parking lot, with an enormous pool of poor, desperate people willing to risk almost anything, and go almost anywhere, for a job. By some estimates, as many as 2 million Nepalese live and work abroad, nearly 10 percent of the population.

The Nepalese are shipped to their jobs via a shadowy global network of labor migration that is rife with abuse, corruption, and exploitation. At the center of the system are middlemen called labor brokers. Typically, brokers in poor countries like Nepal use local agents to trawl through villages and city slums, recruiting workers by promising to send them to jobs in wealthier countries, usually in the Middle East or Asia. In return, the workers borrow money, often from loan sharks, to pay for the chance. The labor brokers in poor countries connect with labor brokers in rich countries in need of workers. If all goes well, the worker takes the new job abroad, pays off the loan with his wages, then begins sending money back home. (Nepal's workers send back more than a billion dollars a year, the country's highest source of foreign currency.)

But often all does not go well. The informal system is filled with risk. Once abroad, workers find themselves with uncertain legal status and few places to turn for help. Many loans are usurious, leaving workers unable to pay them off with the wages they earn. Employers have little incentive to pay decent wages or provide adequate food and housing. Government and police officials in host nations are reluctant to prosecute their own citizens. Women are forced into prostitution. Men find themselves getting paid far less than advertised, or working in different jobs. Reports of physical abuse are common. In Saudi Arabia, for instance, one Nepalese worker dies each month for lack of water. The temptation to remain silent is strong. Workers who complain about conditions are sent home, faced with the burden of the enormous loans. The system "is a sort of slave trade," said Majed Habashneh, the undersecretary for Jordan's Labor Ministry, which has struggled to improve the rights of migrant workers in his country. "No one is taking care of the human rights of these people," he told me.

When the war broke out in Iraq, the United States and its chief contractor, Halliburton, embraced this murky, unregulated system with vigor. The war created an enormous demand for labor to support reconstruction activities and troops on U.S. military bases: someone had to cook the food and ship the gear and clean the toilets for 200,000 soldiers and coalition forces. Although Iraq was filled with millions of jobless men, the military would not hire them to work, considering the risk of insurgent infiltration too high. As a result, commanders insisted on only American or foreign workers. And since contractors were trying to offer the lowest price possible in order to win work, they turned to the cheapest labor available: poor foreigners lured to Iraq by labor brokers. The United States had decided to give the Iraqis more responsibility for rebuilding their country. The people who actually did much of the work were often from abroad.

Most of the hiring was done by Halliburton subsidiary KBR. Between 25,000 and 35,000 of KBR's 50,000 employees in Iraq were third-country nationals, TCNs in contractor parlance. They came streaming in from all over the globe, each filtering into different ghettos of labor, like the émigrés to America in the 1900s. The Pakistanis and Turks drove trucks with fuel and supplies. Filipinos, Nepalese, and Somalis ran the kitchens on military bases. Security guards came from all over: Nepal, South Africa, Colombia, Fiji, and Ukraine.

In theory, America's participation in the labor trafficking system should have reduced the potential for abuse. The United States was certainly aware of the possible dangers. During the 1990s the military had run into trouble in the Balkans when the employees of one contractor, DynCorp, were accused of buying women and girls for use as sex slaves. President Bush declared "zero tolerance" for human trafficking, issuing a national security directive to combat it in February 2003. The State Department produced an annual report ranking the world's countries on their commitment to combat the practice, defining human trafficking to include "debt bondage," the practice by which usurious loans trapped workers into involuntary servitude. The State Department defined such employers as "slave masters." "Cultural practices, illiteracy and unequal power relationships make this traditional form of slavery for low-skilled work particularly difficult to eliminate," the report said.[1] Donald Rumsfeld issued a memo warning about the practice. Commanders "need to be vigilant to the terms and conditions of employment for individuals employed by DoD [Department of Defense] contractors," he wrote in September 2004, according to a memo provided me by the Pentagon. "Trafficking includes involuntary servitude and debt bondage. These trafficking practices will not be tolerated."

The United States also mandated a remarkably generous package of benefits for those who worked on U.S. contracts in foreign lands. Back in the 1940s, when the military first turned to using civilian contractors to build bases overseas, Congress had passed the Defense Base Act to address concerns about the safety of workers, who weren't covered by traditional, state-based worker injury programs. With few exceptions, the legislation required that federal contractors working abroad provide insurance to employees to cover job injuries and death benefits, no matter their nationality nor their position in the subcontracting chain. The benefits were among the most generous in the country, compared to state workers' compensation packages. Injured workers could receive up to $54,000 per year; a widow or child might expect to receive as much as $2 million or $3 million in death benefits over a lifetime.

Given the high-level commitment to ending labor trafficking and the influx of foreign workers, the United States could have turned Iraq into a showcase for the protection of workers' rights. Instead American officials allowed KBR and its subcontractors to engage in the labor trafficking system's most questionable practices.

"KBR believes that all personnel should be treated with dignity and respect, and we are committed to maintaining a work environment that fosters these principles," said Melissa Norcross, a KBR spokeswoman. That commitment was not always clear to KBR's subcontractors in Iraq. A half-dozen Indian workers under a KBR subcontract claimed that they had gone to Kuwait for jobs, then been tricked into working in Iraq. Some six hundred Filipinos went on strike for back pay while working for a KBR subcontractor at an American military base north of Baghdad, a dispute that was settled only with the intervention of the Philippine government.[2]

KBR's own employees were shocked at the unequal treatment given to foreign workers. The minimum salary for an American working for KBR in Iraq was around $60,000. KBR's foreign workers made as little as $3,000 a year, or $60 per week. Sharon Reynolds was a KBR manager from Kirbyville, Texas, who spent nearly a year in Iraq. She recalled that the Americans had an air-conditioned mess hall. The third-country nationals who prepared that food were themselves forced to eat outside in 140-degree heat. The foreign workers "had to stand in line with plates and were served something like curry and fish heads from big old pots," Reynolds said. "It looked like a concentration camp."[3]

There appeared to be different standards for safety as well. Abdul Jaleel Shani, twenty-four, a kitchen worker from India, recounted an explosion at the base where he was working under a KBR subcontract. Other contractors came running out in full battle gear. Shani and his colleagues were told to stand outside near a tent in their pajamas. "At that moment we realized that they are privileged people and we are nothing," Shani said.[4]

America's refusal to crack down on the labor trafficking system turned Iraq into a workers' hell. The poor laborers who streamed into Iraq courtesy of American taxpayers had no rights, no voice, and no advocates. They were commodities, line items in the lowest bid of a corporate overlord who faced no threat of sanction from the United States. The workers were cheated, tricked, and treated like slaves. They were shoved into substandard housing, fed inedible meals, and forced to do without safety gear. They were shot and wounded and sometimes killed. One story, in particular, showed the dangers of the labor trafficking system. It began in Nepal at about the same time the United States was handing over power to the Iraqis and ended in slaughter a few weeks later.

TIME TO PROFIT

On the outskirts of Kathmandu's old Patan neighborhood is a small square where dung sellers pile the flesh, bones, and droppings of the buffalo slaughtered each day in the capital to turn into fertilizer and glue. Just up the street from the stench sits a two-story yellow building behind high fenced walls. It once housed the Moonlight labor agency, one of more than five hundred such outfits operating in Nepal by 2004. Nepalese were especially prized in Iraq. Nepalese trained as soldiers by the British military, known as Gurkhas, had experience sought by private security contractors. And ordinary Nepalese had a reputation as hard workers who were less likely to complain than laborers from other poor countries. "Nepalese don't make too many demands. There's no 'I want this, I want that, I want water.' None of this," said Bigyan Pradhan, the secretary for a trade group for Nepal's labor brokers. Moonlight was owned by a round-faced, dark-haired labor broker named Bala Gam Piri and run by his son. That summer, as the Americans prepared to hand Iraq back to its people, Piri ran an ad in Nepal's largest daily newspaper: "Vacancies in Amman, Jordan." The ad promised jobs with salaries ranging from $200 to $500 per month for butchers, bus drivers, even a "salad man." Preference would be given to candidates who had experience working in hotels.[5]

One of those interested in the work was a skinny, dark-haired boy with almond eyes named Ramesh Khadka. Just nineteen years old, he had been working for three years at a hotel in Kathmandu for $38 a month when he heard about the jobs with Moonlight. He needed money to pay the broker's fee, however, and so he traveled back to his home in a small village called Lele an hour south of the capital. Lele sits in the heart of a river valley of astonishing, verdant beauty. High cliff walls soar toward the sky, covered in a riot of vines and trees. Rice terraces so green they could well have been made of emerald and jade cascade down steep hills. Golden dragonflies buzz in the air and fat water buffalo bathe in roadside ponds.

Khadka's house lies just outside the village, on the right-hand side of a rutted dirt road across from a clear, rushing stream. Khadka's father, Jit Bahadur Khadka, was reluctant to have his son travel abroad. But Ramesh was determined to go. The senior Khadka explained his son's insistence on leaving when I traveled to Nepal in August 2005. A poor farmer, he sat cross-legged on the wooden porch of his home. His tattered gray vest and pants were stained with dirt from the fields. His back was straight, his face solemn. His son, he said, was young and headstrong and independent. The youngest of seven children, Ramesh wanted to make enough money to build a house of concrete next to his family's small two-story mud-and-brick home. "I told him, 'Wait. I'll send you anywhere.' But he didn't want to wait. He wanted to make something of himself," his father said.

Khadka said he was being offered a job as a cook for the U.S. Army at a salary of $200 per month. Moonlight wanted $3,000 as a broker's fee — a small fortune that the family raised by borrowing from local loan sharks and wealthy family friends. At 24 percent interest, the loan would take eighteen months to pay off. He was eager to go. In June 2004, Khadka flew off to Amman from Kathmandu's Tribhuvan International Airport — the first airplane trip of his life. He called his father from the airport just before taking off. "His last words were: 'I'm flying now. Don't worry about me. I'll be back in a few years,'" the elder Khadka recalled. He dabbed his eyes with a handkerchief and looked off in the distance.

As Piri was gathering Khadka and other workers in Nepal, Hayder Aliam was some three thousand miles away in Jordan, helping arrange their transport to Amman. Aliam was the office manager for Morning Star, a Jordanian employment agency that works on the demand side of the labor trafficking business. Aliam's office lies at the end of a narrow hallway with tattered green carpeting in an office building in a busy commercial district of cellular phone stores and car lots. Inside, women from Indonesia and the Philippines stand in corners while wealthy Jordanians sit in overstuffed leather chairs, sorting stacks of files with job candidate applications. In class-conscious Amman, the nationality of your domestic help carries a certain status. Filipinas are the most desirable, and thus most expensive, followed by Indonesians and Sri Lankans. The Nepalese have one advantage, however: unlike other nationalities, Nepalese do not need a visa before their arrival in Jordan.

Thus, when a KBR subcontractor had an urgent need for workers, Morning Star immediately thought of finding them in Nepal. Through a Saudi Arabian businessman, Morning Star and Moonlight worked together to fill the order. Although Morning Star normally imports domestic servants for Jordan, the lure of a $200 fee for each Nepalese for Iraq proved too much to resist. "Iraq was an exception," Aliam told me. "It became a matter of money. It was a time to profit." Morning Star ultimately delivered Khadka and about three dozen other Nepalese to Bisharat & Partners, a dry cleaner that had a contract with Amman-based Daoud & Partners. Daoud in turn had a contract to supply cooks, dishwashers, and laundry services for KBR at a U.S. military base in western Iraq called Al Asad. Bisharat & Partners acknowledged that it "likely" accepted the workers from Morning Star.[6] Daoud, which has political connections to senior Jordanian officials, denied that it had any connection to the workers. KBR has never acknowledged the men were working for one of their subcontractors.

On the morning of August 19, Ramesh Khadka set out in a convoy toward Al Asad across one of the most dangerous stretches of road in Iraq. The highway leading from the Jordanian border to Baghdad is no-man's land, an arid stretch of roadhouses and small villages where kidnappers and highway robbers lie in wait for passing vehicles. The convoy had no security: no armed escorts or bulletproof armor that would have allowed the vehicles to outrun an assault. The two lead vehicles, with Khadka and eleven compatriots, surged ahead of the rest of the cars after a delay at the border crossing. They headed on alone. About forty miles from Al Asad, men dressed like Iraqi security forces stopped the cars at an apparent checkpoint. The Jordanian drivers left the Nepalese at the checkpoint after being told that the Americans would come to pick them up. Hours later the rest of the convoy arrived at Al Asad.

Khadka and the eleven others never made it.[7]

HIT BY A ROCK

On August 20, 2004, Radhika Khadka was at home when a neighbor told her about a grainy Internet video being broadcast repeatedly on Nepalese television. Radhika ran to a store in the village with a television. There Radhika, fifty-five, could see her son crammed into a room with the eleven other men, all holding their passports in front of them. One of the men, with an American flag draped across his chest, read from a statement in halting English. He said the group had been kidnapped by Iraqi insurgents who called themselves the Ansar al Sunna Army. "They said that the situation is not dangerous in Iraq, but we saw the opposite when we entered," the man said. "We ask anyone coming to Iraq not to be cheated by the high salary because they are false and America is lying."

When the camera panned over her son, she saw the look on his face. Her heart broke. A sturdy woman with a face as dark and worn as a saddle, Radhika bowed her head when she recalled the moment. "I felt like I had been hit by a rock," she told me.

The family contacted Piri, the labor broker, who said he would do everything he could to get their son back. Then he disappeared. The Nepalese government did little. The country is so poor that it had only one embassy in the region at the time, in Qatar. The embassy had four employees. In desperation the ambassador turned to Prakash Gurung, a Nepalese businessman who lives in Qatar and runs his own labor agency there. Gurung headed a committee established by the embassy to troubleshoot international labor issues. Lacking contacts in Iraq, Gurung sent an e-mail to a Sunni Muslim group whose address he got from Al Jazeera, the Arab satellite television channel. The group promised to try to help negotiate, but Gurung is not sure whether it did anything at all. "Not anybody else cared about this," Gurung told me. "No other country cared."

Eleven days after the first Internet video, a second surfaced. This time none of the Nepalese workers spoke, except to scream. Unseen hands laid the first worker on the ground, his throat to the sky. A knife descended, slowly sawing through the man's neck as he sputtered and choked, blood gushing from his body. As the video continued, the eleven remaining Nepalese were brought out in pairs, laid on the ground, and shot at close range. Some men doubled up as they were shot, their faces contorted in pain. Khadka's family did not watch the execution video. But a childhood friend did. He said that he immediately recognized Khadka when he was laid in the ditch alongside a second man. The insurgents shot three bullets into the back of Khadka's head. He did not appear to suffer, his friend said. The killings were the worst single incident of violence against foreign contractors in the Iraq war.

In the aftermath Jordan's Ministries of Labor and Interior launched investigations into the killings. Morning Star was shut down for four months but allowed to reopen after promising to stop sending workers to Iraq. Habashneh, the Jordanian labor official, said his office had struggled to prevent the transit of workers through the nation's borders. But migrant workers that I spoke with in Jordan said that the business was thriving. One Filipino woman told me it cost a few thousand dollars to have a Jordanian labor broker smuggle you across the border into a much higher paying job in Iraq.

In the United States the executions barely made the news. A Department of Defense initiative to ban contractors involved in human trafficking got bogged down in disputes between contractors and antitrafficking groups over how best to implement it. KBR said it was "investigating" the incident. A year later the State Department announced it was undertaking its own investigation. But no action was ever taken against KBR, or any of its subcontractors, for possible violations of labor trafficking laws.

The United States also did nothing to enforce the workers' compensation law for overseas federal contractors, the Defense Base Act, even though Khadka and his companions appeared to be covered by its provisions. The Department of Labor, which administers the act, did not even have personnel in Iraq. Instead they relied upon the contractors to report incidents of violence against their employees. There were criminal and civil sanctions available for contractors who failed to do so, but Labor never took action against a federal contractor in Iraq for violating the reporting requirements. One U.S. Army Reserve judge advocate who dealt with injured contract employees criticized the department. "Most executive branches have offices at the U.S. embassy. Why not the Department of Labor?" the judge advocate asked. "It's possible to have more outreach." But of course most executive branches had already shown themselves reluctant to take on a company with Halliburton's clout — and connections.

In Kathmandu the executions touched off a government crisis. Protesters set upon Kathmandu's only mosque, burning it and ripping the Quran to pieces. They also attacked hundreds of labor broker agencies, which are widely reviled in Nepal. In two days of rioting, one protester was shot to death and the government clamped down with a twenty-four-hour curfew. The unrest contributed to the instability that King Gyanendra later cited in dissolving the cabinet and declaring a state of emergency that gave him absolute power in February 2005. "All Nepalese were shocked," said

Bijaya Bishta, the editor of *Shram Weekly*, a newspaper focused on labor is-sues. "We found out that our government is very weak."

The government sought to quell the outrage by revoking Moonlight's li-cense and compensating the survivors. Each family was given nearly $14,000, a fortune in Nepal. Nobody ever offered an apology to the family. "If we had been big shots, they would have said that they were sorry," Rad-hika said, her face creased with worry. "But we're poor people. We're no-body." The Khadkas used their money to pay off Ramesh's debt and for Radhika's medical expenses. (She had fainting spells after the news of her son's death and refused to leave the family's home for seven months.) The family also paid $1,000 to a local sculptor to make a black plaster bust of their son, whose body has never been found. The sculpture was dedicated exactly one year after his execution. Dozens of villagers turned out for the ceremony. A representative of the government also attended. He sat in the front row and read a newspaper.

DEFENSE BASE ACT

If the Khadkas never got rich from the Defense Base Act, the same cannot be said of a particular American insurance company: financial services gi-ant American International Group, Inc. AIG was one of a handful of insur-ance companies that profited off the violence in Iraq by boosting insurance rates to sky-high levels. Indeed the deaths of scores of contractors in Iraq — Americans and foreigners — provided an opportunity that the insurance industry wasted no time exploiting. And when the federal government tried to crack down in an effort to save taxpayers' money and improve the deliv-ery of benefits, AIG and other companies fought the initiative with passion.

AIG was the largest insurance company in the United States, and one of its most aggressive in terms of growth. Its CEO, Maurice R. "Hank" Greenberg, was a legendary figure, an imperious, demanding businessman who over three decades of leadership turned the company into one of the ten most profitable firms in the United States. But a year after the war began in Iraq, Greenberg's practices came under intense scrutiny. New York attorney gen-eral Eliot Spitzer and the U.S. Securities and Exchange Commission initiated a wide-ranging probe of the insurance industry in April 2004 that soon en-snared AIG in questions over bid rigging. Within a year Greenberg was forced to resign and AIG slashed its net worth by $1.77 billion because of accounting irregularities.

By that time, however, AIG had already cashed in on its newest boom business. Prior to the war in Iraq, Defense Base Act insurance was an obscure corner of the underwriting world. There were a few hundred claims filed annually, mostly for routine workplace injuries suffered by contractors at U.S. bases and construction sites. Only four American insurance companies issued the highly specialized Defense Base Act policies, and of those AIG was the dominant carrier. Iraq, however, injected new life into the market. The reconstruction program sent tens of thousands of contractors streaming into the world's most hostile work environment. In Iraq the United States employed perhaps 60,000 American and third-country nationals and more than 100,000 Iraqis. All of them needed Defense Base Act insurance.

As demand for policies increased, insurance rates skyrocketed. Rates, which were calculated as a percentage of a company's payroll, soared from an average of $4–$8 for every $100 of a company's payroll, to $20 for every $100. Insurance for an American engineer making $100,000 a year — not unusual in Iraq — cost $20,000 annually. By 2004 Pentagon officials were estimating that Defense Base Act insurance costs had jumped by more than $1 billion since the September 11 attacks. Ultimately the American taxpayer paid for the increase: the contractors simply folded the higher costs into the price of the contract.

The sudden increase puzzled some in the Pentagon because of another obscure law known as the War Hazards Compensation Act. Passed in the 1940s, the War Hazards Act was designed to quell fears from insurance companies that it was too risky to insure contractors building U.S. bases in the middle of a war. The War Hazards Act guaranteed that the U.S. government would reimburse the insurance companies for any deaths or injuries that stemmed from combat. In the argot of the industry, it was a reinsurance policy. If a worker was injured in a workplace accident, slipping in a garage in the motor pool at Iwo Jima, for instance, the insurance company had to pay. But if the worker was hit by gunfire or injured in an explosion, the U.S. not only picked up the payment but added 15 percent to cover the cost of processing the claim. As one broker told me, it was a dream scenario for the insurance companies: "Who wouldn't want to handle a claim with a fifteen percent profit built in?" he said.

Given that the War Hazards Act removed the insurance companies' risk of paying expensive combat claims, the soaring rates didn't seem to make much sense. Since the insurance companies didn't have to worry about combat injuries, why was Iraq any more dangerous than any other Third World country? In war-torn Colombia, for instance, a contractor flying a helicopter in support of the State Department's antidrug mission paid $3.87 per $100 of payroll. In Iraq a contractor flying a helicopter was paying $90 per $100. "When we saw these rates, eyebrows were raised," one Pentagon official told me. The Government Accountability Office declared the high rates a puzzle: "It really is a big black box," said David Cooper, a GAO investigator. "There's some kind of magic that goes on that makes these rates. We don't have a lot of faith in it."

BUNNY'S REVENGE

One of those alarmed by the growing cost to taxpayers was Bunny Greenhouse. Greenhouse was the Army Corps of Engineers official who took on Halliburton when she objected to a sweetheart deal that gave the company a contract to rebuild Iraq's oil infrastructure. Next in her sights was AIG and the other insurance companies — also powerful forces on the political scene. Greenhouse and others in the Pentagon had talked to the insurance companies to find out about the rate increases. The answer had not impressed them. One Pentagon official involved in the Army Corps effort said a company underwriter explained that the rates were high because "it was 130 degrees. There was a lot of dust," the official told me.

The Pentagon put Greenhouse in charge of a project to bring down the inflated rates, which were eating into funds available for reconstruction projects. At the time, each Defense Department contractor was buying insurance individually. Greenhouse decided to have the Army Corps hold a competitive bidding process in which one insurance company would win the right to cover all Army Corps contractors around the world. The State Department and USAID already had such a blanket policy in place, and it had lowered rates. State and USAID contractors were paying $4–$5 per $100 in payroll for insurance that was costing as much as thirty times more for Defense Department contractors in Iraq.

AIG and its allies responded like a lion protecting its kill. After Greenhouse formally announced her new program in the spring of 2004, AIG led a group of insurance companies and brokers to the Hill and the Pentagon in protest. Several industry representatives met with Deidre Lee, the Pentagon's top contracting official, in June 2004. Also at the meeting were two other companies that issued Defense Base Act policies: the Bermuda-based

ACE and the New Jersey–based Chubb. Industry officials said that Greenhouse's proposal for a competition would "destroy the working marketplace."[8] The AIG representative, Shane McCaffrey, told Lee that AIG and ACE together controlled "close to ninety percent of the business" for Defense Base Act insurance issued to Pentagon contractors, according to one Pentagon official. "That was a fairly stupid thing to say," the official told me. "They were explaining why they didn't want us to go forward with this. . . . It's a de facto monopoly."[9]

AIG and ACE lobbyists also went to Capitol Hill to voice their displeasure, according to lobbying reports and Defense Department officials. At a June 2004 hearing, Representative John B. Larson, a Democrat from Connecticut, upbraided a Pentagon official over Greenhouse's plan: "I am very concerned that such an effort would severely distort the insurance marketplace," Larson said. By August industry representatives crowded into a meeting at Fort Belvoir, Virginia, that Greenhouse convened to listen to the industry's concerns. It was confrontational, with insurance representatives and brokers charging that the government was stealing potentially billions of dollars in business from them, according to government minutes of the meeting.

Insurance officials told Greenhouse that the government was unnecessarily injecting itself into the marketplace. Rates had come down over time — evidence, they said, that the market worked. Although exact figures were hard to come by — no agency actually tracked rates — anecdotal evidence appeared to show that prices had dropped since the beginning of the war, but from an average of about 20 percent of payroll costs to merely 15 percent. "We continue to believe that an open market provides contractors the best opportunity to weigh a number of factors in selecting an insurance carrier, including price, expertise, and claims-handling ability," said Joe Norton, an AIG spokesman. The American Insurance Association, speaking for ACE and Chubb, said it objected to any effort to award all insurance business to a single company. "It's an astounding step for this administration to take," said Bruce C. Wood, an assistant general counsel for the association. "We happen to believe that a competitive market working over time is best, not a government market with government-set prices." Norton added that the rates in Iraq reflected "the hostile work environment," not the violence itself. He said accident rates in Iraq were much higher than in the rest of the world and that Iraq was unique in terms of the type of work being done, stress, climate, and availability of medical care. Norton also said that only 12 percent of AIG's Iraq claims would potentially be covered by the War Hazards Act, and even then the company was not guaranteed payment, since the federal government could reject a claim. For instance, if a contractor died of a heart attack after hearing an explosion, was that combat related or not? "It's the insurer that's at risk," said Eric Oxfeld, a consultant who represented the business community on workers' compensation issues.

Critics saw a different motive behind the objections: protecting a large and mostly unregulated profit center that had exploded during the war on terrorism. The federal government, it turned out, had no power to regulate Defense Base Act rates, unlike states, which have insurance boards to review insurance carrier charges. Sara K. Payne, a senior vice president at Rutherfoord International, a brokerage that handles Defense Base Act insurance, acknowledged that the companies lacked actuarial data to back up rates. The insurance companies "don't know what they're up against. It's a judgment rating. They're picking rates out of the air." That left the federal government, the contractors, and the American taxpayer at the mercy of a small handful of insurance companies to determine fairness. "There's very little oversight," said Robert McGarrah, coordinator for workers' compensation at the AFL-CIO. "You can get away with charging very high rates." And they had, taxpayer money flowing out of Iraq and back into the pockets of the insurance industry with virtually no oversight from the Bush administration.

As Greenhouse pushed onward in her efforts, she found herself increasingly alone. Her battle against Halliburton and the insurance companies had not won her friends in the Army Corps command ranks. After being demoted back in October 2004, she remained in her tiny office without support. Carrying out the contract process essentially alone, Greenhouse took six days of personal vacation to find the time to answer scores of written inquiries from the insurance industry. Finally, in November 2005, nearly two years after she first suggested the idea, the Army Corps awarded a Defense Base Act contract to Chicago-based CNA. The company charged rates between $5 and $8.50 per $100 of payroll — a significant cost saving for taxpayers. "I wanted to make sure this was a success," Greenhouse told me. "It was part of my duty. I tried like the dickens to get everybody to participate. Nobody wanted to." Especially the insurance companies, which had made billions while the government sat on its hands.

HOMEBOY

Bunny Greenhouse's effort to improve the delivery of insurance benefits under the Defense Base Act program came too late for Hayder Kharalla. A slight man with dark eyes and a quick wit, Kharalla was one of the tens of thousands of Iraqis who flocked to work for the American military and companies after the fall of Saddam Hussein. A Sunni, Kharalla watched the bombing of Baghdad in the opening days of the war with fear and relief. The repressive regime that had once threatened to kill his father, a government lawyer, was on its way out. He had high hopes for a new, free Iraq, and he was eager to help his homeland on a path toward democracy.

When U.S. troops came knocking on his door a few days after the invasion, Kharalla impressed them with his English, which he had acquired during a childhood spent in England. The soldiers offered him a job as an interpreter. Kharalla became the voice for the troops. He explained U.S. intentions to rebuild Iraq at neighborhood meetings. He calmed angry crowds of people who swarmed American soldiers. He was at the front door during raids, asking permission to enter. "He got along great with the guys," said Lt. Matt Adamczyk, a commander with the Second Battalion, 325th Airborne Infantry Regiment, Eighty-second Airborne Division. "He was very pro-America, and it showed to us. He was interested in a better Iraq. He believed, like we did, in what we were doing."

The American troops he worked for became his window on a life he had seen only on television. They talked to him about freedom. They played rap music while driving around Baghdad in Humvees. They called him Homeboy, and made him feel like part of something bigger than himself. "It was a dream, honestly," Kharalla told me as we sat together on a worn couch in his family home in a middle-class neighborhood in Baghdad. There was no electricity, so a small generator chugged in the background, supplying just enough power for the television set and a small portable fan. "I loved the people I worked with. I became exactly like them."

In the summer of 2003, the military began to consolidate its interpreters with San Diego–based Titan, now a division of L-3 Communications. Titan had cornered the market on translators in Iraq through a linguistics contract awarded before the war. The contract became the defense contractor's largest source of revenue, worth $657 million by 2004. Airborne soldiers personally took Kharalla to Titan's Baghdad office to make sure that he was hired and assigned to their unit. He was on for ten dollars a day.

A month later, on August 6, 2003, Kharalla was with a platoon conducting a patrol to enforce a curfew in south Baghdad. It was after midnight when they stopped to talk with a man in the road. Kharalla had just begun asking questions when the first shots rang out. Kharalla ducked down, lying against the wheel of an SUV. He barely felt the bullet that severed his right leg. There was a small sting and suddenly his leg was lying next to him in the road, still attached by skin. Another bullet punctured his left calf.

Around him, the firefight raged. Bullets whined past his head, thunking into the SUV. A sergeant fell next to him. Kharalla reached to pull him to safety behind the patrol vehicle, but the man was dead. Another soldier threw Kharalla over his shoulder and staggered backward firing his rifle. Kharalla wound up in a Humvee, headed for a field hospital. Two soldiers were killed and sixteen people were wounded in the incident, including Kharalla.

The next month was spent in a U.S. Army hospital in the Green Zone in a failing effort to reattach his leg. At last doctors decided they had to amputate below the knee. After doctors had put a cast on the leg to prepare for amputation, Kharalla had one physician inscribe a message on it. "It was my honor to work with the Americans. I want to dedicate this leg to all the Americans who died to make Iraq free," he had the doctor write. A nurse started crying.

A logistical and bureaucratic nightmare began with Kharalla's release a month later. U.S. military hospital services in Iraq do not include treatment for amputees. Soldiers with such problems are normally taken to Walter Reed Medical Center in Washington, but as the employee of a private contractor, Kharalla was not eligible. In theory that shouldn't have been a problem: Kharalla was covered under the Defense Base Act insurance policy that Titan held with AIG. First Titan had to transport Kharalla out of the country for treatment. No commercial flights were flying. Kharalla had no passport. He had to obtain a visa to enter other countries, but there were few functioning embassies in Baghdad. E-mails between Titan, AIG, and military officials document the confusion. Military officials rebuffed Titan's attempts to move Kharalla on a military flight; those flights were filled with soldiers, and countries like Kuwait were resistant to accepting Iraqi nationals. Titan next tried to get a visa for Kharalla from Germany or Kuwait. They asked AIG for help and were turned down. "We would have nothing to do with obtaining a visa," AIG wrote to Titan.

As the months progressed, Kharalla's case passed from one company official to another as Titan rotated personnel through Iraq. Several times company officials called Kharalla to tell him his paperwork had been lost. Kharalla said he sent more than twenty photos and three different complete sets of medical records to Titan. The airborne soldiers mounted their own effort to shred the bureaucracy, contacting higher-ups to win permission for Kharalla to leave. Nothing worked. By May 2004 Lt. Col. Kevin King, then the chief operating officer of the Coalition Provisional Authority, wrote an e-mail to Titan demanding to know "why this happened in August '03 and is still kicking around. I want to keep this off of Bremer's plate if at all possible."

Titan declined to comment on the record, citing privacy concerns. Titan did give Kharalla a raise and continued paying his salary at $600 a month. One company official told me that Titan had tried to help Kharalla and other injured translators obtain treatment outside Iraq. "Our insurance company and Titan personnel have been coordinating the movement of this action, but due to the lack of a stable Iraqi government structure, we have not been able to obtain the required travel [documents] and logistics yet needed to make this ongoing effort possible," the official said. But it remains unclear why Titan and AIG had such trouble in transporting Kharalla. Several companies and nongovernmental groups have transported wounded employees abroad for rehabilitation therapy. Kharalla and the soldiers said they asked repeatedly for treatment in the United States, which could grant travel documents. Each time, they said, Titan and AIG told them they could transport Kharalla only to the closest possible country with adequate facilities for an amputee, such as Qatar or Germany. A Titan official added that Kharalla could not be sent to the United States because his case was not considered life threatening. He was trapped between military bureaucracy and private profit taking.

When I met Kharalla in August 2004, he was using a pair of crutches to hop around his home. He had no prosthetic device and was preparing yet another round of documents to send off to Titan seeking transfer to another country for treatment. Baghdad's single hospital for amputees had been looted and destroyed. Kharalla had a new wife and a young boy, Ali, then twenty months old. He was still remarkably upbeat about the possibility that the United States could bring democracy to Iraq. But he was disappointed that he had such trouble getting treatment. He was especially upset that he could not stand and hold his boy in his arms. "I feel inside a little sorry for myself," he told me over a lunch of lamb, rice, and glasses of sweet tea. "I worked so much. And this hurts me so much."

Once again it would be the troops on the ground who would find a solution where the powers that be could not — in this case, soldiers in the 112th Military Police Battalion, a National Guard unit from Mississippi stationed in Iraq. Capt. Steve Lindsley, a certified prosthetician from Louisiana, and Sgt. Chris Cummings, a prosthetic and orthodontics technician from Florida, had taken over treatment of about forty Iraqi amputees after a doctor specializing in prosthetics was killed by a mortar round. Capt. Rob Edwards, a detective from Tupelo, Mississippi, who worked with the men, arranged for Kharalla to be transported to the Green Zone for outfitting for a new leg. "I saw how wronged Hayder had been and decided that we were in a position to help him out," Edwards wrote me in an e-mail. "I am blessed to be an American by having all the medical benefits at my disposal and am more blessed to be able to help someone else out while I am over here. Hayder has been a true inspiration through all that he has gone through."

A few months later, Kharalla was taken to Jordan to undergo rehabilitation. By the time he learned to get around on his new leg, however, he could no longer go back to Iraq. His neighborhood had become an insurgent hotbed. One of his uncles had been killed in a bombing. Kharalla feared he too would be targeted for his work with the Americans. So he remained in Jordan with his wife and child, unable to get a job and unable to go home. He watched from afar as his country grew more violent, more dangerous. He wondered how everything had gone so wrong. "America maybe did something for her policy, but for the Iraqis we lost everything," Kharalla told me in February 2006. "Sorry to say, but democracy in Iraq is just a dream."

Three years after the invasion, Kharalla's disillusionment was shared by many Iraqis. The promises of the reconstruction — to build a newer, better nation for an oppressed people — seemed no more than fantasies. And there was no chimera more vexing than the U.S. pledge to restore light to the Iraqi people. The effort to rebuild Iraq's power grid was a map of the entire reconstruction, a metaphor that traced all its hopes, its flaws, and ultimately its disappointments.

13

Power

Electricity was one of the first things the Americans heard about after they seized Baghdad. When Jerry Bremer gathered his senior advisers around him on the night of his arrival on May 12, 2003, a U.S. Army Corps of Engineers electrical expert named Pete Gibson had told him the country's 300 megawatts of power production was unable to keep the lights on in Baghdad for more than a few hours a day. Bremer had been stunned. The coalition had avoided targeting power plants. "What the hell happened?" he asked.[1]

The answer stretched back more than a decade, to the first Gulf War. In point of fact, the United States helped create the mess it would later have to clean up. First was the American bombing campaign, which deliberately targeted Iraqi power plants and transmission towers. Then, under the Oil-for-Food sanctions that followed the Gulf War, the United States repeatedly blocked the importation of parts needed to repair the power grid. American officials worried about the "dual use" potential of the requested equipment. Saddam could put the parts to use to restart a weapons program. Sanctions critics believed that the U.S. strategy was aimed at slowly eroding the dictator's support by undermining his ability to provide basic services to Iraqis.

In either case, the result was the same. Saddam quickly got the system running after the war, but he could not keep it going. Over the years, Iraq's electrical network slowly crumbled. Iraq's plants were in desperate need of spare parts and new equipment. One plant's transformers, which lift electricity from the plant and onto the national grid, had not been touched other than for minor repairs in a decade. "We were running the units in an unsafe manner," a worker told me.

To keep plants running, Iraq's engineers got creative. They bought equipment and hired technicians from nations whose governments paid only lip service to the UN sanctions. Soon the Iraqi network was a nightmare patchwork of technology, meshing systems from Italy, France, Germany, China, Russia, Yugoslavia, and India. The Iraqis also cannibalized existing systems, stealing parts from one generator to fix another. One American official told me with a mixture of horror and admiration about an Iraqi fix of a power plant turbine, a delicate piece of machinery similar to a jet engine. The thousands of blades in the turbine must be carefully balanced for proper rotation. But when three of the blades in the turbine broke off, the Iraqis had no replacement parts. Instead they simply broke three blades off the opposite side of the turbine, thereby rebalancing it.

Iraq's electrical output peaked in the early 1990s, dropping until it reached about 4,400 megawatts before the war. The United Nations, which oversaw the Oil-for-Food program, documented the decay in a series of publicly issued reports in the 1990s. In 2002, the United Nations described Iraq's electrical system as a "serious problem."[2] Two months before the war began, the United Nations forecast what the United States would find: "The condition of the network has severely deteriorated resulting in frequent and prolonged power cuts to the consumers, including essential services such as hospitals, water treatment and sewage plants, wheat mills, irrigation and drainage pump stations, schools, universities and fuel stations."[3]

By the time of the war Iraq's electrical network was on the verge of collapse. On the night of April 3, as the Third Infantry Division marched toward the Baghdad airport, it went over the edge. American and Iraqi engineers later developed a theory that the fighting accidentally severed a loop of high-voltage power lines that surrounded the besieged city. The resulting imbalance delivered a surge of electricity that tripped an automatic shutdown in large power plants throughout central Iraq. Iraq was plunged into darkness that lasted for ten days. Many of the engineers fled. Looters descended on the abandoned plants, destroying critical equipment and stealing the meager stocks of spare parts to sell for scrap metal. In that ten-day period, Iraq's electrical system essentially short-circuited for good.[4]

POWER FAILURE

Framed by bald foothills, the Bayji power plant juts from flat scrubland on a curve of the Tigris River about 125 miles north of Baghdad. The smokestacks and boxy boiler towers loom over a vast industrial complex of twisting pipes and hissing steam plunked in the desolation, *Lawrence of Arabia* meets *Blade Runner*. Sometimes the plant spews thick, black smoke so heavy with pollutants that rather than rising, it crawls back down the smokestacks, clinging to their sides like poisonous tendrils of ivy. On a good day, Bayji is the largest producer of electricity in Iraq.

During the Persian Gulf War, two Tomahawk cruise missiles slammed into the hulking complex. In a blink of violence one February day in 1991, the United States cut off 10 percent of Iraq's power supply. Old photos now faded to sepia in the narrow hallway leading to the plant manager's office document the destruction. One image shows a pair of electrical transformers the size of Dumpsters crumpled like balls of tissue paper. Another shows transmission towers twisted like trees uprooted by a hurricane. Iraq's engineers were on-site the morning after the attack. Remarkably, they were able to get the plant up and running less than three months later.

Such feats were repeated at plants across Iraq in the aftermath of the 1991 U.S. bombing campaign, with the United Nations estimating that more than 90 percent of Iraq's generating capacity was knocked out by the attacks. But by July, six months after the war began, Iraq's power plants were again satisfying total demand, according to the United Nations. A year later power reached the same level as prior to the war.[5] It helped, of course, that Saddam Hussein remained in charge of the country. For him, restoring Iraq's electricity was proof of his power, a show of strength in the face of devastation. Like all ruthless dictators, he used particularly persuasive methods. Adnan Bashir, a heavyset man with a thick mustache who worked at Bayji at the time as an assistant to the manager, recalled getting a phone call the night of the bombing. "The plant manager called me. He said, 'You have to fix it now!' If we didn't go, there would be a report that said that we're trying to destroy the economy and the consequence is hanging. That was that," Bashir told me.

Bashir's experience with repairing the plant after the second American invasion of Iraq was a remarkable contrast. In 2003 the bombing campaign largely avoided infrastructure, hitting a few major bridges and telephone switching stations, but not much else. Bayji itself was untouched, though a boiler exploded when workers abandoned the plant during the invasion. When engineers from Bechtel arrived at Bayji to fix the damage a few months later, they hired Bashir to help. Nearly a year and a half after the

invasion, the plant was producing only about 550 megawatts of power —
less than half its capacity. Bechtel had burned through more than $170
million in repairs. Bashir merely shrugged when I asked him during a visit
to the plant why the restoration was taking so long.

It was the same story throughout the country. In the long, frustrating
campaign to rebuild Iraq, no task proved more difficult than turning on
the lights. The United States spent more than $6 billion to rebuild Iraq's
electrical system. But three years after the invasion, Iraq was actually generating less power than under Saddam. By the time the Americans completed installing the last new power generator in the winter of 2006, most
Iraqis were getting no more than three or four hours of power per day in
their homes. Blackouts happened constantly, sometimes lasting for a
whole day. In February 2006 Iraq produced about 3,700 megawatts of electricity per day. To light their cities, heat and cool their homes, and run
their industries, the Iraqis needed about 9,000 megawatts. The yawning
gap between those two numbers meant that Iraqis were continuously
plunged into darkness as the power failed. There simply was not enough
electricity to fulfill demand.

The failure was not for lack of trying. The rehabilitation of Iraq's electrical system was the most sustained and well funded program in the reconstruction. The Americans knew that restoring the power grid was the
single most important thing the United States could do to earn Iraqi good
will. "You know that Clinton campaign slogan, 'It's the economy, stupid'?
Here it should be this: 'It's the electricity, guys,' " said Andy Bearpark, a
British development specialist who was Bremer's director of infrastructure. "It determines success or failure. Do it right and you can move forward."[6] Electricity was the symbol of the reconstruction. You could see the
setbacks and the advances, the violence and the chaos, the bad decisions
and new strategies, in the ebb and flow of power to Iraqi homes. The graph
of power production in Iraq was a sharp, jagged line that bounced up and
down but never got close to America's goals. It was a pure, simple metric to
measure U.S. success in restoring Iraq.

At the most basic level, electricity was about making life better for Iraq's
26 million people. During the brutal summers, temperatures soared above
130 degrees inside homes. During frigid winters in the north, it snowed. In
such extremes, children could not sleep, women could not cook, men
stood in long lines to purchase gas for electric generators. Lights didn't
work at night, leading to an increase in crime. Wafi Mnadi, the Electricity

Ministry's director of power plants, put it bluntly: "For our people, electricity is life," he told me.

Electricity was also essential to the economy. Without power, Iraq's oil business could not function. Oil wells could not extract petroleum; pumping stations could not lift crude; refineries could not turn oil into gasoline, kerosene, and other fuels. Without power, factories could not function. At a dairy in Baghdad, owner Ameen Haj explained the cycle: Iraqis bought less milk because they could not refrigerate it. That meant that he had to fire workers to save money. That meant less money for Iraqi families to buy milk. "We were hoping that the Americans would rescue us," Haj said. "Things have just gotten worse."[7]

Power in Iraq was also, quite literally, about power. It was a gauge that the Iraqis used to measure the U.S. occupation. Saddam had gotten the system functioning within months after a far more damaging war. How could the United States — the wealthiest, most powerful, most technologically advanced country in the world — not do the same? The lack of electricity was a constant theme on the airwaves and in the cafés, at government meetings and in sermons at the mosques. The same phrase popped up in nearly any casual conversation with an Iraqi: "Maku kahrabaa" — there's no electricity. "Right now, our issue is electricity," said Raheem Abdul Sadr, a shopkeeper who sold brightly colored tricycles and backpacks in Baghdad's slum of Sadr City. "We have no issues except electricity."

His friend nodded his head in agreement: "Electricity, electricity, electricity."

SCREWED UP

Despite the prewar warning signs, the United States was not prepared for the enormity of what lay ahead. Although the UN had documented the trouble for years, coalition officials expressed surprise when they found out how seriously run-down the system was. "There was a lot more damage than [we] ever realized," said Maj. Erik Stor, operations chief for the Army Corps of Engineers' Restore Iraqi Electricity project. The depth of the ignorance was evident in the resources devoted to the problem in the early months. USAID dedicated only $230 million of Bechtel's $690 million infrastructure contract to rebuild Iraq's electrical system, including limited funds for spare parts. When Bechtel engineers arrived in May, they brought with them only 6 security guards. A year later the number had risen to 169.[8]

The summer of 2003 in Iraq was particularly oppressive. Indoor temperatures routinely passed 130 degrees. Blackouts were constant. Within weeks of the invasion, the Iraqis began complaining about the lack of power. After a promising start, power generation stalled at about 3,400 megawatts by early June. The United States seemed not to notice. Bremer said on June 12 that Baghdad was "producing twenty hours of electricity a day." A few weeks later, he said "most" of the city had power. A little while after that, the city suffered a blackout that lasted several days. In August a State Department official said that the power grid was "more stable" than under Saddam. The next day, there were riots in Basra over the lack of gasoline and electricity.[9] "They sent so many soldiers here to fight," said a bookseller named Saad Abdelrazak. "They should have sent over a few more electricians and engineers."[10]

Part of the problem lay in a fateful decision the coalition made that summer. Saddam had distributed power unevenly, making sure that Baghdad and the homes of his supporters in towns like Tikrit got an almost twenty-four-hour supply, while rural villages and towns in southern Iraq received only a few hours per day. To show the coalition's commitment to democracy, Bremer decided to distribute power more evenly, making sure that all parts of Iraq got the same amount. It was a public relations ploy that backfired badly. David Nash, who arrived after the decision was made, told me it was misguided, if well intentioned: "Electricity wasn't the most important thing to all the people of Iraq. It might have been to Baghdad. But not so much in the rural areas that never had it to begin with." In the political, economic, and media capital of Iraq, 5 million residents suddenly saw their access to electricity plunge dramatically.

By late summer the precarious calm that marked the first few months of the occupation vanished. Iraqis who had been willing to see what the United States occupation would bring now gave up. Protests exploded. In late July the United States military recorded an increase in attacks against coalition soldiers. In August the United Nations building was blown up, prompting Secretary-General Kofi Annan to withdraw most UN workers from Iraq. Later that month, Gen. John Abizaid, head of the war effort, called the major players of the reconstruction together at Central Command headquarters in Tampa, Florida. Those invited included the senior advisers to the Oil, Electricity, and Transportation Ministries. "Why is this screwed up? What we are doing is failing, and the Iraqis are getting damn unhappy," Abizaid told those gathered for the conference, according to senior coalition officials who were present.

Suddenly the electricity effort was flooded with money and manpower. Bush's proposed new aid package included $5.6 billion, not only for rehabilitating old plants but also for building new ones. Another billion dollars of money from the Development Fund for Iraq was added to the mix. The U.S. Army Corps of Engineers brought in three major engineering firms — Fluor, Perini, and Washington Group International — to immediately begin work. In the summer the Coalition Provisional Authority had dedicated five people to the power effort. By the fall, that staff had surpassed fifty. Bremer gave the new effort a name: Task Force 4400. Their job was to boost Iraq's power supplies to their prewar levels by September 30, just six weeks away.

TEAM 4400

Steve Browning, an Army Corps of Engineers official, led the charge. Browning was a rising star in the Army Corps. An environmental engineer by training, he had developed a reputation for his skill at cleaning up messes. Browning was responsible for the Army Corps' response to Hurricane Mitch in Central America. His next disaster was far more daunting: he had been the man chosen to oversee the Army Corps' effort to dispose of the rubble from the Twin Towers disaster in New York. Browning had flown into Iraq with Jay Garner, becoming one of the first three U.S. civilians to arrive in Baghdad after the fall of the city.

Following a quick review, Browning decided that the United States had been too passive. Under Gibson, the first senior adviser to the Electricity Ministry, the U.S. strategy was to empower the Iraqis. The United States would provide advice, but the Iraqis would actually do the repairs and pay for new parts themselves. It wasn't working. "There wasn't really a good plan for moving forward. There were a lot of promises being made and not much [progress]," he later told me.

Browning stepped up the tempo. He paired Iraqi plant operators with U.S. power experts from the Army Corps. He demanded that task force members work from dawn to well past midnight. He created a police force to patrol the transmission towers that were being felled nightly. "The coalition forces were so stretched, it wasn't one of their prime missions. They had bigger things to do," Browning said. (Browning's police force never gelled, in part because of the U.S. military, which insisted that Iraqi security forces conduct no nighttime patrols. Commanders wanted to avoid friendly-fire incidents at night, when night vision–equipped U.S. troops did much of their work. But the commanders also wanted their soldiers chasing insurgents, not patrolling pipelines. The effect was that Iraq's vast system of electrical towers and oil pipelines was left unguarded after dusk. It wasn't until the fall of 2005, two and a half years after the invasion, that the military finally allowed limited patrolling of infrastructure at night. In the interim, the insurgents wreaked havoc.)

Each night Browning and his team gathered to review the day's performance. The pressure was enormous. Deputy Defense Secretary Paul Wolfowitz himself called to review results. "He would say to me, 'I saw your power generation chart today,' every day," Browning said. "When people saw there was a drop, they'd say, 'Oh, you failed today.' "

Not surprisingly, generators began breaking down as they were pushed to their limits. Engineers working twenty-two-hour days made mistakes. (At the Hartha plant, in southern Iraq, somebody left a bundle of wires sitting in a pool of oil. The wires caught fire, taking the plant offline for two weeks.) Some came to believe that the United States was pushing too hard in pursuit of a public relations stunt. "We worked like crazy, but it was all too much," said Gazi Aziz, a plant manager at the Baghdad South power station. When the plant's generators roared to life in early October, the decrepit boilers collapsed. "It fell apart in five days," said Mr. Aziz.[11] One soldier involved in the effort posted a joking entry on his website on September 25. It was titled "TOP 11 WAYS TO REACH 4400 MW (I know it's supposed to be just 10, but it's just as screwed up as the program)."

11. Lie.
10. Pay each Iraqi $5 a day to pedal on a generation bike. (Increase MWs and stimulate the economy.)
9. Dedicate all remaining time to develop a proof that allows us to count imaginary MWs.
8. Count all coalition forces generation, they're in Iraq, too.
7. Attach a generation turbine to the CPA to harness all the hot air into reliable MWs.
6. Develop a new unit, the Iraqi Megawatts (IMW), which is equal to ½ a MW.

5. Report the peak in KW and hope nobody notices.

4. Take a peak reading twice a day and report the sum.

3. Tell the Iraqis it was just a typo, we can only get to 3400 MW.

2. Admit failure and buy all the Iraqis candles.

1. Count Kuwait as part of Iraq, hell it was in the early '90s.[12]

Then on October 5, 2003, just days after the deadline had passed, power production hit 4,417 megawatts. After midnight the power team members gathered around a table at the Rashid Hotel in the middle of Baghdad's fortified Green Zone and bought one another drinks. Someone lit a candle, placed it on the table, and said: "To the people who turned the lights back on in Baghdad." Everyone began applauding.

The excitement didn't last. Bremer announced a new goal almost immediately: 6,000 megawatts by June.

PIPE DREAM

Through the fall of 2003 and spring of 2004, the U.S. Army contracting experts working with Nash's reconstruction agency struggled to bid out thousands of projects, including power plants, dams, and police equipment. Because of the volume of contracts and the backlog, deadlines were pushed back from November to January to February. Amy Burns, Nash's spokeswoman, compared the race to build and refurnish the power plants to trying to build Disney World in downtown Memphis in less than three months. "You couldn't do it any faster than we did," she said.

Contracting officers were overwhelmed by the workload. The electricity team, facing Bremer's target of 6,000 megawatts by June 1, had no more than three contracting officers trying to bid work for $100 million in parts. Orders that were supposed to have been placed in November backed up for months. Nearly a year later, replacement parts had still not arrived. "It was a pipe dream to think that the CPA was going to award and mobilize construction contracts from coalition countries as fast as Admiral Nash wanted them to be," Browning said. "It was just going to take longer."

To speed up the process, the Army Corps used more than $1 billion in Iraqi money, meaning the contracting firms were allowed to buy millions of dollars in parts without competitive bids. Generators that normally would have been transported by sea were shipped in by air, improving speed, but boosting the cost. The Army Corps spent nearly $1 million for each new megawatt added to Iraq's power supply — 30 percent more than Bechtel was spending.[13]

Like so many other efforts in Iraq, despite interest from the very top — the White House and Pentagon got daily briefings on power production — the work was roiled by constantly changing leadership, vision, and emphasis. Between April 2003 and August 2004, seven people were in charge of rebuilding the power system — the equivalent of a new CEO every two and a half months for one of the most complicated and expensive tasks in Iraq. "It was absolutely horrendous," said Michel Gautier, head of the UN's Iraqi infrastructure office, which worked with the Americans on some electrical projects. "We could never collaborate because of the continually changing people. It was extremely inefficient and destructive." It was a problem that was never fixed. When Bill Taylor left his one-year tour as the State Department's reconstruction chief in 2005, he couldn't even recall the names of all the senior advisers he had worked with. The advisers — mostly American power executives on temporary leave of absence from their jobs — each brought a different perspective. Some focused on the generation of electricity, others on security, and still others on fuel sources. The constant change in personnel baffled Americans, Iraqis, and UN officials alike. Senior advisers "would come and spend five weeks getting to know the place, then four weeks of work, and then three weeks getting ready to go back home," the UN's Gautier noted.

In March, Fluor, Washington Group, and Perini each got contracts worth half a billion dollars to carry out Nash's building plan. The surge in violence in April did not stop the reconstruction effort, but it slowed it. When June 1 arrived, Iraq was producing about 4,300 megawatts a day — far from the 6,000-megawatt goal.

Having grown up in dictatorship, Iraqis were used to propaganda. But even the most cynical of them would likely have raised an eyebrow had they encountered the Bush administration's spin on the failure of the coalition's electricity efforts. A question-and-answer section in a report on the coalition website offered clues to the unhappiness over power generation. "People in Baghdad constantly speak of how things were better under Saddam. How do you counter these claims?" one question said. The coalition's answer was that the lack of electricity was actually a sign of a recovering economy. New businesses and consumer spending had resulted in increased demand. "Before the liberation," the report boasted, "Saddam drained power from throughout the country to feed Baghdad, leaving more than 80% of the country to fend for themselves with private generators and whatever power they could scrape together from the grid. Even with this unfair system of power, Saddam was only able to power Baghdad 20–22 hours a day. After the liberation, the power system was re-distributed equitably throughout the nation."[14] Put another way, the coalition was saying that its primary achievement was not providing enough power to Iraq. It was distributing the paucity equitably.

WRONG TECHNOLOGY

By the fall of 2004 the Army Corps' spending spree had caught up with it. The Iraqi money had run out before several electricity projects were completed. Under the new State Department reconstruction plan, Bill Taylor decided to turn the unfinished work over to the Iraqi Ministry of Electricity in the belief that the Iraqis would take over. Instead the Iraqis did nothing, their own budget hampered by the insurgency, inefficient state spending, oil production shortfalls, and persistent corruption. Months passed without any work being done on the abandoned power plants. The poor state of the power system turned into an übertruth of the reconstruction, an excuse repeated over and over by the Americans charged with fixing it.

Scott Hutchins, the newest U.S. senior adviser, realized that the fastest way to boost power production was to finish off the partially completed efforts. In a bit of budget legerdemain, he dedicated an additional $100 million to complete work on the old projects. Thus Project Phoenix was born. The name implied rebirth, but in reality the Americans were simply returning to the work they had abandoned. The United States eventually paid Fluor-AMEC, a U.S.-British joint venture, $93 million to complete the work and add 700 megawatts of power to the grid. The lost months, however, resulted in millions of angry Iraqis having to sweat through another summer. "We started it much too late," admitted Bill Thompson, an Army Corps official who worked on electrical restoration.

Project Phoenix had another goal: fixing one of the most misguided choices of the entire reconstruction effort. Early on, the Army Corps had decided to continue a program begun under Saddam Hussein to install scores of electrical generators that used Iraq's plentiful supply of natural gas for fuel. Americans at the Ministry of Electricity directed hundreds of millions of dollars to purchase and install natural gas–fired generators in electricity plants throughout Iraq. On paper it seemed sensible enough. The problem, however, was that no pipelines existed to actually transport the gas to the power plants. Iraq's Oil Ministry wasn't particularly interested in building them either. Iraqi oil officials — who were backed by American advisers — focused instead on boosting oil production, which brought in hard cash. As a result the pipelines were never built and of twenty-six natural gas turbines installed at seven plants in Iraq — each ranging in cost from a few million dollars to more than $40 million — only seven wound up burning natural gas.

To put the natural gas generators to use, the U.S. Army Corps of Engineers and the State Department had to reconfigure them to burn a different fuel. It was an expensive process that decreased each generator's capacity and increased maintenance. In many cases, heavy fuel oil, a tarry by-product of Iraq's primitive refineries that wreaked havoc on the natural gas generators, was used. One of the gas turbines that I had seen being installed at the Bayji plant in August 2004 at a cost of $40 million had to be replaced a year later. "My concept as a layman [is that] we basically wrecked the unit" by using the wrong kind of fuel, said Dennis Karns, the Army Corps official heading the power sector. The Government Accountability Office reached a similar conclusion in February 2006, warning that power generation at the refurbished plants could be cut in half and maintenance costs tripled. The use of the oil-fueled generators "could result in equipment failure and damage that significantly reduces the life of the equipment," the report said.

Lower power output wasn't the only cost of betting heavily on natural gas. The United States had to cancel other power plants in mid-construction. Taylor decided to shut down a massive new power complex that Bechtel was building northeast of Baghdad in a place called Mansuria. Bechtel engineers believed it to be a "viable project," but Taylor thought it was too big, too costly, and would take too long to get on line. By the time the decision was made in the spring of 2005, the United States had already paid the company $62.7 million for design work, a construction camp, and two generators that were handed over to the Iraqis for future use. Of that amount, $12 million was profit for Bechtel for a plant that was never built.

All through 2005 the United States began to turn over the refurbished power plants to the Iraqis, in keeping with the new State Department philosophy to empower Iraqis and the Bush administration political strategy to prepare for withdrawal. But as the United States stepped back, the Iraqis once again proved themselves unable to do the job. Within months of taking control, they had crippled scores of electrical plants by failing to maintain and operate them properly. By the spring of 2005, USAID officials told me that none of the nineteen power complexes turned over to the Iraqis was being run properly. Dick Dumford, USAID's top electricity expert, said that Iraq's gas and thermal generators, if properly maintained and operated, could produce about 8,000 megawatts a day — almost enough to cover demand. "Operations and maintenance is a big concern for everybody here," Dumford, a retired Siemens engineer, told me. "We do not want [the electrical plants] to go south on us as soon as we walk away. How we do that is a concern we all have."

Nash's program had focused more on dirt-turning than developing the skills Iraqis needed to operate and maintain the expensive equipment that was being installed. The initial contracts overseen by Nash's team had called for a mere three months of follow-up training — a fraction of what their peers in the West might receive. And the Iraqis were decades out of date to begin with. In one incident a contractor hired to train the Iraqis on how to run a new, state-of-the-art power plant instead wound up teaching a Microsoft Windows class. Most of the Iraqis had never used a computer. "In layman's terms, they're very good, like the Cubans, at keeping 1950s cars running," said Spike Stephenson, USAID's director in Iraq. "But we are about to give them eight-cylinder, computer-controlled BMWs that they've never seen before."

Attempts to better the Iraqis' training proved frustratingly hard. In one instance USAID sent scores of Iraqi engineers abroad for training as part of a multimillion-dollar effort to create "tiger teams" that would return and educate other Iraqis. Instead the engineers were dispersed to different plants throughout Iraq and provided very little training. "We never got anything out of them," said Dennis Karns. The Americans tended to blame the indifferent Iraqi work ethic on habits learned under Saddam's regime. Many people held their Saddam-era jobs because of their connections to the regime, not their expertise, and didn't have to worry about being held accountable. The little upkeep that did take place was under threat of harsh punishment — a worry that vanished with the fall of Saddam's regime. Longtime staffers were accustomed to getting paid whether they worked or not. "People are afraid to make decisions," said Aidan Goldsmith, a USAID consultant who was helping train Iraqis. "It's top-down."

Besides training, the Americans also did not give much thought to how much money the Iraqis would need to maintain the new systems. The assumption had always been that oil revenues would pay the bill. But the Americans having failed in their efforts to restore pumping levels, the Iraqi budget was constantly running a deficit. Iraqi officials blamed the United States for not providing adequate funds for upkeep. Iraqi ministries did not have the money to maintain their existing dilapidated systems, much less operate new ones. "The main problem we suffer is our budget. There's simply not enough for our needs," said Mahmoud Ali Ahmed, the head of Iraq's water distribution system. Stuart Bowen, the inspector general, estimated that Iraq would need nearly $1 billion in additional funding per year to sustain operations for its American-financed infrastructure. Congress ignored the warning and appropriated no additional money. For reasons of policy and politics, the State Department was particularly reluctant to ask for more money for fear that the Iraqis would become dependent on American largesse. If the Iraqis wanted to wreck their power plants, that was their choice. The United States would offer advice but not intervene. "This is their country," Bill Taylor told me during a meeting in his office in the Republican Palace one winter day. "They need to take responsibility. We're not going to be responsible for it. If they run it into the ground, we'll be disappointed. But this is their country." It was a kind of tough love approach. Andy Wylegala, who worked at the U.S. embassy in Iraq to help Americans do business there, was even more blunt about the decision to let the Iraqis suffer the costs of the American projects: "No pain, no gain."

THEIR BABY

The handover troubles were not confined to power stations. The United States was beginning to complete water treatment plants and sewer stations as well. Of more than forty such plants run by the Iraqis, not a single one was being operated properly, according to Bechtel. An internal coalition memo said that renovated plants "deteriorate quickly to an alarming state of disrepair and inoperability." One official involved in reconstruction estimated that "hundreds of millions" had been wasted. Jack Hume, a Bechtel engineer who oversaw water projects, recounted his experience at the Kerkh sewage plant. The plant, one of only three in Baghdad, was a top priority for USAID. Saddam had been unable to keep any of the three plants running during sanctions, and Baghdad had had no sewage treatment at all for years prior to the U.S. invasion. The waste of the city's 5 million residents was being shunted directly into the Tigris. The polluted river, in turn, provided drinking and bathing water for poorer Iraqis. Bechtel was on the scene in September 2003 and spent $20 million to fix the plant. But after the keys were handed to the Iraqis in June 2004, Kerkh quickly "went septic" — stopped functioning. The Iraqis began shunting waste directly into the Tigris again. "When I went back out to that plant in November [2004], what I saw was the identical plant that I saw in September 2003," Hume said. "It had reverted back to the same conditions. It was very disappointing." After another year of repair, the United States handed the plant over to the Iraqis again. The plant manager was killed, and by December 2005, Kerkh had once again become nothing more than a collection point to shunt raw sewage into the Tigris.[15]

Jocular, outgoing, and dangerously enthusiastic, Mark Oviatt was one of the first to sound a warning. In two years as USAID's senior water consultant, he constantly toured the country's water and sewer plants in a bulletproof vest, blue blazer, and boat shoes without socks. A bear of a man, tall and overweight, Oviatt towered over his Iraqi counterparts, whom he often greeted with a warm hug. When I met him in February 2005, we were traveling in an armed convoy of three SUVs to the northern Iraqi city of Kirkuk for the dedication of a new water plant. His visits around Iraq had convinced him that the Iraqis had neither the expertise nor the funds necessary to run the plants. He was asking his bosses in Washington for an additional $25 million to train a cadre of expert Iraqi operators. It was a modest program, but even so he was having trouble getting anyone to pay attention to him. The reconstruction process has "not been a waste of money so much as an expensive lesson learned for all parties involved," Oviatt said.

The troubles were clear enough at the water plant, a complex of one-story buildings circled by a ragged cyclone fence and herds of goats. USAID had spent $4.1 million to overhaul the dilapidated plant, which had been producing below capacity after years of neglect. During the final walk-through on a chilly day in February, Oviatt and the Bechtel engineers found a myriad of problems. The Iraqi operators weren't adding chlorine to one part of the treatment process to improve efficiency. Although it had snowed, they hadn't put antifreeze in two backup generators. A basement room was covered with a layer of dirt after Iraqis had failed to clean up a spill of muddy water. A mess of burned cables lay in another part of the plant, the result of a small fire. No workers were wearing safety goggles or boots, even though Bechtel had delivered several cases of them. The overhaul had restored the plant's capability to 95 million gallons of water per day. But the local water director, Abdulkader Muhammad Ameen, wasn't sure how long it would be able to produce that amount.

At the end of the walk-through, Oviatt and Ameen gathered in a small office in the plant's operations center. In an impromptu ceremony, Oviatt officially turned over the plant to the Iraqis. He shook hands with Ameen, who thanked America for its contribution. One of Ameen's deputies took pictures. Then Oviatt and an entourage of security contractors piled into a bulletproof sport utility vehicle. "They have accepted and acknowledged that they are completely responsible," Oviatt said as he and his security detail raced away from the plant for the last time. "It's their baby now."

THE MOST AMAZING MESS

There was no simple answer to the problems of lighting Iraq. The Americans mostly blamed security. Companies such as Bechtel, Siemens, and General Electric suspended operations for weeks on end in response to violent attacks on their technicians. Guerrillas blew up convoys to interrupt the delivery of fuel to power plants. Iraqi workers were targeted for cooperating with the rebuilding effort. Insurgents tumbled transmission towers like dominos: when U.S. assessment teams arrived in Iraq shortly after the invasion, about 30 towers had been knocked down. By September the number had grown to 623 out of 2,554 transmission towers in the country, or nearly a quarter of all towers.[16] "We're just not making progress to the extent we could if it weren't for the security issue," said Mike Moseley, a retired Tennessee Valley Authority executive who served as a senior U.S. consultant on electricity to the Iraqis. "We're moving forward, but not in a sea of water. We're in a sea of molasses on a cold winter day."

The looting that occurred immediately after the war was also a culprit. Rodney Bent, the coalition's budget director, one day toured a complex north of Baghdad in which the control panels had been smashed, apparently to get at the lightbulbs inside. "They got a couple of dollars of benefit at most and did this incalculable harm," he said. Tom Wheelock, USAID's infrastructure director, said much of the looting was done by organized gangs in search of scrap metal. "It was like Pac-Man; they just started at one end of the transmission line and worked their way up, taking down the towers, taking away the valuable metals, smelting it down, selling it into Iran and Kuwait," Wheelock said. So much metal was stolen and sold for scrap from Iraq's power lines that scrap metal prices dropped dramatically throughout the Middle East. Much of the money spent to restore Iraq's power was used not for new equipment but to replace what Iraqis stole from themselves. Wheelock estimated that the looting tripled the cost of getting the lights back on.[17] Clifford G. Mumm, the Bechtel executive who oversaw the company's rebuilding work, had a description for Iraq's electrical system: "The most amazing mess."

Perhaps the biggest American blunder of all was the absence of that most basic tenet of capitalism: pricing based on the law of supply and demand. After the border opened up, electronic goods came flooding into Iraq from Iran, Jordan, and elsewhere. Newly flush with raises implemented by Bremer for people in government jobs, upper- and middle-class Iraqi consumers went on a buying spree soon after the invasion. The upscale Karada district in Baghdad turned into an open-air Best Buy, with washers, dryers, air conditioners, television sets, radios, and refrigerators — mostly brands from Korea and China — cramming the sidewalks, stacked into pillars that soared above store tops. The effect of millions of so-called white goods being plugged in across the country was a tremendous increase in demand for power — and there was nothing to slow it down. Electricity was free in Iraq: neither the United States nor the Iraqis charged for delivering power to homes and businesses. As a result, there was no incentive to turn off lights or air conditioners or anything else. Demand grew unchecked, and the supply could not keep pace.

During the first year of the occupation, when it wielded complete control, the United States could have imposed price controls, but it did not. Bremer and other reconstruction officials knew that the decision to continue Saddam-era subsidies in electricity, food, and oil were warping the economy, but they worried that any increase in prices risked instability. An American senior adviser called the failure to tackle the issue "one of the worst mistakes" of the occupation.[18] After the handover, the United States and the World Bank both attempted to convince the Iraqis to start charging market prices, with limited effect. Again, the objection was instability.

The growing gap between supply and demand made it appear to Iraqis that their electricity supply was actually diminishing. Saddam had been able to fulfill about 65 percent of demand. But even if the United States had matched the output under Saddam — and it didn't — it would have met less than half of the new increased need. In practical terms, Iraqis who had six hours in the early days of the U.S. occupation saw their electrical supply shrink to five, then four, then a mere three hours per day. Even Americans were baffled by the inability to turn the lights on. A fatalistic sense of resignation was common among the Americans as the reconstruction continued to stumble and Iraq veered on the edge of disintegration. "Everybody wants simple answers, and there aren't any," said Dick Dumford, perhaps the longest-serving member of the group of U.S. engineers and experts who labored to get Iraq's electricity running again. "We did our best. Everybody did their best."

For the Iraqis that wasn't good enough. Blackened streets and broken air conditioners were inconveniences. But power failures in hospitals and clinics had deadly consequences. For the family whose child was lost because of an outage that left doctors unable to power an incubator, or whose father died on the operating table as the lights went off, affection for the Americans became a permanently abstract concept.

In December 2005 America completed the last major repair job on an Iraqi power plant. The Khor Zubayr generating station was a pile of gray metal that rose like an island in the vast emptiness outside Basra, in southern Iraq, a wavering hallucination after miles of nothing but sand and highway. Chris Frabott, an earnest, intense young Army Corps official who usually worked on dredging projects on the Interstate Waterway on the East Coast, spent months overseeing an American contractor and hundreds of Iraqis to install two mammoth generators and pipelines. Khor Zubayr was one of the few natural gas generators to actually use natural gas. The Americans had anticipated that Khor Zubayr, capable of producing 500 megawatts of power, would push Iraq's total production to a consistent 5,500 megawatts.

Instead as the Americans handed the plant over to the Iraqis in a brief ceremony, the country's output hovered at around 3,700 megawatts. It was below Iraq's prewar production, below the U.S. goal of 6,000 megawatts, not anywhere close to meeting the country's demand. Insurgents continued to topple transmission towers. Demand continued to rise. Blackouts were constant. It was the best Iraq was going to get.

As Frabott toured the site a few months before the final dedication, he had looked up at one of the generators and patted its side. "It's a lot of work," he said. "A lot of money."

14

Cost of War

Upon arriving from West Point for his new posting in Iraq, Col. Ted Westhusing found himself leading a different kind of army: the private security contractors who served as the foot soldiers of the reconstruction. Westhusing was in Baghdad to work on what the Pentagon considered the most important mission in Iraq: training Iraqi forces to take over security duties from U.S. troops. His specific task was to oversee a private security company, Virginia-based USIS, which had contracts worth $79 million to train a corps of Iraqi police to conduct special operations. Westhusing and USIS had six months to train the elite of the elite, the Iraqis' Emergency Response Unit. The units were designed to provide protection to senior Iraqi dignitaries and act like a SWAT team during kidnapping and ransom cases. There would be three companies of sixty men each. Westhusing had no particular experience in overseeing contractors, or in police tactics, but he plunged into his work with gusto.

Iraq was another chance for self-knowledge, a philosophical quest that he prized above all others. In his PhD dissertation, Westhusing noted how the philosopher Ludwig Wittgenstein refused to discuss the topic of ethics: "To write or talk ethics or religions was to run against the boundaries of language." Westhusing did not appear to care. His dissertation was less concerned with linguistic limitation than it was his own attempt to understand himself. He was seeking, in the heroic acts of others, what he demanded of himself. "Honor, like love, comes in both true and false forms. For the warrior, I will also show that the false forms are particularly bewitching," he wrote.[1]

At first Westhusing was friendly with the contractors and bonded tightly with the new Iraqi cadets, practicing with them daily and even going out on raids. He wrote back home and told friends that Iraq was "high adventure." When one Iraqi officer complained about not getting his check, Westhusing grabbed three Humvees, soldiers, machine guns, and flash grenades and drove to the Ministry of the Interior to force an immediate payday for the man. He recounted to friends back home how his security detail had once just missed being hit by a car bomb that killed two Westerners and an Iraqi on the way to Baghdad airport. An article in *Stars and Stripes,* the military newspaper, featured Westhusing's new unit. In Mosul his first graduates had arrested two "high value" targets suspected of attacking coalition forces, and captured another man suspected of beheading a police officer. "We get a very high level of training from very good instructors and we develop day by day, building our ability, step by step," a twenty-three-year-old member of the Emergency Response Unit told the newspaper. "We are like the lion of Iraq, very brave."[2]

A photograph with the article showed two dozen men in black balaclavas, clad in camouflage and holding AK-47s. Westhusing is off to the side, gazing into the distance, his tongue just poking from his lips, seemingly lost in thought. The unit, he told a friend in an e-mail, was "doing very well against the bad guys." He told another friend that his work required him to apply everything that he had spent so long studying. "If you are not of strong character and know right from wrong, you will leave this place devastated in personal esteem and priceless human beings will be harmed," he wrote. General Petraeus, the training mission's commanding officer, was so impressed that he had Westhusing frocked to colonel, an unusual procedure in which an officer is given immediate higher authority rather than await a scheduled promotion date. Petraeus praised Westhusing's work in an e-mail in March. "You have already exceeded the very lofty expectations all had for you," Petraeus wrote. Westhusing wrote back: "Thanks much, sir, but we can do much better and will."[3]

But by April 2005 Westhusing's mood had darkened as he became increasingly frustrated with the pace of progress in Iraq. The Iraqis' penchant for showing up late deeply irritated him. He worried about training delays and lost equipment like helmets and weapons. He wrote his father that "things [are] not going all that well." He even threatened to resign at one point, telling a captain in his office: "I should just fall on my sword.

I've failed."[4] When he complained to another officer, the response was simply to tell him to buck up. Westhusing briefly rallied. "I will fight it out and either die, [get reassigned] or get fired. I won't give those idiots the satisfaction of me asking them to relieve me," he wrote. But the fire was not sustained.

The contractors on the police training mission he was working with also began to bother him. There had recently been a change in the contract that forced USIS to more closely watch its expenses, and Westhusing began to clash with USIS officials over money issues. He did not understand why they were so concerned about the bottom line and less interested in getting the mission done.

Then, in May, Westhusing received an anonymous four-page letter that contained detailed allegations of wrongdoing and human rights abuses by USIS. The author appeared to be a former USIS employee. He named company officials, had detailed knowledge about the firm's contract, and accurately described numerous USIS operations. He accused USIS of deliberately shorting the government on the number of trainers called for in the contract in order to boost profit margins. More seriously, he detailed two incidents in which USIS contractors allegedly witnessed or participated in the killing of Iraqis. A USIS contractor who accompanied Iraqi police trainees during the assault on Fallujah in November 2004 later boasted about the number of insurgents he had killed, the letter said. In a second case, the letter said, another USIS employee saw Iraqi police trainees kill two innocent Iraqi civilians, but top company officials covered it up. A USIS manager "did not want it reported because he thought it would put his contract at risk."[5]

Westhusing immediately informed his superiors about the allegations, saying that he doubted they were true. U.S. officials found no violations on the narrow question of whether USIS was complying with its contract terms. The more serious charges did not appear to have been thoroughly examined, however. Even if they were true, it was not certain that the crimes could be prosecuted by American officials. The actions had been committed in Iraq, not the United States. "There were real questions about who had jurisdiction," one U.S. official told me.

The letter shook Westhusing. The author had written that he suspected that Westhusing was too friendly with USIS management, and that the company's managers were taking advantage of him because of his lack of knowledge of training or rules of contracting. "The overriding thought is to make as much money as they can with doing as little work as possible," the letter said. USIS, the letter claimed, was boosting its profits in front of Westhusing's nose.

"This is a mess . . . dunno what I will do with this," Westhusing wrote home to his family May 18. He consulted a military attorney. The attorney said Westhusing told him he had no personal knowledge about the truth of the allegations. But Westhusing appeared disturbed. "We were all under incredible pressure there. It was a huge, very difficult mission. There were not enough people to do it the way we would have liked," one U.S. official told me. "Ethics was his thing. To even have somebody suggest that he may have done something improper would explain [why] he seemed to be very bothered."

Westhusing began to complain to colleagues about "his dislike of the contractors," who, he said, "were paid too much money by the government," according to one captain. "The meetings [with contractors] were never easy and always contentious. The contracts were in dispute and always under discussion," an Army Corps of Engineers official told investigators. A contracting officer he worked with said Westhusing was "concerned about overpaying of contractors." His conversations with his family about the contractors were even more blunt, and darker. He even thought that his life might be in danger. He called his wife soon after getting the letter and told her that he was going to quit. "He said he could not be a part of it anymore. The contractors were corrupt, the Iraqis were not trustworthy. He said he lost control. The Iraqi treatment of the insurgents was deplorable and he could not rein them in," his wife, Michelle, said. Terry, Westhusing's mother, said Westhusing called to tell her he was having "difficulties" with the contractors' not doing the "right thing."

SULLIED

By June some of Westhusing's colleagues began to worry about his health. He had lost so much weight that he continually had to hitch up his pants to keep them from falling down. He looked gaunt and worn, sleeping only four to five hours a night. He stopped going to the gym and started chewing smokeless tobacco. His behavior changed too. Although he had never been outgoing, Westhusing seemed even more withdrawn. He stopped participating in social activities like movie night. He began to repeat himself and fidget in the office, sometimes staring off into space for hours.

Westhusing's family was also becoming worried. Westhusing described feeling alone and abandoned. He sent home brief, cryptic e-mails, including one that said, "[I] didn't think I'd make it last night." Westhusing brushed aside entreaties for details, writing that he would say more when he returned home. "Nothing is easy in Iraq, nothing, and everything is important. Couple that with the corruption, evil, etc. etc. and it is tough, but [I'm] persevering," he wrote one of his brothers, Tim. The family responded with an outpouring of e-mails expressing love and support. His wife shipped him beef jerky, a CD player, and a book by Aristotle. She recalled a phone conversation that chilled her. "I heard something in his voice," she said. "There was fear. He did not like the nighttime and being alone." One of his colleagues said Westhusing seemed increasingly anxious about getting out of Iraq. "Ted had an almost desperate desire to get home as quickly as possible," one colleague wrote.

On June 4 Westhusing left his office in the U.S.-controlled Green Zone to view a demonstration of Iraqi police preparedness at Camp Dublin, the USIS headquarters located at Baghdad airport. He gave a briefing that impressed General Petraeus and a visiting scholar. He had meetings with USIS and other contractors the next morning, so he decided to stay overnight at the USIS camp. That night in an office on the compound, a USIS secretary watched Westhusing take out his 9mm pistol and play with it, repeatedly unholstering the weapon and pulling back the chamber. He was staring off into space, fidgeting, scratching and rubbing his legs, and mumbling to himself.

At a meeting the next morning to discuss construction delays, he seemed agitated. He stewed over demands for tighter vetting of police candidates, worried that it would slow the mission. He seemed upset over funding shortfalls. He lashed out at the contractors in attendance, according to one Army Corps official who was present. "Can any one of you tell me why you can't get along?" he shouted. "He was sick of moneygrubbing contractors," the official recounted. Westhusing said that "he had not come over to Iraq for this." The meeting broke up shortly before lunch.

At about 1 p.m. a USIS manager went to look for Westhusing, who was scheduled for a ride back to the Green Zone. After getting no answer at Westhusing's cabin, the manager returned to the pickup point to wait some more. Some fifteen minutes later the manager went back to Westhusing's cabin a second time, this time with another USIS employee. The employee peeked through a window and saw Westhusing lying on the floor in a pool of blood. The manager rushed into the trailer and tried to revive West-husing. The manager later told investigators that he picked up the pistol at Westhusing's feet and tossed it onto the bed. "I knew people would show up," the manager said later in attempting to explain why he had handled the weapon at a crime scene. "With thirty years from military and law enforcement training, I did not want the weapon to get bumped and go off."

After a three-month inquiry, investigators declared Westhusing's death a suicide. A test showed gunpowder residue on his hands. A shell casing in the room bore markings indicating it had been fired from his service weapon.

And there was the note.

Investigators found it lying on Westhusing's bed. It was four pages long, choppy, and filled with abbreviations and underlined words. The handwriting matched his. Parts of the letter lashed out at his two commanders, Petraeus and Gen. Joseph Fil, but most of it was a wrenching account of a struggle for honor in a strange land.[6]

> I cannot support a msn [mission] that leads to corruption, human rights abuse and liars. I am sullied. No more. I didn't volunteer to support corrupt, money hungry contractors, nor work for cdrs [commanders] only interested in themselves. I came to serve honorably and [I] feel dishonored. I trust no Iraqi. I cannot live this way. Death before being dishonored any more. Trust is essential. I don't know whom to trust anymore. Why serve when you cannot accomplish the msn, when you no longer believe in the cause, when your every effort and breath to succeed meets with lies, lack of support and selfishness. No more. Life needs trust. Trust is no more for me here in Iraq.[7]

RIGHT MAN, WRONG WAR

At the time, Westhusing was the highest-ranking military officer to die in Iraq. His suicide touched off a series of inquiries, including one by the army's inspector general. The investigation turned up no wrongdoing by USIS. But it chronicled a collision between the spit-and-shine world of the military and the violent, corrupt culture of the Iraqis. There was "corruption in every single Iraqi organization. We would have to halt our operations to avoid it," one captain wrote. Another officer told investigators that the coalition could not expect to change two thousand years of history in only two. "Unethical behavior is a way of life," the officer said.

As part of a separate investigation known as a commander's inquiry, Lt. Col. Lisa Breitenbach, an army psychologist, conducted an in-depth review of Westhusing's mental state. She reviewed Westhusing's e-mails and interviewed colleagues. She concluded that Westhusing had placed too much pressure on himself to succeed and that he was unusually rigid in his thinking. Westhusing had trouble reconciling his sense of ethics with the chaos of Iraq. "He chose an area of study where ethical and moral issues were prominent matters; and a career in which he espoused and defended them. However, in his current mission, there were no rules or even established procedures to follow which would dictate the proper course of action," she wrote. The anonymous letter had been the "most difficult and probably most painful stressor," she said, triggering a major depressive disorder.

In the miasma of Iraq, Westhusing had met the enemy: it was greed. He seemed continually disappointed by the contractors' concern with money, rather than simply doing the right thing because it was the right thing. He struggled with the idea that monetary values were outweighing moral ones in the war in Iraq. This, Breitenbach said, was a flaw. "Despite his intelligence, his ability to grasp the idea that profit is an important goal for people working in the private sector was surprisingly limited. He could not shift his mind-set from the military notion of completing a mission irrespective of cost, nor could he change his belief that doing the right thing because it was the right thing to do should be the sole motivator for businesses."

Some of Westhusing's family and friends were troubled that he died at Camp Dublin, where he was without a bodyguard, surrounded by the same contractors he suspected of wrongdoing. They wondered why the manager who discovered Westhusing's body and picked up his weapon was not tested for gunpowder residue. Finally, there was the curious matter of the doors. The manager told investigators that the first time he went to check on Westhusing, the door had been locked. The second time, it was open. None of the issues seemed to have been addressed by the military investigators.

Mostly, family and friends wondered how Westhusing — father, husband, son, and expert on doing right — could have found himself in a place so dark that he saw no light. "I don't think he'd give up everything that he'd left behind. It doesn't make a bit of sense to me," said his brother,

Tim. "He's the last person who would commit suicide," said Fichtelberg, his graduate school colleague. "He couldn't have done it. He's just too damn stubborn." Others in Westhusing's family said they had seen signs of trouble from three thousand miles away. Why hadn't the people that he worked with in Baghdad done anything? Why didn't anyone tell Westhusing to get counseling, or just take a vacation when he was physically deteriorating in plain view? "Someone should have been able to detect that [he] was not at full performance and taken measures to get him some assistance," his father said.

For me Westhusing's death captured a central truth about the war in Iraq. Here was one of America's finest soldiers. Smart. Disciplined. Enthusiastic. It did not matter ultimately whether he committed suicide or whether he was killed by greedy contractors looking to silence a whistle-blower. What mattered was that he was thrust into a world where his values — duty, honor, country, the values that America has relied upon in every war we have waged — no longer served as the sole motivation to fight. To a far greater degree than any other conflict in this country's history, the people who fought and rebuilt Iraq were motivated by profit, not by patriotism, or brotherhood, or a belief in what they were doing. To Westhusing, and to many other soldiers and public servants working in Iraq, that reality was disorienting and disheartening.

The greed that so dismayed him was not the conspiracy-theory, hyper-politicized grasping that Democrats attributed to Bush, Cheney, and their oil business buddies. It was the everyday, striving-to-make-a-buck imperative of the average American businessman. Wal-Mart's tactics are not the same as the Eighty-second Airborne's. They work fine in the retail marketplace. But not always on the battlefield. This is no criticism of the individual contractors themselves, many of them ex-military men and women who held values like Westhusing's. But their collective, corporate presence turned the war into a for-profit enterprise that tainted and undermined the entire effort. As one of Westhusing's colleagues put it to military investigators: "You want to fight a war, but contract it out. You can do one, or the other, but not both." There were too many businessmen in Iraq, and not enough believers. Throughout our history, we told our soldiers, men like Col. Ted Westhusing, that war could only be waged by men with honor, courage, and purpose. And then we paid a bunch of contractors to go do the work for us. Why give your life when you can get paid for it? War turned out to be a greedy, dirty, dime-store business after all.

After his death, Westhusing's body was flown back to Dover Air Force Base in Delaware. Waiting to receive it were his family and a close friend from West Point, a lieutenant colonel. In the final military report, the unidentified colonel told investigators that he had turned to Michelle, Westhusing's wife, and asked what happened.

She answered: "Iraq."

Epilogue

In November 2005 Secretary of State Condoleezza Rice made a surprise detour, flying from Bahrain directly to Mosul, a violent city in northern Iraq. Rice and her entourage of aides and reporters landed at the local airport, then traveled by helicopter to a heavily fortified military outpost on the city's outskirts. There, wearing a bulletproof vest under her suit coat, Rice greeted camouflage-clad American troops and local Iraqi leaders in dark jackets. The dramatic visit — the first time in her travels to Iraq that she had been outside Baghdad — was designed to send a message. Too dangerous to drive through or even fly over nearly three years after the invasion, Mosul was chosen to inaugurate the latest rebuilding initiative: provincial reconstruction teams.[1]

The Bush administration's new overall strategy in Iraq was "clear, hold, build." Previously the U.S. military had seized an area from insurgents only to see it slip from control upon the troops' departure. Now the idea was to take a city, establish a military presence, and begin intense, focused reconstruction — a concept that Spike Stephenson and Pete Chiarelli had pioneered in places like Sadr City, and which had spread to a handful of other so-called postbattle cities like Najaf and Fallujah. The success of the tactic had won adherents among development experts back home in the United States. In a widely circulated article in *Foreign Affairs* in the fall of 2005, Andrew Krepinevich had suggested the path to victory in Iraq was deploying "the oil-spot strategy."[2] The Bush administration redubbed it the "ink stain policy" to avoid any suggestion of plundering Iraq's oil riches, but the idea was the same. The economic and political success of one rebuilt city would spread, like ink through paper, to nearby communities.

The provincial reconstruction teams were the mechanism to carry out the new strategy. Ambassador Zalmay Khalilzad had brought the idea of the reconstruction teams with him from Afghanistan, where he had led the U.S. mission before becoming the top American diplomat in Iraq in June 2005.

The teams were supposed to overcome the fissures between State and Pentagon, which Rice and Khalilzad had witnessed firsthand while at the National Security Council, and which had crippled the early days of the rebuilding. Each of Iraq's eighteen provinces would get its own team, fusing officials from across the federal government to work with local Iraqis on smaller-scale rebuilding projects like new wells and classrooms. Rice called such work "reconstruction with a small R," but in announcing the formation of the team in Mosul, she evoked the Marshall Plan and the struggle to rebuild Germany and Japan, just as she had two years earlier when introducing Bush's massive new reconstruction package. "If Iraq does not succeed and should Iraq become a place of despair, generations of Americans would also be condemned to fear and to insecurity," Rice told the soldiers and Iraqis that gathered to hear her speak in a palace once owned by Uday Hussein, Saddam's sadistic son. "Our fates and our futures are very much linked."

A month later President Bush took to the stage in a darkened room at the Omni Shoreham Hotel in Washington to speak to the Council on Foreign Relations. Bush's popularity had plummeted to new lows as a result of the continuing bloodbath in Iraq. His chief political adviser, Karl Rove, had decided the administration needed to make a case for the war, with the president delivering four speeches before Iraqis chose a new government in December 2005 elections. For the first time since the invasion of Iraq, Bush delivered a major speech on the reconstruction. Not coincidentally it was also one of the few times in his presidency that Bush acknowledged problems in Iraq. "Reconstruction has not always gone as well as we had hoped, primarily because of the security challenges on the ground," he told the audience. "Rebuilding a nation devastated by a dictator is a large undertaking. It's even harder when terrorists are trying to blow up that which the Iraqis are trying to build." Bush talked about the successes of the ink stain policy. Americans had been able to reopen schools, spur the growth of small businesses, and even build a soccer field with "new lights and fresh sod." He called it "quiet, steady progress."

By May 2006, however, the teams appeared as troubled as every other rebuilding initiative. Months after Rice's announcement, State and Pentagon continued arguing over the formation of the teams. The State Department wanted each provincial headquarters protected by American military forces — three years of scandals and violence had dampened the gusto for hiring private security contractors. If the American military could be deployed to protect Halliburton, why not the State Department? But the

Pentagon continued to insist that it was too short of troops to protect the new sites, no matter how important they might be to the counterinsurgency effort. "You can't rob Peter to pay Paul," one defense official said.[3]

Nor did Rice's enthusiasm for the reconstruction teams trickle down through the State Department. As the months progressed, the number of teams was cut down from a planned eighteen to half that, with other teams to be manned by coalition partners and the Iraqis. Even filling the slots on the reduced number of teams proved difficult. Hillah, one of the first three teams deployed, was able to fill only about half its 112 positions. The State Department struggled to find qualified applicants for senior offices. Few people wanted to go to Iraq. Even fewer wanted to attach their careers to a floundering effort.[4]

The problems appeared to have depleted the Bush administration's patience and generosity when it came to nation building in Iraq. By the spring of 2006, only about $2 billion was left of the $30 billion that American taxpayers had sent to rebuild a shattered nation. The Army Corps announced that most of the major projects would be finished by the end of 2006 or early in 2007. The Bush administration's new budget contained an additional $5.1 billion for reconstruction — nearly all of it to train and equip Iraq's military. There was only a few hundred million for new projects and democracy-building activities. Gone was Bush's pledge to make Iraq's infrastructure the "best in the region." The city on a hill would instead be no more than a well-laid foundation. "The United States never intended to completely rebuild Iraq — simply to provide Iraq the jumpstart it needed towards progress and prosperity," declared Gen. Bill McCoy, the highest-ranking U.S. Army Corps of Engineers official in Iraq in a December 2005 press conference in Baghdad. Iraq was on its own.

As the reconstruction sped to an end, senior officials did their best to tout its achievements. They announced that the Iraqis had the capacity to generate more than 7,000 megawatts of electricity, to deliver water to an additional 2.3 million people, to mount hundreds of thousands of police officers and soldiers. The key word was capacity — not what the reconstruction was actually delivering to the Iraqis, but what it could deliver if — if there wasn't a war, if the Iraqis were well trained and funded, if the equipment provided by the contractors didn't break down. In other words, if Iraq wasn't Iraq. Like so many other things in the reconstruction, the statistics were spin, an attempt to convince the Americans and Iraqis that their enormous contribution of blood and money had made Iraq into a better place.

Three years after the United States began its first efforts at the rebuilding of Iraq, the reality was otherwise. Oil production was below prewar levels. Every day, Iraq was pumping almost 500,000 fewer barrels of oil per day than under Saddam Hussein. At sky-high world energy prices in 2006, that meant that Iraq was forgoing potential income of more than $10 billion a year — or nearly a third of the money that the United States had pledged to rebuild the country in the first place. If the American plan had invested more, or if its chief contractor, KBR, had performed better, the money would have been available to build new schools, train more troops, or invest in new businesses and democracy-building organizations.

Electricity also sagged below prewar levels. Baghdad, the political, cultural, and media center of the country, which had power nearly twenty-four hours a day under Saddam Hussein was suffering through days in which electricity flowed for only four to six hours. The constant blackouts — along with the daily violence of car bombs, kidnappings, and sectarian violence that scattered mutilated corpses in the street — were a daily reminder to millions of ordinary Iraqis that their quality of life had deteriorated enormously since the American invasion. It was an omnipresent source of frustration, a recruiting tool for the insurgents who killed Iraqis and American soldiers. Contractors like Bechtel, Fluor, Perini, and Washington Group International had worked construction magic in most parts of the world; Iraq was a different story.

Water and sanitation were difficult to measure, but appeared to linger at or below the levels that Iraqis had enjoyed during the Saddam regime. Not that it mattered if Bechtel or Fluor had erected scores of new treatment plants. Most of the clean water never made its way to homes, nor did much raw sewage flow toward treatment plants. Baghdad's water and sewer pipes were constantly cracking from neglect and the effect of heavy American war machines rumbling across roads. By some estimates, as much as 60 percent of the water leaked out of pipes, and 20 percent of the sewage leaked out. In practice that meant that Iraqis were still at risk for waterborne diseases, and still fished, cleaned clothes, and swam in contaminated rivers.

Disease outbreaks like hepatitis might have been manageable had public health shown marked advances. Instead scores of health clinics and hospitals went unfinished after the chief contractor, Parsons, racked up security costs so high that the United States decided to cancel the project. The unpainted, cinder block health clinics rose in poor and destitute neighborhoods throughout Iraq, tantalizing symbols of health care turned into monuments of broken promise. Millions of dollars' worth of new health equipment sat moldering in a warehouse, and thousands of doctors and nurses fled the violence. Reliable statistics were scarce, but most international health experts believed that infant mortality and death from infectious diseases remained about the same in the spring of 2006 as prior to the war.

Even the rebuilding's achievements came with caveats. Perhaps the biggest overall success in the program was in education. The United States used Bechtel and other contractors to rehab more than 5,000 schools — a little more than a third of all schools in Iraq. Some 47,000 teachers went through training sponsored by USAID. U.S. funds purchased millions of new textbooks for Iraqi children. The history texts, however, were missing a key chapter: the overthrow of Saddam. The U.S. invasion was deemed too controversial for inclusion.[5]

The ink stain theory also appeared to have some success. A commitment to spend hundreds of millions of dollars and tight coordination between local military commanders and the rebuilding agencies — USAID, the U.S. Army Corps of Engineers, and the State Department's Iraqi Reconstruction Management Office — resulted in genuine improvements. Sadr City and Najaf — both primarily Shiite communities that suffered under Saddam — had better public services after the rebuilding. Clean water and electricity flowed to homes, many for the first time, and businesses opened along streets once emptied by fighting. Sadr City remained relatively free from violence compared to elsewhere in Baghdad. Najaf was calm enough so that most security duties were turned over to local Iraqi forces.

These bright spots were the exception. For the Iraqis sitting in their homes or businesses or prayer houses, three years of U.S. spending and effort appeared to have left them worse off in terms of the public security and basic services they had enjoyed under Saddam Hussein's dictatorship. They suffered in heat and blackouts. They sickened from dirty water and standing pools of sewage. They watched loved ones die in hospitals without sufficient power or equipment. Worst of all, they witnessed their country wracked by violence, on the verge of all-out civil war. For American troops, civil servants, and individual contractors in Iraq, the U.S. setbacks meant frustration, violence, and death. Without results, commanders and soldiers could not convince the Iraqis that the U.S. presence would materially improve their lives. Iraqi insurgents used their destruction of oil pipelines and transmission towers to demonstrate the impotence of America and its partners in the new Iraqi government. The lack of electrical power was a metaphor for the lack of governing power. There may have been new sod on some soccer fields, but the reconstruction of Iraq failed miserably to do what was most important: turn Iraq into a thriving democracy that would reduce the threat of terrorism against America.

The Bush administration was to blame, from the president himself to senior cabinet officials like Rumsfeld, Rice, and Powell. The fundamental error was not sending enough troops to secure the country. Violence was the single biggest impediment to the success of nation building. Oil pipelines and electrical transmission lines provided easy, convenient targets for insurgents. More than five hundred contractors — Americans and foreigners — working on the reconstruction had been killed by 2006, about one dead for every five American soldiers killed. Thousands of others had been injured. The danger of moving around Iraq kept contractors confined to their quarters on many days, unable to do work. It also affected the quality of projects, with supervisors unable to visit sites to check on standards. The violence drove the explosion of the private security industry in Iraq, adding a vast contingent of armed men to Iraq's battlefields. The security contractors, accountable to no one, clashed frequently with Iraqi and even American troops, complicating efforts to win Iraqi hearts and minds.

From the start the Bush administration's senior officials neglected the nuts and bolts of the reconstruction. Bush, Rice, and Rumsfeld focused on Iraq's political and military problems. Responsibility for rebuilding fell to a succession of second- and third-tier bureaucrats scattered at a handful of government agencies like the U.S. Army Corps of Engineers, USAID, and the State Department. People like Jerry Bremer, David Nash, and Bill Taylor were forced to rely on personnel of uneven quality, many hard workers, but lacking the training or equipment needed for the complexities of building a new society. Nor did the rebuilding leaders have the clout or visibility to fend off constant interference from politicians in Washington who saw Iraq as a golden opportunity for their friends, business partners, and contributors.

The neglect, lack of experience, and the absence of a leader with political power produced violent swings in strategy. Prior to the war, Pentagon planners led by Doug Feith believed the Iraqis would take over. When that turned out not to be the case, the United States contracted out responsibility for the reconstruction to big multinationals with billion-dollar, open-ended contracts. When progress stalled, momentum shifted to hand over control to the Iraqis, who were ill trained and equipped to handle their newfound power. Finally the Bush administration turned to the provincial reconstruction teams as a way to work closely with local Iraqis. But the teams turned into the latest in a long line of half-finished initiatives.

The ever-shifting priorities and lack of oversight led to corruption and waste, which further undermined any chance to renew Iraq. When it came to American taxpayer money, U.S. officials moved too slowly and carefully, paralyzing action and spending millions of dollars on security costs. But Iraqi funds flew out the door, often with little planning or accountability. The corruption and the contractors resulted in the appearance — and often the reality — of a war motivated by greed. Those profiting were not the Americans or the Iraqis, but corporate sharks and shabby swindlers.

The Bush administration's decision to retreat from the effort to rebuild Iraq seemed the final, most tragic mistake of all. The provincial teams — combining a focused effort of U.S. agencies with local Iraqi input and training — appeared to be a promising solution derived from the hard lessons of the past several years. By cutting funding and not pushing harder, the administration risked condemning its rebuilding project to a final defeat. Even at the end Bush was ignoring the lessons of history. The reconstruction in the first few years after World War II had also been disastrous, dubbed Operation Rathole by critics. But American diplomats and political leaders stepped back, adjusted, and created the Marshall Plan, an even larger, more far-sighted response. At the last hour, they rebuilt the reconstruction. It was not too late then. It is not too late now.

Afterword

By the winter of 2006–7, it was impossible to deny that the war in Iraq had gone badly awry. American troops were suffering more attacks in Baghdad than in previous years. Sunnis and Shiites were killing each other in ever greater numbers as part of a blossoming, bloody civil war. Iraqis living on top of one of the world's greatest stores of petroleum continued to lack the kind of basic public services common in all but the poorest third world countries. The $30 billion dedicated to the country's reconstruction — the largest program of its kind since the Marshall Plan — was almost entirely spent. The nation-building project had not delivered on its most fundamental promise to restore light, jobs, and hope to a nation wracked by decades of violence and dictatorship. Iraq had become a will-o'-the-wisp, leading America ever deeper into a quagmire.

The American public signaled its displeasure with President George W. Bush by kicking the Republican Party out of power during midterm elections in November. For the first time in a dozen years, Democrats took control of the House and Senate. The hard slap appeared to shake the administration from its solipsism on Iraq. Bush promptly announced the departure of Defense Secretary Donald Rumsfeld and began an extended review of his Iraq policy, pledging tough new reforms. "We're not succeeding nearly as fast as I wanted," Bush told reporters.

A month after the election, the frustration with America's nation-building failure boiled over in a report by the Iraq Study Group, a bipartisan commission of foreign policy solons seeking answers to Iraq. They dismissed the nation-building efforts to date as "ineffective." "There is a substantial need for continued reconstruction in Iraq, but serious questions remain about the capacity of the U.S. and Iraqi governments," wrote the commission, which was chaired by Lee H. Hamilton, a Democrat, and Republican James A. Baker III, who served as secretary of state for George Bush's father. The commission issued a series of recommendations for a better, smarter rebuilding program. Bush was urged to work closely with multilateral partners like the World Bank and the United Nations, experts in international development. The administration needed to set aside $5 billion per year for the reconstruction efforts. More training and capacity building was needed, and fewer megaprojects. Finally, the reconstruction demanded a single senior official reporting directly to the president to coordinate the entire effort. The suggestions were based on months of study and input from people directly involved in rebuilding. After years of failure, it seemed a blueprint for success.

Bush's response was to largely ignore it. On January 10, 2007, the president stood before the American people in a televised address to offer his latest vision to salvage Iraq from barbarity — his "New Way Forward." Speaking from the library in the basement of the White House, Bush pledged to send tens of thousands of additional troops to diminish the horrific daily violence in Baghdad and elsewhere. He also promised an additional billion dollars for the reconstruction. Only a few months earlier, the president had declared that America was "absolutely" winning the war. Now, chastened, he finally acknowledged mistakes. "The situation in Iraq is unacceptable to the American people — and it is unacceptable to me," Bush told the nation. "Where mistakes have been made, the responsibility rests with me." It was a mea culpa moment for a president previously impervious to acknowledging error.

But the "New Way Forward" was really more of a nostalgic look back. The additional billion dollars paid for expanding existing reconstruction teams in Iraq's provinces and for additional military hearts-and-minds programs. The money would mostly fund small projects in local neighborhoods, things like new schoolrooms and paved roads. The Iraqis were left to bear the brunt of the remaining big-ticket work, with Prime Minister Nouri al-Maliki having to pledge $10 billion toward new power plants and other infrastructure. Instead of a powerful reconstruction czar, Secretary of State Condoleezza Rice announced that she would appoint another bureaucrat in Baghdad as part of a diplomatic surge to complement the military buildup. Bush's new rebuilding initiative was a massively shrunken version of what had come before. It was reconstruction with a small r.

To a great extent, the curtailment was a reflection of political reality. The Bush administration had squandered the capital — political and financial — that had existed at the beginning of the war. The American public, for one, was in no mood to spend more on a rebuilding program that had turned into a money pit. American taxpayers had already shoveled more than $30 billion into the program — more money than the United States had ever spent on any single country, including the war-ravaged nations of Japan and Germany after World War II. But by early 2007, there was still precious little to show for it. Nearly four years after the U.S. invasion, Iraq pumped out less oil than under Saddam Hussein.[1] The supply of electricity in Baghdad had fallen to four to six hours per day. Insurgents had placed the capital under a kind of electrical siege, felling transmission towers and isolating the city from the rest of the country.[2] And U.S.-funded training programs had failed to produce an Iraqi police force or military capable of pacifying the country. The nation-building effort had turned out to be a boondoggle.

There had been some successes, to be sure: millions of children had been vaccinated, and thousands of schools had been refurbished, with new paint and desks. It was something of a miracle that *any* oil or electricity flowed at all, given the horrific attacks against pipelines and other infrastructure. But such advances seemed to make no difference when it came to larger foreign policy goals. If the point of the reconstruction had been to win hearts and minds, it had failed, for Iraqis had grown ever angrier at the American presence. By fall 2006, 71 percent of Iraqis favored a withdrawal of U.S. forces within the year.[3] And if the goal had been to establish a strong, independent Iraq, Iraqis proved themselves unable to operate and maintain the infrastructure projects that the United States had bequeathed them. Technologically advanced power stations burned out after only months of operation. Sewage treatment plants returned to fetid ponds for the collection of human waste. Health clinics languished without supplies or medicine.[4]

When pressed, U.S. officials in charge of the reconstruction rattled off the number of projects completed like an auctioneer driving up bids. But they rarely said what goals had been reached. They even scorned those who had high expectations for the country's restoration. "Some slam the Americans because there is sewage in Sadr City," said Dean G. Popps, the principal deputy assistant secretary of the army for acquisitions, logistics, and technology. "Please."[5] Apparently it was too much to ask for working sewers in a Baghdad slum where the United States had spent four years and $1 billion.

If the sewage remained on Iraq's streets, the money did not. As reconstruction funds began to dry up in the fall of 2006, the U.S. corporations hired to do the work abandoned Iraq. They left behind bills for billions of dollars and unfinished buildings. Bechtel had removed all but two of its employees by the fall, having been paid $2.3 billion and claiming to have completed nearly all its projects.[6] Parsons Corporation struggled to finish up work after the special inspector general for Iraq criticized its performance on nearly all its megaprojects. In one particularly egregious example, the engineering giant had built Iraq's central police academy so shoddily that raw sewage coursed down the walls.[7] The company sent its CEO around to Congress and the press to protest that the job had been too hard. "The entire reconstruction effort was much too ambitious," James McNulty said.[8] McNulty had voiced no such reservations when he signed up for $2 billion worth of contracts in March 2004.

KBR, the single largest contractor in Iraq, paid a price for its wasteful ways. The company had earned more than $14 billion by serving as the military's quartermaster in Iraq and elsewhere. By 2006 the construction and engineering behemoth had served 430 million meals, washed 20 million bundles of laundry, and delivered 28 million bags of mail. The company had also racked up a long list of audits for wasting hundreds of millions of dollars. The Pentagon decided to dump the firm. It restructured KBR's single, massive contract by splitting it into smaller parts that were then sent out for bidding. At the same time, Halliburton decided to distance itself from its troublesome subsidiary, putting KBR up for an initial public offering in November 2006. Officially it was because KBR was making too thin a profit margin, but analysts noted that the negative publicity over the Iraq contract hadn't helped. "The levels of scrutiny have been high for a while, but you're likely to see them escalate now that you have Democrats taking over committee chairmanships," said Poe Fratt, an oil sector analyst with A. G. Edwards & Sons, Inc.[9]

Indeed, as Democrats returned to power, they pledged to introduce one element into the reconstruction program that had long been lacking: accountability. Democrats talked of hearings similar to those of the Truman Commission, which had exposed war profiteering in World War II. Representative Henry Waxman, the Los Angeles Democrat who had waged a frustrating battle to put the foibles of the reconstruction on display, pledged contracting reform legislation. Representative Janice D. Schakowsky, an Illinois Democrat, proclaimed that it was time to crack down. "This is a foggy area where billions and billions of taxpayer dollars are being spent, and we have no sense of how or what they are spending or doing," she said.[10]

It was a fog of daunting opacity. Nearly four years into the war, the contracting world in Iraq remained shrouded in mystery and confusion. It wasn't until 2006 that the United States even tried to determine the exact size of the contractors workforce in Iraq. The military's Central Command conducted a survey that produced a stunning figure: some 100,000 people were at work — a figure that probably underestimated the true number, since subcontractors were not included.[11] Steve Schooner, a professor of government contracting at George Washington University, believed it possible that there was one contractor in Iraq for every American soldier, a ratio never before approached in the history of American warfare.[12] What had been suspected was now confirmed. Contractors were no longer supporting actors who bolstered military capabilities. They were a vital part of the war machine.

The huge and unprecedented phenomenon demanded a strong, robust system of accountability. Americans deserved to know where their money was going and had a right to know what the government was doing. During their control of every branch of the government, Bush and the Republicans had provided few answers. Republicans in Congress had refused to ask hard questions of either the government agencies responsible for the rebuilding or the corporations charged with carrying it out. House and Senate committees had held only a handful of hearings on the reconstruction, and they tended to be sympathetic affairs, lacking tough questions or subpoenas. Representative Tom Davis, the Virginia Republican who controlled oversight as chairman of the House Government Reform Committee, had lambasted Democrats who criticized the performance of Halliburton in Iraq. "Politics is driving this agenda, and I suspect that not even the truth will keep the detractors at bay," Davis thundered at one of the few hearings that he permitted on contracting in Iraq.

As for the executive branch, the "accountability president" showed little affection for his own sobriquet. The Pentagon hardly bestirred itself to recover money that had been wasted or stolen, with Defense Department contracting officials ignoring recommendations from auditors to withhold fat payments to contractors. Despite task forces dedicated to cracking down on contracting fraud, the Justice Department prosecuted only a single case involving a contractor in Iraq — a relatively minor affair involving less than $10 million in kickbacks and bribes. In four years, with at least 100,000 people on the ground, many of them armed and in a war zone, not one other contractor was convicted of committing a crime — a record unbelievable on its face. (Perhaps a crackdown would have hit too close to home. Stuart Bowen, the special inspector general for the reconstruction of Iraq, had found that USAID had cooked its books to hide the spiraling cost of the children's hospital in Basra championed by First Lady Laura Bush. Bechtel's costs had soared to nearly double the original $50 million set aside for the project. Finally the company simply walked away, abandoning the project because of security problems.[13] Neither USAID nor Bechtel faced official sanction from the administration.[14]) For the Bush administration and its private partners, the reconstruction had steamed ahead, business as usual.

The judicial branch proved itself equally ineffective. In the most famous example, a federal judge overturned a jury's verdict in the case of Custer Battles, the private security firm whose owners had been found guilty of scamming the government with shell corporations and inflated bills. U.S. District Judge T. S. Ellis III found "significant" evidence that the company had indeed committed fraud. But he ruled that American laws didn't apply, since Custer Battles held its contract with the Coalition Provisional Authority, the temporary agency that ruled Iraq immediately after the invasion. Although the authority had been formed by the U.S. military, and its leader, Paul Bremer, was appointed by the Pentagon, Ellis decided such conditions weren't sufficient to qualify the CPA as an arm of the U.S. government. Instead, it was more like NATO or other multilateral organizations.[15] The decision amounted to a get-out-of-jail-free card — a message that the United States was not particularly interested in cleaning up the mess it had created.

Even more grave was the deference that judges gave to the Bush administration. A federal judge turned down a request by the *Los Angeles Times* to make public the names of private security companies that shot at Iraqi civilians. U.S. District Judge Florence-Marie Cooper said that she deferred to senior army officers who said the disclosure could "provide an advantage to insurgents" by helping target contractors who provided protection at job sites.[16] In Texas, U.S. District Court Judge Gray Miller dismissed a case in which Halliburton was accused of sending a convoy of truckers to certain death. Miller said that he had no authority to second-guess decisions made regarding the conduct of a war.[17] Private security companies like Blackwater made similar arguments to avoid civil suits brought by the families of contractors who had been killed in Iraq. The rulings were based on the principle that the judiciary could not second-guess the executive branch when it came to decisions of war. The Bush administration had absolved the contractors of responsibility precisely by binding them so closely to the war effort. The Pentagon had, in essence, created a special class: the contractors were bound by neither the military justice that applied to soldiers nor the civilian legal system. In a little-noticed bit of legislation in the fall of 2007, Republican Senator Lindsey Graham of South Carolina tried a quick fix by adding language to a defense bill that would have placed private contractors in Iraq under the military justice system. But it was unclear whether such language would prove constitutional. In a very real sense, the contractors remained beyond the law.[18]

There was perhaps no greater example of American and Iraqi impotence than the case of Aiham Alsammarae, an Iraqi-American engineer who had been appointed by the United States to run the Ministry of Electricity soon after the invasion. Alsammarae had been suspected by Americans and Iraqis alike of corruption when it came to electricity contracts, but the Americans took no action. After the newly elected Iraqi government ousted him from the ministry in May 2005, Alsammarae was put on trial and found guilty of a single count of fraud involving an electricity generator. Alsammarae proclaimed innocence, saying that the charges against him were political, since he was a Sunni and the government was dominated by Shiites. The charge was overturned on appeal, but as Alsammarae waited behind bars to face other charges, he escaped in a mysterious jailbreak in December 2006. He landed in Amman, Jordan, a short while after calling a *New York Times* reporter to gleefully recount his breakout.[19]

How had Alsammarae managed to escape the layers of U.S. and Iraqi security that surrounded him inside his Green Zone prison cell? How had he managed then to penetrate the rings of security that surrounded the Baghdad airport and fly out of the country? The jailbird would give no specifics. Instead he borrowed a line from *The Untouchables* about Al Capone: "The Chicago way," Alsammarae laughed. Alsammarae was in charge of the single most important piece of the reconstruction, the restoration of electricity. He was the highest-ranking Iraqi minister to face corruption charges. And here he was laughing at the inability of either Iraq or the United States to carry out justice.

Alsammarae's escape was an embarrassing coda to the Bush administration's first reconstruction plan, part of its bright, shining vision of reshaping the political wasteland of the Middle East. George Bush had promised to build Iraq into a flourishing democracy that would serve as a model for the future of the region. The money would light homes, create jobs, and build a society based on freedom and free markets. As it slumped toward its end, the program had failed to achieve most of those goals. The president and his men had not created a regional oasis of stability and freedom. They had not even created a sufficient number of new village wells to slake the thirst of a battered and oppressed people.

The collapse of the rebuilding damaged both Iraq and the United States. For the Iraqis, it meant continued suffering under a different kind of tyranny: of hopes raised, then destroyed by a despotism of violence, greed, and incompetence. For America, it meant the destruction of the belief that this country was capable of building a better way of life for another people, a way of life based on liberty and democracy. Bush and his cohorts had promoted that vision. They left behind a sorry history of mangled lives and sordid corruption. The money was gone, and except in canned speeches and prepped press conferences, the vision was gone too. The reconstruction was dead, and it did not appear to be coming back.

Acknowledgments

I am deeply indebted to the many people who took considerable risks to help me tell this story. First among them are the Iraqi staff of the Baghdad bureau of the *Los Angeles Times*. They translated for me and transported me around Iraq, braving violence and intimidation and educating me on the place and people that I was covering. Salar Jaff, Raheem Salman, Suhail Affan, Saif Rasheed, Caesar A. Ahmad, Zainab Bedhani, Asmaa Waguih, and Mohammed Arrawi were my eyes, ears, and voice while I was in Iraq. For safety reasons, I cannot mention all who helped me by name, but I hold all of our staff in the highest esteem for their valor and service to their country. For my money, they and their colleagues at other media outlets in Iraq are the bravest people in journalism.

Second, I owe much to my colleagues at the *Times*. Dean Baquet convinced me to take the job of covering the rebuilding, despite my conviction that it would be a boring beat. To my delight and amazement, editors do sometimes know better than reporters. Marjorie Miller, Scott Kraft, Doyle McManus, and Tom McCarthy gave me the support that I needed to juggle the demands of reporting a complex story across several continents. Don Woutat was my touchstone, providing all that a reporter could ever want in an editor: encouragement, understanding, and patience. Baghdad bureau reporters welcomed the intruder in their midst. Alissa Rubin, Patrick McDonnell, John Daniszewski, Richard Boudreaux, Borzou Daragahi, and Solomon Moore gave me their time and insight. Ranya Kadri in Jordan and Alok Tumbahangphey in Nepal guided me to interviews in their respective countries.

Many of my sources took considerable risk in speaking with me and allowing me access to sensitive documents and e-mails that revealed the problems of the rebuilding process. They did so, I believe, for the same reason that good cops are often willing to talk about bad cops. They wanted to get rid of bad apples. They also must remain unnamed, but they know who they are.

The book would not have happened without my agent, Sandy Dijkstra, who was a fierce advocate, and her supportive staff: Elise Capron, Elisabeth James, and Taryn Fagerness. Geoff Shandler, my editor at Little, Brown, did an amazing job of turning straw into gold — or at least some metal of value, I hope. Junie Dahn worked tirelessly to arrange photographs and maps.

I also have to thank those who took the time to read the book in progress and offer suggestions. My wife, Leslie, and my father and mother, Don and Linda Miller, did heroic work. And friends such as Nic Ammirati, Rick Markoff, Peter Wallsten, and my in-laws, Mike and Lynn Davis, were kind enough to take interest and listen to my gripes. Finally, I want to thank Leslie and my children, George and Oliver. They gave up weekends and many, many hours of free time in order to allow me to complete this book. I love them deeply, and look forward to returning to our long walks in the Secret Forest.

Notes

Unless otherwise cited in the source notes that follow, the information in this book stems from interviews, documents, and official records that I collected during more than two years of reporting on the reconstruction for the *Los Angeles Times*, including four trips to Iraq. Listed below are the people who granted me on-the-record interviews; many of them are quoted in the text, while the others provided valuable background information. Many other sources took considerable risk in speaking with me and allowing me access to documents and correspondence; they must remain unnamed.

ON-THE-RECORD INTERVIEWS

Ibrahim Ali Abbas, July 2005
Lt. Matt Adamczyk, August 2004
Faisal Ahmed, February 2004
Mahmoud Ali Ahmed, February 2005
Delnya Mohammed Ali, February 2005
Hayder Aliam, July 2005
Nihad Alim, February 2005
Jaafar Altaie, July 2005
Capt. Steve Alvarez, U.S. Army,
    multiple occasions
Mahendra Bajgain, August 2005
William "Pete" Baldwin, January 2005
Col. Richard Ballard, January 2005
Nilim Baruah, May 2005
Adnan Bashir, August 2004
Debora Bell, March 2005
Felicia Bell-Carter, March 2005
Rodney Bent, January 2005
Nesreen Berwari, February 2005
Bijaya Bishta, August 2005
Laxmi Bista, August 2005
Lt. Col. William Bland, November 2005
Jack Boese, February 2005
Stuart Bowen, January 2006

Steven Browning, multiple occasions
Amy Burns, multiple occasions
Patrick Burns, multiple occasions
Bonnie Carroll, multiple occasions
Issam Chalabi, July 2005
Alan Chvotkin, April 2005
David Cooper, May 2005
Sachin Devkota, August 2005
Marie deYoung, June 2004
Kanak Dixit, August 2005
Dick Dumford, multiple occasions
Karen Durham-Aguilera, December
    2005
Vice Adm. Joe Dyer, U.S. Navy,
    February 2004
Capt. Rob Edwards, October 2004
A. Huda Farouki, February 2004
George Farrar, February 2004
Doug Feith, January 2006
Aaron Fichtelberg, November 2005
Gen. Joseph Fil, U.S. Army, November
    2005
Ingrid Fisher, March 2005
Nick Fotion, November 2005

Chris Frabott, August 2005

Declan Ganley, April 2004

Richard Garfield, June 2005

Michel Gautier, August 2004

Lt. Col. S. Jamie Gayton, August 2005

Thamour Ghadban, August 2005

Aidan Goldsmith, February 2005

Alan Grayson, multiple occasions

Bunnatine Greenhouse, multiple
occasions

Prakash Gurung, August 2005

Majed Habashneh, July 2005

Edie Hair, August 2004

Wendy Hall, multiple occasions

Tommy Hamill, March 2005

Larry Hartman, February 2005

Mohammed Nouri Hattab, August
2005

Clay Henderson, August 2004

Charlie Hess, multiple occasions

Joe Holladay, November 2005

Nelson Howell, March 2005

Hollie A. Hulett, March 2005

Jack Hume, March 2005

Bob Hunter, April 2005

Abdul Raof Ibraheen, July 2005

Robert Isakson, January 2005

April Johnson, March 2005

Kim Johnson, March 2005

Hassan Jumaa, July 2005

Ahmed Kadhem, August 2004

Dennis Karns, August 2005

Farouk Kasim, June 2005

Bill Keller, May 2005

Jit Bahadur Khadka, August 2005

Radhika Khadka, August 2005

Abdulamir Khafaji, August 2005

Jabbar Abed Khalef, August 2005

Aziz Ibrahim Khalil, August 2005

Hayder Kharalla, multiple occasions

Mike Kohn, February 2006

Victor Kubli, multiple occasions

Bikram Lama, August 2005

Sgt. Hosea Lark, U.S. Army, August
2004

Heather Layman, October 2005

Sen. Patrick Leahy, February 2004

Mark Lemon, June 2004

Jackie Lester, March 2005

David Linker, April 2005

Ramon Lopez, March 2005

Rob McGarrah, May 2005

Jack Martone, April 2005

Mike Means, November 2005

Wafi Mnadi, August 2004

Mike Moseley, August 2004

Fakhir Mousawi, February 2004

Abdul Mutalib, August 2005

David Nash, multiple occasions

Melissa Norcross, multiple occasions

Joe Norton, May 2005

Mahmoud Othman, June 2005

Kadem Oush, July 2005

Mark Oviatt, February 2005

Eric Oxfeld, May 2005

Tom Palaima, April 2006

Charles L. Panayides, June 2004

Sara K. Payne, August 2005

Lawrence Peters, August 2005

Gen. David Petraeus, November
2005

Col. Joseph Philips, U.S. Army,
multiple occasions

Bigyan Pradhan, August 2005

Abdali Qadhim, August 2005

Judge Radhi Radhi, June 2005

Janet Reiser, February 2004

Maj. Gen. Dave Richwine, February
2004

Hawre Riwandizi, February 2005

Earnie Robbins, February 2005

Randy Ross, March 2005

Shakr Jasim Sadi, August 2005

Raheem Abdul Sadr, August 2005

Ayham Sameraei, August 2004

Eddie Sanchez, March 2005

Mark Schaffer, April 2005

Steven Schooner, multiple occasions

Col. Joe Schweitzer, February 2005

Beverly Scippa, March 2005

Brig. Gen. Stephen Seay, U.S. Army, April 2004

Hussain Sharistani, June 2005

Jack Shaw, April 2004

Gyamju Sherpa, August 2005

Muhson Shlash, August 2005

Peter W. Singer, multiple occasions

Fred C. Smith, October 2005

Capt. Jeff Smith, U.S. Army, March 2005

Marjorie Bell Smith, March 2005

Keith Stanley, March 2005

Ray Stannard, March 2005

James "Spike" Stephenson, December 2005

Maj. Erik Stor, U.S. Army, August 2004

Col. David Styles, U.S. Army, October 2005

Dan Sudnick, multiple occasions

Ghiath Sukhtian, February 2004

Norm Szydlowski, May 2005

Bill Taylor, multiple occasions

Bill Thompson, August 2005

Charles Tiefer, multiple occasions

Bob Todor, August 2005

Richard Tollison, March 2005

Col. Tim Trainor, November 2005

Billy Lee Tripp, August 2004

Jacqueline Tunstall, March 2005

Jabbar Ueibi, July 2005

Ibrahim Bahr Uloum, August 2005

Maj. Gen. John Urias, U.S. Army, May 2005

Donald Verene, November 2005

Keith Westhusing, April 2006

Tim Westhusing, April 2006

Capt. Catherine Wilkinson, U.S. Army, August 2004

Frank Willis, January 2005

Melvin Winter, August 2004

William Winter, November 2005

Bruce C. Wood, May 2005

Danny Wood, March 2005

Haita Zamel, August 2005

Doug Zwissler, February 2005

PROMISES

1. Mark Fineman, Robin Wright, and Doyle McManus, "Washington's Battle Plan; Preparing for War, Stumbling to Peace; U.S. Is Paying the Price for Missteps Made on Iraq," *Los Angeles Times*, July 18, 2003, p. A1.
2. David Rieff, "Blueprint for a Mess," *New York Times Magazine*, November 2, 2003, p. 28.
3. Available at http://www.whitehouse.gov/omb/budget/fy2006/pdf/06msr.pdf.
4. James Dobbins et al., *America's Role in Nation-Building: From Germany to Iraq* (Santa Monica: RAND, 2003), p. xxiv.

1: MAN OF HONOR

1. T. S. Westhusing, "The Competitive and Cooperative *Aretai* Within the American Warfighting Ethos" (PhD diss., Emory University, 2003).
2. Aaron Fichtelberg, "Mourning the Loss of a Friend, a Soldier," *Philadelphia Inquirer*, June 19, 2005, p. C7.
3. Ibid.
4. David Lipsky, *Absolutely American: Four Years at West Point* (New York: Random House, 2004), p. 8.

5. Tom Palaima, "Some Plagiarism Serious Enough to Diminish Our Faith," *Austin American-Statesman,* September 28, 2003, p. E1. In the column Palaima said that when he contacted Hedges the reporter blamed "mistaken transcription" for the passage in question and later changed it in paperback editions.

2: HIGH NOON

1. Bob Woodward, *Plan of Attack* (New York: Simon and Schuster Paperbacks, 2004), p. 25.
2. Michael R. Gordon and Gen. Bernard E. Trainor, *Cobra II: The Inside Story of the Invasion and Occupation of Iraq* (New York: Pantheon, 2006), p. 17.
3. Woodward, *Plan of Attack,* p. 62.
4. Ibid., p. 25.
5. Ibid., p. 284.
6. Gordon, *Cobra II,* p. 71.
7. Woodward, *Plan of Attack,* p. 254.
8. Don Van Natta Jr., "Bush Was Set on Path to War, Memo by British Adviser Says," *New York Times,* March 27, 2006, p. A1.
9. Bob Drogin and John Goetz, "The Curveball Saga," *Los Angeles Times,* November 20, 2005, p. A1.
10. Woodward, *Plan of Attack,* p. 342.
11. I owe much of my reconstruction of the events surrounding the creation of the Office of Reconstruction and Humanitarian Aid to reporting done by my colleagues Mark Fineman, Robin Wright, and Doyle McManus. The three put together one of the earliest and most definitive accounts of the fiasco that surrounded prewar planning. Fineman later died in Iraq of a heart attack. See Fineman, Wright, and McManus, "Washington's Battle Plan."
12. David L. Phillips, *Losing Iraq: Inside the Postwar Reconstruction Fiasco* (Boulder, Colo.: Westview Press, 2005), p. 37.
13. Daniel Williams and Peter Slevin, "Leagues Apart, Iraqi Exiles Convene in London; Infighting, Absence of Key Figures and Diminished Importance to U.S. Will Limit Meeting's Relevance," *Washington Post,* December 13, 2002, p. A50.
14. Eric Schmitt and Joel Brinkley, "State Department Study Foresaw Trouble Now Plaguing Iraq," *New York Times,* October 19, 2003, p. 1.
15. Doug Feith and William Luti. Pentagon briefing, June 4, 2003.
16. Jeff Gerth, "Report Offered Bleak Outlook About Iraq Oil," *New York Times,* October 5, 2003, p. A1.
17. Woodward, *Plan of Attack,* p. 62.
18. Gordon, *Cobra II,* p. 140.
19. Ibid., p. 459.
20. Ibid., p. 141.
21. Ibid., p. 144.
22. Ibid., p. 142.

23. Rieff, "Blueprint for a Mess."
24. Woodward, *Plan of Attack*, p. 413.
25. Phillips, *Losing Iraq*, p. 127.
26. Fineman, Wright, and McManus, "Washington's Battle Plan."
27. Phillips, *Losing Iraq*, p. 16.
28. Sydney J. Freedberg Jr., Corine Hegland, and John Maggs, "A Postwar Who's Who," *National Journal*, March 29, 2003.
29. George Packer, *The Assassins' Gate: America in Iraq* (New York: Farrar, Straus, and Giroux, 2005), p. 123.
30. Fineman, Wright, and McManus, "Washington's Battle Plan."
31. Larry Crandall, interview by Larry Plotkin, United States Institute of Peace, September 20, 2004.
32. Packer, *Assassins' Gate*, p. 124.
33. Ibid., p. 133.
34. Robin Raphel, interview by Charles Stuart Kennedy, United States Institute of Peace, July 13, 2004.
35. Fineman, Wright, and McManus, "Washington's Battle Plan."
36. David Dunford, interview by Bernard Engel, United States Institute of Peace, August 25, 2004.
37. Fineman, Wright, and McManus, "Washington's Battle Plan."
38. Ibid.
39. Ibid.
40. Dunford interview.
41. Fineman, Wright, and McManus, "Washington's Battle Plan."
42. L. Paul Bremer III, *My Year in Iraq: The Struggle to Build a Future of Hope* (New York: Simon and Schuster, 2006), p. 18.
43. Ibid., pp. 54–67.
44. Ibid., p. 18.
45. Daniel W. Drezner, blog entry, May 28, 2004. Available at http://www.daniel drezner.com/archives/001326.html.
46. Joshua Micah Marshall, Laura Rozen, and Colin Soloway, "The Washington Monthly's Who's Who," *Washington Monthly*, December 2003.
47. Yochi J. Dreazen, "One Baby-Faced American Is Tasked with Delivering a Reborn Iraq Stock Market — Playing a Lead Role from a Trailer, Mr. Hallen, 24, Shows Growing Pains," *Wall Street Journal*, January 28, 2004, p. A1.
48. Ariana Eunjung Cha, "In Iraq, the Job Opportunity of a Lifetime; Managing a $13 Billion Budget with No Experience," *Washington Post*, May 23, 2004, p. A1.
49. Stephen Braun, Judy Pasternak, and T. Christian Miller, "Blacklisted Russian Tied to Iraq Deals; The Alleged Arms Broker Is Behind Four Air Cargo Firms Used by U.S. Contractors, Officials Say," *Los Angeles Times*, December 14, 2004, p. A1.
50. Raphel interview.

3: BACK AT THE RANCH

1. Bremer, *My Year,* p. 109.
2. Larry Crandall, interview by Larry Plotkin, United States Institute of Peace, September 20, 2004.
3. Bremer, *My Year,* p. 119.
4. Bush's statement is instructive. There was never a single, clear policy statement on the overall goal of the reconstruction. Would America only repair war-related damage? Would it return Iraq's services to prewar levels? Or would it try to improve living conditions? Bush's declaration was one of the few unambiguous pledges to better infrastructure.
5. David Firestone, "Lawmakers Back Request by Bush on Funds for Iraq," *New York Times,* October 18, 2003, p. 1.
6. Nicole Foy, "Injury Sent UTHSC Chief Down Path of Self-discovery," *San Antonio Express-News,* February 6, 2000, p. B1.
7. Ala'din Alwan, *Health in Iraq: The Current Situation, Our Vision for the Future and Areas of Work* (Iraq Ministry of Health, 2nd ed., December 2004), p. 54.
8. Seth G. Jones et al., "Securing Health: Lessons from Nation-Building Missions," Rand Center for Domestic and International Health Security, 2006. Available at http://www.rand.org/pubs/monographs/2006/RAND_MG321.pdf.
9. Available at http://www.qualcomm.com/press/releases/1998/press811_print .html.
10. Interview with Daniel Sudnick.
11. Interviews with Shaw friends in May and June 2004.
12. Department of Defense official biography, John A. Shaw.
13. Executive Branch Personnel Public Financial Disclosure Report for John A. Shaw, Department of Defense, 2001.
14. Citizens Against Government Waste, *2005 Congressional Pig Book* (Washington, DC, 2005). Available at http://www.cagw.org.
15. Chuck Neubauer, "Scrutinized Investment Made Senator $822,000," *Los Angeles Times,* June 15, 2005, p. A13.
16. Congressional Record, 108th Session. Debate on Emergency Supplemental Appropriations for Iraq and Afghanistan Security and Reconstruction Act, 2004, p. S12354.
17. The list of board members of the two companies was obtained from confidential bidding documents from the Coalition Provisional Authority reviewed by the author, and from a presentation by NANA to Shaw made in the Pentagon on January 12, 2004, a copy of which was obtained by author. A side-by-side list of the boards of directors was also made part of the criminal investigative file.
18. Joshua Chaffin, James Drummond, Stephen Fidler, Roula Khalaf, Nicolas Pelham, and Demetri Sevastopulo, "Reconstruction on Hold — How the Contest for Iraq's Mobile Telephone Contracts Sank into Disarray," *Financial Times,* November 26, 2003, p. 19.
19. State Department Cable from Secretary of State Colin Powell to Amb. L. Paul Bremer, March 9, 2004. Author copy.

20. E-mail from Declan Ganley to Jack Shaw, April 28, 2004. Author copy. Ganley reacted angrily to a question over whether Shaw had any financial interest in the deal. He said "the very concept of that is preposterous" in a phone interview in April 2004. Later Ganley's lawyers threatened to sue, saying that the articles that I wrote on the issue were "seriously defamatory." No suit was ever filed.

21. E-mail from Jack Shaw to Daniel Sudnick, March 11, 2004. Author copy.

22. Senator Grassley, who championed whistle-blowers, accused Schmitz of stonewalling the investigations of several Republican officials in the Bush administration, including Shaw. Grassley focused on a press release that Schmitz helped draft in August 2004. The release appeared to exonerate Shaw, stating that he "is not now, nor has he ever been, under investigation" by the inspector general. It was a lie, and Schmitz resigned in August 2005 as Grassley's inquiry was ongoing. Schmitz attributed his decision to leave to a job offer with the parent company of Blackwater USA, the private security company active in Iraq.

23. Preliminary Findings: Report to the Inspector General into Mobile Telecommunications Licenses in Iraq. International Armament and Technology Trade Director. Office of the Deputy Undersecretary of Defense, May 11, 2004.

24. Letter from Jack Shaw to Donald Rumsfeld, December 3, 2004. Author copy.

25. James Glanz, William J. Broad, and David E. Sanger, "Huge Cache of Explosives Vanished from Site in Iraq," *New York Times*, October 25, 2004, p. 1.

26. "Rumsfeld Discounts Report of Russian Assistance," Associated Press, October 29, 2004; *Seattle Times*, p. A10.

27. E-mail from Jack Shaw to Ray DuBois and Jim O'Beirne, November 18, 2004. Author copy.

28. Kenneth R. Timmerman, "Ex-Official: Russia Moved Saddam's WMD," NewsMax.com, February 19, 2006. Available at http://newsmax.com/archives/articles/2006/2/18/233023.shtml.

4: THE HALLIBURTON GANG

1. "Halliburton's Questioned and Unsupported Costs in Iraq Exceed $1.4 Billion." Minority Report by the House Government Reform Committee and the Senate Democratic Policy Committee, June 27, 2005.

2. Cheney took steps to neutralize potential conflicts of interest with Halliburton after he agreed to run for vice president, long before the war in Iraq became an issue. As part of his retirement package, Cheney got stock options worth potentially millions of dollars as well as "deferred compensation" — essentially a delayed paycheck — worth hundreds of thousands of dollars annually. Cheney pledged to donate to charity any proceeds from the stock options. He bought an insurance policy that guaranteed payment of the deferred salary no matter what the company's fortunes. But the nonpartisan Congressional Research Service determined that the measures weren't sufficient. Cheney still had "a financial interest." He had created the buffers; he could also take them away.

3. Interviewed by Tim Russert, *Meet the Press*, September 14, 2003.

4. E-mail from William Ryals to David L. Petersen, July 29, 2004. Author copy.

5. Jane Mayer, "Contract Sport," *The New Yorker*, February 16, 2004.

6. Col. Steven J. Zamparelli, "Contractors on the Battlefield: What Have We Signed Up For?" *Air Force Journal of Logistics* 23, no. 3 (fall 1999).

7. Ibid.

8. Ibid.

9. Ibid.

10. Peter Elkind, "The Truth About Halliburton: No-bid Contracts, Cronyism, Profiteering — Scandal Clings to This Company Like Lint on a $100 Bag of Laundry. But the Really Ugly Tale About Halliburton? Its Business," *Fortune*, April 18, 2005, p. 190.

11. Dan Briody, *The Halliburton Agenda: The Politics of Oil and Money* (Hoboken, N.J.: Wiley, 2004), p. 130.

12. Ibid., p. 169.

13. James M. Carter, "The Merchants of Blood: War Profiteering from Vietnam to Iraq," *CounterPunch*, December 11, 2003. Available at http://www.counter punch.org/carter12112003.html.

14. Ibid.

15. Briody, *Halliburton*, p. 196.

16. Ibid., p. 184.

17. Elkind, "The Truth About Halliburton."

18. KBR press release, July 2004.

19. Defense Contract Audit Agency, "Memorandum for Corporate Administrative Contracting Officer," January 13, 2004, p. 2.

20. U.S. Army Field Support Command, Press Release, April 5, 2005.

21. "Halliburton's Questioned and Unsupported Costs in Iraq Exceed $1.4 Billion." Minority Report by the House Government Reform Committee and the Senate Democratic Policy Committee, June 27, 2005.

22. David Walker, Testimony Before the House Government Reform Committee, June 15, 2004.

23. Ibid.

24. Freedberg, Hegland, and Maggs, "A Postwar Who's Who."

25. Much of the information concerning Mobbs's role comes from interviews with the staff of Representative Henry Waxman's office, who received a briefing from Mobbs. While their account of that briefing may be biased, it has never been disputed. Mobbs declined an interview request.

26. DOD planners believed that the planning contract "would result in Kellogg Brown & Root being uniquely qualified to initially execute the plan." David Walker, congressional testimony.

27. Rumsfeld memorandum cited in "Justification for Other Than Full and Open Competition," Section E, Contract DACA63-03-D-0005, obtained through Judicial Watch Freedom of Information Act request.

28. Col. Emmett Du Bose Jr., Testimony Before the House Government Reform Committee, June 21, 2004.

29. Representative Henry Waxman, letter to Condoleezza Rice, January 15, 2004.
30. E-mail to Amb. Richard H. Jones describing background of Altanmia Company, December 3, 2003, obtained by Representative Henry Waxman through a Freedom of Information Act request.
31. Humaidhi has never spoken publicly about his accusations, and the Kuwaiti parliament dropped an inquiry into the ownership of Altanmia.
32. An e-mail released as part of Waxman's Freedom of Information Act request provides a fuller version of the story. As related by Camille Geha, the sales manager at the Kuwait City Hilton Resort, Mrs. Crum lost her "diamond encrusted" watch at the resort and asked the hotel staff for help finding it. After several days went by, Crum called Geha and reminded him that Halliburton was spending $750,000 to $1.5 million a month at the hotel. He told Geha to "get off your fucking ass, put my wife in a car and go get her a watch." Geha did a quick cost-benefit analysis and did exactly as Crum had requested, opening a store at a swank Kuwaiti mall in the middle of the night.
33. E-mail to Amb. Richard H. Jones describing background of Altanmia Company, December 3, 2003.
34. E-mail from Richard Jones to U.S. embassy official in Kuwait, December 2, 2003, obtained by the author.
35. Letter from Mary Robinson, U.S. Army Corps of Engineers, December 6, 2003. Author copy.
36. Jackie Spinner, "Corps of Engineers Defends KBR Deal; Fuel Averted Crisis, General Says," *Washington Post,* January 13, 2004, p. E01.
37. James Glanz, "Army to Pay Halliburton Unit Most Costs Disputed by Audit," *New York Times,* February 27, 2006, p. A1.
38. Lt. Col. Albert Castaldo, U.S. Army Corps of Engineers. Memorandum for the record, July 21, 2004. Author copy.

5: THE MOTHER LODE

1. A revealing fact about the reconstruction is that nobody really knows how much oil is coming out of the ground in Iraq. Unlike most petroleum-producing nations, Iraq until recently had no monitors measuring well output. Nor until recently did the United States get around to installing any, despite repeated pleadings from the United Nations. Oil production estimates are derived from the amount of petroleum transiting through the system. But that, of course, allows for an untold amount of pilfering between the wellhead and the pipeline or tanker truck. Estimates of the amount of oil smuggled out of Iraq run up to 100,000 barrels per day.
2. Eric Schmitt, "Iraq Facing Hurdles, U.S. General Warns," *New York Times,* January 6, 2006, p. 10.
3. Iraq Pipeline Watch, Institute for the Analysis of Global Security. Available at http://www.iags.org/iraqpipelinewatch.htm.
4. Daniel Yergin, *The Prize: The Epic Quest for Oil, Money, and Power* (New York: Free Press, 1992), p. 184.

5. Ibid., p. 204.

6. U.S. Energy Information Administration, Iraq Country Analysis, December 2005. Available at http://www.eia.doe.gov/emeu/cabs/Iraq/oil.html.

7. United Nations, "Report of the Group of Experts Established Pursuant to Paragraph 12 of Security Council Resolution 1153," 1998, p. 6.

8. Final Report, Independent Inquiry Committee into the United Nations Oil-for-Food Programme [also known as the Volcker Commission], October 27, 2005. Available at http://www.iic-offp.org/story27oct05.htm. Of far greater magnitude, though much less notoriety, Hussein also illegally transported $11 billion in oil to Syria, Jordan, and Turkey during the sanctions period. The smuggling was an open secret, but the United States tolerated the shipments because they aided U.S. allies.

9. U.S. Energy Administration Information, Iraq Country Analysis, December 2005.

10. Government Accountability Office, "Rebuilding Iraq: Stabilization, Reconstruction, and Financing Challenges," February 8, 2006, p. 15.

11. "Unocal and Bidas Pulling Taliban for Gas Pipeline," *Alexander's Gas and Oil Connections,* December 8, 1997. Available at http://www.gasandoil.com/goc/company/cnc80415.htm.

12. Alfred Neffgen, Statement to U.S. House Committee on Government Reform, July 22, 2004.

13. Charles "Stoney" Cox, Statement to U.S House Committee on Government Reform, July 22, 2004.

14. U.S. Energy Information Administration, Iraq Country Analysis, December 2005.

15. Mike Wynn, Testimony Before the House Armed Services Readiness Subcommittee, June 24, 2004.

16. Chip Cummins and Hassan Hafidh, "Iraqi Oil Output Sinks as New Woes Surface — Battles of Politics and Regionalization Quash Earlier Gains," *Wall Street Journal,* February 21, 2006, p. A2.

17. Chris Kraul, "Decline in Oil Output Dims Iraq's Recovery; As U.S. Financial Aid Winds Down, Concerns Grow, with No Quick Turnaround in Sight," *Los Angeles Times,* January 25, 2006, p. A1.

18. Special Inspector General for the Reconstruction of Iraq, "Al Fathah River Crossing Tie Ins," March 15, 2006; U.S. Energy Information Administration, Iraq Country Analysis, December 2005.

19. Joanna Chung and Clay Harris, "Shell Puts Iraq Project on Hold," *Financial Times,* May 5, 2004, p. 23.

6: THE BUILDER

1. Jackie Spinner, "Contract Meeting Draws 1,300; U.S. Sponsors Conference on Iraq Reconstruction Awards," *Washington Post,* November 20, 2003, p. E6.

2. The Seabees were created in 1942 precisely because the navy in that era de-

cided that civilian contractors did not belong in the combat zones of World War II — a marked contrast from Iraq, where the military invited civilians into harm's way.

3. Patrick McCartney, "Port Hueneme Base Commander Is Made Rear Admiral," *Los Angeles Times,* January 23, 1993, p. 2.

4. The United States has experimented with nation-building exercises of varying ambition in the aftermath of seven conflicts: Germany, Japan, Somalia, Haiti, Bosnia, Kosovo, and Afghanistan (Dobbins et al., *America's Role*).

5. Lisa Zagaroli, "Three Years After Iraq War Began, Reconstruction Still Is Unsteady," *Fresno Bee,* March 12, 2006, p. A12.

6. Robin Wright and Dana Milbank, "Bush Defends Barring Foes of War from Iraq Business; Concerns Raised by Republicans as Well as Germany and France," *Washington Post,* December 12, 2003, p. A01.

7. Neil King Jr. and Yochi Dreazen, "Bush to Defer Some Iraq Work Until After Transfer of Power," *Wall Street Journal,* December 31, 2003, p. A2.

8. Department of Defense, Press Release, "Iraqi Rebuilding Contracts Proceeding Well, Nash Reports," March 10, 2004.

9. Martin A. Schain, ed., *The Marshall Plan: Fifty Years After* (New York: Palgrave, 2001), p. 42.

10. Ibid., p. 285.

11. Available at http://citadel.edu/r3/pao/addresses/pres_bush.html.

12. Gordon, *Cobra II,* pp. 103–4.

13. Bremer, *My Year,* p. 10.

14. Michael J. Hogan, *The Marshall Plan: America, Britain, and the Reconstruction of Western Europe, 1947–1952* (Cambridge: Cambridge University Press, 1987), p. 138.

15. Allen W. Dulles, *The Marshall Plan* (Providence, R.I.: Berg, 1993), p. 96.

16. Schain, *Marshall Plan,* p. 191.

17. Hogan, *Marshall Plan,* p. 156.

18. Ibid., pp. 138–39.

19. Schain, *Marshall Plan,* p. 201.

20. Ibid., p. 288.

21. Hogan, *Marshall Plan,* p. 432.

22. Statement of Work. Solicitation FY5866-04-R-0001 Battalion Sets.

23. American Export Group International Services bankruptcy proceedings. Memorandum of Points and Authorities of the National Bank of Washington and First American Bank N.A. in Support of Motion for Reconsideration of the Order Appointing Cappello & Foley as Special Counsel. U.S. Bankruptcy Court for the District of Columbia, Case no. 87-00369.

24. Knut Royce, "Start-up Company with Connections," *Newsday,* February 15, 2004, p. A7.

25. Much of the information for this section stems from bidding documents submitted by the Defense Equipment Supply Group, or DES, in response to the battalion sets supply contract, solicitation FY5866-04-R-0001, which were reviewed by the author.

26. Royce, "Start-up Company."

27. U.S. Army Inspector General, Report of Investigation (Case 05-030), September 20, 2005.

28. My colleague Solomon Moore conducted extensive interviews in October 2004 with Shaalan in Amman, Jordan, and with Cattan in Warsaw, Poland. The information cited stems from previously unpublished portions of those interviews. Shaalan and Roman Baczynski, Bumar CEO, also held a press conference in Warsaw, Poland, on September 29, 2005. Transcript and translation provided by Ela Kasprzycka.

7: THE SHOOTING STARTS

1. Much of the section on Fern Holland and Bob Zangas is based on reporting by two journalists, one of them a colleague. Alissa J. Rubin of the *Los Angeles Times* and Elizabeth Rubin of the *New York Times Magazine* both recognized Holland as a case study in the well-intentioned zeal for reform that brought many young Americans to Iraq.

2. Alissa J. Rubin, "American Put Her Life on the Line for Iraqi Women," *Los Angeles Times,* March 16, 2004, p. A1.

3. Elizabeth Rubin, "Fern Holland's War," *New York Times Magazine,* September 19, 2004, p. 66.

4. Marcella Bombardieri, "Courage Under Fire: Bob Zangas Improved Lives and Saved Others in Two Visits to Iraq," *Boston Globe,* March 22, 2004, p. B7.

5. Robert Zangas, "Bob Zangas' Journey in Iraq," March 6, 2004. Zangas's blog is archived and available at http://web.archive.org/web/20040318122636/http://zangasiniraq.militarypages.com/.

6. Much of the reporting for this section is based on a lawsuit filed by the families of the Blackwater workers killed in Fallujah and on "The Bridge," a richly detailed series by reporters Jay Price and Joseph Neff that appeared in the *News & Observer* (Raleigh, N.C.) in the summer of 2004.

7. Ted Roelofs, "Neither Party Well Off Here as Primary Nears," *Grand Rapids Press,* February 23, 1992, p. A1.

8. Joseph Neff and Jay Price, "Contractors in Iraq Make Costs Balloon," *News & Observer,* October 24, 2004, p. A1.

9. *Richard P. Nordon et al. v. Blackwater Security Consulting, LLC.* Complaint. North Carolina Superior Court for Wake County, p. 8.

10. Available at: http://www.pbs.org/wgbh/pages/frontline/shows/warriors/contractors/helvemail.html.

11. Alissa J. Rubin and Doyle McManus, "The Fight for Iraq; Why America Has Waged a Losing Battle on Fallujah," *Los Angeles Times,* October 24, 2004, p. A1.

12. Halliburton gave me permission to ride with one of its convoys in August 2004. I was escorted by a Halliburton spokeswoman most of the time, though I rode alone with Melvin Winter, the driver, during our trip from Balad to Baghdad airport. Halliburton provided me wide access to its drivers and op-

erations, though the company placed some restrictions on what I could write regarding security issues.

13. The reporting reconstructing the events of April 9 relies on interviews with nine of the thirteen surviving drivers, the families of four of those killed, several army officers, and the 280-page U.S. Army Report of Commander's Inquiry of the 724th Transportation Company Hostile Engagement, dated August 2, 2004.

14. Jarob D. Walsh, "The Real Story Behind the April 9th Insurgency in Iraq," *Intellectual Conservative,* May 17, 2004. Available at http://www.intellectualconservative.com/article3444.html.

8: PRIVATE ARMIES

1. Federal agents came looking for the blueprints prior to the outbreak of the war, believing that Hussein might have used them to design an underground network beneath his palace. Parsons had long ago disposed of them.

2. Special Inspector General for the Reconstruction of Iraq, "Management of Personnel Assigned to the Coalition Provisional Authority," pp. 3–4.

3. Special Inspector General for the Reconstruction of Iraq, "Administration of Iraq Relief and Reconstruction Fund Contract Files," p. 4.

4. Parsons allowed me to interview their Iraqi workers only on condition that I not publish their names, to ensure their safety.

5. James Glanz, "Army Cancels Contract for New Iraqi Prison," *New York Times,* June 20, 2006, p. A9.

6. Government Accountability Office, "Rebuilding Iraq," June 2004.

7. James Glanz, "Violence in Iraq Curbs Work of 2 Big Contractors," *New York Times,* April 22, 2004, p. 1; James Glanz, "Contractors Return to Iraq, But Numbers Are Still Down," *New York Times,* May 8, 2004, p. 10; Elizabeth Becker, "Heavy Toll of Violence on Iraq Rebuilding," *New York Times,* April 14, 2004, p. 11.

8. E-mail from Don Kerbow, KBR Theater Transportation Mission manager, April 8, 2004. Author copy.

9. Agence France Presse, "U.S. Marines Start to Ration Food in Troubled Al-Anbar Province," April 19, 2004.

10. Bremer, *My Year,* p. 342.

11. Daniel Bergner, "The Other Army," *New York Times Magazine,* August 14, 2005, p. 29.

12. David Barstow, James Glanz, Richard A. Oppel Jr., and Kate Zernike, "Security Companies: Shadow Soldiers in Iraq," *New York Times,* April 19, 2004, p. 1.

13. P. W. Singer, *Corporate Warriors: The Rise of the Privatized Military Industry* (Ithaca: Cornell University Press, 2003), pp. 21–28.

14. Ibid., p. 50.

15. Ibid., p. 67.

16. Ibid., p. 78.

17. Barstow et al., "Security Companies."

18. Bergner, "The Other Army."
19. David Barstow, "Security Firm Says Its Workers Were Lured into Iraqi Ambush," *New York Times,* April 9, 2004, p. A1.
20. I am deeply indebted to my colleagues Borzou Daragahi, Saad Fakhrildeen, and Asmaa Waguih for help in reporting on this incident.
21. One soldier, Sgt. First Class Paul R. Smith, became the war's first Medal of Honor winner. He was killed while holding off scores of Iraqi soldiers threatening to overrun a handful of soldiers near the airport's eastern entrance.
22. Neil King Jr. and Yochi J. Dreazen, "Willing to Take a Risk, Security Firm Discovers Big Opportunity in Iraq — Using Army Experience, Custer Battles Is Rare Business Success in Baghdad — A Swimming Pool for Its Employees," *Wall Street Journal,* August 13, 2004, p. A1.
23. Much of the reporting in this section is built upon documents, letters, and e-mails contained in a lawsuit, *United States Ex. Rel. DRC Inc. v. Custer Battles, LLC,* U.S. District Court, Eastern District of Virginia; a report by the Defense Department, Inspector General's Defense Criminal Investigative Services, 200400237A-06-NOV-2004-60DC-E0; and a suspension notice and supporting documents from the U.S. Air Force, dated September 30, 2004.
24. Pete Baldwin statement in U.S. Air Force suspension file. Author copy.
25. Ibid.
26. Letter from attorney for Custer Battles in U.S. Air Force suspension file. Author copy.
27. *United States Ex. Rel. DRC Inc. v. Custer Battles, LLC.* Michael Battles, October 2005 deposition.
28. Interview, FAA official, March 2005.
29. Mike Battles interview in U.S. Air Force suspension file. Author copy.
30. Interview, Pete Baldwin, January 2005.
31. Letter from attorney for Custer Battles in U.S. Air Force suspension file. Author copy. Google Inc. secured its seed funding of $100,000 in September 1998, and a second round of funding for $25 million nine months later. Google corporate history available at http://www.google.com/intl/en/corporate/history.html.
32. King and Dreazen, "Willing to Take a Risk."
33. *United States Ex. Rel. DRC Inc. v. Custer Battles, LLC.* Hugh Tant, October 2005 deposition.
34. Michael Corkery, "Newport Man Out to Strike. It Rich in Iraq," *Providence Journal,* January 25, 2004, p. A1.
35. King and Dreazen, "Willing to Take a Risk."
36. Michael Corkery, "Battling for Voters, One Mile at a Time," *Providence Journal,* August 14, 2002, p. B1.
37. Interview, Frank Willis, January 2005.
38. Hugh Tant, interview by Mark Gribbin, United States Institute of Peace, October 22, 2004.
39. Internal memo from Coalition Provisional Authority. Author copy.

40. Ottenbreit memo, Defense Criminal Investigative Service Case #200400237A-06-NOV-2004-60DC-E0. Author copy.
41. Ibid.
42. *United States Ex. Rel. DRC Inc. v. Custer Battles, LLC.* Hugh Tant, October 2005 deposition.
43. Iraq Currency Exchange Spreadsheet, Defense Criminal Investigative Service Case #200400237A-06-NOV-2004-60DC-E0. Author copy.
44. March 1, 2004, memo from Pete Miscovich to file. Author copy.
45. February 28, 2004, memo from Pete Miscovich to Charles Baumann. Author copy.
46. Interview with Custer Battles official, December 2004.
47. Joe Morris statement to investigators on January 15, 2004, Defense Criminal Investigative Service Case #200400237A-06-NOV-2004-60DC-E0. Author copy.
48. Interview with Custer Battles officials and attorneys.
49. Ottenbreit memo.
50. Runnels memo, Defense Criminal Investigative Service Case #200400237A-06-NOV-2004-60DC-E0. Author copy.
51. Frank Willis, Testimony to Senate Democratic Policy Committee, February 14, 2005.

9: BLIND MICE

1. Demetri Sevastopulo, "Former Bush Aide Set to Inspect Iraq Authority," *Financial Times,* January 14, 2004.
2. Jackie Spinner and Ariana Eunjung Cha, "U.S. Decisions on Iraq Spending Made in Private," *Washington Post,* December 27, 2003, p. A1.
3. Ariana Eunjung Cha, "$1.9 Billion of Iraq's Money Goes to U.S. Contractors," *Washington Post,* August 4, 2004, p. A1.
4. Ibid.
5. Spinner and Cha, "U.S. Decisions on Iraq Spending."
6. Bremer, *My Year,* p. 358.
7. U.S. House of Representatives, Committee on Government Reform — Minority Staff, Special Investigations Division, "Rebuilding Iraq: U.S. Mismanagement of Iraqi Funds," June 2005.
8. It was months later that a UN-hired auditing team determined that the money had been deposited in full.
9. Bremer, *My Year,* p. 394.
10. The official did not respond to requests for comment, though a friend of his defended his actions as a good faith effort to move projects along quickly.
11. Special Inspector General for the Reconstruction of Iraq, "Oversight of Funds Provided to Iraqi Ministries Through the National Budget Process," January 30, 2005, p. 7.
12. Ibid., pp. 33–40.
13. James Glanz, "U.S. Aide Accused of Graft in Iraq Had a Shadowy Past," *New York Times,* November 19, 2005, p. 8.

14. *U.S. v. Robert J. Stein.* U.S. District Court for the District of Columbia. Plea agreement.
15. Special Inspector General for Iraq Reconstruction, "Management of Rapid Regional Response Program Contracts in South Central Iraq," January 23, 2006, p. 14.
16. *U.S. v. Robert J. Stein.* Plea agreement.
17. Ibid.
18. Glanz, "U.S. Aide Accused of Graft."
19. Associated Press, "N.C. Man Charged in Iraqi Kickback Scheme Has Shaky Past," November 19, 2005.
20. Glanz, "U.S. Aide Accused of Graft."
21. Charles R. Babcock, "2nd Officer Accused in Iraq Bid-Rigging Case," *Washington Post*, December 16, 2005, p. A25.
22. Special Inspector General for the Reconstruction of Iraq, "Management of the Contracts and Grants Used to Construct and Operate the Babylon Police Academy," October 26, 2005.
23. Special Inspector General for the Reconstruction of Iraq, "Management of the Contracts, Grants and Micro-Purchases Used to Rehabilitate the Karbala Library," October 26, 2005.
24. The Hillah outpost, formally known as the Coalition Provisional Authority South Central, also bought thirty thousand books for the library from a variety of contractors. According to the library manager, none were delivered.
25. Javed Ahmad Ghamidi and Shehzad Saleem, "What Is *Diyat.*" Available at http://www.renaissance.com.pk/septrefl2y2.html.

10: BOOM TOWN

1. Interview with senior U.S. reconstruction official.
2. Special Inspector General for the Reconstruction of Iraq, "Challenges Faced in Carrying Out Iraq Relief and Reconstruction Fund Activities," January 26, 2006.
3. James Glanz, "Security vs. Rebuilding: Kurdish Town Loses Out," *New York Times,* April 16, 2005, p. 1.
4. Scott Wilson, "A Different Street Fight in Iraq: U.S. General Turns to Public Works in Battle for Hearts and Minds," *Washington Post,* May 27, 2004, p. A1.
5. Ibid.
6. Katarina Kratovac, "American Troops in Baghdad Slum See Their Reconstruction Effort as Blueprint for Fallujah," Associated Press, November 18, 2004.

11: THE FIX

1. Peter J. Boyer, "The Believer: Paul Wolfowitz Defends His War," *The New Yorker*, November 1, 2004.
2. Jim Krane, "Iraqi Military Won't Get Tanks, Offensive Capabilities," Associated Press, June 26, 2004.

3. Boyer, "The Believer."

4. Information on the Iraqi audit and its findings regarding Ziad Cattan is based on an English-language translation of the Iraqi Supreme Board of Audit review, May 2005. Author copy.

5. Patrick Cockburn, "What Has Happened to Iraq's Missing $1Bn?" *The Independent,* September 19, 2005, p. 1.

6. I worked with several colleagues on a series of stories about the scandals at the Iraqi Defense Ministry. Much of the reporting in this chapter is based on extensive interviews that my colleague Solomon Moore conducted with Prime Minister Ayad Allawi in Baghdad, Roman Baczynski and Ziad Cattan in Poland, and former Iraqi defense minister Hazim Shaalan in Jordan.

7. Ziad Cattan, "My History." Available at http://www.ziadcattan.com/en/historia.html.

8. Ibid.

9. Maynulet, who insisted he shot the Iraqi man to prevent further suffering, was convicted of assault with intent to commit voluntary manslaughter and was dismissed from the military. "Convicted GI Will Not Serve Time," Associated Press, April 2, 2005.

10. Prior to the U.S. invasion, the hardscrabble neighborhood adjacent to impoverished Sadr City was known as Seven Nisan, or April 7, the date of the founding of the Iraqi Baath Party. Americans redubbed it to mark the day of the collapse of Saddam's regime.

11. Bremer, *My Year,* p. 179. Inexplicably, Bremer denied knowing Cattan six months prior to the publication of his book. "To his knowledge, he'd never met him," Bremer's spokesman, Dan Senor, told a Knight Ridder reporter in August 2005.

12. Col. P. J. Dermer, interview by Arma Jane Karaer, United States Institute of Peace, August 22, 2004.

13. Donna Miles, "Petraeus Cites Highs and Lows of Iraqi Deployment," American Forces Press Service, March 17, 2004.

14. Ken Silverstein, a colleague of mine, provided much of the information on the murdered American contractor Dale Stoffel, who had been a personal friend. Aram Roston, "Unquiet American," *Washington Monthly,* June 1, 2005, profiles Stoffel and was the inspiration for the heading of this section.

15. Roston, "Unquiet American."

16. Ibid.

17. Ibid.

18. Ibid.

19. Ibid.

20. Another Lebanese businessman, Mohammed abu Darwish, worked with Zayna's firm, General Investment Group, on the contract with Stoffel, e-mails and interviews showed. It was not Darwish's first brush with a company accused of corruption. Darwish had a business partnership with Custer Battles, the American security contractor. The Pentagon suspended Darwish and Custer Battles in September 2004 from receiving future American con-

tracts because of their alleged involvement in a scheme to defraud the U.S. of millions of dollars on a security contract in Iraq, according to a U.S. Air Force document.

21. Neither Zayna nor Sarraf responded to requests for comment on the deal when I attempted to contact them. Later Zayna and Sarraf's attorney, who insisted on anonymity, sent a letter to the *Washington Monthly* which disputed Stoffel's account of Zayna's role. The attorney said it was Stoffel who brought the Lebanese financier into the project, not the Ministry of Defense. Additionally, the letter said Zayna was working with Stoffel in a joint venture, not as a middleman. The letter said Stoffel made "extraordinary and outlandish demands for immediate payments of cash" to which he wasn't entitled. Zayna had done nothing wrong and the company was continuing to safeguard funds associated with the tank project.

22. Sarraf, the Ministry of Defense adviser, provided the *Washington Monthly* a written statement in which he said that no one at the ministry would have made such a demand.

23. By bizarre coincidence, Stoffel used a lobbying connection to meet with Jack Shaw, the Pentagon official involved in Iraq's cellular phone scandal. Shaw was the Pentagon official charged with monitoring weapons sales in Iraq, and Stoffel warned him in a letter I obtained that the weapons contract "has fallen prey to . . . corruption and self-dealing." Failing to stop the alleged corruption "will set a very negative precedent for subsequent dealings with the Iraqi military, harm U.S. companies seeking to do business according to U.S. law, and be the source of embarrassment and political tension to the Bush administration with respect to the effort in Iraq."

24. Roston, "Unquiet American."

25. Deborah Hastings, "Corruption, Missing Millions, and Two Dead Contractors," Associated Press, January 28, 2006.

26. U.S. Army Maj. Charles Miller and U.S. Army Capt. Elizabeth Young, "Army Day Celebrates Service and Sacrifice," *The Advisor: The Multi-National Security Transition Command — Iraq Weekly Command Information Reporter*, January 2005, p. 4.

27. Hannah Allam, "Audit: Fraud Drained $1 Billion from Iraq's Defense Efforts," Knight Ridder, August 12, 2005.

28. Cockburn, "What Has Happened to Iraq's Missing $1Bn?"

29. Roston, "Unquiet American."

30. Hannah Allam, "Iraq Seen Wasting $300 Million on Substandard Military Equipment," Knight Ridder, July 15, 2005.

31. Fred Kaplan, "Supplemental Insecurity: The Revelations Buried in Bush's Latest Supplemental Budget Request," *Slate*, February 15, 2005.

32. Senate Armed Services Committee Hearing on United States Military Strategy and Operations in Iraq and the Central Command Area, September 29, 2005.

12: HIRED HANDS

1. United States Department of State, Trafficking in Persons Report, 2005, p. 15.
2. David Phinney, "Blood, Sweat, and Tears: Asia's Poor Build U.S. Bases in Iraq," *Corpwatch,* October 3, 2005. Available at http://www.corpwatch.org/article .php?id=12675.
3. Ibid.
4. Ariana Eunjung Cha, "Underclass of Workers Created in Iraq; Many Foreign Laborers Receive Inferior Pay, Food, and Shelter," *Washington Post,* July 1, 2004, p. A1.
5. Cam Simpson, "Desperate for Work, Lured into Danger," *Chicago Tribune,* October 9, 2005, p. 1.
6. Cam Simpson, "Into a War Zone, on a Deadly Road," *Chicago Tribune,* October 10, 2005, p. 1.
7. Ibid.
8. Insurance industry presentation. June 2004. Author copy.
9. AIG denied that McCaffrey made such a statement. A company spokesman said AIG did not publicly comment on its share of individual insurance markets. According to figures maintained by the Labor Department, AIG accounted for 80 percent and ACE for 10 percent of the 2,732 claims for deaths and injuries in Iraq and Afghanistan filed by June 2005. The AIG spokesman said the percentage of claims filed in Iraq and Afghanistan was not necessarily an indication of market percentage.

13: POWER

1. Bremer, *My Year,* p. 18.
2. United Nations, Iraqi Distribution Plan Phase XII, June 13, 2002. Available at http://www.iraqwatch.org/un/Index_UN_Iraq.html.
3. United Nations, Iraqi Distribution Plan Phase XIII, January 3, 2003. Available at http://www.iraqwatch.org/un/Index_UN_Iraq.html.
4. Rajiv Chandrasekaran, "Crossed Wires Deprived Iraqis of Electric Power," *Washington Post,* September 25, 2003, p. A1.
5. United Nations, "Reconstruction of Iraq: An Arab Economic and Social View," July 2003. Available at http://www.escwa.org.lb/information/iraq/docs/RecIq .pdf.
6. David Streitfeld, "Starved for Power in Baghdad," *Los Angeles Times,* September 23, 2003, p. A1.
7. Neela Banerjee, "No Power, No Rebirth in Iraqi Business," *New York Times,* May 25, 2003, p. 1.
8. Neil King Jr., "Power Struggle: Race to Get Lights On in Iraq Shows Perils of Reconstruction," *Wall Street Journal,* April 2, 2004, p. A1.
9. Streitfeld, "Starved for Power in Baghdad."
10. Rajiv Chandrasekaran and Peter Slevin, "Iraq's Ragged Reconstruction: A Month After Baghdad's Fall, U.S. Efforts Founder," *Washington Post,* May 9, 2003, p. A1.
11. King, "Power Struggle."

12. Available at http://www.geocities.com/j_mengers/oeb.html.
13. King, "Power Struggle."
14. Coalition Provisional Authority, "An Historic Review of CPA Accomplishments," June 28, 2003.
15. John Ward Anderson and Bassam Sebti, "Billion-Dollar Start Falls Short in Iraq: U.S. Officials Worry About Leaving Baghdad Without Basic Services," *Washington Post*, April 16, 2006, p. A11.
16. Streitfeld, "Starved for Power in Baghdad."
17. Tom Wheelock, interviewed by W. Haven North, United States Institute of Peace, September 8, 2004.
18. Anne Ellen Henderson, "The Coalition Provisional Authority's Experience with Economic Reconstruction in Iraq," United States Institute of Peace, p. 12.

14: COST OF WAR

1. Westhusing, "The Competitive and Cooperative *Aretai*," pp. 286–87.
2. Sandra Jontz, "Elite Iraqi Police Put Training to Use on Streets," *Stars and Stripes*, April 14, 2005.
3. U.S. Army Criminal Investigation Command, Report of Investigation, #05-CID259-36276-5P2, p. 298. Much of the information for this chapter, including e-mails from Westhusing and comments from his friends and colleagues, comes from the three reports by the U.S. Army in the possession of the author: the U.S. Army Criminal Investigation Command, Final Report of Investigation, #05-CID259-36276, dated August 27, 2005; U.S. Army Inspector General, Report of Investigation (Case 05-030), September 20, 2005; and the Joint Contracting Command — Iraq, Letter to U.S. Investigative Service, May 24, 2005.
4. U.S. Army Criminal Investigation Command, Report of Investigation, #05-CID259-36276–5P2, p. 46.
5. Author copy.
6. Both generals later told investigators that they had not criticized Westhusing or heard negative comments from him. An army review was complimentary of the command climate under the two men. Both men declined to comment on the investigation when I contacted them, but both had high praise for Westhusing. He was "an extremely bright, highly competent, completely professional, and exceedingly hardworking officer. His death was truly tragic and was a tremendous blow," Petraeus told me.
7. The author was allowed to review a copy of the note by a U.S. government source.

EPILOGUE

1. Steven R. Weisman, "Rice, in Stops in Iraq, Urges Sunnis to Reject Insurgency," *New York Times*, November 12, 2005, p. 8.; Tyler Marshall, "The World: Rice Makes Surprise Side Visit to Northern Iraq," *Los Angeles Times*, November 11, 2005, p. A13.

2. Andrew F. Krepinevich Jr., "How to Win in Iraq," *Foreign Affairs,* September/October 2005.
3. Bradley Graham and Glenn Kessler, "Iraq Security for U.S. Teams Uncertain; Use of Reconstruction Coordinators Has Been Approved," *Washington Post,* March 3, 2006, p. A11.
4. Glenn Kessler, "Iraq Reconstruction Teams Delayed at State Department," *Washington Post,* April 13, 2006, p. A19; Paul Richter, "Staffing, Security Issues Stall Provincial Program; Only Three of 18 Teams Have Been Fielded in a U.S. Reconstruction Effort to Build Up Local Governments in Iraq and Improve Public Services," *Los Angeles Times,* April 2, 2006, p. A28.
5. Jonathan Finer, "For Iraqi Students, Hussein's Arrival Is End of History," *Washington Post,* April 15, 2006, p. A1.

AFTERWORD

1. State Department, "Iraq Weekly Status Report," November 29, 2006. Available at http://www.state.gov/documents/organization/77251.pdf.
2. James Glanz, "Iraq Insurgents Starve Capital of Electricity," *New York Times,* December 19, 2006, p. A1.
3. Program on International Policy Attitudes, Center for International and Security Studies. University of Maryland, "The Iraqi Public on the U.S. Presence and the Future of Iraq." September 27, 2006.
4. Personal interview with former USAID official, September 2006.
5. Rowan Scarborough, "Rebuilding in Iraq Tops 4,000 Projects; Pentagon Compares Scope to That of Marshall Plan," *Washington Times,* November 20, 2006, p. A1.
6. David Streitfeld, "Bechtel Calls It Quits After More Than 3 Years in Iraq; Violence Has Left Few of the Company's Infrastructure Projects in the War-torn Country Operating as Planned," *Los Angeles Times,* November 3, 2006, p. C1.
7. Special Inspector General for the Iraq Reconstruction, "Quick Reaction Report on the Baghdad Police College," September 27, 2006.
8. Griff Witte, "The Builder Who Bombed in Iraq; Battered Over Failed Projects, Parsons's CEO Fires Back at Government Critics," *Washington Post,* December 22, 2006, p. D1.
9. Griff Witte, "KBR Shares Up 22% on 1st Day of Trading; Halliburton Spins Off Troublesome Unit," *Washington Post,* November 17, 2006, p. D3.
10. Griff Witte and Renae Merle, "Contractors Face More Scrutiny, Pinched Purses; Democrats Vow to Examine Large Deals," *Washington Post,* November 28, 2006, p. D1.
11. Renae Merle, "Census Counts 100,000 Contractors in Iraq; Civilian Number, Duties Are Issues," *Washington Post,* December 5, 2006, p. D1.
12. Personal interview, Steve Schooner, December 2006.
13. Special Inspector General for the Iraq Reconstruction, "Review of the U.S. Agency for International Development's Management of the Basrah Children's Hospital Project," July 28, 2006.

14. The same could not be said of Bowen. Representative Duncan Hunter, the California archconservative, slipped a last-minute provision into a spending bill that would have shut down Bowen's office before the reconstruction ended. Only a last-minute compromise with Democrats and moderate Republicans after the November elections saved the inspector general's office from disappearing sooner than expected. James Glanz, "Watchdog Agency for Iraq Projects Survives," *New York Times,* December 9, 2006, p. A10.

15. *United States Ex Rel. DRC Inc. v. Custer Battles.* U.S. District Court for the Eastern District of Virginia. Memorandum Opinion.

16. David G. Savage, "U.S. Can Withhold Security Firm Data; The Times Loses Its Bid in Court for the Names of Contractors Involved in Shootings in Iraq," *Los Angeles Times,* July 27, 2006, p. A18.

17. David Ivanovich, "Judge Dismisses Lawsuit Against Halliburton; Truck Drivers Will Appeal in Iraq Ambush Case," *Houston Chronicle,* September 23, 2006, p. A1.

18. Farah Stockman, "Contractors in War Zones Lose Immunity," *Boston Globe,* January 7, 2007, p. A1.

19. James Glanz, "Escaped Minister Says He Fled Iraqi Jail 'the Chicago Way,'" *New York Times,* December 20, 2006, p. A16, and "Final and Bitter Detour for Expatriate Back in Iraq," *New York Times,* December 15, 2006, p. A18.

Selected Bibliography

These are the books I found most helpful on the reconstruction.

Anderson, Liam, and Gareth Stansfield. *The Future of Iraq: Dictatorship, Democracy, or Division?* New York: Palgrave MacMillan, 2004.

Bremer, L. Paul, III. *My Year in Iraq: The Struggle to Build a Future of Hope.* New York: Simon and Schuster, 2006.

Briody, Dan. *The Halliburton Agenda: The Politics of Oil and Money.* Hoboken, N.J.: John Wiley and Sons, Inc., 2004.

Chatterjee, Pratap. *Iraq, Inc.: A Profitable Occupation.* New York: Seven Stories Press, 2004.

Diamond, Larry. *Squandered Victory: The American Occupation and the Bungled Effort to Bring Democracy to Iraq.* New York: Times Books, 2005.

Dobbins, James, et al. *America's Role in Nation-Building: From Germany to Iraq.* Santa Monica: RAND, 2003.

Dulles, Allen W. *The Marshall Plan.* Providence, R.I.: Berg Publishers, Inc., 1993.

Feldman, Noah. *What We Owe Iraq: War and the Ethics of Nation Building.* Princeton, N.J.: Princeton University Press, 2004.

Fukuyama, Francis. *State-Building: Governance and the World Order in the Twenty-first Century.* Ithaca: Cornell University Press, 2004.

Glantz, Aaron. *How America Lost Iraq.* New York: Penguin Group, 2005.

Gordon, Michael R., and General Bernard E. Trainor. *Cobra II: The Inside Story of the Invasion and Occupation of Iraq.* New York: Pantheon Books, 2006.

Hamill, Thomas, and Paul T. Brown. *Escape in Iraq: The Thomas Hamill Story.* Accokeek, Md.: Stoeger Publishing, 2004.

Hartung, William D. *How Much Are You Making on the War, Daddy?: A Quick and Dirty Guide to War Profiteering in the Bush Administration.* New York: Nation Books, 2003.

Hogan, Michael J. *The Marshall Plan: America, Britain, and the Reconstruction of Western Europe, 1947–1952.* Cambridge: Cambridge University Press, 1987.

Holmes, Eric. *Iraq: Providing Hope.* Allen, Tx.: Timberwolf Press, Inc., 2004.

Lipsky, David. *Absolutely American: Four Years at West Point.* New York: Random House, 2004.

Mack, Robert T., Jr. *Raising the World's Standard of Living: The Coordination and Effectiveness of Point Four, United Nations Technical Assistance, and Related Programs.* Birmingham, N.Y.: Citadel Press, 1953.

McDermott, Terry. *Perfect Soldiers*. New York: HarperCollins Publishers, Inc., 2005.

Packer, George. *The Assassins' Gate: America in Iraq*. New York: Farrar, Straus and Giroux, 2005.

Phillips, David L. *Losing Iraq: Inside the Postwar Reconstruction Fiasco*. Boulder, Colo.: Westview Press, 2005.

Risen, James. *State of War: The Secret History of the CIA and the Bush Administration*. New York: Free Press, 2006.

Schain, Martin A., ed. *The Marshall Plan: Fifty Years After*. New York: Palgrave, 2001.

Schultheis, Robert. *Waging Peace: A Special Operations Team's Battle to Rebuild Iraq*. New York: Gotham, 2005.

Shadid, Anthony. *Night Draws Near: Iraq's People in the Shadow of America's War*. New York: Henry Holt and Company, LLC., 2005.

Singer, P. W. *Corporate Warriors: The Rise of the Privatized Military Industry*. Ithaca: Cornell University Press, 2003.

Woodward, Bob. *Plan of Attack*. New York: Simon and Schuster Paperbacks, 2004.

Westhusing, T. S. "The Competitive and Cooperative *Aretai* Within the American Warfighting Ethos." PhD diss., Emory University, 2003.

Yergin, Daniel. *The Prize: The Epic Quest for Oil, Money, and Power*. New York: Free Press, 1992.

Zucchino, David. *Thunder Run: The Armored Strike to Capture Baghdad*. New York: Atlantic Monthly Press, 2004.

Index

About the Author

T. Christian Miller is an award-winning investigative reporter who writes for the *Los Angeles Times*'s Washington bureau. In his ten years as a professional journalist, he has covered four wars and a presidential campaign, and has reported from more than two dozen countries. He is a graduate of the University of California at Berkeley and lives in Washington, DC, with his wife and two young children.